D1155312

WORLD CHRISTIANITY

World Christianity

Perspectives and Insights

Essays in Honor of Peter C. Phan

Editors
Jonathan Y. Tan
&
Anh Q. Tran, S.J.

ORBIS BOOKS
www.orbisbooks.com

Founded in 1970, Orbis Books endeavors to publish works that enlighten the mind, nourish the spirit, and challenge the conscience. The publishing arm of the Maryknoll Fathers and Brothers, Orbis seeks to explore the global dimensions of the Christian faith and mission, to invite dialogue with diverse cultures and religious traditions, and to serve the cause of reconciliation and peace. The books published reflect the views of their authors and do not represent the official position of the Maryknoll Society. To learn more about Maryknoll and Orbis Books, please visit our website at www.maryknollsociety.org.

Copyright © 2016 by Jonathan Y. Tan and Anh Q. Tran

Published by Orbis Books, Maryknoll, New York 10545-0302.
Manufactured in the United States of America.

All rights reserved. No part of this publication may be reproduced or transmitted in any form or by any means, electronic or mechanical, including photocopying, recording or any information storage or retrieval system, without prior permission in writing from the publisher.

Queries regarding rights and permissions should be addressed to: Orbis Books, P.O. Box 302, Maryknoll, New York 10545-0302.

Library of Congress Cataloging-in-Publication Data

Names: Phan, Peter C., 1943- honouree. | Tan, Jonathan Y., editor.
Title: World Christianity : perspectives and insights : essays in honor of
    Peter C. Phan / editors, Jonathan Y. Tan & Anh Q. Tran, S.J.
Description: Maryknoll : Orbis Books, 2017. | Includes index.
Identifiers: LCCN 2015040800 | ISBN 9781626981690 (pbk.)
Subjects: LCSH : Christianity.
Classification: LCC BR145.3 .W67 2017 | DDC 270.8/3—dc23 LC record
    available at http://lccn.loc.gov/2015040800

To

Peter C. Phan

Theologian, Scholar, Colleague,

Collaborator, Mentor, Friend

for his significant contributions to

the study of

World Christianity and Asian Christianity

on the occasion of his

seventieth birthday.

七十而從心所欲, 不踰矩

(論語 2:4)

From seventy I could be unfettered in my heart-and-mind

without any fear of transgressing boundaries

(Analects 2:4)

Contents

Part III
The Pastoral and Practical Dimensions of World Christianity

Part IV
Peter C. Phan's Contributions to World Christianity:
Two Perspectives

ACKNOWLEDGMENTS

The impetus for this book came from the many discussions by members of the Asian/Asian American Theological Consultation of the Catholic Society of America (CTSA) who were looking for a way to honor Peter C. Phan on the occasion of his seventieth birthday, a momentous milestone within the Confucian tradition of his Vietnamese background and upbringing. From these discussions, an initial consensus formed that we should put together a book celebrating Peter's wide-ranging contributions to World Christianity, in general, and Asian and Asian American Christianity in particular.

The editors would like to thank Orbis Books for taking on this book project, and in particular Robert Ellsberg, Jim Keane, and their wonderful team at Orbis for ensuring the successful completion and publication of this book. More importantly, the editors owe a great debt of gratitude to all the contributors for their willingness to share their time and impart their wisdom and insights in their essays. This book would not exist today without their contributions. Finally, the publication of this title is made possible in part by a grant from Georgetown College of Georgetown University, Washington DC. Orbis Books and the editors express their gratitude to Dean Chester Gillis for facilitating this funding arrangement.

Jonathan Y. Tan & Anh Q. Tran

Contributors

Christina A. Astorga is Professor and Chair of the Department of Theology at the University of Portland in Oregon.

Stephen Bevans, SVD, is Louis J. Luzbetak, SVD Professor Emeritus of Mission and Culture at Catholic Theological Union in Chicago, IL.

William R. Burrows is Managing Editor Emeritus, Orbis Books, Maryknoll, NY; Research Professor of Missiology, New York Theological Seminary; and Fellow in the A. F. Walls Center for the Study of Christianity in Africa and Asia at Liverpool Hope University.

Joseph Cheah, OSM, is Associate Professor of Comparative Theology and Chair of the Department of Philosophy, Theology, and Religious Studies at the University of Saint Joseph in West Hartford, CT.

Edmund Kee-Fook Chia is Senior Lecturer in Theology and Convener for Interreligious Dialogue at Australian Catholic University.

Gemma Tulud Cruz is Senior Lecturer in Theology at Australian Catholic University.

Frans Dokman is Director of the Nijmegen Institute for Mission Studies and Senior Researcher in the Centre for World Christianity and Interreligious Studies at Radboud University, the Netherlands.

Jojo M. Fung, SJ, is Assistant Professor of Contextual Theology at the Loyola School of Theology of Ateneo de Manila University and Lecturer at the East Asian Pastoral Institute.

Ruben L. F. Habito is Professor of World Religions and Spirituality at Perkins School of Theology, Southern Methodist University, and also serves as Guiding Teacher of Maria Kannon Zen Center in Dallas, TX.

Dale T. Irvin is President and Professor of World Christianity at New York Theological Seminary.

Julius-Kei Kato is Associate Professor of Religious Studies at King's University College at Western University, London, Canada.

Lim Swee Hong (林瑞峰) is Deer Park Assistant Professor of Sacred Music and directs the Master of Sacred Music program at Emmanuel College of Victoria University in the University of Toronto.

Gerard Mannion is Joseph and Winifred Amaturo Professor in Catholic Studies at Georgetown University, and Senior Research Fellow and Co-Director of the Church and World Program of the Berkley Center for Religion, Peace and World Affairs at the Berkley Center at Georgetown University.

vanThanh Nguyen, SVD, is Associate Professor of New Testament Studies and holder of the Bishop Francis X. Ford, M.M., Chair of Catholic Missiology at Catholic Theological Union.

Kenan Osborne, OFM, is Professor Emeritus of the Franciscan School of Theology, California.

Elaine Padilla is Assistant Professor of Constructive Theology at New York Theological Seminary.

Scott Sunquist is Dean and Professor of World Christianity in the School of Intercultural Studies at Fuller Theological Seminary.

Jonathan Y. Tan is Archbishop Paul J. Hallinan Professor of Catholic Studies at Case Western Reserve University.

Anh Q. Tran, SJ, is Assistant Professor of Historical and Systematic Theology at the Jesuit School of Theology of Santa Clara University.

Amos Yong is Professor of Theology and Mission and Director of the Center for Missiological Research at Fuller Theological Seminary.

INTRODUCTION

Jonathan Y. Tan

In his seminal study, *The Cross-Cultural Process in Christian History: Studies in the Transmission and Appropriation of Faith*, Andrew Walls spoke of Christianity's center of gravity shifting away from Europe and North America to Africa, Asia, Latin America, and the Pacific.[1] He made the point that while Christianity may have begun the twentieth century as a *Western religion*, it ended the century as a truly global and world religion, that is, as *World Christianity*.

Since the beginning of the twenty-first century, the discipline of World Christianity has grown in stature, challenging and transforming how Christianity is studied, taught, and articulated as a global or world religion. This was the context for Peter Phan's lecture, "World Christianity: Its Implications for History, Religious Studies, and Theology," at the Burke Lectureship on Religion and Society at the University of California San Diego on October 13, 2011.[2] In his paper, Phan spoke on the reality of World Christianity emerging from the massive global demographic movements of Christians and explored its implications for reshaping discussions on church history, religious studies, and theology in diverse and hybridized forms beyond the Western or Eurocentric orientation. After tracing the development and key characteristics of World Christianity, he outlined possibilities for rethinking the history of Christianity, the teaching of World Christianity in religious studies, and reshaping a theology of church that is responsible to this emergent reality.

In response to Peter Phan's invitation to explore new possibilities for reshaping theological discussion within the framework of World Christianity, this book seeks to present a comprehensive overview of major themes and topics in World Christianity, and gather the best insights from an ecumenical team of scholars and theologians in a single and easily accessible

---

[1] Andrew Walls, *The Cross-Cultural Process in Christian History: Studies in the Transmission and Appropriation of Faith* (Maryknoll, NY: Orbis Books, 2002), 84.

[2] Peter C. Phan, "World Christianity: Its Implications for History, Religious Studies and Theology," *Horizons* 39/2 (2012): 171–88.

volume. It is our hope that this book will serve as a seminal resource and reference work for scholars, researchers, and students alike.

For ease of reference, this book is divided into four parts. In Part I, readers are introduced to World Christianity and its many faces around the world with Dale Irvin's introduction to the academic discipline of World Christianity and Scott Sunquist's discussion of how World Christianity is transforming our understanding and study of church history. Their essays are followed by Amos Yong's insights on the relationship between World Christianity and Global Renewal Christianity, Frans Dokman's examination of World Christianity changing the face of European Christianity, and Gemma Tulud Cruz's analysis of the impact of migration from the Global South on World Christianity.

Part II focuses on various broad theological topics that have traditionally been discussed within frameworks that assumed the primacy of European and North American contexts and experiences. The contributions in this part explore how the various theological disciplines are being transformed or reshaped by World Christianity. Here, readers will find a broad cross-section of theological experts engaging in critical conversation with World Christianity in their discussions of biblical exegesis and interpretation (Nguyen), missiology (Burrows), contextual theologizing (Bevans), Trinitarian theology (Habito), Christology (Tran), church and ecclesiology (Mannion), liturgy and sacraments (Osborne), theological bioethics (Astorga), as well as theological anthropology and aesthetics (Padilla).

The third part of this book highlights the pastoral and practical dimensions of World Christianity with essays focusing on indigenous Christians (Fung), Catholics negotiating their complex identities (Cheah), ecumenical and interchurch engagements (Chia), and world church music (Lim). Their essays remind us that the discipline of World Christianity transcends theoretical and systematic discussions to encompass practical and pastoral implications that seek to decenter Christianity from its uncritical Eurocentric axis.

The final part of this book features two tributes by Julius-Kei Kato and Gerard Mannion representing the younger generation and senior echelon of theological scholars, respectively, who have been influenced by the wide-ranging and prodigious theological oeuvre of Peter Phan, to whom this book is dedicated. If there is anyone who deserves to be honored for advocating, developing, and advancing the discipline of World Christianity to take its rightful place in the academe, it would be Peter Phan. His election in 2001 as the first non-European to be president of the Catholic Theological Society of America (CTSA) and the subsequent conferral upon him of the CTSA's highest honor, the John Courtney Murray Award in 2010, is testimony to his peers' esteem of his theological stature. Together with Dale Irvin, Peter is instrumental in the establishment of the World Christianity Group in the American Academy of Religion, cementing the increasingly important role that World Christianity plays in academic discourses on religion.

The various contributors of this book, who count Peter as colleague, collaborator, mentor, and friend, together with its two editors who also call Peter their *doktorvater* offer this volume to him in celebration of his many contributions to the study of World Christianity and Asian Christianity on his seventieth birthday. As Peter celebrates this milestone, may he continue to embody the wisdom of Master Kong—to be unfettered in his heart and mind and in his theological writings, breaking new ground and laying the path for others without any fear of transgressing boundaries (cf. Analects 2:4).

Part I

The Many Faces of World Christianity

1

WHAT IS WORLD CHRISTIANITY?

Dale T. Irvin

*The call comes to us to weld the two branches of ecumenical
Christianity [ecumenics and missions] into one
ssingle world Christian movement.*

HENRY P. VAN DUSEN[1]

Over the past several decades, the phrase *World Christianity* has gained
popularity as shorthand for the contemporary global configurations of the
Christian religion in all their complexities.[2] The phrase carries an implicit

---

* This is a revised version of an earlier article first published in the *Journal of World Christianity* 1/1 (2008): 1–26.

[1] Henry P. Van Dusen, *World Christianity: Yesterday, Today, Tomorrow* (New York: Abingdon-Cokesbury Press, 1947), 107.

[2] Francis John McConnell, *Human Needs and World Christianity* (New York: Friendship Press, 1929) is one of the first uses of the phrase World Christianity in print. For a comprehensive overview of the Christianity as a world religion in 2010, see Todd M. Johnson and Kenneth R. Ross, eds., *Atlas of Global Christianity 1910–2010* (Edinburgh: Edinburgh University Press, 2009). Among the excellent introductions to World Christianity are Douglas Jacobsen, *The World's Christians: Who They Are, Where They Are, and How They Got There* (Oxford: Wiley-Blackwell, 2011); Sebastian Kim and Kirsteen Kim, *Christianity as a World Religion* (London: Bloomsbury, 2008); and Charles E. Farhadian, ed., *Introducing World Christianity* (Malden, MA: Blackwell Publishing, 2012). A concise review of the history of the study of World Christianity and some of the problems inherent in the field, can be found in M. Thomas Thangaraj, "An Overview: Asian and Oceanic Christianity in an Age of World Christianity," in Heup Young Kim, Fumitaka Matsuoka and Anri Morimoto, eds., *Asian and Oceanic Christianities in Conversation: Exploring Theological Identities at Home and in Diaspora* (Amsterdam: Rodopi, 2011), 11–21. An overview of major critical themes that are occupying scholarship in the field is provided by Ogbu U. Kalu, "Changing Tides: Some Currents in World Christianity at the Opening of the Twenty-First Century," in Ogbu

admission within it. The term *Christianity* without any qualifier has often referred only to the dominant Western historical form or forms of this religion, rendering the broader global Christian reality invisible. In contrast, the study of World Christianity seeks to investigate and understand Christian communities, faith, and practice as they are found on six continents, expressed in diverse ecclesial traditions, and informed by the multitude of historical and cultural experiences in a world transformed by globalization. It is concerned with both the diversity of local expressions of Christian life and faith throughout the world, and the variety of ways these interact with one another critically and constructively across time and space. It is particularly concerned with marginalized experiences or expressions of Christian faith that have been underrepresented in scholarship and underappreciated for their wider contributions. This last point requires the study of World Christianity to pay greater attention to the experiences of Christian communities that were not part of Western Christendom, the experiences of marginalized communities and the poor throughout the world, and the experiences of women.

As a field of study, World Christianity has its historical roots in the study of missions, ecumenics, and world religions.[3] It continues to pursue a threefold conversation, across borders of culture (historically the domain of mission studies), across borders of confession or communion (historically the domain of ecumenics), and across borders with other religious faiths (historically the domain of world religions).[4] Beyond these, it also seeks to

---

U. Kalu and Alaine Low, eds., *Interpreting Contemporary Christianity: Global Processes and Local Identities* (Grand Rapids, MI: Wm. B. Eerdmans Publishing, 2008), 3–23; and Namsoon Kang, "Whose/Which World in World Christianity? Toward World Christianity as Christianity of Worldly-Responsibility," in Akintunde E. Akinade, ed., *A New Day. Essays on World Christianity in Honor of Lamin Sanneh* (New York: Peter Lang Publishing, 2010), 31–48. The manner in which understanding Christianity from a world perspective rather than from a Eurocentric perspective has reshaped church historiography is explored by Mark A. Noll, *The New Shape of World Christianity: How American Experience Reflects Global Faith* (Downers Grove, IL: IVP Academic, 2009); and Justo L. González, *The Changing Shape of Church History* (St. Louis: Chalice Press, 2002).

[3] These first two were explicitly included in the scope of Henry P. Van Dusen's ground-breaking study from 1947, cited above. The third was implicitly a part of the field for much of the twentieth century, becoming more pronounced by the twenty-first. A caution, however, regarding the notion of world religions is sounded in Tomoko Masuzawa, *The Invention of World Religions: Or, How European Universalism Was Preserved in the Language of Pluralism* (Chicago: University of Chicago Press, 2005).

[4] The theme of border crossing will be pursued in greater detail below, but for a

engage other areas of the theological curriculum and the social sciences. A critical goal of World Christianity in the first decades of the twenty-first century is to call into account the disciplines and fields of study in the theological curriculum (including its own) insofar as they have represented various local forms of knowledge as being universal. One of its constructive tasks is to offer space for differential methods, theories, and practices, and to foster new rationalities and knowledge beyond those generated from various traditions and locations in isolation on their own.[5] In this regard, World Christianity seeks to foster the study and practice of both local and translocal ways of knowing and doing. It is concerned with both the local and the global. It is an attempt to broaden the universe of Christian understanding to reflect the open-ended nature of the divine.[6]

The Horizons of the *World* in the Long History of World Christianity

Christianity in all of its various forms through the ages has always shown to some degree an inclination toward what can be called world-mindedness.[7] In the pages of the New Testament, one encounters a fundamental

---

general introduction to the notion of borders and border crossing in theology, see María Pilar Aquino and Roberto S. Goizueta, eds., *Theology: Expanding the Borders* (Mystic, CT: Twenty-Third Publications, 1998); Peter C. Phan, "Crossing the Borders: A Spirituality for Mission in Our Times," in *In Our Own Tongues: Perspectives from Asia on Mission and Inculturation* (Maryknoll, NY: Orbis Books, 2003), 130–50; and Elaine Padilla, "Border-Crossing and Exile: A Latina's Theological Encounter with Shekhinah," *CrossCurrents* 60/4 (2010): 526–48.

[5] See Chela Sandoval, *Methodology of the Oppressed*, vol. 18, in *Theory out of Bounds* (Minneapolis: University of Minnesota Press, 2000).

[6] For a theo-missiological reading of this phrase, see Dale T. Irvin, "The Mission of Hospitality: To Open the Universe a Little More," in *The Agitated Mind of God: The Theology of Kosuke Koyama*, ed. Dale T. Irvin and Akintunde E. Akinade (Maryknoll, NY: Orbis Books, 1996), 173–87.

[7] The New Testament uses three Greek terms that are usually rendered world in English language translations. The first and most common of these is kosmos, which encompasses all human beings, all nature, and even the heavenly realms of the sun, moon, and stars. The second is oikoumene and refers to that portion of the cosmos that is inhabited by human beings. This second term often carried more limited political connotations in the Greco–Roman world that confined its meaning to the Roman Empire, but the New Testament refers to nations outside the Roman Empire as well, thereby enlarging its meaning. The third term, aion, might be better translated as age and refers to a limited historical era or world, as in this present age. The term *world* (in

desire to bring to "all nations" (*panta ta ethne,* Matt. 28:19) the message of
Jesus Christ, literally to be witnesses to "the ends of the earth" (*eschatou toss
gas,* Acts 1:8). Those first disciples of Jesus in Western Asia could hardly
have imagined how vast that world actually was. At every turn, however,
they appeared ready to engage it. Acts 2 introduces Parthians and others
from the Persian Empire, while Acts 8 introduces us to a court official from
an independent African kingdom south of Egypt the text calls "Ethiopia,"
but whose capital at the time was the city of Meroë. The book of Revelation
extends the range much further with the help of active merchants who were
busy bringing their goods into the city of Babylon the Great (chapter 18).
Among the luxury items, one finds listed on verse 12 is silk (*serikos*), which
in the first century came only from China. The kings of the earth return in
the visionary world of Revelation 21:24, to bring their glory not to Babylon
but to the New Jerusalem, to honor it and its ruler, the Christ.

The expansionist dreams of those first-century disciples were not
supported by military force. They rode the commercial networks of international trade as artisans and merchants, inspired by a vision and a power that
they attributed to the Holy Spirit. In various cities around the Mediterranean, south into Africa via the Nile and eastward into Persia, wherever they
went they told the story of Jesus and gathered those who accepted it into
a community that formed around his name. Those who joined themselves
to the first communities of faith that the apostles of Jesus founded likewise
had no armies or grand strategies for conquest. These new followers were
enjoined to abandon all previous commitments to other gods, although
not their language and customs of life or culture. The majority underwent a
ritual initiation ceremony of immersion in water (baptism), regularly shared
a common ritual thanksgiving meal (the *Eucharist*), and followed basic
teachings about God and the world that handed on from those who had
originally been with Jesus when he walked on earth in the flesh.

Not all who remembered Jesus of Nazareth or gathered in his name considered themselves members of the apostolic community in the first centuries.[8]
Even among those who did follow the apostolic teachings demonstrated consid-

---

all three of these senses) has carried both positive and negative connotations throughout
Christian history, the world being both a place where evil rules but also the arena of
God's redemption. All three originating Greek concepts and both sets of meaning (posi-
tive and negative) must be engaged by the study of World Christianity.

   [8] See, for instance, Bart D. Ehrman, *Lost Christianities: The Battles for Scriptures and
Faiths We Never Knew* (New York: Oxford University Press, 2003).

erable diversity in the details of their beliefs.[9] The churches in various parts of the Mediterranean world and across the Persian Empire formed a polyglot network of communities that were linked together mostly by the communication of their leadership, the bishops. *Koine* Greek, the common language of merchants used from India to Spain, provided an initial vehicle of communication, most notably through the apostolic writings, but the message soon took root in new linguistic and cultural locations. Space does not permit a detailed description of how this expansion took place.[10] What is important to note here is that the Christian world self-consciously reached beyond the known horizons of any one group. Writing in the fourth century, Cyril of Jerusalem concluded his listing of peoples among whom Christian faith had spread with those "for whom we have no names; for of many of the nations not even the names have reached us."[11]

A momentous turning point in the story of World Christianity occurred over the course of the fourth century with the conversion of the Roman imperial household to Christian faith. The greatest areas of numerical Christian growth up to this time had been in the Roman Empire. After the fourth century, Christianity became politically dominant as well in this part of the world. Christians in the Roman world had previously tended to make use of imperial rhetoric, often (but not always) to oppose imperial ways.[12] Now they embraced the imperial order, or at least a significant number of them did, giving rise to a new form of imperial Christianity.

The seventh century witnessed another major turning point in the reception of the message of the Prophet Muhammad and the consolidation

---

[9] The classic statement of this is found in Walter Bauer, *Orthodoxy and Heresy in Earliest Christianity*, trans. Robert A. Kraft and Gerhard Krodel. (Philadelphia: Fortress Press, 1971), German original 1934.

[10] See Dale T. Irvin and Scott W. Sunquist, *History of the World Christian Movement, vol. 1: Earliest Christianity to 1453* (Maryknoll, NY: Orbis Books, 2001).

[11] Cyril of Jerusalem writes, "For consider, I pray, with mind enlightened by Him, how many Christians there are in all this diocese, and how many in the whole province of Palestine, and carry forward thy mind from this province to the whole Roman Empire; and after this, consider the whole world; races of Persians, and nations of Indians, Goths and Samaritans, and Moors, Libyans and Ethiopians, and the rest for whom we have no names; for of many of the nations not even the names have reached us." In "The Catechetical Lectures," XVI, para. 22, in *Nicene and Post-Nicene Fathers of the Christian Church*, vol. 7, ed. P. Schaff and H. Ware (New York: Christian Literature, 1894), 121.

[12] See Averil Cameron, *Christianity and the Rhetoric of Empire: The Development of Christian Discourse* (Berkeley: University of California Press, 1994); and Gay Byron, *Symbolic Blackness and Ethnic Difference in Early Christian Literature* (New York: Routledge Press, 2002).

of Islam under his successors in the form of a new empire under the Arabs. The Arab empire explicitly and persistently opposed the Roman Empire and the established position that Christianity occupied within it. Within a one hundred year period, from 632 to 732 CE, roughly half of the Christians on earth came to find themselves living under Muslim political rule. These Christians found their world drastically changed forever as a new chapter in the history of Christian interfaith relations unfolded.

By the eighth century, the cultural axis of Christian life in the western Mediterranean region had shifted drastically. The city of Rome, a repository of apostolic heritage and tradition, had turned its attention to the north and forged a new set of alliances with more recently converted Germanic peoples. Over the course of the next seven centuries—from roughly 700 to 1400 CE—the horizons of World Christianity shifted dramatically. While Christianity steadily shrunk in the east in Asia and to the south in Africa, it expanded north and west in Europe. By the twelfth century, Christianity had become primarily a European religion. Meanwhile from the twelfth to the fifteenth centuries, Europe underwent a tremendous transformation in its material economic life, setting in place the conditions for its explosive geographic expansion that began in the fifteenth century.

World Christianity and the Modern World

Five hundred years ago, a new chapter in world history began, characterized by tendencies and trajectories that would come to be identifying characteristics of what we now call the modern era, or in its ideological form modernity.[13] The early modern world that emerged after 1500 ushered in a new global vision. For the first time, peoples from all continents on earth

---

[13] C. A. Bayly, *The Birth of the Modern World 1780–1914: Global Connections and Comparisons* (Malden, MA: Blackwell Publishers, 2004) argues for reserving the phrase "the modern world" for the global construction that emerged at the end of the eighteenth century. But he also acknowledges that the argument is mostly a matter of "scope and scale" (ibid., 11). The key factors defining modernity for Bayly are the rise of the nation-state and the massive expansion of global commercial and intellectual links. I find both to be sufficiently under way by 1500 to argue the modern was beginning then but would allow for a more careful delineation of early modern, high modern, and postmodern sensibilities, with the second of these fitting what Bayly simply terms the modern. The global contours of modernity are already in view in the fifteenth century, I will argue, although the systems necessary to sustain its global pretensions were not sufficiently developed until the eighteenth century when Europe's economic and political power were sufficient to truly achieve world domination.

were tied together in a unified picture of the whole. The driving engines of what is now called modernity were (and in many respects still are) the engines of Western European political and economic expansion. Europeans traveling to Asia, Africa, and the Americas had set in motion the processes that gave rise to what we call the modern world. However, Europe did not build this modern world alone. The indigenous peoples of Africa, Asia, and the Americas north and south contributed much not only to the material production of what after 1500 became an increasingly integrated world economy but to the multiple cultural and ideological constructions of the modern world as well. The contributions of Africans, Asians, and Native Americans were (and in many cases continue to be) made from what has often been called the underside or the peripheries of modernity, that is, from subaltern or marginal locations, so much so that any depiction of the modern that excludes them remains deficient and incomplete.

Modernity drew upon knowledge and power from peoples on all continents. Its cross-cultural, transregional, and polycentric practices accelerated over the course of five centuries as the era unfolded,[14] but already at its inception, one discerns various forms of consciousness and perceptions that can be called global.[15] As a movement and an ideology, modernity has often been a significantly destabilizing force. Its corrosive effects have brought about tremendous losses to local cultures globally. However, modernity has also preserved much that it has touched. Whole languages and cultures have been preserved by its documentation processes and amplified by its communicative practices, often done unwittingly by those seeking to dominate. New formations derived from the multiple global pasts in many cases now thrive in an emerging postmodern space.[16]

---

[14] On the polycentric nature of World Christianity, see Klaus Koschorke and Adrian Hermann, eds., *Polycentric Structures in the History of World Christianity/ Polyzentrische strukturen in der geschichte des Weltchristentums* (Wiesbaden: Harrassowitz Verlag, 2014). A special edition of the *Journal of World Christianity* on the method of polycentric historiography in the study of World Christianity that Professor Koschorke and his students have pioneered at Munich is forthcoming in the *Journal of World Christianity* in 2016.

[15] In the paragraphs that follow I am drawing upon insights from Immanuel Wallerstein, especially his recent book, *The End of the World As We Know It: Social Science for the Twenty-First Century* (Minneapolis: University of Minnesota Press, 2001). A previous version of these paragraphs appeared in an earlier form in Dale T. Irvin, "Global Faith: Not Made in the USA," *Christian Century* 121/15 (July 27, 2004): 28–31.

[16] See Marshall Berman, *All That Is Solid Melts into Air: The Experience of Moder-*

Christianity was little more than the regional religion of the patchwork of societies that inhabited the geographical continent of Europe at the beginning of the fifteenth century. In other regions of the world where Christians had once dominated, in North Africa, Egypt, Nubia, Palestine, Syria, Asia Minor, Mesopotamia, and Persia, churches had been reduced to a remnant living as subjugated minorities hemmed in by the laws of *dhimmi* (protected minority) under Islamic governments, or had ceased altogether to exist. An earlier Christian missionary expansion into Central Asia and China had sputtered to an end. A small but significant Christian community numbering in the tens of thousands could still be found in the south of India. Although relatively isolated from the rest of World Christianity and integrated into their surrounding Indian culture as a caste, they maintained a strong Christian identity that reached back through memory and tradition to St. Thomas, the Apostle to the East. In Africa, only the ancient Christian kingdom of Ethiopia remained as a place where Christians exercised a meaningful presence. Ethiopia was also the only African nation in which Christianity continued into the modern era to be established politically as the religion of the state.

In Europe, the process of bringing the entire continent under Christian domination had only been recently completed by the beginning of the fifteenth century.[17] The last non-Christian tribes on Europe's northwestern frontier were only converted on the eve of the Protestant Reformation, while the last Islamic kingdom in Spain was defeated the year Columbus set sail for the Indies. Internally within Europe, the integrated religious–cultural formation called Christendom that had been under construction for almost a thousand years was beginning to break apart under the weight of a number of factors, not least of them the emergence of a new political entity that became the modern nation state.

Externally these emerging European nation-states, starting with Portugal and Spain, launched out on voyages of discovery and conquest into other parts of the world in the fifteenth century. Their military forces took Christianity in its diverse Western cultural forms with them, first in Roman

---

nity (New York: Penguin Books, 1988); Peter L. Berger, Brigitte Berger, and Hansfried Kellner, *The Homeless Mind: Modernization and Consciousness* (New York: Random House, 1973); and Peter L. Berger and Samuel P. Huntington, *Many Globalizations: Cultural Diversity in the Contemporary World* (New York: Oxford University Press, 2003).

[17] See Lionel Rothkrug, *Religious Practices and Collective Perceptions: Hidden Homologies in the Renaissance and Reformation, Historical Reflections*, vol. 7, no. 1 (Waterloo, Ontario: Historical Reflections Press, Spring 1980).

Catholic and then later in various Protestant or Evangelical missions. The concept of a mission as an extension of the church within Christendom took root, giving rise to a new agent of foreign affairs called a missionary.[18] The modern missionary movement accelerated through the nineteenth century to epic proportions, bringing agents of various forms of Western Christianity to virtually every corner of the world.

The great truth of World Christianity over the last five hundred years is that these missionary efforts were successful.[19] Nevertheless, they have not necessarily been successful in the way that the Western Christian missionaries themselves, their strategists in Western churches, or their more recent critics from around the world have often depicted them as being. What Western missionaries intended and what indigenous agents of conversion apprehended in the communication of the message of Jesus Christ were often two different things, creating a fundamental borderline that continues to run through all of World Christianity today.

That boundary was obvious throughout much of the modern missionary era to anyone who cared to take notice. The landscape of World Christianity for the past several hundred years is littered with such phrases as *Christian lands/mission lands* or more recently *historic churches/younger churches*. Lamin Sanneh has suggested that this divide between the territorial forms of Christianity that dominated in Europe and nonterritorial forms of Christianity that emerged beyond Christendom's frontiers can also be understood in terms of structure and antistructural.[20] Along its contours, following Sanneh, we can see the space open up for a new understanding of World Christianity.

---

[18] David J. Bosch, *Transforming Mission: Paradigm Shift in Theology of Mission* (Maryknoll, NY: Orbis Books, 1991) points out that many of the modern connotations of the word, mission can be dated only back to the sixteenth century. Prior to that time, the word was reserved in Christian theology to refer to what God did. According to Bosch, a new usage was introduced by Ignatius of Loyola and the Jesuits to designate ecclesiastical agents who were sent to regions being colonized by the kings of Spain and Portugal in order to propagate the reign of Christ. An intimate connection between colonialism and this new conception of Christian mission was thereby established. Bosch argues, "The new word, 'mission,' is historically linked indissolubly with the colonial era and with the idea of a magisterial commissioning. The term presupposes an established church in Europe which dispatched delegates to convert overseas peoples and was as such an attendant phenomenon of European expansion" (ibid., 28).

[19] This is an argument advanced most recently by Andrew Walls in *The Cross-Cultural Process in Christian History* (Maryknoll, NY: Orbis Books, 2002).

[20] Lamin Sanneh, *Abolitionists Abroad: American Blacks and the Making of Modern West Africa* (Cambridge, MA: Harvard University Press, 2001).

The modern era, in both its early and high formations as noted above, had been a global phenomenon from its inception. Its construction has entailed the contributions not just of Europeans, but of Asians, Africans, and indigenous Americans as well, even if the latter have contributed from a place on the underside of this history. In the same way, modern World Christianity has been a global phenomenon long before the twentieth century. Although Western forms of thinking have dominated the world Christian experience these past five hundred years, they have not been the only way Christians have expressed their faith. Recovering the memory of those diversities and understanding their implications for theory, method, and practice today is one of the fundamental tasks that the study of World Christianity has to undertake.

Now at the end of the five-hundred-year period that we call the modern age, the success of that missionary project (and especially of the apprehension of the message of Jesus Christ along the indigenous side of the border between missionary and convert) emerges as arguably the most important factor in world Christian life. Coupled with the de-Christianization of the traditional European *homeland* of Western Christendom, the shift is transparent. Christianity, long identified in world historical consciousness as primarily a Western European religion, is so no longer. Christianity is now predominantly a religion of African, Asian, and the Americas (North, Central, and South). It is estimated that as many as 60 percent of the world's Christians are now living in the southern hemisphere. From a statistical perspective, the average Christian is now better represented as living in São Paulo, Dar es Salaam, or Manila rather than in Rome, Geneva, or London. The forms of expression that Christian faith takes in day-to-day practice, the ideas that people have of what it means to be a faithful disciple of Jesus Christ, and the languages they use to express themselves in worship and salvation are proliferating beyond those of European Christian descent. A new world Christian reality has emerged.

For many Christians, especially those living in regions that are considered as *the West*, there is unfortunately a serious intellectual lag in coming to grips with what this new reality means. In this regard, there is a critical need in our theological work for new theoretical ways of seeing this reality, in order for us to engage it both faithfully and productively. "The assumptions that have governed our understanding of Christian history during the past several centuries were all formed in the European context where the church was identified with the cultural and religious majority and attention was focused largely on its institutional life," argues Wilbert

R. Shenk.[21] "There is no way in which African and Asian church history can be incorporated within a traditional Western-type syllabus; nor can they be appendages to Western church history," Andrew Walls continues.[22] As Sanneh observes,

> People want to interpret Christianity by standards of exegesis and doctrine familiar to them, something that the Christendom model of the church warranted. World Christianity, by contrast, must be interpreted by a plurality of models of inculturation in line with the variety of local idioms and practices. The mental habits of Christendom predispose us to look for one essence of the faith, with a corresponding global political structure as safeguard, whereas world Christianity challenges us to pay attention to the dynamic of power of the gospel and the open-ended character of communities of faith.[23]

The notion that the study of World Christianity requires a multiplicity of models and theoretical productions that are open to new expressions of faith points us in two directions. Sanneh argues that, on the one hand, we need to attend carefully to "the principles of local agency and indigenous cultural appropriation" and, on the other, to the overall framework of World Christianity in its diversity within which these local realities are located.[24] There is no single standard for defining this framework, no universal Christian history or truth apart from what we encounter in the diversity of Christian cultures and communities through time, against which to measure our various Christian constructions and endeavors.[25] Instead, ecumenical networks, overlapping commonalities, recurring themes, multiple structures of communication, and various demands for accountability allow us to draw connections and make judgments.

---

[21] Wilbert R. Shenk, ed., *Enlarging the Story: Perspectives on Writing World Christian History* (Maryknoll, NY: Orbis Books, 2002), xiii.

[22] Shenk, Enlarging the Story, 8.

[23] Lamin Sanneh, *Whose Religion Is Christianity? The Gospel beyond the West* (Grand Rapids, MI: Wm. B. Eerdmans Publishing, 2003), 35.

[24] Lamin Sanneh, "World Christianity and the New Historiography," in Shenk, *Enlarging the Story*, 94–114.

[25] As Peter C. Phan notes, "There is not, nor has there ever been, one Christianity; rather there exist Christianities (in the plural), all over the world and all the time." Peter C. Phan, "World Christianity: Its Implications for History, Religious Studies, and Theology," *Horizons* 39/2 (2012): 175.

This last point is a critical one to make, for what often passes as a global or universal truth is in reality a local strategy that has been amplified to global dimensions. This is an argument that Enrique Dussel and Walter D. Mignolo have made in their work in postcolonial studies.[26] The modern West sought to impose its own definitions and designs on peoples and cultures far removed from its centers and interests. What is often depicted by Western writers as *universal history* is in fact little more than a tribal history, an ethnocentric telling of the larger global story from an exclusively European perspective. What Mignolo calls "global designs" were "brewed, so to speak, in the local histories of the metropolitan countries" and "implemented, exported, and enacted differently in particular places."[27] Be they embedded in the universal claims of Western Christendom, or offered in a more secularized version, such as Hegel's universal world history, such global designs were and are local histories amplified by world-dominating pretensions.

The modern era witnessed the successful expansion of Western European colonialism to impose its designs on other histories and cultures with varying degrees of success across the planet. However, colonialism did not extinguish other histories, other cultures, and other traditions. A more dynamic and contentious interaction took place. "Today, local histories are coming to the forefront and, by the same token, revealing the local histories from which global designs emerge in their universal drive," Mignolo concludes.[28] In the words of Michel Foucault, we are witnessing the "insurrection of subjugated knowledges."[29]

The Modern/Colonial

Mignolo identifies the border as the line that runs between the global designs of one particular group of local histories, those from the West, and the rest of the local histories that populate our globe. As a line running between the *modern* and the *colonial*, it cuts through every region, every nation, and every culture on the face of the earth. Mignolo acknowledges that the modern

---

[26] Enrique Dussel, "Beyond Eurocentrism: The World-System and the Limits of Modernity," in *The Cultures of Globalization*, ed. Fredric Jameson and Masao Miyoshi (Durham, NC: Duke University Press, 1998), 3–31; and Walter D. Mignolo, *Local Histories/Global Designs: Coloniality, Subaltern Knowledges, and Border Thinking* (Princeton, NJ: Princeton University Press, 2000).

[27] Mignolo, *Local Histories/Global Designs*, 65.

[28] Ibid., 21.

[29] Michel Foucault, *Power/Knowledge: Selected Interviews and Other Writings, 1972–1977*, ed. Colin Gordon (Brighton, UK: Harvester Press, 1980), 81.

was defined as being centered in the West and that modernity is in this sense by definition Eurocentric.[30] Along with other postcolonial theorists such as Edward Said (*metropolis* and *colony*) and Gayatri Chakravorty Spivak (*center* and *margins*), Mignolo recognizes that the West succeeded to a great degree in realizing its global designs precisely by defining itself as being at the center of the modern.[31] The ability the West had to impose this construct on distant lands far removed from its geographical center is very much a part of what makes the modern a global phenomenon.

At this point, we need to stop and ask what precisely is meant by the terms *Western* or *the West*. The geographical concept, Jasper M. Trautsch argues, goes back for millennia, but the notion of the West as a coherent political, economic, and cultural world is more recent.[32] Trautsch traces its emergence in the nineteenth century as an invention of Russian intellectuals in the debates around Peter the Great's attempt to "Europeanize" Russia.[33] In these debates, *the West* generally meant Great Britain and France. Germany was still considered *Central Europe*. At the beginning of the twentieth century for reasons that had largely to do with the United States' emergence as both a major industrial and a foreign colonial power, the United States began ideologically to identify itself as part of *Western Civilization* and *the West*. After 1945, the United States in turn facilitated West Germany's reemergence as a part of the West. From 1946 to 1989, the East–West divide of the Cold War was a dominant global political reality shaping political, economic, social, and cultural discourses.

Meanwhile powerful revolutionary and global anticolonial struggles that had been going on for centuries began to gain significant ground after 1945 on the global political agenda. A new alignment of Asian, African, and Latin American nations emerged under such terms as *the Third World* or *the non-Western World* in this period. The new alignments did not always exactly fit older cultural realities. For reasons that had much to do with the political and economic dominance of the North Atlantic nations, Latin America, for

---

[30] See Dale T. Irvin, *Christian Histories, Christian Traditioning: Rendering Accounts* (Maryknoll NY: Orbis Books, 1998); and Dale T. Irvin, "From One Story to Many: An Ecumenical Reappraisal of Church History," *Journal of Ecumenical Studies* 28/4 (Fall 1991): 537–54.

[31] Edward W. Said, *Culture and Imperialism* (New York: Vintage Books, 1993); and Gayatri Chakravorty Spivak, *In Other Worlds: Essays in Cultural Politics* (New York: Routledge, 1988). See also Dussel, "Beyond Eurocentrism."

[32] Jasper M. Trautsch, "The Invention of the 'West,'" *Bulletin of the German Historical Institute* 53 (2013): 89–102.

[33] Trautsch, "The Invention of the 'West,'" 91.

instance, which is arguably more a part of European civilization historically than the United States, came to be regarded as *non-Western*. Nevertheless, the alignment took hold: Europe and North America constituted the center, or *the West*, while Asia, Africa, and Latin America constituted the periphery or *the Rest*.[34]

In much critical discourse in recent decades, the West has come to be identified with the modern, and the Rest has come to be identified as the colonial. Assigning geographical locations to these identities (*modern* and *colonial*) has become quite problematic however. Given the history of the past five hundred years, the reality of the contemporary world system, and the effects of the integrated world economy, Mignolo argues that the border running between the modern and the colonial does not exist as a geographical line drawn around the North Atlantic nations, but rather found in every local history today.

Here the conception of the *modern* as discussed above takes on greater complexity in the form of the modern/colonial. The slash that runs through the middle of the phrase, says Mignolo, represents a border, a fissure that runs through every region, every culture, and every history in the world today. It is found in those regions that were colonized by European nations. It is immediately obvious in the imposed territorial structures of modern nation-states, in the intellectual dominance exercised by European forms of knowledge in universities everywhere, and in the ever-present cultural artifacts of the Western (United States and Western European) consumerism that proliferate around the globe. It is also found in the territories of Europe and later the United States from whence global dominance was enacted. One finds it represented, for instance, by the potatoes and tomatoes that Europeans now eat, foods that first came from the Americas, and by the coffee, chocolate, tobacco, and tea that peoples of European descent now consume, all foods that arrived in Europe in the first days of the modern age.[35] In religion, it is seen in the lingering structures and practices of Euro-

---

[34] Stuart Hall, "The West and the Rest: Discourse and Power," in *Formations of Modernity*, ed. Stuart Hall and Brian Gieben (Cambridge: Polity Press, 1992), 275–330.

[35] Mignolo, *Local Histories/Global Designs*, 15 quotes Fernando Ortiz's 1940 book, *Cuban Counterpoint: Tobacco and Sugar:* "Tobacco reached the [Western] Christian world along with the revolutions of the Renaissance and the Reformation, when the Middle Ages were crumbling and the modern epoch, with its rationalism, was beginning. One might say that reason, starved and benumbed by theology, to revive and free itself, needed the help of some harmless stimulant that should not intoxicate it with enthusiasm and then stupefy it with illusions and bestiality, as happens with

pean and later North American missionary (or colonial) Christianity found in Asia, Africa, and in other parts of the Americas. It is also seen in new forms of Christianity that emerged in the mixing that took place across the Americas and in Europe. It is still taking place especially in global Pentecostalism today, challenging the sufficiency of truths forged in the former Western Christian center, and challenging those who consider themselves part of the West itself to embrace a more diverse Christian future.[36]

Church/Mission

Mignolo's argument provides a critical insight into the nature of World Christianity today. The modern/colonial border that he articulates was reproduced in World Christianity over the past five hundred years in numerous ways in the form of a border between church and mission. Churches sent missions overseas as agents of ecclesiastical extension, following colonial patterns. For the most part these missions almost immediately began to give rise to believing communities that were extensions under the rule of the existing Western churches (although here there were important exceptions). Church and mission continued to exist in a colonial relationship well into the twentieth century around the globe. In most cases, missions did indeed eventually give rise to new churches, however, constituting a double border of mission/church that was crossed in numerous instances and not without significant local struggle. Missionaries and local

---

the old alcoholic drinks that lead to drunkenness. For this, to help sick reason, tobacco came from America. And with it chocolate. And from Abyssinia and Arabia, about the same time, came coffee. And tea made its appearance from the Far East." See also K. M. Panikkar, *Asia and Western Dominance: A Survey of the Vasco Da Gama Epoch of Asian History 1498–1945* (London: George Allen and Unwin, 1953).

[36] Historical analysis, cultural reflection, and social theory remain inadequate without attending to the presence of this border. Given the multiplicity of its historical locations, it is logical that it take a variety of shapes or manifestations. "The colonial difference is the space where local histories inventing and implementing global designs meet local histories, the space in which global designs have to be adapted, adopted, rejected, integrated, or ignored" writes Mignolo (*Local Histories/Global Designs*, ix.). He points in this regard to the "double-consciousness" of African Americans about which W. E. B. DuBois wrote at the beginning of the century; the mestiza consciousness that Gloria Anzaldúa has referred to more recently; or the recognition of *une pensée autre* in the work of Abdelkhebir Khatibi as incidents of border thinking. In each case, the distinctive nature of local histories gives shape to a distinctive type of border thinking that follows along the modern/colonial divide, giving rise to new and distinctive configurations of thought.

agents of evangelization often parted ways in order for these new churches to arise. When they did, they permanently reproduced within them the memory of this border. Indeed, the double boundaries of church/mission and mission/church runs like scars through Christian communities and communions throughout the world still today.

The implications for the study of World Christianity are enormous. One cannot understand Christian history, practice biblical or theological studies, or engage in pastoral practice without attending to the complex and multi-faceted church/mission and mission/church borders that run through each Christian community globally today. The line that runs between church and mission is found in every place, and in every local Christian community. Moreover, this line is continuously being redrawn and redefined. It cannot be reduced to natal descent, nor can it be identified simply with missionary outreach. Churches that grew out of mission work over the past five centu-ries in Asia, Africa, and the Americas have never been merely reflections of the missionizing efforts, even if they engaged in what Homi Bhabha calls colonial mimicry.[37] Churches in Europe and the United States that consider themselves descendants of European historical tradition are no less places where mission is taking place.

Telling the more complex story of World Christianity today entails a more complex practice of border crossing than the reigning paradigms and models of church history have allowed. Church historiography for the most part remains ill prepared to attend to local dynamics and indigenous expressions of Christianity that emerged on the mission side of the mission/church border.[38] It is my contention here that the story of church history even within Europe and North America, or *the West*, cannot be narrated apart from the story of missions and the practice of missions in the modern era. *The Other*, most

---

[37] See Homi K. Bhabha, *The Location of Culture* (London: Routledge, 1994).

[38] Contextual theologies have made an important contribution over the past fifty years to developing theological insights that lie on the other side of the border. Their influence on the main structures of systematic theology as it is produced and taught in the West, however, remains hampered by the perception that they are (hyphenated) local projects, and thus not on the same level of importance as those (unhyphenated) global and universal, if confessional, systematic theologies of the West. On the origin of contex-tualization, see Shoki Coe, "In Search of Renewal in Theological Education," *Theological Education* 9/4 (1973): 233–43. Regarding the diversity of contextual theologies, see Hans Waldenfels, *"Kontextuelle Theologie," Lexikon missionstheologischer Grundbegriffe* (Berlin: Dietrich Reimer, 1987), 224–30; Justin Ukpong, "What Is Contextualization?" *Neue Zeitschrift für Missionswissenschaft* 43 (1987): 161–68; and Stephen B. Bevans, *Models of Contextual Theology*, 2nd ed. (Maryknoll, NY: Orbis Books, 2002).

often represented in modern church history through the figure of *missions*, is constitutive of modernity in fundamental ways that cannot be dismissed. [39] To understand World Christianity today, the divide between church history and mission history must be crossed in order that the church/mission or mission/church border can be located clearly within our historiography. [40]

In this regard, the strange bifurcation of the history of Christianity into church history and mission history has seriously distorted our understanding of World Christianity in its long history over the last two millennia. [41] A quick survey of the courses and curricular materials in almost any Bible school or theological school throughout the world reveals an operative consensus that church history proper, or the history of Christianity, concerns itself with the history of church and theology in Europe and later in the United States; while mission history studies the expansion of Christianity primarily in the modern period from the west to the south and east. The former concerns itself with the growth and development of the Christian church proper, while the latter is concerned with the extension of Christianity into new contexts and situations. Church history (which is usually taught and studied in the introductory course) is thus closely related to the history and development of doctrine, while mission history (taught and studied in an elective course) is concerned with the application and extension of doctrine and practices *overseas*. As a result, the histories of Christian communities outside the main lines of Western European Christendom remain underrepresented or invisible within the history curriculum. The history of Christianity in places like Latin America becomes severely distorted, as if it is apart from the universal history of the church. [42] One or more tribal forms of Christianity, those that were forged in European experiences, pass themselves as the universal history of World Christianity. [43]

---

[39] See especially Enrique Dussel, *Invention of the Americas: Eclipse of "the Other" and the Myth of Modernity*, vol. 1 (New York: Continuum International Publishing Group, 1995).

[40] This has been one of the guiding methodological principles of Dale T. Irvin and Scott W. Sunquist, *History of the World Christian Movement*, vol 1: *Earliest Christianity to 1453* (Maryknoll, NY: Orbis Books, 2001) and vol 2: *The Modern Era* (Maryknoll, NY: Orbis Books, 2005).

[41] See Irvin, *Christian Histories, Christian Traditioning*.

[42] The election of Jorge Mario Bergoglio as Pope Francis, in 2013 has put to rest for good any notion that the history of Latin American Christianity is not an integral part of the Latin experience often identified with the West.

[43] Walls, in *The Cross-Cultural Process in Christian History*, 220, writes, "In its essence, Western Christianity is tribal religion; and tribal religion is fundamentally

This is the surprising truth concerning World Christianity today: the most important event in modern church history, viewed from the perspective of World Christianity, is not the European Enlightenment and the concomitant rise of modern theology in the West, but the modern missionary movement that took Christianity beyond European places in such decisive ways.[44] Much that is celebrated regarding cultural diversity in Christian theological circles today is the direct result of the growth of Christian communities around the world, many of whom trace their histories in part to the Western European missionary movement of the past several centuries. The shift in theological agenda that is often associated with various liberation theologies, a shift from addressing concerns raised by Europe's intellectual elite to addressing concerns raised by the poor, can likewise be attributed in part to the global shift in location and commitment. One cannot tell the story of modern global Christian history without putting the history of missions at the center. We cannot understand World Christianity without building a bridge between the disciplines of church history and mission history.

Building a bridge, or navigating the divide, between mission history and church history challenges the privileged perspective that the Western church (Europe and North America) has received in the historiography of World Christianity over the past century. There have been other Christian communities on this earth whose culture and historical identity was not European. Their numbers diminished in the past, but never so rapidly as the numbers of faithful European Christians have diminished in the last one hundred years. In centuries past, many Christian communities were diminished by political forces of oppression that were external to them, whereas the recent decline in European Christianity came from *self-inflicted wounds* of secularization, which only in Europe has accompanied modernity.[45] In many cases

---

more about acknowledged symbols, and custom and recognized practice, than about faith."

[44] This is a point that Walls makes throughout *The Cross-Cultural Process in Christian History*.

[45] It is important to note that I am not equating secularism with modernity or secularization with modernization, nor am I rejecting the critical intellectual projects of thinkers such as Marx, Freud, and Nietzsche who have been so closely identified with secularization and modernity in the West. Sociologist Grace Davie argues that only in Western Europe was modernity accompanied by secularization and the diminishment of institutions of religion. Elsewhere in the world, in Asia, Africa, Latin America, and even North America, modernity and religion have not been antagonistic. The modern period has even been accompanied by a revitalization of religion and religiosity. See

Christians from Africa, Asia, and the Americas have represented history from the underside of modernity, a heritage that is becoming increasingly recognized as important for the future of World Christianity.

The development of a fuller historiographical bridge resulting in a clearer understanding of the border that runs between church history and mission history in the modern period is a necessary step toward overcoming the reduction of the history of churches in Asia, Africa, and parts of the Americas to the history of European missions, or to being extensions of North Atlantic church history. Nevertheless, it is also necessary to understanding more clearly the history of Christianity in the European West. The diversity of Christian history in the Greco–Roman world, and later in that part of the world now generally referred to as Europe, is as much a part of the history of missions as is the diversity of Asian, African, American, and Pacific Christian history. Churches throughout the world, especially those claiming the spaces of *orthodoxy* defined by Nicaea and Chalcedon, can benefit from missiological readings of church history, the history of doctrine, and systematic theology.[46] The insights of mission studies are critical for understanding the transmission of faith across any historical border of time. As Letty Russell has reminded us, the handing on of tradition itself is best understood as mission.[47]

Grace Davie, *Religion in Modern Europe: A Memory Mutates* (Oxford: Oxford University Press, 2000); and Grace Davie, *Europe: The Exceptional Case: Parameters of Faith in the Modern World* (London: Darton, Longman & Todd, 2002).

[46] The reduction of the diversity one meets in the history of World Christianity, either in the name of what is significant or what is orthodox, has been a central feature of Western church historiography for several centuries. The result has been an uncritical dismissal of large portions of the history of Christianity as simply being insignificant. In this regard, the term heresy has played a particularly critical role. Even as it is being rethought in a number of confessional locations as a direct result of ecumenical dialogue between and among communions, it continues to be used in historical discourse to mark the border between the Christian self and other. Church historiography simply needs to catch up. Groups that have been culturally marginalized by the dominant historiographies need to be examined in a less prejudicial manner. See Irvin, *Christian Histories, Christian Traditioning*; and Irvin and Sunquist, *History of the World Christian Movement*.

[47] Letty M. Russell, *Church in the Round: Feminist Interpretation of the Church* (Louisville: Westminster John Knox, 1993), 90 writes, "I myself have always recognized the links in my feminist liberation theology to the theological understanding of God's Mission. It is no accident that I wrote my doctoral thesis on the understanding of Tradition as Mission, nor that the person who pioneered this . . . reinterpretation of Mission in the World Council of Churches was my late husband, the Dutch missiologist Hans

Toward the Future of World Christianity

Over the last century, mission studies in the Western European and North American academic world led the way in understanding theological processes of contextualization. Questions of inculturation and dialogue are as old as the Christian movement itself. However, the discipline of mission studies has given them fresh articulations in the postcolonial context of the late twentieth century. The emergence of these questions and concerns in the study of theology first emerged from mission departments in the theological schools and mission boards in the churches of Europe and North America. In recent years, there has been a growing awareness in many quarters that the recovery of the fuller *missional* identity of the Christian movement is necessary not just for the future of Christian faith in those regions that were never part of historical Christendom. Recovering a fuller understanding of the missionary nature of the church is necessary for there to be a future of Christianity in all parts of the world. The *missional church* movement has been forcefully making the case that mission is not what churches do but what churches are in their very structure and nature.[48] Our academic work would do well to acknowledge the contribution mission studies has made to the contextual diversity that has become so much an accepted part of contemporary Christian life. Likewise, our theological work would do well to attend to the missionary nature of the church if there is to be another generation of faithful Christians on earth.

We would also do well in our academic work, both as religious scholars who are studying Christianity as a world religion and as theologians for whom faith is constantly seeking understanding, to be more cognizant of the manner in which the confessional boundaries that define various communions or traditions that once seemed to be so secure have in fact become quite porous. The twentieth century ecumenical movement made the realization of full, visible unity among the churches one of its main pursuits, if not its primary goal.[49] It has become common to read today of the demise

---

Hoekendijk." See also Johannes C. Hoekendijk, *The Church Inside Out* (Philadelphia: Westminster Press, 1964).

   [48] J. E. Lesslie Newbigin, *The Household of God: Lectures on the Nature of the Church* (London: SCM Press, 1953; J. E. Lesslie Newbigin, *The Gospel in a Pluralist Society* (Grand Rapids, MI: Wm. B. Eerdmans Publishing, 1989); and Darrell L. Guder, *Missional Church: A Vision for the Sending of the Church in North America* (Grand Rapids, MI: Wm. B. Eerdmans Publishing, 1998).

   [49] The reduction of the ecumenical movement to being primarily or even exclusively a movement for the realized unity of the churches in both popular and scholarly

of the ecumenical movement or the emergence of an "ecumenical winter."[50] If one were only to be attending to official church statements and policies, it would indeed appear that the effort to bring about full communion among the separated churches appears to have stumbled. Yet in terms of actual experiences, quite the opposite is in fact proving to be the case. On the level of actual church life, one finds throughout the world on every continent a lively, if unorganized, ecumenical reality emerging. Throughout the world, one finds people attending churches in traditions other than the one into which they were baptized. More and more people are not just attending more than one Christian church sequentially, going from being Catholic to Pentecostal for instance, but in an increasing number of cases, people are attending and participating in more than one church community at the same time. The borders between and among churches and traditions that keep them from officially recognizing each other's faith or sharing communion are not being brought down. The faithful are simply crossing those borders and participating in forms of undocumented ecumenism. Nor is it only the laity who are doing so, and not just minor or marginal figures. The experience of Cardinal Bergoglio (now Pope Francis) joining Evangelical and Pentecostal pastors regularly for prayer while he served as Archbishop of Buenos Aires, and even asking Evangelical and Pentecostal leaders to pray over him with laying on of hands prior to his taking the podium to speak in June 2006 at the Communion of Renewed Evangelicals and Catholics, is quintessential in this regard.[51]

---

understanding is a relatively recent phenomenon. Earlier understandings of the movement following the Edinburgh Missionary Conference of 1910 consistently emphasized the close relationship between unity and mission in the ecumenical movement. By the 1920s, the question of dialogue with other religions was also beginning to appear on the ecumenical agenda, to blossom in the 1960s. Through the 1980s, the Faith and Order Commission, which by all accounts was the ecumenical instrument most committed to realizing the visible unity of the churches, embarked on a study process on the unity and renewal of the whole of humanity, This culminated in the publication of a Faith and Order study document *Church and World: The Unity of the Church and the Renewal of Human Community* (Geneva: World Council of Churches, 1990). Such concerns have been largely absent from Faith and Order since 1990. For a fuller reading of the broader agenda of the modern ecumenical movement, see Dale T. Irvin, *Hearing Many Voices: Dialogue and Diversity in the Ecumenical Movement* (Lanham, MD: University Press of America, 1994).

[50] See William G. Rusch, "The State and Future of the Ecumenical Movement," *Pro Ecclesia* 9/1 (2000): 8–18; and Ola Tjørhom, "An 'Ecumenical Winter'? Challenges in Contemporary Catholic Ecumenism," *Heythrop Journal* 49/5 (2008): 841–59.

[51] Austen Ivereigh recounts the story in *The Great Reformer: Francis and the Making*

On the level of theological reflection, one finds the borders between and among traditions being crossed at the most profound levels. Roman Catholic, Orthodox, Protestant, Evangelical, Pentecostal, and charismatic scholars working in biblical studies, theology, ethics, church history, and pastoral studies are drawing upon each other's work with deep appreciation and with profound results. The result has not been a movement toward homogenization, but rather a new kind of lively ecumenical intellectual life where multiple traditions interact on a deep level, and fresh theological insights emerge on all sides. As Peter Phan has noted,

> the rise of the concept of World Christianity has brought to the fore the realities of different and multiple Christianities, with their distinctive traditions in theology, liturgy, spirituality, and ecclesiastical organization. This heightened consciousness of ecclesial variety and multiplicity in turn fosters new and diverse theological methodologies.[52]

The third area of border-crossing in World Christianity, that between Christianity and other religions, is likewise only going to increase in the future. Religious pluralism is not a new phenomenon in human history. Not even European Christendom at the apex of its uniformity in the twelfth through fifteenth centuries was entirely monolithic in its religious faith and practices. On the other hand, the depth and extent of pluralism that characterizes the world today has no parallel in previous human historical experience. Mass migration and easy access to information through the Internet on a global scale are bringing about increased interaction among members of different religious communities and the ideas that are part of their various religious worldviews. On a formal theological level, the work of scholars such as Peter C. Phan, Marjorie Hewitt Suchocki, Raimundo Panikkar, Lamin Sanneh, Elaine Padilla, S. Mark Heim, and many others demonstrates decisively the positive gains to be found when Christian theologians dare to cross religious borders and engage in constructive dialogue with other religions.[53]

---

of a Radical Pope (New York: Henry Holt, 2014), 290–94. Pope Francis's close personal relationship with Bishop Tony Palmer of the Communion of Evangelical Episcopal Churches and the new pope's subsequent initiatives engaging other global Pentecostal and charismatic leaders is recounted in the same volume on pages 326–28 and 389–90.

[52] Phan, "World Christianity: Its Implications for History, Religious Studies, and Theology," 183.

[53] See, for instance, Peter C. Phan, *Being Religious Interreligiously: Asian Perspectives on Interfaith Dialogue* (Maryknoll, NY: Orbis Books, 2004); Peter C. Phan and

The modern age bequeathed, to any who would accept it, a model of history that was represented as a linear narrative running from the ancient world (reduced to the Greeks) through the Christian medieval West, to the modern global world.[54] Thinking along the borders disrupts this singular narrative and calls us to a more critical historical accounting.[55] The outcome will be multiple historical accountings and historical narratives that relate differences in common or simultaneous events, in an attempt to provide a more diversified and complex accounting of the past. Bringing these insights to bear not only upon theoretical studies but upon theological and pastoral practices is a critical task on the part of World Christianity. The study of World Christianity, I have suggested, takes place along the borders. Nevertheless, as Paul Tillich pointed out eight decades ago in his essay, "On the Boundary," a border is also a limit.[56] Each of our theologies in some sense serves as a limit to the others in World Christianity. It is part of the task of the study of World Christianity to draw upon the insights of the limits to reveal just how limited and limiting so many of our grand theological constructions really are. World Christianity has the opportunity in this regard especially today to

---

Jonathan S. Ray, eds., *Understanding Religious Pluralism: Perspectives from Religious Studies and Theology* (Eugene, OR: Pickwick Press, 2014); Marjorie Hewitt Suchocki, *Divinity and Diversity: A Christian Affirmation of Religious Pluralism* (Nashville: Abingdon Press, 2003); Raimundo Panikkar, *The Unknown Christ of Hinduism: Towards an Ecumenical Christophany* (Maryknoll, NY: Orbis Books, 1981); Raimundo Panikkar, *The Intra-Religious Dialogue* (New York: Paulist Press, 1998); Lamin Sanneh, *Piety and Power: Muslims and Christians in West Africa* (Maryknoll, NY: Orbis Books, 1996); Elaine Padilla, "Expanding Space: A Possibility of a Cavernous Mode of Dwelling," in *Contemporary Issues of Migration and Theology*, ed. Elaine Padilla and Peter C. Phan (New York: Palgrave MacMillan, 2013), 53–72; S. Mark Heim, *Salvations: Truth and Difference in Religion* (Maryknoll, NY: Orbis Books, 1995); and S. Mark Heim, *The Depth of Riches: A Trinitarian Theology of Religious Ends* (Grand Rapid, MI: Wm. B. Eerdmans Publishing, 2001).

[54] See Irvin, *Christian Histories, Christian Traditioning*, chaps. 2–4.

[55] See Hjamil A. Martinez Vazquez, "Shifting the Destructive Space: A Post-Colonial Approach to U.S. Religious Historiography" (Ph.D. diss., Lutheran School of Theology, 2003).

[56] Paul Tillich, "On the Boundary," in *The Interpretation of History* (New York: Charles Scribner, 1936), 32, wrote, "To stand on many border lines means to experience in many forms the unrest, insecurity, and inner limitation of existence, and to know the inability of attaining serenity, security, and perfection.... [T]here is a boundary of human activity which is no longer the dividing line between two possibilities, but a limitation through that which is beyond any human possibility—the Good and the True. In its presence, even the very center of our being is only a boundary, and our utmost perfection only a fragment."

go beyond the boundaries of Western rationality and the reigning discursive regimes of hermeneutics and epistemology that have governed the dominant theologies drawn from European experience, liberal and conservative, since the Enlightenment.[57] In doing so, it offers the promise of realizing a greater degree of emancipation than even the most enlightened of the European Enlightenment thinkers could have ever dreamed.

The study of World Christianity is a prelude to engaged activity. New rationalities and new knowledge are manifest not only on theories and methods but also in practices. Diverse experiences of pastoral care, cultural life, gender identity, healing, and sexual orientation are sources of new theological insight and reflection. Questions regarding liturgy and proclamation are reshaped when explored in different locations and contexts.[58] The distinctions made in the dominant Eurocentric or Western curriculum between theoretical and practical knowledge simply do not hold up when subjected to the scrutiny of Christian experience from diverse regions of the world. The study of World Christianity is as much a call to faithful living as it is a topic for academic discussion. The practice of World Christianity is a vocation, calling us to a new anticipation of a world that is yet to come. In the words of Peter C. Phan,

> the important thing for Christians to remember is that the future of World Christianity is not in Christians' hands, though of course they do have a part to play. Rather, its future lies in the faithfulness and loving mercy of God—God's *emet* and *hesed,* to use two descriptions of God in the Hebrew Bible, which Jesus himself embodies in his promise: "I am with you always, to the end of the age." (Matt. 28:20).[59]

---

[57] See Valentin Y. Mudimbe, *The Invention of Africa: Gnosis, Philosophy, and the Order of Knowledge* (Bloomington: Indiana University Press, 1988). Gustavo Gutierrez, *The Power of the Poor in History* (Maryknoll, NY: Orbis Books, 1983), 190, writes, "Our question is not how to speak of God in an adult world. That was the old question posed by progressivist theology. No, the interlocutor of the theology of liberation is the 'nonperson,' the human being who is not considered human by the present order, the exploited classes, marginalized ethnic groups, and despised cultures. Our question is how to tell the nonperson, the nonhuman, that God is love, and that this makes us all brothers and sisters."

[58] See, for example, Phan, *In Our Own Tongue*, especially Part II, "Worship and Prayer in the Asian Way," 65–150.

[59] Phan, "World Christianity," 188.

2

WORLD CHRISTIANITY
TRANSFORMING CHURCH HISTORY

Scott W. Sunquist

World Christianity, in all its recent surprising developments and global connections, has transformed the study of church history. No one predicted it, and most historians have yet to embrace the new reality. For centuries it has been common to see church history as the history of the Western church (mostly Roman Catholic and Protestant) with some discussion of Orthodoxy and missionary work to the non-Western world. However, when Christianity outside of the West is discussed, the assumption is that eventually Western forms and ideas will develop in every village and among every language. Church unity has been understood as all churches, in each context, becoming Western and thinking Western, theologically speaking. Most people would not express it this way today, but old habits die hard and the habit of rooting normative Christianity in Western theological statements, Western liturgies, and Western creeds still dominates the church ecumenical.

The Christianity of today, as Dale Irvin explains in Chapter 1 of this book, is not what we thought it was. What we are talking about is not just the writing of church history, but the very understanding of Christianity. The great theological debates and ecumenical traditions of most of the twentieth century had no language or concepts for what World Christianity was becoming in Africa, China, or Brazil. The basic debates regarding Christology, the Eucharist, church unity, ethics, and ecclesiology were all using the discourse and assumptions of the Western church. The framework of these discussions assumed the history of the Western church as normative. But the big surprise is that Christianity could develop, almost bubble up or emerge, from non-Western cultures, with no Western initiative. Many of these indigenous expressions have come to challenge our basic assumptions of what Christianity really is. Christian life in community is not as rational or scholastic as we thought.

My argument in the following pages is twofold. First, I would like to argue that the newer writing of church history as World Christianity is foundational for the task of doing theology today. This is evident in the discussions by the other contributors in this book. Thus, we must understand the history of Christianity in Ethiopia and China on their own terms if we are going to be involved in honest ecumenical or ethical discussions. The nature and meaning of the church (ecclesiology) is not just a Western discourse, but it requires some knowledge of the understanding of the church traditionally held by Coptic and Persian as well as French and Caribbean Christians. All of these discussions must be historically grounded in a more globally inclusive, less Western dominated, Christian story. Even our reading and study of the Bible requires a more inclusive historical awareness of the history of interpretation. History is important.

My second argument relates to diversity and unity. I posit that the newer study of church history as World Christianity requires newer questions to be asked (mostly related to local cultures), yet this preoccupation with diversity does not mitigate the early church assumption that Christianity is one (*one, holy, catholic, and apostolic*). Let me explain.

It is common today to emphasize that the great diversity of Christian expressions in the twenty-first century—a diversity that we are far more aware of than ever before—points to essential differences. To express it with a biological analogy, it is like these different Christianities have different DNA strands and are therefore genetically or essentially different. I think it is more accurate to describe the great diversity (as with plants) as an expression of the same genotype but expressed in a variety of phenotypes. In other words, we are talking about the same plant, but the different expressions of that plant (here, the diversity of Christianity) is determined also by environmental and epigenetic factors. Plants with the exact same genetic structure may look and behave differently depending upon the environment and which genetic codes are turned on or off (epigenetic factors). So Christianity, as it may be expressed in different contexts with a variety of languages and cultures, is still Christianity. This argument does not take away from the obvious truth that there are expressions of the Christian tradition that are not truly Christian, but that debate and the various ways we identify what is Christian, does not take away from the fact that we can study Christianity as *a particular belief-life system*. Still, we know that biologists often have to retract decisions about plant families and species; historians are no different.

Church History as the Study of
World Christianity Will Transform Theological Disciplines

When teaching pastors and missionaries from ten countries who were working in seven different countries in southeast Asia, I was amazed to discover the variety of ways these men and women were involved in outreach and ministry. One of the pastors, who was also a professor, told me he was working on a book on systematic theology from the Thai perspective. This would be one of the first theology books written in Thai. Still thinking about our discussions in class I asked, "How are you going to handle ancestors and spirits? Do you have a separate chapter on spirits?" His response showed me how much the dominant Western story (history) has shaped local theologies. "I haven't thought about the spirits. But I guess you are right, I need to talk about a theology of 'spirits' since that is so much a part of Thai culture."

What good is a systematic theology if it does not answer questions presented by a local culture, and how could a Thai Christian think of writing a theology that does not mention what every Thai sees every day: spirit houses? The answer is both simple and troubling. Most theology that has been written, even by Asians, assumes a Western historical tradition and thus deals with themes related to Greek philosophy and the Western church tradition. I have found that when Asian Christians study church history as a worldwide Christian movement, they are more able to engage their local culture in thinking about the nature of the church, liturgy, and biblical interpretations. Church history as the history of the world Christian movement enables theological studies for each context.

What follows are themes in the newer study of church history and a brief presentation of how these themes will redirect the theological enterprise. My point is that each of these important themes of World Christianity must now guide historical Christian studies. The inclusion of these themes will change the way we do theological studies.

End of Christendom

Christianity flourished in the West in the context of governments and empires that worked with or in some way supported Christian teachings and practices. Much has been written on the mixed history of Christendom, but more important than studying this mixed history is to recognize what it means that Christendom is now gone. For the first time since the fourth century, Christianity is now flourishing in places where governments and local authorities only tolerate, restrict, or persecute the church. In Africa and Asia, where Christianity seems most vital (numerical growth, new institutions, etc.), Christians live under rulers and constitutions that at best tolerate and at worst persecute Christians. In most places, there are restrictions on Christian life and practices. Western Christians are just beginning to experience what has been the normal Christian life in Asia as Western governments drop Christian identity from their historic memories.[1] Historians were lulled into the assumption that Christianity works toward Christendom with all of its shared power and shared ideals. We had forgotten that from the beginning Christianity grew and flourished under great opposition, as a minority faith resisting majority narratives of life.

This new understanding will determine how we teach ethics. Under Christendom, the church saw it as the responsibility of Christians to speak prophetic words to power, to participate in the marketplace of ideas in bringing about more just societies. The approach of previous generations, such as the invitation for theologians to speak on important public and political issues, will no longer be possible. The difference between Christendom and what we see now in the marginalization of Christianity in non-Christian societies, I first learned while living in the Republic of Singapore. Issues of justice came before me when I heard about the treatment of foreign workers, especially of female *amahs* from the Philippines. Roman Catholic priests spoke up about this and provided free legal counsel for foreign workers who had been mistreated. These priests were exiled from the country. Soon the Protestant ecumenical body, the Christian Conference of Asia (CCA) was also sent out of the country on twenty-four hours' notice. Is it not possible to engage in public debate and service, I thought?

Christian ethics in a Buddhist or Muslim country will look very different than ethics in a Christendom context. Teaching and writing about ethical concerns will be more of an interreligious task as well as a missional task. The contexts will determine the issues and the expression. Christians in Kenya, both Kikuyu and as well as missionaries, have had to deal with the issue of female circumcision, a cultural trait of the Kikuyu. Contexts shape theological and ethical discourse.[2] Writing about ethics and the Christian life in northern Nigeria, where children are kidnapped and churches burned,

---

[1] See Michael O'Neill, *The Struggle for the European Constitution: A Past and Future History* (New York: Routledge, 2009), 244–46.

[2] Kevin Ward, "African Identities in the Historic 'Mainline Churches': A Case Study of the Negotiation of Local and Global within African Anglicanism," in *African Identities and World Christianity in the Twentieth Century*, ed. Klaus Koschorke (Wiesbaden: Harrassowitz Verlag, 2005), 49–62.

will be very different. But it will be very different not only for those living in Nigeria, but it should be different for all Christian communities. The global context should inform parochial parish thought and life, and these local discussions should, in turn, reshape global theological awareness.

Culture and Theology

The writing of Christian history must now pay more attention to the cultural contexts of Christian life. This has always been true, but only now do we see how important this is to explain the diverse expressions of Christianity. What this means is that when writing about the early church we must continue to pay attention to Roman values, deities, and philosophies; but we also need to pay attention to astrology and Zoroastrian dualism of the Persian Empire, and Buddhism, Taoism, and Confucianism in the Chinese realm. In the past, it was the more exotic regions that drew the attention of mission historians (ancestor worship and foot binding in China or Indian practices of settee and child brides in India). But it is more than the exotic that requires our attention. We must understand basic myths, cultural values, and cultural histories in which Christianity develops.

Following the indigenizing or incarnational principle described by Andrew Walls, historians must make sense of local incarnations of Christianity by giving greater attention to indigenous customs, beliefs, and practices. In writing about Christianity in West Africa, the Christian historian must first explain basic beliefs that are held in common from various ethnic groups. There are some common beliefs regarding a creator God, ancestors, the spirit realm, and the use of charms or fetishes. All of these local customs and beliefs are part of the context that will help to explain the growth and conflicts that occur in Christian development. Language and translation is one of the most important cultural issues. Christianity in East Asia develops very differently than in West Africa because of the deeply ingrained Confucian values of most East Asian people. Christianity in India develops differently than in Indonesia because of local *adat* or customs as well as the dominant overlay of Islamic culture in Indonesia. Thus, theological development, interpretation of scriptures, and ethical concerns will all be shaped by local cultural contexts. Both macrocultural themes (such as views of ancestors or Islamic heritage) as well as micro-(local) cultural themes are important in explaining historical developments and practices.

The local contexts of Christian development include social and political realities as well. Church histories of the past were generally alert to social and political movements, but today the movements are not just local rulers and governments, for global movements also shape the church. Christian history writing must be alert to issues of international trade, human trafficking, and migration, all that connect church developments in distant regions. The growing economy of China, which is related to trade sanctions and permissions, has created a whole class of global Chinese. Many of these Chinese are Christian, or they become Christian when they are involved in education or trade in the West or in Africa or South Asia. African and Asian migration to the United States today is related to the 1965 Immigration and Nationality Act, which removed the preference for European immigrants and opened the door to Asians and Africans for the first time since 1921. As a result, Christianity has become more global in the United States than ever before. Globalization is a dimension of cultural awareness that is required in church history writing today.

Indigenous Movements

Another major theme of World Christianity and therefore of historical writing is the remarkable number of indigenous movements that were nurtured under colonialism and its aftermath. Most of the earliest movements were in Africa, beginning in the late nineteenth century. By the early twentieth century, the new phenomenon was occurring throughout Africa, Asia, and in some regions of Latin America. Some of these movements were closely related to the rise of Pentecostalism, but most were catalyzed as a resistance to colonialism. In China indigenous movements like the Jesus Family, Jesus Church, or Christian Tabernacle were started by Chinese leaders who were often overlooked or undervalued by missionaries and their missions. Indigenous leadership began to bubble up apart from the Western-dominated mission structures. In Korea the rapid indigenization was related to Japanese imperialism, and in Africa it was related to British, French, and Belgic imperialism. Prophets like William Wade Harris proclaimed a Christian faith that resisted American domination of Liberia, and Simon Kimbangu, son of a traditional healer, proclaimed a faith of conversion and healing that resisted the Catholic Church and the Belgic authorities. The Kimbanguist Church was seen as a nationalist movement. Many indigenous movements of recent history are closely related to independence movements: independence from missionary control, and independence from colonial powers.

Other indigenous movements have challenged Western and traditional understandings of the church (ecclesiology). China has witnessed a movement of *culture Christians*: believers who meet in homes for Bible study, fellowship, and prayer, but who do not share in the sacraments and do not *join* a church. Political and social considerations are reshaping Christian identity. In India there are movements of *unbaptized believers*: believers who follow Jesus and read the Bible but do not get baptized because of the social or religious stigma in a conservative Hindu or Muslim community.

Indigenous movements in Islamic contexts are more complex. Only in the past four decades have we now seen movements of people who follow Jesus but who do not drop the name *Muslim* from their identity. These movements of Muslim followers of Jesus have been a challenge for Western theologians as they try to make sense of a church where members attend the mosque rather than church and do not get baptized (or only do so secretly at night). Some of these Muslim believers groups eventually become a church, but others never will. They are emerging as embedded followers of Jesus in Muslim villages and neighborhoods.

The variety of indigenous movements that have sprung up in the past century is not like anything witnessed before. In the past millennium, indigenous movements have come from Christians who sensed that they were to reform the church. Lutheran and Reformed movements were *indigenous* and often nationalistic, but they were not like the indigenous movements of today that spring up out of non-Christian cultures. Recent indigenous movements have come about within other religions (or ideologies as in China) or as resistance to the Western church. It will be necessary to include these movements, describing both what they oppose and how they express themselves as Christian. Again, this will have a great impact upon theological study today since it comes as new evidence regarding ecclesiology, missiology, and pneumatology.

Can Historians and Theologians Be Friends?

This means that the teaching and writing of theology, ethics, ecumenics, and other theological disciplines is going to have to change. We are not talking about replacing systematic theology with contextual theology. All theology must be more explicit in its cultural engagement and still be systematic in its presentation. The change is much more profound and simple. Theological discourse built around the Western frameworks of the past, answering questions of the past, will not do for the future. Theological discourse must ask the questions and describe the situation of all of Christian history but particularly the recent history. Again, what happened in the twentieth century was never predicted because our theological language and our theological frameworks were inadequate. Historians must help theologians write with this newer understanding or mind-set, and theologians must remind historians that ideas about God need to develop in ways that are still fully Trinitarian and connected with the Great Tradition. We cannot afford to jettison the tradition that we are part of, but we must see it as a developing (not static) tradition involving the worldwide church.

One simple example may help: pneumatology. How do we write about the Holy Spirit in writing Christian history, and how do we write about the Holy Spirit when writing theology? Earliest Christian histories were quick to see God at work through the Holy Spirit in every miraculous or seemingly miraculous event. It is a little uncomfortable for us today when we see some of these histories and how they give credit to God's Holy Spirit for battles won and natural disasters coming upon God's enemies. After the Enlightenment historical writing was much more scientific and mention of the Holy Spirit for most all historians today (Christian or not) has been eschewed. We ignore the Holy Spirit except when describing how a church or leaders explain what has happened in history. We do not claim that the Holy Spirit did anything specific but merely report what people say when they make spiritual claims.

Theologians until very recently spoke little about the Holy Spirit. The Spirit was the small, shy person in the Trinity. This is changing today as spiritual forms of Christianity grow and develop throughout the world. Amos Yong[3] and Veli-Matti Kärkkäinen[4] are two Pentecostal theologians who are developing theologies that are centered on the Holy Spirit (Yong) or are infused with the Holy Spirit and global concerns (Kärkkäinen). These and, I would argue, all theology today must take into account indigenous movements that have no other explanation for their genesis and continued existence except for a dream, or series of dreams. Some indigenous movements are rooted in a vision, a voice, or a dream that point to Jesus and the concern for a more rigorous and dedicated life in a particular context. Can such visions and words that have changed whole

---

[3] Among the many books and articles Amos Yong has written regarding a systematic theology centered on the Holy Spirit, are *The Spirit Poured out upon All Flesh: Pentecostalism and the Possibility of Global Theology* (Grand Rapids, MI: Baker Academic, 2005); and *The Spirit of Creation: Modern Science and Divine Action in the Pentecostal-Charismatic Imagination* (Grand Rapids, MI: Wm. B. Eerdmans Publishing, 2011).

[4] Veli-Matti Kärkkäinen's works include *Pneumatology: The Holy Spirit in Ecumenical, International and Contextual Perspective* (Grand Rapids, MI: Baker Academic, 2002); and edited with Jurgen Moltmann, *The Spirit in the World: Emerging Pentecostal Theologies in Global Context* (Grand Rapids, MI: Wm. B. Eerdmans Publishing, 2009).

communities become the *stuff* of theological reflection—the *facts* that will begin to reshape our Reformed and Anabaptist and Thomist theologies? I hope so. If our systems do not explain such Christian existence, they are too small.

Christianity as One; Christianity as Diverse

As a reminder, my second thesis relates to the unity and diversity of Christianity: I posit that the newer study of church history as World Christianity requires newer questions to be asked (mostly related to local cultures), yet this preoccupation with diversity does not mitigate the early church assumption that Christianity is one (*one, holy, catholic, and apostolic*). We are concerned with the greater diversity that comes about when we look at all the new questions and all the areas of the world, but we are also looking for what holds it together: unity and diversity.

History reveals that Christians have a hard time staying united. It is easier to call our neighbor a heretic (or so it seems) than to try to understand differences and learn to love. Religious wars in the Christian past are not all that different from religious wars of the Muslim present. We can learn from both about how to write history. Often these wars are about power, control, and ethnic identity, all masked as religious conflict. Still, differences persist within Christianity, and these differences, whether they create conflict or not, are of many origins. Some differences express the rich variety of languages and cultures. Other differences reflect a decentering of Christian teaching and practice by secular rulers or even by Christian leaders. In this section I would like to suggest how we can understand Christian unity and diversity through the newer study of church history. Our overriding concern is to tell a more accurate and complete Christian story: a story that includes what is necessary and releases what is extraneous. This has always been the challenge of historical writing, but the process has changed. That is what this section seeks to explain.

Writing History Is a Matter of What to Throw Out

In our work on writing *History of the World Christian Movement*,[5] we had to decide what to include as *Christian* and therefore what to *throw out*. This becomes more of a problem when we are trying to write a thicker description of history than when a more exclusively Western history is

---

[5] Dale T. Irvin and Scott W. Sunquist, *History of the World Christian Movement*, vol. 1 (Maryknoll, NY: Orbis Books, 2001); and Dale T. Irvin and Scott W. Sunquist, *History of the World Christian Movement*, vol. 2 (Maryknoll, NY: Orbis Books, 2012).

written. Do we include movements that claim to be Christian and yet are not included in any Christian list of major churches? Is it enough to say you are Christian to actually be a Christian? Of course the dominant American splinter groups come up in all of these discussions: Jehovah's Witnesses, Mormons, various Adventist groups, and Christian Science. But what about other African-initiated religions and what about the apocalyptic *Christian* movements like the Taiping Heavenly Kingdom in nineteenth-century China? Christians may not want to claim all of these splinter groups (and many others that are considered more orthodox), but on what basis can (or should) we include or not include? Everyone is not in the same story, even though our stories are not absolutely exclusive.

I believe there are two ways we have sorted this out in the past. One way is to establish our own orthodox filter that filters out all groups that do not fit our standard of what it means to be Christian. Groups that have done this in the past have ended up with a very small fellowship of other Christians. This tendency we might call the *minimalist* approach. Lutherans, Reformed theologians, Brethren, Catholics, Methodists—we have all been guilty of a minimalist approach to Christian unity, and all of these approaches are based on an inadequate history that is dishonest with the facts. One of the most helpful pieces of advice I received in how to study church history was given to me by Richard Lovelace in the first church history class I took. I must admit my Reformed heritage was severely bruised by this reminder. "One of the most difficult lessons we will learn in the study of church history is that God often blesses the people who have bad theology." What he meant here is that the minimalist approach to church history, built around our particular theology, is inadequate to explain the facts. What Lovelace calls bad theology is often the theology that we and our tradition have resisted or have rejected. Catholics find that Lutherans and their missionary work is often blessed (or so it seems). Reformed Christians find that Arminians and Catholics are blessed. If we have a minimalist approach to what must be included in the Christian story, we end up with a small church and a small God.

The second tendency is the *uncritical* approach to historical Christian studies. This approach uncritically wants to include all who claim to be Christian. However, we find that even though this sounds reasonable, inclusive, and open, it is in fact an impossible position to hold. The Taiping Rebellion (causing over twenty million deaths) and the Unification Church have a different center and a different goal (eschatology) from most Christian traditions, and yet they have claimed to be part of the larger Christian story. Although greatly influenced by Christian teaching and even the reading of the Bible,[6] groups like Jim Jones' People's Temple were centered on something very different and had a very different understanding of purpose and *end*. We may know this intuitively, but how can we write about it historically?

It is neither accurate nor possible to include every group that has been influenced by Christian teaching. On the other hand, it is both helpful and necessary to be honest about our study and writing of Christian history to ask critical questions before we end up including wolves in sheep's clothing. Some religious groups have certain elements of the discourse and resources of Christians, but that does not make them a Christian group.

Church histories have always had to make decisions about who is in and who is out of the Christian family, and many times we have had to repent of bad decisions. The newer openness of the Vatican to the Protestant Church, beginning with Pope John Paul II on the anniversary of the birth of Martin Luther, is an indication that our judgments can change. The Roman Catholic Church declared Lutheran and the earlier Waldensian movements as heretical, outside of the Christian story. In the past, Protestants included Waldensians as Protestant forerunners, but until recently these same Protestants have had great difficulty, including the Roman Catholic Church. But today many Evangelical Protestants claim Pope Francis as their pope! Judgments change, but on what basis do we change our judgments?

Looked at from another angle, most Christians have consistently seen the Unification Church as outside of the Christian family. This judgment has changed very little. In contrast, some groups start as Christian influenced groups, outside of the Christian family, but then they later recenter and become part of the Christian family.[7]

Historians can and should provide guidance for the church in these questions. Historical writing is not a neutral science. What we include, what we exclude, how we describe, and how we decry are important decisions that cannot be avoided. These decisions are part of creating the discourse for all other theological discussions. Below we will look at four major themes that help us understand the nature of Christian diversity in historical writing. This

---

[6] See especially Jonathan Spence, *God's Chinese Son: The Taiping Heavenly Kingdom of Hong Xiuquan* (New York: W. W. Norton, 1996).

[7] I am thinking here of the Worldwide Church of God (Herbert W. Armstrong) later to become Grace Communion International. Upon the founder's death, theological statements were rewritten, and under the new theology and openness to other Christian organizations what was a marginal group has become part of the worldwide Christian story.

section concludes with a brief discussion of where we find the unity in Christianity as we write about Christianity as a diverse worldwide movement.

Migration: Forcing the Issues

As a number of authors have shown us in recent years, migration is a major issue in understanding the development of Christianity.[8] Although migration has always been important in Christian history, it has taken on new meaning today with the massive numbers of people moving and the large distances they travel. We now find that in major cities of the West, it is common to find Asian, African, and Latin American churches. Cities like New York, Toronto, London, Munich, and Los Angeles have growing West African as well as Korean and Chinese churches. These churches fit into the local Christian climate only uncomfortably. They bring with them different ways of worshipping, different questions and answers, and they often worship and teach in different languages. They quickly change their patterns as the second and third generations express different cultural forms of Christianity.

One way of looking at this is that migration brings together the ecumenical church in local proximity like never before. Rather than ecumenical discussions being held only among an elite group of Christian leaders in a special space, migration forces ecumenical discussions at a local and common practice level. We observe each other, pray together, sometimes we worship together, and this forces us to rethink commonly accepted Christian norms. We absolutely must adjust our understanding of what it means to be Christian in light of our new locally present global Christian life. One example will help us see how this will affect our understanding of what unites the Christian global community.

My wife and I attended a multicultural church in the east end of Pittsburgh for about eight years. During our time there, our church leadership was approached by Christian leaders who migrated from Francophone Africa. Their numbers were growing and they were looking for a local church where they could meet for worship, education, and prayer. Most of these leaders were Presbyterian or at least had some type of Reformed background so they came to our Presbyterian Church. We had some wonderful

---

[8] See Jehu Hanciles, *Beyond Christendom: Globalization, African Migration and Transformation of the West* (Maryknoll, NY: Orbis Books, 2009); and Mark Gornik, *Word Made Global: Stories of African Christianity in New York City* (Grand Rapids, MI: Wm. B. Eerdmans Publishing, 2011).

meetings learning to listen to each other. They were surprised at how short our worship service was, and we were surprised about their all-night prayer meetings (*fire night*). The real conflict that we all remember was about the possibility of combining our youth fellowship groups. It seemed to be obvious that since all our children, African and African American, spoke English, they could combine forces: a wonderful place to ground our Christian unity.

However, no sooner was it suggested by our pastor that we could combine youth groups, than all three African leaders said, "No. That will never work." Their point was clear. The African American youth did not want to gather only for Bible study and prayer meetings like the African youth. The cultures, values, and understanding of the Christian life were too different for them to work together. Hopefully this situation will change in a generation, but it may not. Migration brings up new themes for the church to study, and new challenges and opportunities for Christian unity.

Some migrant communities are large enough that they can plant their own *Presbyterian Church of East Africa* in Philadelphia or London. Other groups worship with people of their own language, even if they have to compromise some on the worship liturgy, music, and even sacraments. I recently ran into a group of Malabar Christians from Austin, Texas, who worship together as Roman Catholics, Eastern Catholics, St. Thomas Christians, Mar Thoma, and still others are Orthodox Syrian. They do not all worship together each week, but they come together quite often for worship and meals and celebrations mostly for the sake of the children. Migration creates new theological issues and new issues and opportunities for church unity.[9]

Power and the Poor

Most of the Christians in the world are not *for* the poor, they *are* poor. Christian growth has been greater among the outcasts and the powerless than among the powerful and influential. It has always been the case, but the past centuries of colonial and Christendom Christianity has clouded our memory. Before the middle of the twentieth century, we thought of Christians as Western people living in modern and fairly wealthy cultures. The great shock in nineteenth- and twentieth-century missions was when

---

[9] Space does not allow here for a full discussion of Korean churches and Chinese churches in the West. Issues of unity, division, different generations (first versus 1.5 and 2.0), language, and their Confucian heritage are very complex.

missionaries discovered the great poverty and disease of many tropical and subtropical peoples. Thus, missionary work during this period was framed as a theology of progress and advancement, even civilization. Becoming Christian required social progress.

The focus on the poor came from two directions: from Latin America and from Africa. In Latin America, the church leadership was very much a Christendom leadership working closely with powerful and wealthy rulers. Many of these rulers were corrupt, and many of the church leaders were complicit in their support of an unjust social and political structure. Theologies of liberation developed as expressions of the gospel with and from the poor and oppressed. A model of theological reflection also developed that required theological reflection to be rooted in identity with the poor and in praxis. Theology is not theology unless it is lived theology, and it is not lived, unless it is lived with and for the poor.

In Africa, the rapid Christianization that took place in the last half of the twentieth century was not dependent on missionaries, on colonial empires, or on large institutions. A church developed rapidly among the poor, both through missionary churches and the newly instituted churches.[10] These churches were indebted to, but not dependent on, mission schools and mission hospitals. Many of the converts were very poor subsistence farmers whose literacy was very low. However, churches grew and forms of Christian ritual and life began to develop through, rather than opposed to, local customs and beliefs.

The rapid growth of the church of the poor has created other challenges for Christian unity. Theologies of liberation often develop out of opposition to the traditional church. Theologies of liberation can also be very costly as they develop a discourse that exposes false beliefs and the oppressive structures of military elites. The church of the poor is the majority church. How can this church express unity both in local contexts and with the churches in the West who often represent what was resisted by the poor? Can a liberationist church from Latin America be in fellowship with a church rooted in Western capitalism in the West?

---

[10] There is much writing on the various movements of spiritual renewal, Ethiopianism, and independency in Africa. One of the more insightful is Ogbu Kalu's "Ethiopianism in African Christianity: Power and Contested Identities—'Princes Shall Come out of Egypt; Ethiopia Shall Soon Stretch out Her Hands unto God,'" in *African Identities and World Christianity in the Twentieth Century*, ed. Klaus Koschorke (Wiesbaden: Harrassowitz Verlag, 2005), 19–48.

Spiritual Christianity

Not even recognized or known in 1900, barely recognized by historians in midcentury, the spiritual family of Christians is now a dominant form of worldwide Christianity.[11] At this time, we do not need to go over the statistics or the many streams of spiritual Christianity that have developed in the past century.[12] Suffice it to say that this is one of the three most important transformations of Christianity that took place in the twentieth century.[13] Spiritual Christianity has a power and influence that has brought about changes in individuals and societies. Some of this power, however, brings about divisions because many loyal Pentecostals or charismatics have left their traditional churches. For example, many of the spiritual Christians in the West were raised Anglicans, Presbyterians, or Lutherans. Many from the Church of South India have become Pentecostal, and we could go on and on.

There are at present a variety of approaches to writing about the spiritual family of Christians, but there is no one agreed method or style. In some ways it was easier when we had a limited number of mainline and traditional churches with only a few *splinter groups*. The fragmentation that has occurred in institutional Christianity makes it difficult to tell about Christian history as a story. We can no longer tell the story of the newer spiritual family as a side story, or as an annex of the church universal, for in many regions these churches and movements are now the main story of Christianity. Some of these churches start out as Christian movements, but then they move away from the main story—they focus on themes or practices that oppose commonly accepted Christian teaching. How do we talk about these movements when they move away from continuity with the Christian story?

---

[11] We use the phrase *spiritual Christianity* here as we use it in Irvin and Sunquist, *History of the World Christian Movement*, to mean one of the four major families of Christianity: Roman Catholic, Orthodox, Protestant, and Spiritual. We include those churches who primarily find authority and guidance in the Holy Spirit (Pentecostal, African-initiated churches (AICs), many indigenous churches in the non-Western world, as well as charismatic churches).

[12] See Scott W. Sunquist, *The Unexpected Christian Century: The Reversal and Transformation of Global Christianity, 1900–2000* (Grand Rapids, MI: Baker Academic, 2015), 124–33.

[13] The rise of non-Western Christianity and the ecumenical movement would be the two others.

Women

A final important theme that must be explicitly included, but that seems to invite further division, is the role and place of women in the church. Three major historical themes have made the place of women central to our history today. First was the modern missionary movement, which was often (after the middle of the nineteenth century) dominated by women. In unprecedented numbers, women, many very well educated, were sent out by mission societies to work with their husbands as equal partners planting churches or running schools. Later, single women were sent out to work with women who could not be reached through traditional methods. Often called *zenana* missions, they were devoted to reaching Hindu and Muslim women who were isolated to the *zenana* region of the house.[14] Thus, the overwhelming majority of Protestant missionaries sent out before World War II were women, maybe as much as two-thirds.

Second, as the concern for reaching women increased, a whole movement of women's mission (*women's work for woman*) developed, and these new institutions were led mostly by women. Thus, women were running missionary institutions and establishing schools, hospitals, and churches. Missionary gatherings included women leaders who often spoke on an equal level with the male missionary leaders.

Third, the recent growth of Christianity in the non-Western world is at the heart a women's movement according to Dana Robert.[15] Many Christians in Africa or Asia know this through their daily experience. The Chinese church, the fastest growing church in the world for decades, is dominated by women in leadership. Even with the resistance of women in leadership that is often part of Confucian societies, women are leaders in large numbers of churches throughout East Asia. In Africa, many of the African-initiated churches have been started by women who had dreams or visions that they identify as their call to evangelism or to lead churches.

Of course such a strong movement of women in church leadership puts pressure on churches that have traditionally not supported women in the highest levels of leadership (not only Roman Catholic and Orthodox). What does church unity mean when women are leading church movements in some cultures and countries, but in other church traditions women are

---

[14] The region of the house reserved for women only.

[15] Dana L. Robert, "World Christianity as a Women's Movement," *International Bulletin of Missionary Research* 30/4 (2006): 180–88.

not to teach, pastor, or lead men in any area of the church? Again, where do we find unity, and how do we write about such movement in our newer historiography?

Unity: What Holds Christianity Together?

What the above discussion should make clear is that as these newer issues in the worldwide Christian movement become larger in our Christian discourse, we will be forced again and again to ask, "Where is our unity?" Can we write about "Christianity" as a story? The answers of the twentieth-century ecumenical movement, of the nineteenth-century Roman Curia, or of the Orthodox Church are not sufficient. These issues today, studied through our newer historical awareness, force the church to find unity in ideas, practices, and traditions that empower the Jesus story to continue to make its historical impact in a unified witness (John 17).

Many approaches to church unity have filled library shelves in the past century or so. Ecumenical discussions (the reversal of the Reformation) have been a major theme of twentieth-century Christianity. Unity has been sought after in missionary work (the foundation of modern ecumenism[16]), in common witness and service in society, in common confession, and in shared liturgy and sacraments. All of these are difficult and have particular histories of successes and failures. Our approach here is not to bring about some type of corporate unity, either theoretical or organic. Instead I would like to offer a simple explanation for what holds Christianity together. For even if we talk about *Christianities*, we can and must still talk about Christianity.

Another way of framing our concern here is to answer the questions, "What is the absolute core of Christianity without which we would not have Christianity? What is essential in the Christian faith and tradition?" These questions have been answered by using confessions, but all confessions are ad hoc, written to and in a particular context. Other answers have started with particular doctrines that have come out of particular cultural contexts: belief in God as Triune, or Jesus as fully human and fully divine, or belief in the inerrancy or infallibility of the Bible (or of the pope!). We may believe one or most of these, but this does not answer our question. Our question must be asked of the whole church, this church that we see now is both incarnational and pilgrim.[17] What is it that holds together Christianity

---

[16] Willem A. Saayman, *Unity and Mission* (Pretoria: University of South Africa, 1984).

[17] It is really not possible to discuss this issue without reference to Wall's famous

in all of its diverse expressions throughout time and throughout the world? Looked at from another angle, we might ask, "What is it that is only true of Christianity, but not of other beliefs or other communities?"

The World Council of Churches (WCC) has an answer to this, as do most church traditions.[18] What is helpful about the WCC *basis* is that it is not limited to beliefs (a weakness of most of the Western Christian tradition), but it points toward participation or embodiment of those beliefs. Andrew Walls gives a suggestive description of what gives coherence, connection, or continuity to Christianity. In an oft quoted paragraph he says,

> Our observer is therefore led to recognize an essential continuity in Christianity: continuity of thought about the *final significance of Jesus*, continuity of a certain *consciousness about history*, continuity in *the use of the Scriptures,* of *bread and wine*, of *water*. But he recognizes that these continuities are cloaked with such heavy veils belonging to their environment that Christians of different times and places must often be unrecognizable to others, or indeed even to themselves, as manifestations of a single phenomenon.[19]

We might summarize this as man, story, book, bread, and water. Again, this is very suggestive and minimalist, but it comes from a historian who has held together the church, in all of its diversity, in his historical writing over the past four decades. We should take this very seriously, knowing that each of these words requires expansion. Walls has done us a great service in opening up an awareness of Christian coherence that is not found in Western theology or Western Christian practices.

After working for the past decades on writing Asian Christian history and history of the worldwide Christian movement, I would like to suggest a framework for understanding the essential elements of Christian continuity. There are elements in Walls's *essential continuity* that I believe are missing.

---

essay, "The Gospel as Prisoner and Liberator of Culture," in his *The Missionary Movement in Christian History: Studies in the Transmission of Faith* (Maryknoll, NY: Orbis Books 1996), 3–15.

[18] The basis of the WCC, as reformulated in 1961 and adopted by the Third Assembly, is expressed in the following manner: "The World Council of Churches is "a fellowship of churches which confess the Lord Jesus Christ as God and Saviour according to the scriptures, and therefore seek to fulfill together their common calling to the glory of the one God, Father, Son and Holy Spirit."

[19] Walls, "Gospel as Prisoner," 7 (emphasis added).

Two of the most important, which I believe give clearer coherence, are the *Holy Spirit* and the *mission of God*. Throughout history, as Christian presence develops in each place and language and culture, the missionary nature of the story and awareness of God's active presence through the Holy Spirit provide coherence and continuity. Therefore, I would like to suggest the following five elements as giving the church in each context a common story and a common family identity.

Christian coherence is found in that Christians in all their diverse beliefs and practices find *their identity in Jesus Christ, they look to the Scriptures* to explain who he is and who they are to be as *they gather to remember, honor, and spread the teachings and practices* that Jesus commends, and they are aware that *God is somehow active through his Spirit* in what they do and say.

To expand this a little, continuity according to this coherence model would mean that the local Christian community would see itself as part of the tradition that points back to the life of Jesus of Nazareth. They would not see themselves as absolutely unique, but part of a larger story. It is hard to find a community in the history of Christianity that does not find its primary identity in and through Jesus Christ or that does not see that in light of Jesus's life, they as a local community are part of the continuing life of Jesus in their context. Mission, social witness, evangelism, and public theology are all indications of this life in Jesus. Any of these tones may become weak and hardly audible, but they are still present if a community is a Christian community.

In addition, the phrase r*emember, honor, and spread* expresses the integral relationship of worship (remember and honor) and mission (spread). Christians gather to do both, and we see it throughout history and throughout the world. Historical Christian writing, I believe, recognizes the great diversities of Christianities but at the same time remembers the coherence that holds them together.

Finally, I believe Christians in all places and time recognize the ongoing work of God through his Holy Spirit. This is a major theme in Orthodox liturgy, indigenous churches in Africa, Asia and Latin America, and it is inescapable in Roman Catholic and Protestant teachings and practices. Can we really call a community *Christian* if the community sees that all that it does and says is purely this worldly, *secular*? Certainly the emergence of the Holy Spirit in the twentieth and twenty-first centuries should remind us that Christian coherence is in some way or in some dimension a Spirit and spiritual matter.

Reconception, Re-vision, and Retradition[20]

What was beginning to be recognized by Henry P. Van Dusen[21] in 1945 and by Walbert Bühlmann[22] in 1974 has become much clearer with the reflections of writers like Andrew Walls, Dale Irvin, and Peter Phan.[23] What they call for, and what historians are now engaged in is reconceiving, re-visioning, and retraditioning the past with an understanding that the Western Christian tradition is not the only norm. The challenge is to embrace the full diversity of Christian life and belief, the many cultural expressions of followers of Jesus, and to tell a story that is still a single story. Like the migrant family from Ireland that a few generations after migrating to North America find that they have Italians, Swedes, Hispanics, and Afro-Caribbean relatives, Christianity is no longer Western. Actually it never was.

The retraditioning that is needed involves recovering the many lost themes mentioned above, but it also involves recovering the topographic diversity that has been part of the original DNA of the followers of Jesus. Christianity was born at the intersection of three continents and on the border of two empires.[24] From the beginning followers of Jesus spoke

---

[20] These three concepts come from Andrew Wall's essay, "Eusebius Tries Again: The Task of Reconceiving and Re-visioning the Study of Christian History," found in *Enlarging the Story: Perspectives on Writing World Christian History*, ed. Wilbert Shenk (Maryknoll, NY: Orbis Books, 2002), 1–21; and Dale T. Irvin, *Christian Histories, Christian Traditioning, Rendering Accounts* (Maryknoll, NY: Orbis Books, 1998).

[21] Van Dusen wrote about World Christianity and endowed two chairs at Union Theological Seminary in the area of ecumenics and World Christianity. But, his understanding of what was happening was very limited. Van Dusen still saw this *World Christianity* as somehow Western Christianity now finding greater unity as led by the West. Thus, most of his volume *World Christianity, Yesterday, Today, Tomorrow* (New York: Abingdon-Cokesbury Press, 1947) focuses on the (now waning) ecumenical movement. His vision of World Christianity was a Western vision empowered by Western institutions and thinking. He could never have guessed, writing during World War II, what would happen in the shadow of global imperialisms. The above book was first delivered as lectures in 1945 at Emory University.

[22] Walbert Bühlmann, *Es kommt die dritte kirche: Eine analyse der kirchlichern gegenwart und zukunft*, original German edition of 1974, published in English as *The Coming of the Third Church* (London: St. Pauls Publications, 1976).

[23] Among others, Peter C. Phan, *Vietnamese-American Catholics* (Mawhah, NJ: Paulist Press, 2005); and Peter C. Phan and Elaine Padilla, eds., *Theology of Migration in the Abrahamic Religions* (New York: Palgrave-McMillian, 2014).

[24] See Scott W. Sunquist, *The Unexpected Christian Century: The Reversal and Transformation of Christianity, 1900–2000* (Grand Rapids, MI: Baker Academic, 2015), 1.

different languages (see Acts 2), ate different foods, and lived under different rulers and governments. Theology developed as it always does, answering questions posed by local cultures, in and through a community seeking to be faithful to Jesus and all his teachings. Worship patterns and patterns of living also were Christian responses to local cultural customs and assumptions. In the Greek-speaking world of the eastern Mediterranean, it was important to make sense of creation and the cosmos in light of Christian teaching. Thus, statements like the Nicene Creed and theologies like those of the Cappadocians made perfect sense. However, these were not the questions or concerns of Persian Christians, nor of Ethiopians, nor even of Latin-speaking Christians of Italy or England. Earliest Chinese theological developments, dating back to the seventh century, were responding to another set of issues. They did not develop a *Nicene Creed*, but they responded to Buddhism and Daoism in their earliest writings.

Writing Christian history today involves *norming* the story as a global story recovering both the variety of traditions of the distant past and reciting the diverse stories of the recent past. It is neither helpful nor accurate to follow the Western theological tradition alone. From the start, and throughout the narrative, Christian diversity and lines of unity must both be carefully traced by the historian. In the end we find that the fabric of the Christian church is more of a paisley or plaid than it is a solid color. Still, it is a single fabric.

3

GLOBAL RENEWAL CHRISTIANITY AND WORLD CHRISTIANITY: TREKS, TRENDS, AND TRAJECTORIES

Amos Yong

One can hardly speak coherently about global renewal Christianity, much less its interface with World Christianity, in the scope of one chapter.[1] Hence, I will focus here on select treks (historical analyses), trends (contemporary realities), and trajectories (potential, if not probable, future developments) of the global renewal movement in order to highlight some of the intersecting issues relevant to the field of World Christianity.[2] The

---

[1] Here I cannot adjudicate the present and ongoing debates regarding the nature and study of World Christianity. Instead, the following is presented as one angle through which ongoing discussions in this arena can be viewed and engaged. One might say that this chapter represents an approach to the field of World Christianity from the perspective of pentecostal–charismatic renewal as a global phenomenon. It can be read as an extension of the argument proffered in my "Pentecostal and Charismatic Theology," in *The Routledge Companion to Modern Christian Thought* ed. Chad Meister and James Beilby (New York: Routledge, 2013), 636–46.

[2] I come to this essay having completed much of the editorial work for four volumes on the global renewal movement, and it is with this work fresh in mind that the following thoughts have emerged; see Vinson Synan and Amos Yong, eds., *Global Renewal Christianity: Spirit-Empowered Movements Past, Present, and Future*, vol. 1: *Asia and Oceania* (Lake Mary, FL: Charisma House Publishers, 2015); Vinson Synan, Amos Yong, and Miguel Alvarez, eds., *Global Renewal Christianity: Spirit-Empowered Movements Past, Present, and Future*, vol. 2: *Latin America* (Lake Mary, FL: Charisma House Publishers, 2015); Vinson Synan, Amos Yong, and J. Kwabena Asamoah-Gyadu, eds., *Global Renewal Christianity: Spirit-Empowered Movements Past, Present, and Future*, vol. 3: *Africa* (Lake Mary, FL: Charisma House Publishers, 2016); and Vinson Synan and Amos Yong, eds., *Global Renewal Christianity: Spirit-Empowered Movements Past, Present, and Future*, vol. 4: *Europe and North America* (Lake Mary, FL: Charisma House Publishers, 2016).

main question explored in what follows is how what is happening in the former may illuminate discussions in the latter.[3]

Treks

What is *renewal Christianity*? The term *renewalist* came into prominence in the 2006 report by the Pew Research Center, "Spirit and Power: A 10-Country Survey of Pentecostals," wherein it was used "as an umbrella term throughout the report to refer to pentecostals and charismatics as a group."[4] I will adopt this all-inclusive designation in this essay, although it will become clear, especially in the next section, that what comes under the *charismatic* label is much more complicated than considered by most conventions. Here in the next few pages, my focus will be on the pentecostal movement, particularly debates within the field of pentecostal history and historiography, not only in order to understand better the complexities of contemporary global renewal but also to get perspective on similar discussions that have unfolded in the field of World Christianity.

Most historical accounts of the modern pentecostal story begin with either the outbreak of glossolalia at Charles Fox Parham's Bethel Bible College in Topeka, Kansas, on the first day of the new year in 1901, or at William J. Seymour's Azusa Street mission in Los Angeles in the spring of 1906. To be more precise, it has only been during the last quarter of the twentieth century that the latter has become prominent in the historiography of modern pentecostal origins. Part of the explanation for this shift may be due to the fact that the initial scholarly accounts that emerged around midcentury were written by the first generation of trained historians who belonged to white pentecostal denominations such

---

[3] This chapter is but a small token of my appreciation to Peter C. Phan for his exemplary leadership as an Asian Christian theologian, his exceedingly wide-ranging contributions across the theological disciplines, and his personal collegiality to me over the last fifteen years. I first *met* him through Peter C. Phan and Jung Young Lee, eds., *Journeys at the Margin: Toward an Autobiographical Theology in American-Asian Perspective* (Collegeville, MN: Liturgical Press, 1999), and through that was exposed to and have followed closely his work at the nexus where systematics, Asian Christian theology, and World Christianity meet. The following attempts to inhabit, from a pentecostal and renewal perspective (my background, upbringing, and Christian identity of choice), the theological and theoretical *space* his efforts have opened up at this nexus.

[4] See http://www.pewforum.org/2006/10/05/spirit-and-power/; following the Pew survey, I will not capitalize *pentecostal* when used adjectivally, but I do so otherwise when used as a proper name.

as the Assemblies of God,[5] for whom the defining feature of pentecostal spirituality was encapsulated in the movement's distinctive doctrinal contribution: that of tongues-speaking as an evidence or sign of the reception or baptism of the Holy Spirit. By this time, white pentecostal churches had already begun the process of assimilation into the broader North American evangelical subculture. This was evinced by the inclusion of the Assemblies of God in the founding of the National Association of Evangelicals in 1942. Thus, it was to be expected that the theology of tongues and Spirit baptism was accentuated as what distinguished Pentecostalism from its evangelical cousins. Toward this end, Charles Parham's Bible College was viewed as the natural launch of the modern pentecostal revival specifically because the teaching of evidential tongues was formulated within and promulgated from that site.[6]

It is in the work of Walter Hollenweger, now widely recognized as the doyen of pentecostal studies, that a gradual shift began to take place in foregrounding Seymour's Azusa Street mission over Parham's Topeka school for pentecostal origins. Whereas his first English language publication on Pentecostalism, a distillation of his massive ten-volume German-language doctoral dissertation, moves expectedly from Parham to Seymour,[7] from the beginning Hollenweger had been attentive to both the complexity of the worldwide pentecostal movement and the peculiar characteristics of pentecostal spirituality, especially as shaped by the multicultural constituencies of the Azusa Street mission. More specifically, Hollenweger noted Seymour's African American Holiness background, and this suggested that even in the North American context, the form of Pentecostalism unleashed in the Los Angeles mission was shaped as much by black slave spirituality as by either Parham's or Seymour's Holiness religiosity.

---

[5] Klaude Kendrick, *The Promise Fulfilled: A History of the Modern Pentecostal Movement* (Springfield, MO: Gospel Publishing House, 1961), chap. 4; and William W. Menzies, *Anointed to Serve: The Story of the Assemblies of God* (Springfield, MO: Gospel Publishing House, 1971).

[6] For more on Parham's role in the development of this unique pentecostal teaching, see James R. Goff, Jr., *Fields White unto Harvest: Charles F. Parham and the Missionary Origins of Pentecostalism* (Fayetteville: University of Arkansas Press, 1988), chap. 3.

[7] Walter J. Hollenweger, *The Pentecostals: The Charismatic Movement in the Churches*, trans. R. A. Wilson (Minneapolis: Augsburg Publishing House, 1972), 22–24. Hollenweger's Ph.D. thesis was published as *Handbuch der pfingstbewegung*, 10 vols. (Geneva: Universität Zürich, 1965–67).

Hollenweger identified in his magnum opus[8] the root influences nurturing the modern pentecostal movement: the black oral root related to the Africanisms that persisted in African American religion and that was transmuted through Seymour's leadership at an Azusa Street mission that featured *koinonia* between people from different cultural, racial, and linguistic backgrounds (it ought to be emphasized); a catholic and (distinct but yet related) evangelical root related to John Wesley and the American Holiness movement's streams carried by Parham, Seymour, and many other pentecostal ministers of the first generation; a critical root that characterized Pentecostalism's nonconventional spirituality, at least when measured by modern and Enlightenment modes of rationality; and an ecumenical root related to the fact that converts to the pentecostal movement in the early years came not only from Holiness but many other Protestant traditions both in North America and in Europe, if not also elsewhere. For our purposes, however, the black oral root is primary in this account, leading Hollenweger to ask whether Parham or Seymour ought to be recognized as being at the head of the movement. Aside from the well-documented racism of Parham, Hollenweger casts his lot with Seymour, less for historical than theological reasons: although "there is hardly a Pentecostal movement in the world that is not built on Seymour's oral black modes of communication," the important question is this: "Where does one see the decisive contribution of Pentecost: in the religious experience of speaking in tongues as seen by Parham, or in the reconciling Pentecostal experience of Pentecost as seen by Seymour (which of course includes glossolalia and gives it an important role)?"[9]

Hollenweger's point is well taken. It is not the initial evidence doctrine that sets Pentecostalism apart, notwithstanding the fact that at the doctrinal level, it is this one claim that separates pentecostal denominations from other more ecclesial confessions in the broader evangelical movement. Rather, it is the pentecostal form of worship and spirituality that is embodied and affective, rather than primarily cerebral, that not only distinguishes Pentecostalism from other Christian traditions but also accounts for its resonance with and expansion across the majority world. The point is less that there are multiple originating sites to what is now known as the global pentecostal movement, and more that Pentecostalism's explosive growth

---

[8] Walter J. Hollenweger, *Pentecostalism: Origins and Developments Worldwide* (Peabody, MA: Hendrickson Publishers, 1997).

[9] Ibid., 23.

in Asia, Africa, and Latin America are arguably due to its oral culturality, manifest palpably in Seymour's Azusa Street mission, and then dispersed by its missionaries around the world.[10] Again, the issue is not to dismiss either local agency or even the appearance of pentecostal-type revivals around the world before 1906 but to emphasize that the pentecostal mission from Azusa Street was as effective as it was precisely because its oral modality, informed by what Hollenweger calls the black root, was consistent with, if not altogether similar to, the oral spiritualities that nurtured the revivals in these other parts of the world.

It is in this context that we can appreciate the contributions of one of Hollenweger's most influential students, Allan Anderson, who complicates if not undermines the North American origins thesis by calling attention to how Azusa Street missionaries were received in other parts of the world precisely because the ground had been prepared beforehand by indigenous pentecostal-type revivals.[11] Anderson's point, consistent with and extending Hollenweger's argument, is that the pentecostal spirituality of Azusa Street was convergent with the oral spirituality of revivals happening worldwide preceding and following 1906. What ought not be underestimated about Seymour's mission was its catalytic role in establishing a worldwide network connecting these otherwise disparate centers of revival. In that sense, the missionary fervor and impulses precipitated by the Azusa Street mission can be acknowledged: whatever else might be said about its oral spirituality, its essential missionary nature and commitments are as, if not more, important for understanding its expansive scope and global reach.[12]

The preceding observations about pentecostal origins and historiography may helpfully illuminate the contested question in World Christianity scholarship about the relationship between *the West* and *the rest*. If in earlier generations the emphasis was on *church history* that told the story of Christianity from the perspective of the ecclesiastical and institutional centers in

---

[10] Harvey G. Cox, *Fire from Heaven: The Rise of Pentecostal Spirituality and the Reshaping of Religion in the Twenty-First Century* (Reading, MA: Addison-Wesley, 1995), identifies Hollenweger's black oral root as a *primal spirituality* that is indigenous to cultural and religious traditions around the world.

[11] Allan Anderson has different versions of this argument in his various books, the two most important and relevant on this issue being *An Introduction to Pentecostalism: Global Charismatic Christianity* (Cambridge: Cambridge University Press, 2004); and *To the Ends of the Earth: Pentecostalism and the Transformation of World Christianity* (Oxford: Oxford University Press, 2013).

[12] See also Allan Anderson, *Spreading Fires: The Missionary Nature of Early Pentecostalism* (London: SCM Press, 2007).

the Latin and Western world, contemporary scholarship prefers a *Christian history* approach that highlights local agency especially in the non-Western world. I would like to suggest that the gradual shift in pentecostal historiography from Parham to Seymour and Hollenweger's spirituality hypothesis provides instructive parallels at least on two related fronts. First, whatever the historical facts are—which may generate consensus or contestation, as the case may be—there are good reasons to adopt one or a number of other theological rationales to understand the history of Christianity as, from the beginnings at the Day of Pentecost, being carried by many peoples, cultures, languages, and nations. Second, and building on the first, the point is not to minimize the contributions of the Western tradition but to provide a more complete account of non-Western agency and roles in history of Christianity. Along this line, then, it does not matter whether the priority of Western missionaries can be documented since in the end (in some cases, these will be inconclusive and in a few others, no Western missionary presence will be discernible), local reception depends in part on local agents and factors, and these will often have at least historical roots antedating the missionary arrival.

The historical work of Dale Irvin and Scott Sunquist and the historiographic contributions of Lamin Sanneh are helpful along these lines. Irvin and Sunquist are engaged in a multivolume project that seeks to retell the history of Christianity as including but being irreducible to Western developments.[13] If Hollenweger and Anderson aid us in seeing that there are not only multiple roots to the modern pentecostal movement but that the roles of indigenous receptors of the pentecostal message are crucial to understanding its global spread and appeal, then Irvin and Sunquist assist our comprehension of the multiple strands and *diverse trajectories* of the early and worldwide Christian movement[14] and how local agents have played important roles in the reception, planting, and nurturing of the Christian message both in the West and among the rest. Sanneh's work, meanwhile, complements these others not only because of his emphasis on Christian mission as essentially about translation of the gospel and the Christian scriptures into vernacular languages and local idiom but also that this task of translation is theologically rooted in the early Christian movement as

---

[13] See Dale T. Irvin and Scott W. Sunquist, *History of the World Christian Movement*, 2 vols. (Maryknoll, NY: Orbis Books, 2001–2012).

[14] Part II of volume 1 of Irvin and Sunquist is titled, "Diverse Trajectories of the Early Christian Movement."

well as instantiated in its holy texts.[15] Thus, Sanneh also suggests that we
can understand the history of Christianity, not only the history of Christian mission, as unfolding amidst, in, and through indigenous if not oral
cultural dynamics, and this regardless of the extent of the role of Western
missionary efforts and initiatives.[16] The point so far can be summarized
thus: that developments in pentecostal studies and especially historiography
reflect the shift of focus, however contested, from the North American West
to the majority world, even as the emergence of World Christianity as a
field of inquiry is itself demanded by the increasing awareness of the roles
of non-Western agents and perspectives, again however understood, in the
worldwide history of the Christian movement.

Trends

I now want to fast forward to current trends that I will argue have
persisted for the last half century. Here we move forward from the first
generation of the modern pentecostal movement, what sociologists have
called *classical Pentecostalism*, to dynamic and fluid developments initiated
with the *charismatic renewal* movement—hereafter CRMs—that emerged
in the mainline Protestant denominations and the Roman Catholic and
Orthodox communions in the 1960s. These CRMs have been called variously not only *charismatic* or *neopentecostal* but also *Jesus People* movements,
among others. Many, including myself, have distinguished between these
CRMs that have their origins in the 1960s from later Pentecostal- and
charismatic-type movements like the Vineyard, apostolic, and other more
or less independent ministries and churches from the late 1970s and into
the 1980s, and collected these under the category of *neocharismatic* or *Third
Wave*.[17] While there are distinctions that might be helpfully made between
these *second* and *third* streams of the global renewal movement—for
instance the ecclesially rooted character of much of the second as opposed
to the independent, primarily free church character of the third *waves*—
they will be combined for the purposes of our discussion. My point to be

---

[15] See Lamin Sanneh, *Translating the Message: The Missionary Impact on Culture*,
rev. and expanded (Maryknoll, NY: Orbis Books, 2009).

[16] See my theological appropriation of Sanneh's work vis-à-vis that of Hollenweger's contributions in Amos Yong, *The Future of Evangelical Theology: Soundings from
the Asian American Diaspora* (Downers Grove, IL: IVP Academic, 2014), 39–43.

[17] For example, C. Peter Wagner, *The Third Wave of the Holy Spirit* (Ann Arbor,
MI: Servant Publications, 1988).

unpacked here is that current trends in global renewal Christianity include but cannot be reduced to even these three streams or waves (the classical pentecostal, CRM, and neocharismatic, if we were to use those terms), and such ferment is in part why understanding global renewalism is imperative for the field of World Christianity writ larger.

To press this main point, I note that CRMs, while perhaps less energetic in some mainline Protestant denominations in North America, where most of these originated a half century ago, are quite central to the growth of the Christian churches in the majority world. By this, I am observing at least two phenomena: first, that the growth and expansion of Protestantism in the Global South, on the African continent especially, remains fueled by CRMs within the historic churches; and second, that the ongoing vivacity of contemporary Roman Catholicism worldwide is sustained by charismatic renewal within its ranks. The former point has been documented amply by researchers such that most observers of Christianity, particularly in the African context, realize that Anglicanism, Presbyterianism, and Lutheranism, for instance, are growing in that environment primarily as pentecostalized or charismatized movements.[18] When we examine the East Asian context, this is further borne out: large Protestant denominations in South Korea are essentially pentecostal in spirituality if not in name, even as the explosive growth of Christianity in rural China is sustained by pentecostal and charismatic practices, certainly not nomenclature.[19] The latter point regarding contemporary Roman Catholicism as a global phenomenon is as remarkable: Roman Catholic scholars themselves are arguing that charismatic renewal is not only pervasive, if not predominant, where the faith is most vigorous, but perhaps has even salvaged Catholic Christianity, specifically in and through developments in the Latin American hemisphere.[20] Interestingly, then, when

---

[18] See, for example, J. Kwabena Asamoah-Gyadu, *African Charismatics: Current Developments within Independent Indigenous Pentecostalism in Ghana* (Leiden: Brill, 2004); Cephas N. Omenyo, *Pentecost Outside Pentecostalism: A Study of the Development of Charismatic Renewal in the Mainline Churches of Ghana* (Zoetermeer, the Netherlands: Boekencentrum, 2006); and Kevin Ward and Emma Wild-Wood, eds., *The East African Revival: History and Legacies* (Farnham, UK: Ashgate, 2012).

[19] For example, Timothy S. Lee, *Born Again: Evangelicalism in Korea* (Honolulu: University of Hawai'i Press, 2010); Luke Wesley, *The Church in China: Persecuted, Pentecostal, and* Powerful (Baguio, Philippines: AJPS Books, 2004); and Lian Xi, *Redeemed by Fire: The Rise of Popular Christianity in Modern China* (New Haven, CT: Yale University Press, 2010).

[20] Again, for example, Katherine L. Wiegele, *Investing in Miracles: El Shaddai and*

charismatic renewal first emerged in mainline Protestantism and the Roman Catholic Church in the 1960s, the task was to understand these in relationship to the modern (classical) pentecostal movement. Five decades later, the quest is to clarify how pentecostal and charismatic spirituality might itself be essential to the ongoing life and evangelistic mission of the church. This is true especially in the majority world context where these historic churches are growing and even expanding precisely as pentecostal and charismatic movements.

Yet such pentecostalizing and charismatizing trends are prevalent not only in these historic churches but also across the broad scope of evangelical Christianity around the world. If Anglo-American postdenominational impulses are threatening the survival of mainline Protestantism, these same dynamics are transforming evangelical *free church* traditions so that congregational independence and networks of relationships are now at the vanguard of missional Christianity. It has been precisely in this environment that *Third Wavers, apostolics*, and other movements have emerged, and a wide range of independent pentecostal and charismatic groups and organizations have flourished. The result is the dual pentecostalization of evangelicalism and evangelicalization of Pentecostalism at least on the Anglo-American scene. This means both that classical pentecostal churches are progressively indistinguishable from evangelical churches, at least on the surface of what happens at their weekly worship services, and that evangelical spirituality, piety, and worship are increasingly exhibiting pentecostal and charismatic features. Nondenominational churches and congregations are developing into megachurches with their own networks of relationships, and more often than not, these are intentionally pentecostal or charismatic in orientation, if not at least implicitly imbibing of such spirituality in practice. Out of this milieu, the so-called Third Wave has washed ashore a myriad of independent congregations, networks, and movements nationally and internationally, drawn together by common spirituality, values, and missional commitments.[21]

---

the *Transformation of Popular Catholicism in the Philippines* (Honolulu: University of Hawai'i Press, 2004); and the work of Edward L. Cleary, *How Latin America Saved the Soul of the Catholic Church* (New York: Paulist Press, 2010); and Edward L. Cleary, *The Rise of Charismatic Catholicism in Latin America* (Gainesville, FL: University of Florida Press, 2011).

[21] Although focused on the United Kingdom, William K. Kay, *Apostolic Networks in Britain: A New Way of Being Church* (Milton Keynes, UK: Paternoster Press, 2007), applies equally to developments on the North American side.

In a global context, things are increasingly difficult to name. There are certainly pentecostal, charismatic, evangelical, and even denominational and historic churches and traditions, but there are many *independent*-type movements that may or may not go by any of these names as a primary means of self-identification but yet feel they have loose or other kinds of connections and relationships with one or more of these labels to the point that adherents may even embrace such a description in some sense of their own overall Christian identity. It is in part for such reasons that observers of the coming and in many ways already here *global Christianity* recognize the centrality of pentecostal–charismatic features but yet are reluctant to name such according to these labels. Thus, Philip Jenkins, for instance, realizes that even as the center of gravity of Christianity has shifted to the Global South, majority world Christians are Bible believers, albeit not in the North American fundamentalist or evangelical mold but in the pentecostal–charismatic oral mode (that which is described well by Hollenweger, I might add).[22] Generally speaking, then, what appears as the most vigorous form of Christianity at the world Christian frontline might well be characterized as evangelical–pentecostal–charismatic type, which is in that sense what I in this essay am calling *renewalist* as an overarching category.

There is one more point I want to make, however, before turning more explicitly to consider interfaces with the field of World Christianity. This picks up from my comment above about the growth of renewal Christianity especially in inland and rural China. Although more recently, with the reopening of China to the outside world, Western influences are leaving their mark, for almost a generation during the Maoist and Cultural Revolution eras, Christianity existed on Chinese soil due almost exclusively to indigenous efforts. Thus, the form of renewal Christianity in China is quite autochthonous, nurtured by distinctively Chinese adaptations of the faith mediated from earlier periods rather than shaped by Western or missionary legacies. Yet these developments are certainly not unique to the Chinese front but are to be found around the world, perhaps most intensely in the African context over the last few centuries. What is interesting to note especially in sub-Saharan Africa is that the late nineteenth and early twentieth century indigenous African Christianities were forged on a similar anvil as that which facilitated the arrival and growth of pentecostal and charismatic

---

[22] See Philip Jenkins, *The Next Christendom: The Coming of Global Christianity* (Oxford: Oxford University Press, 2002); and Philip Jenkins, *The New Faces of Christianity: Believing the Bible in the Global South* (Oxford: Oxford University Press, 2006).

renewal movements on African shores.[23] African independent or instituted churches were thus not only those founded by Africans for Africans
(rather than established by the missionaries) but also almost always pneumatic in their overall orientation. It was and is in this latter sense that these
African indigenous churches have been similar to those emergent from out
of pentecostal–charismatic Christianity in the African context. Although
most pentecostal and charismatic believers would reject or be suspicious
about African indigenous Christianity (primarily because of the presence
of African traditional religious and cultural features carried over into the
Christian sphere) and even if those who inhabit the latter social and religious space do not usually identify with either of these labels, members and
adherents are united across both spectrums by the prominent if not preemi-
nent role of the Holy Spirit in their spirituality, worship, and piety.[24] Hence,
renewalism often includes not only pentecostal and charismatic types but
also indigenous and independent churches and movements whose spirituality is pneumatic and in that sense difficult to ignore when considering the
vitality of renewal in Christian Africa.

Although I want to turn explicitly to asking about the relevance of
contemporary renewal Christianity for the study of World Christianity, it
should be obvious by now that many of the issues that have been unearthed
in the preceding paragraphs have been and remain central to the latter
field of inquiry. Because renewal movements, understood according to the
broad scope covered in this section and chapter, have been at the forefront
of world Christian growth and expansion, studies in World Christianity
have not only been embroiled in renewalism but have been effectively
shaped by these movements. Thus, there is increasing consideration of the
charismatization and even *pentecostalization* of Christianity, especially in
a global context.[25] It is thus becoming increasingly difficult to speak about

---

[23] See Ane Marie Bak Rasmussen, *Modern African Spirituality: The Indepen-
dent Holy Spirit Churches in East Africa* (London: I. B. Tauris, 1996); and Allan H.
Anderson, *African Reformation: African Initiated Christianity in the 20th Century*
(Trenton, NJ: Africa World Press, 2001).

[24] For example, Caleb Oluremi Oladipo, *The Development of the Doctrine of the
Holy Spirit in the Yoruba (African) Indigenous Christian Movement* (New York: Peter
Lang, 1997); and David Tonghou Ngong, *The Holy Spirit and Salvation in African Chris-
tian Theology: Imagining a More Hopeful Future for Africa* (New York: Peter Lang, 2011).

[25] For example, Young-Gi Hong, "Encounter with Modernity: The 'McDon-
aldization' and 'Charismatization' of Korean Mega-Churches," *Cyberjournal of
Pentecostal-Charismatic Research* 15 (2006), http://www.pctii.org/cyberj/cyber15.html;
and Jakob Egeris Thorsen, *Charismatic Practice and Catholic Parish Life: The Incipient*

renewal Christianity and World Christianity disparately.[26] Nevertheless, three cautions are appropriate in this connection. First, it is appropriate for students of renewal Christianity to press questions specific to these movements, regardless of how diffusive they may be in reality; we are still only at the very beginning stages of comprehending renewalism in its various facets and complexities so sustained exploration and focused consideration on such is still needed. Second, despite the palpability of renewalism across the world Christian landscape, such nevertheless provides only one set of lenses for scholarly analysis; to focus on World Christianity only through renewalist refractions will be reductionistic not only given the limitations of any single analytical lens but also because of the breadth and richness of the Christian tradition in its global permutations. But finally, then, if renewalists have from the beginning of the modern pentecostal movement understood their contribution not as a displacement of the existing Christian tradition but its revitalization, then in that sense we can understand renewal studies as complementary to the study of World Christianity; in this case, distinctive trajectories of research and inquiry will benefit both sides. In particular, students of renewalism can learn much from the research and scholarship on World Christianity, especially since the latter's interdisciplinary interfaces will continue to generate new and innovative perspectives and questions on the field, even as students of World Christianity can be helped by attentiveness to the questions and concerns registered by one of the most vibrant segments of the world Christian movement.

Trajectories

In this final section, I want to put on my explicitly theological hat and ask theological questions that bubble up at this intersection where renewal studies meets studies in World Christianity. The trajectories I propose to explore, then, are theological in nature. Specifically, I want to ask what renewalism contributes to World Christianity besides its spirituality, missionary zeal, and reinvigoration. Actually, the question is more accurately put this way: what are the implications of renewal spirituality, missiology, and vitality for Christian theology more generally?[27] As a theo-

---

Pentecostalization of the Church in Guatemala and Latin America (Leiden: Brill, 2015).

[26] See my review essay, Amos Yong, "The Emerging Field of World Christianity: A Renewal Reading of the *Cambridge Dictionary of Christianity*," *Journal of World Christianity* 4/1 (2011): 27–43.

[27] Initially charted in Amos Yong, "Poured Out on All Flesh: The Spirit, World

logian, I have been driven over the last two decades primarily by this and related questions: if pentecostal–charismatic piety is supposed to renew the church catholic, then might pentecostal–charismatic spirituality also renew the Christian theological tradition?[28] Let me essay some reflections at three levels: historically, missionally, and biblically.

What are the theological implications of the renewal historiography unfolded in the preceding? How does or should renewal history inform renewal theology? What theological lessons might be derived, for instance, from the orality of renewal spirituality and its amenableness to flourishing in the indigenous ground of World Christianity? Two considerations present themselves, one looking backward, and the other looking ahead.

From the perspective of a historical theologian, I suggest that the oral spirituality of renewal Christianity invites a reconsideration of Christian historiography itself, one that shifts the gaze of the historian and historical theologian in two interrelated directions: toward nonliterary sources, to the degree that such can be mined for historical insight, and toward the affective dimensions embedded in or discernible within historical data.[29] To rely solely on written texts or documentary evidence is to privilege the perspective of the literate and elite, while to read texts or other historical data only for their cognitive content is to miss the communicative affect through which oral cultures relate.[30] The point is that the multiculturality of contemporary renewalism that is constituted by and constitutive of many sites of linguistic, symbolic, and semiotic importance quite apart from any

---

Pentecostalism, and the Performance of Renewal Theology," *PentecoStudies: An Inter-disciplinary Journal for Research on the Pentecostal and Charismatic Movements* 6/1 (2007): 16–46.

[28] I began asking these questions while working on the theology of religions, the subject of my doctoral dissertation, published as Amos Yong, *Discerning the Spirit(s): A Pentecostal-Charismatic Contribution to Christian Theology of Religions* (Sheffield, UK: Sheffield Academic Press, 2000). I have since turned in a variety of other directions—theological method, political theology, disability theology, theology and science, Buddhist–Christian dialogue, Asian American theology, etc.—but always motivated by this same general question: how can pentecostal–charismatic perspectives add to these wider theological discussions?

[29] I develop these ideas in Amos Yong, "The Affective Spirit: Historiographic Revitalization in the Christian Theological Tradition," which is the concluding chapter of Dale Coulter and Amos Yong, eds., *The Spirit, the Affections, and the Christian Tradition* (Notre Dame: University of Notre Dame Press, 2016).

[30] For more on affective communication, see Amos Yong, "Proclamation and the Third Article: Toward a Pneumatology of Preaching," in *Third Article Theology: A Pneumatological Dogmatics*, ed. Myk Habets (Minneapolis: Fortress Press, 2016).

dominant (imperial or ecclesiastical) center presses the question of how the histories of renewal can be told in the history of the Christian tradition itself, emanating as they have from multiple spaces, localities, and times. The renewal of Christian history requires a renewal historiography, one attentive to multiplicity not only in terms of historical sites but also in terms of modalities of communicative media.

Looking ahead, similarly, our shift into the multimedia and multisensory era of a telecommunicative age is promising for the development, articulation, and preservation of renewalism's manifold expressivism. Toward this end, the renewal of Christian theology in the twenty-first century might be facilitated at least in part through the many tongues of renewal spirituality. Ideally, the multiplicity of global renewalism foregrounds the need for a dialogical theological method, one attentive to the many levels of theological engagement—spiritually in its many expressions, discursively in the ecumenicity of renewal movements and catholicity of World Christianity, and methodologically in engagement with the full range of humanistic and even scientific disciplines.[31] Renewal theologians face steep challenges at this juncture, however, not only in having to contend with and against the anti-intellectualism prevalent across wide swaths of the global renewal movement but also in then needing to translate renewal values, commitments, and insights into the discursivity of other churches, guilds, and disciplines. Yet such crossing of ecclesial, academic, and disciplinary boundaries ought to be expected for renewalists, and this leads to our specifically missiological considerations.

Renewalists have been motivated perennially by the promise of Pentecost in the book of Acts: "But you will receive power when the Holy Spirit has come upon you; and you will be my witnesses in Jerusalem, in all Judea and Samaria, and to the ends of the earth" (1:8). From this starting point, they have been emboldened, encouraged, and motivated to go, to explore, and to reach beyond the confines of the comfortable. This missionary dynamic of modern renewalists has already been noted above, so it is not surprising to mention that renewalists have emerged first in the theological academy in the field of missiology. As expected, their contributions have unfolded from out of their spirituality and its implications for mission: the foregrounding of indigeneity; the role of the charismata, especially miracles, healings, and signs and wonders; and, most importantly, the centrality of the person and work

---

[31] I sketch such a dialogical theological method in Amos Yong, *The Dialogical Spirit: Christian Reason and Theological Method for the Third Millennium* (Eugene, OR: Cascade Books, 2014).

of the Holy Spirit.[32] I suggest that renewal missiology can fruitfully interact with at least the following two trajectories of missiological inquiry: those connecting studies in World Christianity with Christian mission history, and those connecting missiology with mission theology and vice versa.

The first potential renewalist missiological contribution springs off many of the openings afforded by the discussions in the earlier sections of this essay. This involves not only the history of renewalist mission among (classical) pentecostal and charismatic movements in the twentieth century but also analysis of mission strategies and their effectiveness as instructive for present and future missiological work.[33] Such studies triangulate methodologically by drawing from analytical perspectives in renewal studies, missiology, or the history of missions, and studies in World Christianity. Each of these disciplinary angles can draw from the other two even as the findings can extend discussions in these various directions. If the lines are blurred between where the discipline of Christian history leaves off and the field of World Christianity begins, then lessons can be learned also from where the history of Pentecostalism blends into the emerging area of pentecostal mission history. Parallels between how each of these conversations is being adjudicated can be mutually informative. If historians of Pentecostalism and of pentecostal mission history can learn from developments in the wider world Christian historical field, then those laboring in the latter can also gain from the very dynamic arena of global renewalism as a contemporary instance that can shed light on how the past is to be investigated and understood.

As a theologian, however, I am also interested in how pentecostal mission history opens up to pentecostal, and by extension, Christian mission theology. If theology is a second order discourse grounded in and emergent from out of what is happening on the ecclesial ground, then, pentecostal

---

[32] I discuss these themes in renewal missiology variously in Amos Yong "Many Tongues, Many Practices: Pentecost and Theology of Mission at 2010," in *Mission after Christendom: Emergent Themes in Contemporary Mission*, ed. Ogbu U. Kalu, Edmund Kee-Fook Chia, and Peter Vethanayagamony (Louisville, KY: Westminster John Knox Press, 2010), 43–58; and Amos Yong (with Tony Richie) "Missiology and the Interreligious Encounter," in *Studying Global Pentecostalism: Theories and Methods,* ed. Allan Anderson, Michael Bergunder, André Droogers, and Cornelis van der Laan (Berkeley: University of California Press, 2010), 245–67; see also the pentecostal missiological literature cited in these two essays.

[33] Exemplary in this regard is the work of Connie Au, *Revival in Political Turmoil: Early Pentecostal Missions in China, 1900–1949*, CHARIS: Christianity and Renewal—Interdisciplinary Studies series (New York: Palgrave Macmillan, forthcoming).

mission history provides the data, context, and material for pentecostal mission theology in particular and pentecostal theology in general, even as both trajectories of the latter also have the potential to feed into broader developments in Christian mission theology and theological discourse in general. Both the challenges and opportunities confronting pentecostal expansion (mission) and understanding (theology) combine to indicate less and more promising directions for thinking in the present fluid and dynamic world Christian context. For instance, the transmutation of the primarily Latin and occidentally dominated Christian tradition into the majority world signals upheavals for the theological task in the twenty-first century that pentecostal mission history and theology may well be able to facilitate. This has to do not only with the putative correlation between pentecostal spirituality and indigenous cosmologies but also with the fact of Pentecostalism being equally at home in a modern and postmodern Western world. Hence, pentecostal pneumatology can be queried for insight into theological issues in global context, both in the *West* and in relationship to the *rest*. Herein may lie the promise of a pentecostal pneumatological missiology and holistic theology for the third millennium, one that resists the bifurcations and dualism of West/rest and natural/spiritual, among others.[34]

In the end, though, the promise of pentecostal historiography and missiology and missiological theology are dependent, at least for Protestant Pentecostals (if not also increasingly and even fundamentally for Roman Catholic and Orthodox charismatics), on their biblical moorings. Biblically, renewalists would want to say that they seek no more than a restoration of apostolic Christianity. As restorationists in at least this respect, renewalists are focused on the apostolic teachings and way of life. It is not necessarily a desire to emulate literally the apostolic examples, although in some circles that may well be what such restorationism is presumed to be. Instead, the point is to live as people of the Spirit, as the apostles were Spirit-filled and empowered to accomplish their tasks. Such a restorationist hermeneutic guides renewal readings, retrievals, and reappropriations of the apostolic writings. In part for these reasons, Pentecostals envision that their own lives unfold from out of the apostolic path, opening up, as it were, to the rest of the church and its histories being various versions of the twenty-ninth chapter of the Book of Acts.[35]

---

[34] I explore the contours of such in Amos Yong, *The Missiological Spirit: Christian Mission Theology for the Third Millennium Global Context* (Eugene, OR: Cascade Books, 2014).

[35] I unpack these hermeneutical intuitions in Amos Yong, "Reading Scripture

To be sure, there is no agreement about the normative character of such twenty-ninth chapter across the global renewal movement. Many renewalists focus on the allegedly supernatural manifestations of the Spirit's apostolic work and insist on their ongoing validity for the contemporary church and world, although others (unfortunately so far a minority) would counter that such supernaturalist rhetoric is more a legacy of the Enlightenment paradigm that depends on the contrast with its own (reductionistic) naturalism.[36] Despite a lack of consensus about what apostolicity means in the present time, renewalists across the spectrum agree that the Acts of the Apostles are neither more nor less than the Acts of the Holy Spirit, and in that sense, what is aspired toward and hoped for is a more rather than less pneumatically charged Christian existence and witness, regardless of how, wherein, and whence such unfolds.[37] If the Day of Pentecost narrative provides the ongoing template for how to understand the presence and activity of the Spirit of Jesus Christ and of the living God in the world, then the plurality of such witnesses and testimonies in the many tongues, languages, and cultural traditions of World Christianity will remain going forward.

If nothing else, observations about global renewal vis-à-vis World Christianity will continue to press a question that has been around since the time of the apostles: "what does this mean?" (Acts 2:12). A millennium later, Joachim, abbot of Fiore, picked up this query and wondered if a fulfillment of the promise of the Spirit was nigh, and almost a millennium after that, modern renewalists have been assuming that theirs is the culmination of the age of the Spirit (the latter rain of the Spirit's outpouring, classical Pentecostals aver). If pentecostal and charismatic theologians have now considered that the contemporary global renewal movement is the harbinger of the fully Trinitarian theology undergirded by a robust theology of the Third Article—a pneumatological theology—consonant

---

and Nature: Pentecostal Hermeneutics and Their Implications for the Contemporary Evangelical Theology and Science Conversation," *Perspectives on Science and Christian Faith* 63/1 (2011): 1–13; cf. also for the monograph version of the argument Amos Yong *Spirit-Word-Community: Theological Hermeneutics in Trinitarian Perspective*, New Critical Thinking in Religion, Theology and Biblical Studies Series (Burlington, VT,: Ashgate Publishing Ltd.; reprint, Eugene, OR: Wipf & Stock, 2002).

[36] I attempt to get us beyond the early modern natural–supernatural dichotomy in Amos Yong, *The Spirit Poured Out on All Flesh: Pentecostalism and the Possibility of Global Theology* (Grand Rapids, MI: Baker Academic, 2005), chap. 7.

[37] See also Amos Yong, *Who Is the Holy Spirit? A Walk with the Apostles* (Brewster, MA: Paraclete Press, 2011).

with the pluralism and diversity of the many tongues of World Christianity in the twenty-first century,[38] outside observers of this same renewal ferment are also considering this as being at the vanguard of the age of the Spirit for the third Christian millennium.[39] From such a theological standpoint, it is never inappropriate to invoke, "Come Holy Spirit."[40]

---

[38] See D. Lyle Dabney, "Otherwise Engaged in the Spirit: A First Theology for the Twenty-first Century," in *The Future of Theology: Essays in Honor of Jürgen Moltmann,* ed. Miroslav Volf, Carmen Krieg, and Thomas Kucharz (Grand Rapids: Wm. B. Eerdmans Publishing, 1996), 154–63, whose pneumatological theological method I build on and expand in Amos Yong, *Renewing Christian Theology: Systematics for a Global Christianity*, images and commentary by Jonathan A. Anderson (Waco, TX: Baylor University Press, 2014).

[39] For example, Phylis Tickle, *The Age of the Spirit: How the Ghost of an Ancient Controversy Is Shaping the Church* (Grand Rapids, MI: Baker Books, 2014); cf. also Harvey Cox, *The Future of Faith* (San Francisco: HarperOne, 2009).

[40] Thanks to my graduate assistant Ryan Seow for proofreading this chapter, and to the editors of this volume for inviting my contribution and help with the final draft; needless to say, all errors of fact or interpretation remain my own responsibility.

4

EUROPE AND THE WORLD: WORLD CHRISTIANITY AND THE TRANSFORMATION OF CHRISTIANITY IN THE NETHERLANDS

Frans Dokman

This chapter explores the relationship between World Christianity and the transformation of Christianity in Europe, analyzing the diversity and the encounter between Western and non-Western orientations in European society. As Grace Davie points out in her book *Europe: The Exceptional Case*, secularized Europe is an exception to the spread and growth of religions worldwide.[1] Secularization has transformed societies from predominantly Christian to a point where religion and Christianity are marginalized. Nevertheless, Frans J. Verstraelen rightly claims that next to a secular Europe, there is also a religious and a Christian Europe in which religions and Christianity do play an important role.[2]

Indeed, Europe is experiencing a growing religiosity that results from globalization and migration. After September 11, 2001, the fear of religious violence by Muslims started to dominate the public debate across Europe. Meanwhile, people from diverse cultures and religions are more and more living and working side by side in contemporary European societies. In turn, a new Christian Europe is emerging in which native and migrant believers may be members of the same church while worshipping in different parishes.

This chapter will focus on the Netherlands and the Roman Catholic Church as the prime examples of what is happening in Europe. The Neth-

---

[1] Grace Davie, *Europe: The Exceptional Case: Parameters of Faith in the Modern World* (London: Darton, Longman & Todd, 2002).

[2] Frans J. Verstraelen, "Jenkins' *The Next Christendom* and Europe," in *Global Christianity: Contested Claims*, ed. Frans Wijsen and Robert Schreiter (Amsterdam: Rodopi, 2007), 95–115.

erlands is relevant because it is commonly regarded as one of the most secularized countries in the world. Likewise, the Dutch Roman Catholic Church is facing a significant transformation in view of the rising number of migrant Catholics and the growing number of religious orders and congregations affected by migration. Another reason for concentrating on the Catholic Church is the conclusion by Peter Phan that "there is a skewed perception that Christianity is a Western religion, especially Roman Catholicism, with its papacy, its centralizing hierarchical structure, its numerous cadres of missionaries, its canon law, its uniform liturgy, and the Vatican State."[3]

It is useful to highlight the following key features of Dutch society and the Roman Catholic Church as we ponder the transformation of Christianity in Europe: secularization, diversity in society and church in relation to migrants, internationalization of orders and congregations, and the diversity of orientations. The objectives of this chapter are threefold. First, it affords insight into a European society that is becoming more and more culturally and interreligiously diverse. Second, it focuses attention on the Roman Catholic Church as well as religious orders and congregations that are becoming more and more culturally and intrareligiously diverse in Europe. Third, it explores the meeting between Western and non-Western orientations within these contexts and its meaning for World Christianity.

Secularization and the Netherlands

The Netherlands is a small and, with around sixteen million inhabitants, heavily populated country located in Western Europe. Until the 1970s, its religion was mainly Christianity. Today the Netherlands is perceived as one of the most secular countries in the world. This hypothesis, however, needs some further exploring.

In 1999, Peter Berger gave his book *The De-secularization of the World* the meaningful subtitle, *Resurgent Religion and World Politics*. Berger, a pioneer on the de-secularization theory, writes,

> My point is that the assumption that we live in a secularized world is false. The world today, with some exceptions to which I will come presently, is as furiously religious as it ever was, and in some places more so than ever. This means that a whole body of literature by

---

[3] Peter Phan, "World Christianity and Christian Mission: Are They Compatible? Insights from the Asian Churches," *International Bulletin of Missionary Review* 32/4 (2008): 194.

historians and social scientists loosely labelled "secularization theory" is essentially mistaken.[4]

Specifically, Berger attributes the worldwide resurgence of religion to the fact that religion gives people something to hang on to in uncertain times. Many sociologists of religion maintain that secularization theory is fashionable mainly in the culture of the elite. By contrast, the masses have always been committed to some sort of religion. It is in this context that Grace Davie perceives that Europe is remarkable for being the exception to the growth and flourishing of religions globally. Nevertheless, Davie's claim that Europe is an exception to the rule needs further validation.

A decisive factor is the definition of the terms *religious* and *secular*. There is a persistent trend to regard sociology of religion as a sociology of the church(es), and to define secularization as abandoning the church. That is a fallacy. As Grace Davie puts it, there are phenomena like "believing without belonging" and "belonging without believing."[5] In response to secularization theory, it is commonly assumed in religious studies that we should speak of a transformation of religion rather than a decline of religiosity. People are religious but not necessarily in the churches.

Dutch Catholicism is facing difficult challenges as the number of Catholics drops dramatically from one low to another. Sunday church attendance has become an exception and results in the closure and the merger of many parishes. The number of churchgoers fell in the period 1990–2011 by 720,000 to 249,000. In the same period, the number of churches decreased from 1,896 to 1,632.[6]

Joep de Hart concludes that secularization in the Netherlands does not mean that people no longer believe.[7] Europeans are less secular than is usually assumed. They may not go to church, but they attach great importance to religion. French and Vietnamese respondents respond similarly to the question, "Is religion part of your daily life?" Scores in Japan and Hong Kong are as low as those in Great Britain, and in the United States, they are as high as in Argentina.[8]

---

[4] Peter Berger, ed., *The De-secularization of the World: Resurgent Religion and World Politics* (Washington, DC: EPPC, 1999), 2.

[5] Grace Davie, *Religion in Britain since 1945: Believing without Belonging* (Oxford: Blackwell, 1994).

[6] T. Bernts, *Ruimte voor Religie* (Nijmegen, Netherlands: NIM Symposium, 2012).

[7] Joep de Hart, *Zwevende gelovigen. Oude religie en nieuwe spiritualiteit* (Amsterdam: Bakker, 2011).

[8] S. Crabtree, "Religiosity Highest in World's Poorest Nations," *Gallup Global*

In the Netherlands, 61 percent of respondents express some or great interest in the sacred or the supernatural.[9] This percentage is just as high as that found in countries that are commonly regarded as typically Catholic—Italy (61 percent) and Ireland (61 percent)—and higher than those in neighboring countries like Germany (43 percent), Belgium (49 percent) and the United Kingdom (51 percent).[10]

These statistics show that in Europe and in Dutch society, religion still plays a major role. It is also noteworthy that secularization is not an exclusively European matter. Shorter and Onyancha demonstrated that church attendance in Nairobi is as low as, or even lower, than that in some European cities, as secularization takes root among urban poor, the newly rich, and the intellectuals of Nairobi.[11] In other words, many Africans are less notoriously religious[12] and Europeans are not as secular as usually assumed.

Diversity in Society

According to the Dutch Central Bureau of Statistics, there were almost two million non-Western migrants living in the Netherlands on January 1, 2014. Non-Western migrants are defined as inhabitants with at least one of the parents born in a non-Western country. Their countries of origin are African, Latin American, and Asian (including Turkey but not Japan or Indonesia). Non-Western migrants are most strongly represented in the big cities in the so-called Randstad area. Rotterdam has the highest proportion of non-Western migrants: 37 percent. Amsterdam and Den Haag take second and third place, with 35 percent. Then Almere (29 percent), Schiedam (27 percent), Diemen (27 percent), Utrecht (22 percent), and Capelle aan den IJssel (21 percent).

Within each national group of migrants, there are differences in religion, gender, language, age, social class, and education. This means that a focus on national identity does not represent the actual diversity of people adequately. Diversity refers to differences between individuals on any

---

Reports August 31, 2010. http://www.gallup.com/poll/142727/religiosity-highest-world-poorest-nations.aspx.

[9] P. L. Bernts, G. Dekker, and J. de Hart, *God in the Netherlands* (Kampen, the Netherlands: Ten Have, 2007).

[10] *European Values Studies*, ed. Loek Halman and Paul de Graaf (Leiden: Brill, 2008).

[11] A. Shorter and E. Onyancha, *Secularism in Africa. A Case Study: Nairobi City* (Nairobi, Kenya: Pauline Publications Africa, 1997).

[12] J. Mbiti, *African Religions and Philosophy* (London: Heinemann, 1969), 1.

aspect that may lead to the perception that another person is different from self. Diversity may thus refer to an almost endless number of dimensions. The effects of diversity may be studied at the individual level as well as at the group level.[13] Diversity research focuses mainly on gender, age, race/ethnicity, tenure, educational background, and functional background. Because of globalization, it seems that worldwide lifestyles are homogenizing. Nevertheless, beneath the surface, there is a continuing cultural and religious diversity.

The processes of globalization and migration have an effect on diversity within society and church. Steven Vertovec speaks even of superdiversity that affects the integration of migrants. The concept of superdiversity is characterized by an interaction of variables that connects the usual dimensions (migrants' nationality, ethnicity, language, gender, religion, age, education) with less usual dimensions like legal status, social networks, and labor market niches.

The notion of superdiversity emphasizes that an ethnicity-focused approach to understanding and engaging various migrants groups is inadequate and often inappropriate for dealing with individual migrants' needs or understanding the dynamics of inclusion or exclusion.[14]

As societies become more diverse, competing values and standards will make policy choices more controversial. Public policies are aimed at promoting cooperation and communication between people with different orientations. Social cohesion comes under pressure when people experience that their orientations are not recognized or acknowledged. Therefore, Vertovec pleads for recognizing the variables of migrants' identity:

> The concept of super-diversity points to the necessity of considering multi-dimensional conditions and processes affecting immigrants in contemporary society. Its recognition will hopefully lead to public policies better suited to the needs and conditions of immigrants, ethnic minorities and the wider population of which they are inherently part.[15]

---

[13] D. Knippenberg, S.A. Haslam, M. J. Platow, *Unity through Diversity: Value-in-Diversity Beliefs, Work Group Diversity, and Group Identification* (Rotterdam: ERIM, 2007).

[14] Steven Vertovec, *New Complexities of Cohesion in Britain. Super-diversity, Transnationalism and Civil-integration.* (Wetherby, UK: Communities and Local Government Publications, 2007).

[15] Steven Vertovec, *Migration and Diversity* (Cheltenham, UK: Edward Elgar Publishing, 2014), 733.

Social cohesion is also supported by recognizing that for the vast majority of non-Western people in general, and non-Western people in diasporic situations in particular, religion is an important factor in determining identity. However, it is difficult to isolate religion from other factors such as national, ethnic, social, or dimensions of diversity. We rarely, if ever, meet a Muslim, but rather, Dutch of Turkish, Iraqi, or Syrian origins who also define themselves as Muslim. The diversity of identities resulting from religion, education, gender, ethnicity, legal status, work, and the like is considerable. Likewise, in the Netherlands, there are secular academics, African Catholic businesspeople, Dutch–Turkish Muslim government officials, and so forth. At work, in urban neighborhoods, and in the public arena, people increasingly have contact with others who have diverse social, cultural, and religious identities. In a superdiverse society, people deal with one another based on one of their many identities that extend beyond cultural background. There are religiously and culturally diverse communities in which no particular religion or culture dominates. Thus, the Netherlands can be labeled as a society where inhabitants have a superdiverse identity, including superdiverse religious identities.

Religious identity features more and more prominently in a Dutch society that used to restrict religion to the private domain. Religion in the public domain is back with a vengeance. Where religion was regarded for years as a private affair, religion is now increasingly an issue that national and local authorities, schools and hospitals, and even companies need to take into account. This is partly a result of immigration of non-Western peoples with embedded religious identities to the Netherlands. The manifestation of religion in the public arena, especially the presence of Islam remains controversial. The Netherlands has about 825,000 inhabitants with an Islamic background, mostly Dutch–Turkish or Dutch–Moroccan. In contemporary Dutch society, Muslim immigrants are under a microscope in the aftermath of September 11 and the murder of Theo van Gogh by a Dutch–Moroccan Muslim in 2004. Anti-Islam sentiments are further fueled by disruptive behavior by some Islamic youth (for example, petty crime, discrimination based on sexual orientation, or anti-Semitism), as well as the severe public criticism of Islam by politicians like Geert Wilders.[16] Fortunately, there are also positive developments in support of the multicultural and multireligious society. A notable example is the Moroccan–Dutch politician, Ahmed Aboutaleb, mayor of Rotterdam since 2009 and the first mayor of a large

---

[16] H. Vroom, *Dialogue with Islam: Facing the Challenge of Muslim Integration in France, Netherlands, Germany* (Brussels: Centre for European Studies, 2010), 15.

city in the Netherlands of migrant descent and a Muslim. Mayor Aboutaleb has garnered accolades for building bridges between native and migrant, secular and Islamic, communities.

Diversity in Church

Along with a superdiverse society, one can also start to speak about a superdiverse church. The Christian faith communities in the Netherlands have acquired a culturally diverse character. There are an estimated 520,000 to 640,000 non-European Christians in the Netherlands. Their social class varies from working for multinationals or embassies to refugees. This number includes migrant Catholic faith communities with an estimated 360,000 believers. The largest group of Catholic migrants comes from the Netherlands Antilles and Aruba, about 106,000. The next group consists of Surinamese Catholic migrants, of whom there are an estimated 100,000 in Netherlands (see Table 1).

The Nijmegen Centre for World Christianity and Interreligious Studies investigates the number of migrants who are Catholic churchgoers, allowing a good comparison with the number of native Catholic churchgoers. While the Netherlands has about 4 million Catholics, only 249,000 believers visit their local church regularly.

From the perspective of the Roman Catholic Church as a world church (and from the perspective of World Christianity), the arrival of migrant Catholic believers is valuable because their presence contributes to the realization of a church in which migrants and natives can constitute a unity in diversity. This is a hopeful paradigm for both church and society. However, at this moment, both native and migrants churches have preferred to form territorial and categorical communities based on nationality, culture, ethnicity, legal, and social status. The research of the Nijmegen Institute for Mission Studies among African Catholics in the Netherlands shows that going to church is much valued as an opportunity to meet with fellow African migrants.[17] In their experience, they can be among themselves on Sunday. By contrast, they feel the stress of adapting to an unfamiliar society on other days of the week. The opposite is true of native Dutch Catholics. As the result of this major difference, native Dutch Catholics have not been able to find common ground with migrant Catholics. Rather than merging declining

---

[17] N. van der Meer, *Believers in the Universal Church: Processes of Self-Identification among Catholic Immigrants of African Descent in the Dutch Religious Landscape* (Zurich: LIT, 2010).

Table 1
Estimated Number of Non-European Catholic Migrants in 2012

Origin	Number
Former Dutch Antilles and Aruba	106,000
Suriname	100,000
Africa	26,000
Cape Verde Islands	17,000
The Philippines	14,000
Brazil	13,000
Indonesia	11,000
Colombia	11,000
Dominican Republic	9,000
US	8,000
Canada	6.000
Other	39,000
Total	*360,000*
Non-European Christian	520,000–640,000
Estimated Polish Catholics	130,000

Source: J. Castillo Guerra, F. Wijsen, and M. Steggerda, *Een gebedshuis voor alle volken* (Zoetermeer, the Netherlands: Uitgeverij Boekencentrum, 2012).

native Dutch Catholic parishes with thriving migrant parishes, the declining native Dutch parishes have been content with merging among themselves.

The present distance between native and migrant churches is also affected by different worldviews. Most migrants tend to perceive the Netherlands as a godless and lawless society that is affected by all kinds of evil: pornography, drug addiction, gambling, abortion, homosexuality, birth control, HIV/AIDS, divorce, and single-parent families.[18] Most migrants are unable to accept the legalization of abortion, prostitution, euthanasia, soft drugs, and same-sex marriages that are accepted as normal by a majority of the Dutch people.

[18] F. J. S. Wijsen, "Global Christianity: A European Perspective," *Exchange (Journal of Missiological and Ecumenical Research)* 39/2 (2009): 147–60.

The process of inner-church cooperation between native and migrant believers continues to be impacted by the diversity of worldviews based on cultural, religious, socioeconomic, and political features. People from various countries and cultures have different values and standards, especially on the issue of what constitutes the *common good*. At the same time, churches are able to create space for building communities and social networks among people of diverse age, cultural, and national origins, promoting encounters between members of various population groups and supporting the building of sustainable relationships within church and society.

Churches are able to contribute to the social cohesion within Dutch society through their members who comprise a part of Dutch population and participate as citizens in Dutch society. Notwithstanding the church–state separation in the Netherlands, the Dutch government approaches religious organizations as partners, especially in recent years. Dutch public policy makers continue to promote the constructive social roles of churches and mosques, as well as appreciate migrant churches for their community outreach endeavors.

Hence, many government officials recognize the contributions of migrant religious organizations to nurturing social cohesion and contributing to socio-economic and financial well-being in contemporary Dutch society, resulting in the passage of the so-called Social Support Act (*Wet Maatschappelijke Ondersteuning*), which became law on January 1, 2015. This law heralds a new phase in the relationship between church and state. Local governments are required to acknowledge and facilitate the social works of churches. Vice versa, the churches are asked to support the social policy of the municipalities and to contribute to their implementation via their outreach efforts. The Social Support Act demonstrates that the rigid boundary separating church and state is slowly being eroded as it legitimizes a direct connection between the public domain and religion, between church and state.

Migrant faith communities bring a new stimulus and dynamic within the Dutch society in general, and Dutch Catholicism in particular. In superdiverse parishes, Christian natives and migrants will increasingly communicate intrareligious with fellow believers from diverse backgrounds. On the one hand, because of their reduced number, native parishes will increasingly relate with other local churches, including migrant churches in metropolitan regions. On the other hand, despite their desire for intense contact with family and friends in their country of origin, migrants are challenged to reorient themselves to the Dutch church and society as they settle down in the Netherlands.

At this moment, many migrants experience alienation as foreigners who are marginalized as outsiders in Dutch society. In this regard, migrants are following in the footsteps of Jesus, who not only showed solidarity with strangers but also was a stranger himself (Matt. 25:28) and regarded as such (Luke 24:18). Such social foreignness may be compared to theological foreignness inasmuch as the encounter of Christians with adherents of other faiths confronts them with the totally Other, the absolute Mystery of life, as the Swiss missiologist Richard Friedli explains so well in his groundbreaking work *Fremdheit als heimat* (*Strangeness as Home*).[19]

Diversity within Orders and Congregations

Social and theological foreignness are very familiar to missionaries. It was experienced by young Dutch men and women who went for mission to distant countries. They were idealists bringing the gospel across the globe. Between World War I and the Second Vatican Council, Dutch missionary congregations *exported* a great number of missionaries.[20] During this period, one in nine Catholic missionaries was Dutch.[21] By contrast, the Netherlands has become a mission country itself. Mission cannot any longer be associated with the world beyond Europe. Mission is contextually, rather than geographically, determined. Mission also takes place in a traditionally Christian region as Europe, a region affected by secularization.

From other continents, young people have migrated to the Netherlands and are plunging headlong into the missionary challenge of secularization, bringing the liberative dimensions of the gospel to both native and migrant Catholics alike. Table 2 below shows the arrival of *new* missionaries that has fueled the growth of Dutch clergy and religious. In turn, these new missionaries experience social and theological foreignness as they grapple with learning Dutch, studying theology, and serving in Catholic parishes and institutions.

The arrival of the new missionaries (as *foreign* missionaries are called) and especially of foreign priests brings up critical reactions. Some native

---

[19] Richard Friedli, *Fremdheit als Heimat: Auf der suche nach einem kriterium für den dialog zwischen den religionen* (Fribourg, Switzerland: Universitätsverlag, 1974).

[20] Peter C. Phan, "World Christianity and Christian Mission: Are they compatible? Insights from the Asian Churches," *International Bulletin of Missionary Review* 32/4 (2008): 193–200.

[21] J. Roes, *Het groote missie-uur. De missiemotivatie van de Nederlandse katholieken* (Baarn, the Netherlands: Ambo, 1974).

Table 2
Growth of *New* Missionaries in the Netherlands

	2006	2013
Priests	45	101
Brothers	10	19
Sisters	130	353
Total	185	473

Source: Database of the Conference of Dutch Clergy and Religious Communities.

Catholics argue that the influx of foreign clergy marginalizes nascent lay leadership roles in favor of traditional clericalism. In addition, many Dutch religious orders that invested in lay missionaries in the face of declining vocations since the 1970s perceive lay missionaries as the successors of their religious communities. Some new missionaries have found innovative ways to work with large parishes where laypeople have always exercised crucial leadership roles in the absence of clerical leadership. By contrast, migrant faith communities welcome new missionaries with much enthusiasm. One would hope that the pastoral work of new missionaries could contribute to the realization of a church in which migrants and natives develop a unity in diversity. This is a hopeful paradigm for both church and society.

The arrival of new missionaries also affects their own religious communities. In their concern about working for a better world and spreading or proclaiming the Christian faith, international orders and congregations have always confronted with a diversity of cultures. Missionary orders and congregations are accustomed to dealing with the challenges of global diversity. However, as the center of gravity of Christianity shifts southward and eastward from Europe, historic European religious communities are experiencing major transformation with new members of diverse ethnic and national origins. This phenomenon is evident in the missionary movement in the Netherlands. Toward the end of the twentieth century, many religious institutes, originally Dutch but later others as well, started bringing non-European members to the Netherlands, thereby diversifying the ethnic and national origin character of these religious communities. In so doing, these religious communities have become less Eurocentric and more international. There are 473 new missionaries living and working in the Netherlands. Many of them, especially those from Asia, come from environments that are highly diverse culturally and religiously.

Many of these new missionaries experience cultural shock arising from secularization and the inferior status of Catholic clergy and religious in Dutch society. At the same time, many congregations in the Netherlands interpret mission as presence. Ideally, the presence of new missionaries incarnates the message of the gospel and expresses the Catholic way of life. By viewing mission as presence, new missionaries are challenged to transcend their distinctive ethnic and national origins, reorienting themselves to Dutch society and serve the Dutch Catholic Church. This is no easy task, as these new missionaries confront their experiences of social and theological foreignness not only in the surrounding society but also within their own religious communities.

In this situation of theological and social foreignness, knowledge of and insight into cultural and religious diversity is required for the well-being of all members. Within religious communities, an increasing number of members from diverse cultures share life, work, and spirituality side by side, resulting in the transformation of the historic Eurocentric character of these religious communities. In turn, this increasing diversity has a healthy impact on communication and collaboration, management style, leadership, formation, and spiritual formation within these religious communities.

Diversity in religious communities often leads to a spiritual learning process in which their members encounter disillusionment, doubt, misunderstanding, and resistance. This raises new questions: Why does a religious from a different culture behave or believe differently? Why is it sometimes difficult to get close to each other? How do I deal with my cultural foreignness? How do I resolve the clash of cultures in my religious community?

Ideally, these challenging questions would form part of a learning process that would lead to new insights, breakthroughs, recognition, solidarity, and communication within any religious community. Contact with foreignness puts members of religious communities in contact with the Other and with the absolute Mystery of life. The shared spirituality within a congregation offers an opportunity to transcend cultural foreignness. Internationalization deepens the spirituality of religious and their communities. In so doing, diversity becomes a process of enrichment rather than clash or challenge.

However, the relations between the native and new missionaries are affected by diverse orientations that, if unchecked could lead to estrangement among members of a religious community. In particular, new missionaries tend to think in holistic terms, eschewing dualistic dichotomies in favor of integration of spirit and matter. Often, many new missionaries complain of not being taken seriously and being excluded from leadership roles in their communities in the face of a superiority complex among the native Dutch missionaries.

As far back as 2005, the Indian Jesuit theologian Michael Amaladoss has warned religious institutions of the challenges arising from cultural dominance. He points out strongly that within an international congregation, there is always the chance that a dominant culture emerges to monopolize the functional and financial positions of power within that institution. The European culture continues to be a dominant culture within religious institutions partly due to the financial contributions of the European provinces. More importantly, Amaladoss explains that cultural diversity does not automatically result in equality: "Cultural pluralism is welcome and can be enriching. The problem is that in most situations the cultures do not encounter each other as equals. One culture always tends to dominate over the others. The reasons can be cultural, financial or political."[22]

Notwithstanding the passage of time, Amaladoss's analysis remains valid. Within the general boards of many international congregations, tensions continue to fester among their native European and international members, aggravated by a continued Western hegemony in finances and management that persists despite the actual diverse composition of their general boards and leadership roles. It is a truism that the gatekeepers to financial resources also control the decision-making process within any religious congregation.

Until recently, many new missionaries felt sidelined in leadership roles within their communities. However, slowly this situation is changing as many religious communities implement policies to diversify their leadership by appointing members from outside Europe to major leadership roles. This transfer of leadership has profound implications for dismantling the European hegemonic structures and transforming the identity and character of a religious community to reflect its global and transnational dimensions.

Diversity in Orientations

The identities of people are changing all over the world, transformed by processes of diversity. As globalization and internationalization shape increasingly diverse societies, churches, and religious congregations, the emerging dimensions of superdiversity challenge uncritical essentialist understandings of ethnicities as inadequate and inappropriate. For example, a typical uncritical essentialist perspective would take for granted that

---

[22] Michael Amaladoss, "Mission Institutes in the Millenium," in *The West and the Rest of the World in Theology, Mission and Co-funding,* ed. Frans Dokman (Nijmegen, Netherlands: NIM, 2005), at 74.

Dutch people are secular while African migrants are religious. However, as mentioned earlier, a critical understanding would recognize that the idea that the Dutch have a secular worldview has to be carefully nuanced. At the same time, Shorter and Onyancha discuss examples of Africans being both religious and secular.[23]

The foregoing discussion demonstrates that an essentialist view is inadequate in the face of the complexities arising from global diversity. An essentialist way of thinking means that people are inseparable from the roots of their culture, and religion, sharing only equal dimensions. Consequently, cultures and religions become permanent blocks between which no transfers are possible. The result of such an essentialist and static view is that the actions of people are determined by their cultural and religious backgrounds. An essentialist thinking denies the ability of people to construct an identity that would transcend the borders of their original cultural and religious orientations.

The constructions of one's identity occur across intra- or intercultural, as well as intra- or interreligious encounters. In general, we identify ourselves by referring to the differences with others. This discourse of *differences* may not connect to reality. We categorize *the other* based on our own values, norms, and ideas. On the one hand, life without categories is not possible. On the other hand, an uncritical use of categories could lead to absolute contrasts.

We learn positive and negative values within our cultures through family, school, and community. These values are internalized and influence our thinking, acting, and feeling. The French philosopher and sociologist Pierre Bourdieu speaks about *habitus*.[24] The cultural *habitus* of internalized values reveals how we relate to community and time. Do we, for instance, come from a culture where obedience to authority is strongly emphasized?

Alongside cultural *habitus*, we can also talk about spiritual *habitus*: the internalized religious and spiritual dimensions that affect our relations with other people, nature, and society. This is visible in the diversity within the Catholic Church, with its Asian, African, Latin American, North American, and European Catholics. Moreover, within the ecumenical movement there are also many diverse Christian churches with various expressions and symbols.

According to Halleh Ghorashi, while people act on the basis of their *habitus*, they are also able to transcend their *habitus* once they feel

---

[23] See discussion in Shorter and Onyancha, *Secularism in Africa*.

[24] Pierre Bourdieu, "The Forms of Capital," in *Handbook of Theory and Research in the Sociology of Education*, ed. J. G. Richardson (New York: Greenwald Press, 1986), 241–58.

safe.[25] Eventually, people do not act on the basis of their *mental programming* but on the basis of their *situational logic*. Hence, it becomes critical that a safe environment be created where people can explore their spirituality, feel seen, feel safe, and work toward overcoming misconceptions.

A nonessentialist attitude offers the opportunity to emphasize the potential benefits of diversity, where shared orientations can be emphasized without concealing mutual differences. An inclusive attitude promotes the willingness to accept that the other is different, thereby giving space to diversity in society, church, religious orders, and congregations. There is a need to distance oneself from categorical and essentialist thinking in favor of developing a spirit and sensitivity for the diversity of fellow citizens, atheists, Catholics, Christians, and adherents of other faiths.

By contrast, an essentialist perception of the other leaves little room for diversity. An essentialist conception assumes that culture and religion can be clearly distinguished from other dimensions, for example, Dutch are secular versus Africans are religious. From this *us and them* view, there is no common ground among members of diverse ethnic and cultural backgrounds in parishes and religious orders or congregations. As a result, an essentialist way of thinking creates separation and division.

As more and more people with diverse backgrounds live, work, and believe together in community, church, and religious congregations, challenges arise when people's worldviews and identities simultaneously converge and conflict. People connect and disconnect, understand and misunderstand. In such a context, it is important to identify common ground to establish connections without denying the disconnections. This leads to the next question: what would be the contribution of World Christianity to this discussion?

Diversity and World Christianity

In 2013, the Nijmegen Institute for Mission Studies celebrated its twentieth anniversary with a symposium devoted to diversity. In his contribution to this symposium, Mark-Robin Hoogland takes the Thomistic point of view on diversity as an expression of the goodness of God:

> First of all, because it comes directly from God. Thomas does not refer explicitly to Psalms 19:2 and 104:24, but his line of thought

---

[25] Halleh Ghorashi, *Paradoxen van culturele erkenning. Management van diversiteit in Nieuw Nederland* (Amsterdam: Vrije Universiteit, 2006).

echoes these and similar texts. He adds that such a rich and ordered diversity does not just come forth from coincidental natural changes (generation and corruption) to one single created thing. Hence, what God creates—diversity—must have been intended by Him. And so it is good.[26]

Hoogland goes on to explain that for Aquinas, this does not mean that all different things are equal. Rather, Thomas asks us to appreciate the richness of the diversity because it reveals to us the splendid goodness of God. However, instead of merely trying to understand one another, diversity invites us to question:

> Do I understand the difference, the diversity, *and* can it be recognized as an expression of the great goodness of God? And if so, in what way? For, random diversity may lead to chaos, whereas the manifold diversity in creation is one in God, namely His one and only goodness.[27]

World Christianity is Christianity characterized by diversity. According to Peter Phan, World Christianity refers to "the historical, sociological, cultural and theological diversity and multiplicity of Christianity, from its very beginning, throughout its two millennia history, and arguably more so in the future."[28]

Christianity is unified in the common faith in God revealed by Jesus and in God's reign. Throughout history, this faith has been expressed and practiced in diverse ways. Christianity has been received by different people and indigenized in different locations. This rich diversity makes up World Christianity, raising intriguing theological challenges. Within World Christianity, there are no victors, interpretations, or normative and privileged forms of Christianity. Diverse expressions of Christianity are valuable because they express God's goodness in different ways. All participating diversities unify in their reference to God.

---

[26] M. R. Hoogland, "Diversity as an Expression of the Goodness of God," in *Celebrating Diversity. Lectures on the Occasion of the 20th Anniversary of the Nijmegen Institute for Mission Studies,* ed. Frans Dokman (Nijmegen, Netherlands: NIM, 2014), at 17.

[27] Ibid., 18.

[28] Peter C. Phan, "World Christianity: Its Implications for History, Religious Studies and Theology," *Horizons* 39/2 (2012): 171.

Conclusion

After five hundred years of European expansion around the world, the center of gravity of Christianity is no longer in Europe. It has shifted southward and eastward. In 1937, Hendrik Kraemer wrote,

> The Western hegemony in the affairs of the world belongs to the past . . . all prognosis about the future religious and spiritual development of mankind will have to adjust itself to the new fact that all great religions and conceptions of life may become world-wide in their effects and possibilities.[29]

Nonetheless, it appears that European Christians are still struggling to respond to the massive transformations and changes of the past decades. As Michael Amaladoss reminds us, those with access to financial resources continue to control the decision-making process within religious orders and congregations. New missionaries complain that they are not taken very seriously and that they continue to exercise little influence on the policy of their orders and congregations. Nonetheless, the increasing diversity arising from globalization and migration that has transformed international religious orders, and congregations have also changed Dutch society in general and Dutch Catholicism in particular. One could argue that international religious communities highlight the rich diversity of World Christianity in Europe in general, and the Netherlands in particular, as Christians with diverse ethnic, cultural, and spiritual orientations strive to live, work, and pray together on an equal basis.

The resulting superdiversity in contemporary Dutch society since the 1970s has eroded the dominance of the Dutch Roman Catholic Church, which is less experienced with bridge building with other religious traditions than, for instance, the Catholic churches in Asia.[30] The question for Dutch bishops is how to relate intra- and interreligious to diversity and secularism. The answer to this question implies new roles for migrants and new missionaries. Those newcomers have experience with diversified societies and manifest church and Christianity less dominated by Eurocentric

---

[29] H. Kraemer, *The Christian Message in a Non-Christian World* (Edinburgh: Edinburgh House Press, 1937), 21.

[30] Jonathan Tan, "*Missio inter gentes*: Towards a new Paradigm in the Mission Theology of the Federation of Asian Bishop's Conferences (FABC)," *Mission Studies* 21/1 (2004): 70.

orientations. We see how the Dutch government recognizes the important contributions of migrant churches to building social cohesion through the passage of the Social Support Act (*Wet Maatschappelijke Ondersteuning*), which allows the government to sidestep the church–state separation in its outreach to migrants in the fullness of their diverse cultures and religions.

A key aspect of World Christianity is the transformation of a unipolar world with spiritual centers in Europe that are centered in Rome, Geneva, and Canterbury to a multipolar world that Manila, Nairobi, and Sao Paulo represent in their own unique way, emerging and thriving incarnations of the Christian gospel in local contexts. Thomas Aquinas asks us to appreciate the richness of diversity because it reveals the goodness of God. However, instead of merely trying to understand one another, diversity invites us to question the ways in which the goodness of God is expressed, as we acknowledge that we will never receive and interpret God's message in a perfect way because we are imperfect humans.

As the centers of Christianity continue to shift southward and eastward from Europe, one has to acknowledge that the spiritual centers are still centralized in Europe largely because leadership roles are still intertwined with financial control. In this respect, terms such as *Western* and *non-Western* Christianity continue to be used to express the status quo. Nonetheless, this does not lessen the reality that Christianity is changing and diversifying throughout Europe in general, and in the Netherlands in particular, at a rapid rate. This process of diversification engendered by the presence of World Christianity in Europe is still uneven and faces challenges from natives who struggle to cling on to power and control. Nevertheless, society, churches, and religious communities are slowly but surely undergoing a process of transformation in which people with superdiverse identities and orientations live, work, and believe next to each other.

At the same time, one has to acknowledge that there are still roadblocks to diversity that arise from the continued separation between natives, on the one hand, and migrants and their European-born progeny, on the other. Indeed, within the Dutch Roman Catholic Church, native and migrant churches continue to exist separately, and native Dutch worldviews continue to clash with migrant worldviews. Nonetheless, within international religious orders and congregations, the diversity of membership has given rise to new ways of building community life and shared spirituality that builds on rather than suppressing diversity.

In conclusion, the *mission* of World Christianity is to reveal the diverse incarnations of Christianity worldwide and liberate us from rigid categorical thinking and misplaced superiorities. Missiologists and intercultural theologians, including Peter Phan play an important role in this mission by virtue of living in different cultures, learning other languages, and studying local expressions of Christianity and contextual theologies. More importantly, these missiologists and intercultural theologians also act as bridge builders between churches, fellow colleagues, and Christians. They can create an environment in which Christians can explore theology in diverse and hybridized forms beyond the Western versus non-Western dichotomy, helping people to transcend their *habitus,* heal misconceptions, and overcome social and theological foreignness.

5

LIGHT OF THE WORLD?
CHRISTIANITY AND IMMIGRANTS
FROM THE GLOBAL SOUTH

Gemma Tulud Cruz

The Global South is the collective name of the nations of Africa, Central and Latin America, and most of Asia, including the Middle East, which have less developed or severely limited resources as compared to the richer and more developed regions of North America, Western Europe, and developed parts of East Asia, which are referred to as the Global North. While Global North countries are wealthy, technologically advanced, politically stable, and aging as their societies tend toward zero population growth, the opposite is the case with Global South countries. Moreover, while Global South countries are agrarian based, dependent economically and politically on the Global North, countries in the latter category have continued to dominate and direct the Global South in international trade and politics.[1] Clearly, *Global North* and *Global South* are not so much geographic labels but socioeconomic and political categories.[2]

The people of the Global South, which includes nearly 157 of a total of 184 recognized states in the world, bear the brunt of some of the greatest challenges facing the international community: poverty, environmental degradation, human and civil rights abuses, ethnic and regional conflicts, mass displacements of refugees, hunger, and disease. Thus, for many people in the Global South, moving across borders is the best if not the only way to cope with the risks and challenges, at least for those who can afford it or, in the case of asylum seekers, those brave enough to do it.

---

[1] See Lemuel Ekedegwa Odeh, "A Comparative Analysis of Global North and Global South Economies," *Journal of Sustainable Development in Africa* 12/3 (2010): 338–48.

[2] Australia and Israel, for example, are technically considered as part of the Global North.

Migration is obviously both a cause and effect of broader development processes and an intrinsic feature of our ever globalizing world. The twenty-first century has been called the age of migration[3] essentially because there are more migrants in the world today than ever before. Of the 136 million international migrants living in the north, 82 million or 60 percent originated from countries in the Global South, while 54 million or 40 percent were born in the north. Further, 82 million or 86 percent of the 96 million international migrants residing in the developing world in 2013 originated from the south, while 14 million or 14 percent were born in the north. This predominance of migration among people from the Global South, particularly to the Global North, is illustrated in the analysis of international migration from 1990 to 2013.[4] Although the annual growth rate in international migrant stock in the south outpaced the growth rate in the north since 2000, of the 53 million international migrants added in the north between 1990 and 2013, 42 million or 78 percent were born in the south. The remaining 12 million international migrants, or 22 percent, originated from a country in the north.[5]

Not surprisingly, the implications or effects of the movement of massive number of people from the Global South have been the subject of considerable scholarly attention in the past decade, including Samuel Huntington's claims regarding a "clash of civilizations."[6] Indeed, the changes and transformations brought by the movement of people from the Global South, whether it is to northern or to other southern countries, go beyond demographics and it is to the religious character and implications of this movement that this essay now turns.

Faces of Christianity among
Christian Immigrants from the Global South

In the last decades, religion, particularly Christianity, has experienced revitalization because globalization provided fluid transnational networks

---

[3] See Stephen Castles and Mark Miller, *The Age of Migration: International Population Movements in the Modern World*, 4th ed. (Basingstoke, UK: Palgrave MacMillan, 2009).

[4] J. D. Payne goes even further by tracing the migration to the West from 1500 to 2010. J. D. Payne, *Strangers Next Door: Immigration, Migration and Mission* (Downers Grove, IL: Intervarsity Press, 2012), 86–94.

[5] See United Nations Department of Economic and Social Affairs, *International Migration Report 2013* (New York: United Nations, 2013), 17.

[6] See Samuel Huntington, *The Clash of Civilizations and the Remaking of the World Order* (New York: Simon and Schuster, 2011), 183–206.

that help transport religious messages from local to global audiences. As far as Christianity is concerned, this revitalization involved the emergence of new religious movements in post-Socialist countries and the global explosion of Pentecostal Christianity. Without a doubt, migrant Christians, who make up the majority of believers on the move and in diaspora,[7] play an important role in this ongoing revitalization of Christianity. Philip Jenkins gives voice to this significant role of migrant Christians, especially in Europe:

> Accounts of the collapse of Christianity neglect the growth of immigrant churches among Africans, East Asians, and Latin Americans. Though far less numerous than Muslims, immigrant Christians represent a potent cultural and religious force. Even if we accept the most pessimistic view of the fate of Christianity among Europe's old stock white populations, these thriving new churches represent an exciting new planting, even potentially a kind of re-evangelization.[8]

In what follows, this essay will unpack this potent cultural and religious force by exploring the faces of Christianity among Christians from the Global South who move(d) across borders, with a particular focus on Asian and African immigrants in developed countries or the Global North.

Ethnic and Multicultural

When people move, they bring invisible baggage. This invisible baggage is the migrant's ethnic markers that consists of, among others, language; cuisine; music; and, intertwined with these, their faith. Christianity in the context of migration from the Global South inevitably takes on an ethnic face as southern immigrants, regardless of religion, resort to what Paul Eid calls the "ethnicization of religion."[9] This ethnicization entails the almost complete fusion of ethnic identity with religious identity such that religion

---

[7] Todd Johnson and Gina Bellofatto, "Migration, Religious Diasporas, and Religious Diversity," *Mission Studies* 29/1 (2012): 8.

[8] Philip Jenkins, *God's Continent: Christianity, Islam and Europe's Crisis* (Oxford: Oxford University Press, 2007), 87.

[9] See Paul Eid, "The Interplay between Ethnicity, Religion, and Gender among Second-Generation Christian and Muslim Arabs in Montreal," *Canadian Ethnic Studies* 35/2 (2003): 30–60. A noteworthy critique of the implications of calling migrant churches as "ethnic churches" is presented in Amélé Adamavi-Abo Ekué, "Migrant Christians: Believing Wanderers between Cultures and Nations," *Ecumenical Review* 61/4 (December 2009): 394–95.

becomes a powerful source or means of constructing, negotiating, and maintaining one's ethnic identity.

While ethnicization of religion is generally true for first-generation or earlier batches of immigrants across race, ethnicity, or socioeconomic conditions, it is particularly true among southern immigrants in the past and at present as social–psychological needs, exacerbated by economic and political marginalization, force them to turn to religion for comfort and hope. For example, in a comparative study of the (Egyptian) Coptic and (Dutch) Calvinist immigrant churches in Canada, Joanne Van Dijk and Ghada Botros point out that while ethnic identity was an equally strong and important factor in the establishment of churches among the former, religious identity was more important than ethnic identity among the latter. Van Dijk and Botros contend that for Coptic Christian immigrants in North America, in general, churches are not only "vessels of faith" but, just as strongly, a source of emotional rejuvenation to nostalgic immigrants and facilitators for the integration of newcomers.[10] In 1991, Coptic immigrants in Australia even established Saint Mary's Coptic Orthodox College in Melbourne, the first Coptic Orthodox school outside of Egypt. Similar Coptic schools have since been built in North America.

To be sure, the establishment of immigrant religious institutions and other social institutions such as schools that are attached to parishes and churches become the means to achieve cultural reproduction, pass on the heritage and religion to their children, negotiate and construct ethno-religious identities, and integrate newcomers.[11] In fact, more recent immigrants have even more elaborate, if not comprehensive, approaches in the use of socioreligious institutions to construct, achieve, and maintain ethno-religious identities including the integration of newcomers. The Indonesian Family Church in Perth, Australia, for example, has ministries that cater to different groups and different ages. It also runs various social projects overseas and in Australia such as an orphanage, home for the elderly, and scholarship for Indonesian students.[12]

---

[10] Joanne Van Dijk and Ghada Botros, "The Importance of Ethnicity and Religion in the Life Cycle of Immigrant Churches: A Comparison of Coptic and Calvinist Churches," *Canadian Ethnic Studies* 41/1–2 (2009): 192.

[11] See S. Akhtar, *Immigration and Identity: Turmoil, Treatment and Transformation* (Northvale, NJ: Jason Aronson, 1999); and S. Warner and J. Wittner, *Gatherings in Diaspora: Religious Communities and the New Immigration* (Philadelphia: Temple University Press, 1998), 16.

[12] See http://www.gerejaoikos.org.au/.

In some cases, ethnic churches are used by southern immigrants for purposes of moral legitimation. For example, in the context of the government crackdown on the use of marriage by many Ghanaians to access the Dutch welfare state, one of the important functions of the more or less thirty Ghanaian Pentecostal churches in the Netherlands is to create a context of morality and legitimacy in which marriages, which are perceived as lawful and righteous in the eyes of the immigrant community, can be officiated.[13] Other more Evangelical churches like the Wenzhou Christian churches in Paris serve as bastions of culturally related religious conservatism, for example, patriarchal morality that is fueled by the perceived lack of morals in receiving societies. The values of the French-born youths in these churches are heavily influenced and controlled by the first-generation immigrants. Moreover, church leaders insist on the necessity of training the younger generation in a distinctively Wenzhou Christian way so that they will not mingle with the French mainstream, which is perceived as a cultural and religious threat in the passing of the "authentic faith"[14] and true Wenzhou culture. This conservative Evangelical orientation can also be found among Chinese Christian churches in the United States,[15] and it is aimed, as well, at preserving desired Chinese cultural traits among the second-generation Chinese Americans. However, unlike Chinese American Christians, who generally hold positive attitudes toward assimilation, Parisian Wenzhou Christians embed themselves in a religious diaspora and in a unique transnational Chinese space centered on the Wenzhou identity.[16] For example, like other immigrants from Confucian cultures, Taiwanese immigrants find that their Confucian family traditions are difficult to maintain in the United States. However, while they also use their churches to shield their children from the perceived loose morals of American society, their churches have become an important community institution that offers new models of parenting and family life as well. Carolyn Chen's study of

[13] Rijk van Dijk, "Negotiating Marriage: Questions of Morality and Legitimacy in the Ghanaian Pentecostal Diaspora," *Journal of Religion in Africa* 34/4 (2004): 441.

[14] Nanlai Cao, "Renegotiating Locality and Morality in a Chinese Religious Diaspora: Wenzhou Christian Merchants in Paris, France," *Asia Pacific Journal of Anthropology* 14/1 (2013): 90, 93.

[15] See Nanlai Cao, "The Church as a Surrogate Family for Working Class Immigrant Chinese Youth: An Ethnography of Segmented Assimilation," *Sociology of Religion* 66/2 (2005): 183–200.

[16] See P. Nyiri, "Moving Targets: Chinese Christian Proselytizing among Transnational Migrants from the People's Republic of China," *European Journal of East Asian Studies* 2/2 (2003): 263–301.

Taiwanese American Evangelical Christians and their families shows how through the influence of Evangelical Christianity, the church reconstructs Taiwanese immigrant families by (1) shifting the moral vocabulary of the family from one of filial duty to religious responsibility, (2) democratizing relationships between parents and children, and (3) consecrating the individuality and autonomy of children.[17] Hence, while the establishment of immigrant churches or pastoral centers provide, for immigrants, what could be the single most important source of cultural continuity in their world that has changed in so many ways these churches can also challenge and transform ethnic traditions.

The various cultural groups that usually characterize ethnic churches in destination countries, especially in the Global North, also mean that Christianity has become even more multicultural. Such multiculturalism is reflected in not only the multicolored faces that make up the worshipping community, but also the various flags and ethnic saints that adorn the churches, the various languages in which religious services are held, and the intermittent ethnic feasts and celebrations. Not surprisingly, the multicultural character contributes to conflicts and tensions within these churches. Take the case of the Word of Life Assembly (WOLA) in South Africa, which has 95 percent Congolese who are mostly refugees, 2 percent South African, 1 percent Angolan, and 2 percent from other African countries such as Nigeria, Zimbabwe, Zambia, Cameroon, and Rwanda. Local (South African) women members clash with the Congolese members on the issue of clothing in church. The former do not see any problem wearing shorts in a church whereas the latter are culturally used to wearing conservative clothes, especially to church. Thus, as a South African female member of the church opines "the only problem we have lies with the foreign women who do not feel comfortable when we are around; they tell us not to wear short skirts, and command to cover whatever . . . Maybe they think that we are going to take their husbands."[18] In such multicultural settings, lack of cultural knowledge or sensitivity can be problematic. This can serve as a factor in the break-up or splintering of migrant congregations, albeit the most common cause of church break-up is less problematic as it has to do with the simple desire to have a church in one's own language and with one's own group.

---

[17] Carolyn Chen, "From Filial Piety to Religious Piety: Evangelical Christianity Reconstructing Taiwanese Immigrant Families in the United States," *International Migration Review* 40/3 (2006): 573–602.

[18] Vedaste Nyazabino, "The Role of Refugee-Established Churches in Integrating Forced Migrants: A Case Study of Word of Life Assembly in Yeoville, Johannesburg," *HTS Theological Studies* 66/1 (2010): 7.

Folk and Pentecostal

Most scholars on Christianity agree that migration has a way of revitalizing the religion. Time and again, whether it is in the United States, Great Britain, Canada, or Australia, immigrants have not only transformed the religious landscape of receiving countries but also reinvigorated it. The story of Transfiguration Church in New York's Chinatown illustrates this. The church, which was built in 1801, was first used by Dutch Lutherans. As Manhattan became less Dutch and more English, it evolved to serve an Episcopal congregation. The Roman Catholic Church then bought the building in 1853 to serve a parish created by a Cuban exile priest who directed his services to poor Irish immigrants. As the Irish assimilated, the pews came to be filled by Italians. Then as the Italians grew older and their children moved out of the area, the church leaders sought out the new immigrants, that is, the Chinese. Without the Chinese the church could have died.[19]

Today, immigrants from the Global South like the above-mentioned Chinese Catholics in New York are doing the same thing in their destination countries, perhaps even more so, as new immigrant Christian groups in both North America and Europe bring new life and vitality in the worship and spirituality of their host churches, because they reproduce or exhibit the same dynamic, creative, and celebratory character of religious rituals in their homeland. Such dynamic, creative, and celebratory character of Christianity in the context of southern-derived immigrant congregations is largely because it is folk and Pentecostal.[20]

Folk Christianity generally involves the quest for more simple, more direct, and more profitable relationships with the divine.[21] It usually comes in three forms: (1) devotions to Christ, Mary, and the saints; (2) rites related to the liturgical year; and (3) institutions and religious objects that are often connected with the first two forms. Examples for the first form include various Marian devotions such as Guadalupe (Mexicans), Our Lady of Perpetual Help (Filipinos), and Our Lady of La Vang (Vietnamese).

---

[19] Jennifer Lee, "In Chinatown a Church Speaks in Several Languages but with One Strong Voice," *New York Times*, December 25, 2007.

[20] Pentecostalism or Pentecostal Christianity is used here as an umbrella term for forms of Christianity that differ greatly historically and culturally but nevertheless all assign a central role to the Holy Spirit. These include, among others, the charismatic, revivalist and *born-again* movements.

[21] Luis Maldonado, "Popular Religion: Its Dimensions, Levels and Types," in *Popular Religion*, ed. Norbert Greinacher and Norbert Mette (London: T &T Clark, 1986), 4.

In Canada and other parts of the world where Filipino immigrants have settled, devotions to Mary also include festive religious processions such as *Santacruzan* or *Flores de Mayo*.[22] Examples for the second form include the Filipino immigrants' practice of *Simbang Gabi, Visita Iglesia*, and *salubong*.[23] The home-based prayer circles among Filipino American Catholics in northeast Florida, in the meantime, serves as an example of the third form.[24]

Pentecostal Christianity is noted for its focus on healing, deliverance, and faith, as well as its basic features of faith healing, glossolalia, being filled by the Holy Spirit, and positive understanding of the material, which is often described in terms of a *prosperity gospel*. It is precisely because of these focus and features, combined with the lack of a central(ized) hierarchy or authority, that newer Pentecostal churches are springing up among migrants, particularly among African migrants. Based on a study of Nigerian migrants in Johannesburg, South Africa, where there are scores of newer Pentecostal churches of Nigerian origin, Caroline Jeannerat contends that migrants are attracted to Pentecostalism for three reasons: (1) the manner in which Pentecostalism employs the body in prayer allows migrants to achieve successful connection and communication with the ultimate more easily; (2) Pentecostalism's theology of deliverance, through which a believer is enabled to break out of the bounds of evil, allows migrants to deal with the social, economic, political, and kinship forces that they see as causing the misfortune they are experiencing; and (3) Pentecostalism's theology of evil allows migrants to deal with their kin relationships, which are strained when migrants achieve some form of prosperity.[25] Vietnamese immigrants in Germany, for example, are attracted to Pentecostalism since its *gospel of prosperity* encompasses happiness, health, and economic success.[26] Korean

---

[22] See Marisa Roque, "Fil-Canadians Bring Flores de Mayo Tradition to Their Local Parish," http://globalnation.inquirer.net.

[23] *Simbang Gabi* refers to the nine-day novena Masses held from December 16 to 24 in connection with Christmas. *Visita Iglesia* is a practice of visiting more or less seven churches on Holy Thursday. *Salubong* is an Easter Sunday predawn ritual that reenacts the Risen Christ's meeting with His mother.

[24] Rachel Bundang, "May You Storm Heaven with Your Prayers: Devotions to Mary and Jesus in Filipino-American Catholic Life," in *Off the Menu: Asian and Asian North American Women's Religion and Theology*, ed. Rita Nakashima Brock et al. (Louisville, KY: Westminster John Knox Press, 2007), 89, 91.

[25] See Caroline Jeannerat, "Of Lizards, Misfortune and Deliverance: Pentecostal Soteriology in the Life of a Migrant," *African Studies* 68/2 (2009): 251–71.

[26] Gertrud Hüwelmeier, "Socialist Cosmopolitanism Meets Global Pentecostalism: Charismatic Christianity among Vietnamese Migrants after the Fall of the Berlin Wall," *Ethnic and Racial Studies* 34/3 (2011): 446.

immigrants in Los Angeles exhibit, as well, the above-mentioned aspects of Pentecostalism. As Connie Kang writes,

> Six days a week in Koreatown hundreds of people converge on Oriental Mission Church for a prayer service before sunrise. Some worshipers inch their way to the base of the cross on their knees. Others raise their arms heavenward, calling out, "Hana-nim Aboji! (Father God), or Joo-yoh! (Lord Jesus)." Some just sit, weeping. The scene is repeated at Korean congregations throughout Southern California, with thousands of Korean Americans packing churches for predawn services before hustling off to work or school.[27]

Pentecostal Christianity, indeed, is also characterized by the narrativity of its theology and orality of its liturgy. Thus, when examining the beliefs of and motivations within Pentecostal immigrant congregations "it is imperative to analyze not only what is documented, but more importantly, what is articulated and practiced within that community. It is the spoken word, melodic songs, rhythmic clapping and dance that one encounters the (religious) community's theology, and impact upon the lives of its members."[28] Songs and music, for example, help West Indian migrants in the United States and Britain to maintain and renegotiate their distinctive immigrant identities, particularly in the context of their experience of isolation, discrimination, and marginalization. It is in the context of their search and hope for *somebodiness* that they sing "It is alright, alright. It is alright, alright. As long as I have my Lord beside me it is alright. As long as I have his hands to hold, as long as he watches over my soul, as long as I am under his control. It is alright."[29]

The central role of music in the Pentecostal expression and celebration of the faith as a means of forging subjectivity could also be seen among the Asaphs of Seraph, a Yoruba Christian group based in the United States. In this group, the focus on religious music and its religious performance "emphasizes the affective ties and modes of practice that allow people to feel connected . . . mediate relationships between heaven and earth, God and

---

[27] K. Connie Kang, "Korean Churches Growing Rapidly," *Los Angeles Times*, November 1, 2008.

[28] Janice McLean, "Make a Joyful Noise unto the Lord: Music and Songs within Pentecostal West Indian Immigrant Religious Communities in Diaspora," *Studies in World Christianity* 13/2 (2007): 130.

[29] Emphasis in original. As quoted in McLean, "Make a Joyful Noise unto the Lord," 132.

human, past and present, here and there, and similarity and difference. This musical mediation is at once institutional and embodied, affective and material, political and moral."[30]

In most cases, the folk and Pentecostal character of Christianity among southern immigrants is rooted in how religion becomes a means to struggle against the alienating forces embedded in migration. Away from their home country and in search of company, intimacy, identity, and better living conditions, immigrants find in religion a formidable anchor for their lives. Consequently, religious acts, rituals, symbols, and institutions permeate and inform almost every aspect of their lives. According to Roberto Goizueta, popular piety or folk Christianity denotes "much more than a series of religious practices, symbols, narratives, devotions" but also "a particular worldview, an epistemological framework that infuses and defines every aspect of the community's life" such that it becomes not only a particular way of being "religious" but also a particular way of living life.[31] Orlando Espín pushes this perspective further in *The Faith of the People* by arguing that popular piety could be regarded as an epistemology of suffering insofar as it is the religion of those treated as subaltern by both society and the church.[32]

Missionary and Transnational

Christianity has always been a migratory religion. The most extensive missionary movement in Christianity's history corresponded with one of the great migrations in human history, that is, the European expansion, especially between 1800 and 1925. In the past, it was the clergy and missionaries from Europe or the West, who moved to what is now known as the Global South, who were the primary proselytizers and carriers of the Christian faith. Today, however, it is the millions of ordinary Christians on the move who are, directly or indirectly, increasingly playing a major role in the expansion of Christianity.

In their new *home* or destination country, religious assembly and affiliation constitute the most powerful means available to southern immigrants in

---

[30] See Vicki Brennan, "'Truly We Have a Good Heritage': Musical Meditations in a Yoruba Christian Diaspora," *Journal of Religion in Africa* 42/1 (2012): 5, 7.

[31] Roberto Goizueta, "Reflecting on America as a Single Entity: Catholicism and U.S. Latinos," in *Many Faces, One Church: Cultural Diversity and the American Catholic Experience,* ed. Peter Phan and Diana Hayes (Lanham, MD: Rowman and Littlefield, 2005), 73.

[32] Orlando Espín, *The Faith of the People: Theological Reflections on Popular Catholicism* (Maryknoll, NY: Orbis Books, 1997).

their search for self-identity, communal acceptance, and social integration. Consequently, immigrant congregations, especially those built and maintained by immigrants from the Global South, potentially have a missionary function, not only because they represent the most effective instruments through which immigrants can impact the wider society, but also because immigrant churches model religious commitment, apply the message of the gospel directly to daily exigencies, and comprise communities that interact on a daily basis with other marginalized segments of society.[33]

To be sure, many immigrants from the Global South take their missionary role seriously. Gerrie ter Haar, for example, notes how "many African Christians in Europe have come to see themselves as charged with a divine mission to re-evangelise a continent that they consider to have lost its Christian faith."[34] For these Africans and other southern immigrants, Europe is a *de-Christianized* continent, allegorically identified with the "valley of the dry bones" (Ezek. 37), deprived of its spiritual foundation and in desperate need of revitalization.

This combination of messianic and missionary impulse toward a secularized Europe among Africans is expressed eloquently by the leader of the (Angolan) Tokoist Church,[35] Bishop Alfonso Nunes, in his exhortation to Tokoists in Lisbon to be more courageous and expand their proselytism and evangelization efforts:

> In a hymn we sang before we said: "God visits Africa and darkness dissipates." The darkness was removed from Africa, but returned

---

[33] Jehu Hanciles, *Beyond Christendom: Globalization, African Migration and the Transformation of the West* (Maryknoll, NY: Orbis Books, 2008), 277–78.

[34] Gerrie Ter Haar, "African Christians in Europe: A Mission in Reverse," in *Changing Relations between Churches in Europe and Africa: The Internationalization of Christianity and Politics in the 20th Century*, ed. Katharina Kunter and Jens Holger Schjorring (Wiesbaden: Harassowitz Verlag, 2008), 241. See also Gerrie Ter Haar's earlier work *Halfway to Paradise: African Christians in Europe* (Cardiff: Cardiff Academic Press, 1998).

[35] The Tokoist Church is a Christian prophetic church founded by Angolan Simão Toko in the Angola and Lower Congo region in the 1940s and 1950s. The group arose out of the religious and political turmoil in the region and have experienced some persecution itself notably imprisonment and expulsion from the Belgian Congo to Angola where the group expanded despite violent persecution from Portuguese colonial authorities due to the active proselytism of the Tokoists in and around the *colonatos* (labor camps). Ruy Llera Blanes, "Double Presence: Proselytism and Belonging in an Angolan Prophetic Church's Diaspora in Europe," *Journal of Religion in Europe* 4/3 (2011): 409–28.

to Europe. In another time Portugal was a country of God adorers, of true God adorers but today . . . the churches are empty. . . . Do you want to end up like Sodom and Gomorrah? [No sir!] We must not compare ourselves to the world, because we are church, and not from the world—we must seek to transform it, take the good news to those who are lost.[36]

As the first Tokoist Church branch in the diaspora in Europe, Tokoist Christians in Lisbon proudly follow the orders coming from the hierarchy in Luanda, Angola, and see themselves as simultaneously performing as spearheads of an institutional expansion outside of Africa. Such missionary gaze toward Europe and Europeans is also reflected in a Vietnamese-German pastor who is head and founder of a Pentecostal church based in Berlin with networks spanning Asia and North America. For this pastor, there is a need for a *return mission*, that is, to reclaim Germany, the land of Martin Luther, for Jesus.[37]

Missionary orientation and practice among immigrants from the Global South is even more pronounced among Pentecostal Christians. In fact, the emergence of Pentecostal churches founded by immigrants, particularly in Europe, is arguably the most striking feature of the religious sphere in the diaspora. This is illustrated in two large Nigerian-led Pentecostal churches in Europe—the Church of the Embassy of the Blessed Kingdom of God for All Nations based in Kiev, Ukraine, which has twenty-five thousand adult members scattered throughout Eastern Europe, and the Kingsway International Christian Center (KICC), which has a membership of more than ten thousand adults in its main church in east London. J. Kwabena Asamoah-Gyadu contends that, at least based on their size and history, these two African-led Pentecostal churches are the champions of Christian mission in both Western and Eastern Europe. The latter has even overtaken the Church of England as the church with the single largest *active* congregation in Western Europe.[38]

---

[36] As quoted in ibid., 425.

[37] Emphasis in original. Hüwelmeier, "Socialist Cosmopolitanism," 437–39.

[38] Emphasis in original. See J. Kwabena Asamoah-Gyadu, "'To the Ends of the Earth': Mission, Migration and the Impact of African-led Pentecostal Churches in the European Diaspora," *Mission Studies* 29/1 (2012): 25. See also David Garbin, "Symbolic Geographies of the Sacred: Diasporic Territorialization and Charismatic Power in a Transnational Congolese Prophetic Church," in *Travelling Spirits, Migrants, Markets and Mobilities*, ed. G. Hüwelmeier and K. Krause (Oxford: Routledge, 2010), 145–64; R. van Dijk, "The Moral Life of the Gift in Ghanaian Pentecostal Churches

For centuries, Christianity has sought new followers across the globe. Today, Pentecostal forms of Christianity are the dominant force behind Christian missionizing. As missionization is a central character of global Pentecostalism, religious experts, as well as ordinary believers, become mobile people, traveling to various places in order to proselytize. In fact, in contrast to nineteenth-century evangelicalism, which was embedded in a "colonial modernity," with missionaries seen as part of the bourgeois and the privileged elite, and where the flow of religious messages was directed "from the West to the rest," the new kind of multidirectional interaction and global outreach of today's Pentecostals, particularly among southern immigrants, creates religious practitioners from below. Many of the leading Evangelists of Vietnamese Pentecostal churches in Germany, for example, are former refugees working in factories. For example, a pastor and former refugee profiled in a study of a charismatic Pentecostal church with headquarters in Berlin, Germany, started from a small-sized German city before founding many branches in West Germany in cities such as Stuttgart and Munich, as well as in small towns and the countryside. This evangelism then spread to parts of former Eastern Socialist Europe, and every summer about five hundred believers travel from various regions of Germany, Poland, Russia, Bulgaria, the Czech Republic, Switzerland, Canada, and Vietnam to gather at the Loreley, a famous rock by the Rhine River.[39]

Still, it is increasingly not easy to proclaim and spread the gospel, especially in Europe, as proselytization and evangelism have become contentious in recent times because of issues of civil rights, freedom of belief, individual will, democratization, and globalization. Such criticism extends to the so-called reverse mission. Historically, processes of mobility and mission were uncontested in what was once a predominantly Christian Europe, which sent thousands of missionaries overseas itself. Today, however, talks of reverse mission feed the recurring fears of the advocates of new atheism, anti-immigration apologists, and other discursive stances.[40] This has forced religious movements to engage in rhetoric of evangelization, proselytism,

---

in the Diaspora," in *Commodification, Things, Agency, and Identities: The Social Life of Things Revisited*, ed. W. M. J. van Binsbergen and P. L. Geschiere (Munster, Germany: Lit Verlag, 2005), 201–24; and B. Nieswand, "Ghanaian Migrants in Germany and the Social Construction of Diaspora," *African Diaspora* 1/1-2 (2008): 1–25 for other examples in England, the Netherlands, and Germany, respectively.

[39] Hüwelmeier, "Socialist Cosmopolitanism," 436–37.

[40] See, for example, Danielle Koning, "Place, Space, and Authority: The Mission and Reversed Mission of the Ghanaian Seventh-day Adventist Church in Amsterdam," *African Diaspora* 2/2 (2009): 203–26.

and conversion to either decry or advocate them in the name of their own moral and ethical frameworks.

Such contested atmosphere poses problems for currents of contemporary global Christianity where evangelization, proselytism, and conversion play very explicit roles such as in Pentecostalism. Ruy Llera Blanes argues, however, that one can find alternative perspectives regarding proselytism and evangelization among prophetic movements such as the Tokoist Church in Lisbon. Blanes posits that Tokoist Christians fulfill their mission to proselytize and evangelize through the production of "double presence," which is achieved through the process of mobility and circulation. This "double presence," which is obviously born out of the intricacies of the process of migration, implies that the process of "circulating" creates new cartographies through which Christian migrants dwell and operate, opening new fields of interaction between host and homeland, religious, political, and identity-related spheres.[41] More specifically, double presence means that, on the one hand, proselytism is mainly practiced by Tokoists through family networks and in the church's Sunday schools, so much so that a *new Tokoist* in the church is usually the son, daughter, or relative of an older one. On the other hand, they engage in implicit proselytism through the various activities they conduct in order to make themselves visible in the local communities, which include social work activities, such as collecting food and clothes for the poor; organizing events in public spaces, such as pavilions; and using media to promote the group.[42] Mission in this sense becomes a testimonial proselytism and evangelization that does not necessarily imply an active, verbal transmission of the gospel and where the immigrant church's example is expected to attract others.

Privilege and power present complications in the missionary work of southern immigrants. In spite of such limitations, many southern-derived immigrant churches do reach out. Lao Canadians send members to Laos to teach in Bible schools. Iranian American churches broadcast extensively into Iran and provide a platoon of volunteers who respond to e-mail correspondents. Korean American churches, in the meantime, create jobs in North Korea through businesses that they establish.[43]

To be sure, missionary work for these immigrants is greatly aided by their transnationalism. Transnationalism seeks to understand how people take

---

[41] Blanes, "Double Presence," 413.

[42] Ibid., 423–24.

[43] Miriam Adeney, "'Colorful Initiatives': North American Diasporas in Mission," *Missiology: An International Review* 39/1 (2011): 16.

part in multilateral national contexts through their economic, political, and social activities. As Thomas Csordas contends, religious transnationalism, in the case of migrant believers, is linked with processes of missionization, migration, mediatization, and mobility.[44] Afe Adogame notes this transnationalism among Africans:

> The significance of local and global networks among African churches in both home and host contexts cannot be overemphasized. Such networks are assuming increasing importance for African migrants. The range and nature of ties include new ecumenical affiliations, pastoral exchanges between Africa, Europe, and the US, special events and conferences, prayer networks, internet sites, international ministries, publications, audio/video, and tele-evangelism. The "flow" between the links is two-directional, sending and receiving—globally and locally.[45]

In most cases, especially for Christian churches founded in and associated with a particular country, transnationalism is aimed at keeping migrants connected to the home church. In the case of the previously mentioned Asaphs of Seraph, musical performances at annual conventions, which rotate between cities in the United States with large Nigerian populations, are partly a way of keeping members connected to Cherubim and Seraphim communities back home in Nigeria since many members of the group, who now live in the United States, attended the same church (Cherubim and Seraphim Movement Ayo ni o Church) in Lagos prior to moving to the United States. Many members also continue to have family and friends who are part of the church in Lagos. Transnationalism is also built and maintained by the attendance at the annual convention by church members from Lagos and by Prophet S. F. Korode, the choirmaster of the church in Lagos who serves as an anchoring point for the group and a pivot between the geographically located church in Lagos and the more ephemeral body that

---

[44] See Thomas Csordas, *Transnational Transcendence: Essays on Religion and Globalization* (Berkeley: University of California Press, 2009). See also Steven Vertovec, *Transnationalism* (London: Routledge, 2009).

[45] Afe Adogame, "Contesting the Ambivalences of Modernity in a Global Context: The Redeemed Christian Church of God, North America," *Studies in World Christianity* 10/1 (2004): 29. See also David Garbin and Manuel Vasquez, "'Sacred Connections': Religious Spaces, Transnational Communication and the Congolese Diaspora," in *Migrations, Diaspora and Information Technology in Global Societies*, ed. L. Fortunati, P. Pertierra, and J. Vincent (New York: Routledge, 2011): 156–71.

is the Asaphs of Seraph.[46] The same is true for the Tokoist Church in Lisbon
that is recognized as a national branch within the church hierarchy in
Luanda (Angola). The church has a discernible circulation of people coming
to and from Angola (or from other European countries) visiting, leaving, or
returning to the community. Moreover, the home church in Luanda remains
as the spiritual and administrative center. Among West Indian immigrants
in the United States, in the meantime, the expansion of transnational ties
between the United States and the *home* countries has resulted in the establishment of several branches of religious communities. Moreover, for many
of these branches, the model used for the liturgy, administration structure,
and more does not come from the new context but from the home context.[47]
In doing so, the ties with the home church and, by association, the homeland
are maintained.

Marginal and Inclusive

As people who are usually in the minority and tend to have a lower
socioeconomic status, as well as a (religious) culture that is different from
the dominant members of the local faith community, immigrant Christians
from the Global South live on the margins both in society and, in some
cases, the local faith community. Such marginalization is often intensified
by anti-immigrant rhetoric and immigration policies in destination countries. Not surprisingly, Christianity with the face of southern immigrants is
marginal and, to a certain extent, inclusive.

Due to personal, social, economic, and political circumstances,
immigrants from the Global South tend to live in the urban fringes or
economically challenged areas. Hence, many immigrant congregations start
from urban peripheries and remain in these marginal places not only because
that is where most of the members live but also because they are forced to
remain there for purposes of cheaper rents or due to government policies
and initiatives.[48] The small group of ten young Angolan men who started
the Tokoist Christian Church in Lisbon, for example, initially gathered in

---

46   Brennan, "Truly We Have a Good Heritage," 9.

47   McLean, "Make a Joyful Noise unto the Lord," 136.

48   For example, KICC, a large church in London that was founded by a Nigerian pastor and composed mainly of members with (West) African backgrounds and
some from British Caribbean communities, had to move out of their headquarters in an
industrial park to make way for the large-scale regeneration of the area in preparation
for the 2012 London Olympics.

old pensions in downtown Lisbon or their own apartments. The previously mentioned WOLA in South Africa was started by a Congolese pastor from his rented flat until it moved to a hotel, then to a hall, before it moved to its current site. Ninety-eight percent of WOLA's members are foreigners who are predominantly refugees (about 95 percent) from Congo.[49] To be sure, particular spatial configurations and locations constitute objective expressions of social status and symbolic positionalities, particularly in the ghettoized environments of developed destination countries.

For many southern immigrants, the church is not just the principal site of celebration for ethnic identity and community. It is also their refuge in times of crisis and their home when they want to shout for joy. In fact, the major driving forces for the establishment of self-identified, for example, black-led and independent African and Caribbean churches in Britain are the experience of socioeconomic marginalization and, more so, the resentment and rejection felt in both society and in local church communities.[50] As Dominic Pasura affirms in his case study of Zimbabwean Catholics in Britain's second largest city of Birmingham, diasporic congregations provide migrants with spaces to escape exclusion, racism, and discrimination in the destination country and, consequently, help in forging group solidarity. As Nyarai, a member in the parish Pasura studied, says,

> Where I live, it was hard to see black people walking around. If you saw one, most often they were Jamaicans and they wouldn't stop and talk to you. Most Jamaicans don't like Africans so it was very hard for me. When I heard about this church [Zimbabwean], I was so happy because I was feeling so lonely. You go to school to pick up your kids and the [white] mothers won't speak to you. They speak to your kids but not to you. That is quite sad.[51]

It is worse, of course, when racism or discrimination creeps into the parish or congregation. As a priest laments,

---

[49]   See Vedaste Nyazabino, "The Role of Refugee-Established Churches in Integrating Forced Migrants: A Case Study of Word of Life Assembly in Yeoville, Johannesburg," *HTS Theological Studies* 66/1 (2010): 1–9.

[50]   In most cases, self-identification among these churches serves to create a coherent communal approach. See Ekué, "Migrant Christians," 391–92.

[51]   As quoted in Dominic Pasura, "Religious Transnationalism: The Case of Zimbabwean Catholics in Britain," *Journal of Religion in Africa* 42/1 (2012): 36.

Somebody said to me, "Lots of dark faces in the church, father" and I just said, "Yes, and they are all Catholics" (laugh). We are not having it: in the parish next door, this sounds bad, two families came to the priest and said, "We are not coming to the church because there are too many dark faces and we are going to so and so because they don't have any dark faces there." And the priest said, and I wouldn't have said that, "Don't ever come here again," which is bad. He was rejecting them because they were rejecting others. You should never reject people like that; you should always encourage them, whatever community of race or wherever people come from.[52]

As faith communities made up of marginal(ized) people based in marginal(ized) areas, southern-derived congregations are increasingly filling the void for outreach to these areas and sections of the population that need serious and urgent attention. In fact, they play a strategic role, whether they like it or not, serving constituencies (both immigrant and native) long abandoned by more established and affluent congregations precisely because they are predominantly located in urban neighborhoods and often forced to occupy the most unlikely places—cramped living rooms, hotel ballrooms, thousands of storefronts, rented halls or office buildings, crumbling buildings in industrial areas, even ornate churches whose membership has declined.

African Christians in Europe, for instance, have set up evangelistic initiatives to reach out to groups of people that are rarely directly targeted by indigenous missionaries. These groups include drug addicts, alcoholics, prostitutes, victims of human trafficking, juvenile delinquents, and unauthorized migrants.[53] Part of the success of these African-led churches with these groups is how these churches link personal identity with destiny as well as individual and divine agency.[54] As the late Otto Maduro affirms, "in these dire circumstances it is often only religious congregations—especially those founded by migrants, with migrants, and for migrants—that are left to care for the 'collateral damages' wrought by national xenophobia, white

---

[52] As quoted in Pasura, "Religious Transnationalism," 46. The parish has members from Ghana, Nigeria, Cameroon, Ireland, Poland, and *indigenous* British people.

[53] See Asamoah-Gyadu, "To the Ends of the Earth," 30–31; and Pasura, "Religious Transnationalism," 37.

[54] For an illustrative discussion, see Boris Nieswand, "Enacted Destiny: West African Charismatic Christians in Berlin and the Immanence of God," *Journal of Religion in Africa* 40/1 (2010): 33–59.

supremacy and nativism."[55] Thus, the very marginality of these migrants is actually giving birth to some sense of inclusivity on the basis of their pastoral work among cross-sections of the urban poor and, to a certain extent, the membership and participation of other racial and ethnic groups. Sebastian Onah and Johan Leman posit: "In such circumstances, under the religious umbrella, groups who may have previously been at arm's length begin to move towards one another, appreciating the other's ethnic particularities, finding and suggesting opportunities to one another, and putting aside inter-group inhibitions."[56]

In some cases, the marginal status of these immigrants paves the way toward forms of inclusivity at the ecumenical level. It is common, for example, that other more established Christian parishes or congregations adopt or provide a space for these immigrants until they decide or are able to stand on their own. The Tokoist Church in Lisbon officially inaugurated their church after celebrating a service in a Presbyterian church. In the subsequent years, the Tokoists also connected with other Angolan Christians such as Pentecostals with whom they shared resources and worship spaces around the city center before finding their own place.[57] As argued by David Garbin in the case of Afro-Christian churches, particularly as shown in his study of the Congolese Kimbaguist Church in London and Atlanta, what is clear is that marginal(ized) immigrant religious groups are also engaged, in their own terms, in a transformative project of spatial appropriation, regeneration, and reenchantment of the urban landscape.[58] These Afro-Christian churches engage, in other words, in the politics of emplacement by forming, through their religious practices, particular spaces of alterity, often at the margin of urban experience. In doing so, they create or provide glimpses for possibilities for inclusive relationships at the cultural, economic, ecumenical, and interreligious levels.

---

[55] Otto Maduro, "2012 Presidential Address: Migrants' Religions under Imperial Duress: Reflections on Epistemology, Ethics and Politics in the Study of the Religious 'Stranger,'" *Journal of the American Academy of Religion* 82/1 (2014): 45.

[56] Sebastian Onah and Johan Leman, "Cosmological and Religious Fundamentals among Igbo Immigrants in Belgium: The Way Out of Segregation," *Social Compass* 52/4 (2005): 521.

[57] Blanes, "Double Presence," 420.

[58] David Garbin, "The Visibility and Invisibility of Migrant Faith in the City: Diaspora Religion and the Politics of Emplacement of Afro-Christian Churches," *Journal of Ethnic and Migration Studies* 39/5 (2013): 677–96.

Conclusion

Philip Jenkins's book *The Next Christendom: The Coming of Global Christianity,*[59] the first in a trilogy on the future of Christianity, has been hailed as a landmark in our understanding of modern Christianity. One of the important points raised in this book, which is echoed in the two other books that make up the trilogy,[60] is how contemporary migration is reshaping and redefining not just human geography but also the religious features and landscape, particularly of Christianity. Jenkins notes how the survival, future, and vitality of churches in destination countries are significantly influenced by southern-derived immigrant churches. This essay illustrates Jenkins's point by showing how immigrants from the Global South, especially in developed and more secularized societies, are bringing renewal and expansion to Christianity.

One can conclude that Christianity in the context of the experience of immigrant Christians from the Global South is, in the words of the Bible, the "light of the world." It shines a light on the dark corners of our world where these immigrants come from and the forgotten people and places in our cities where these immigrants have pitched their tent. At the same time, it puts the spotlight on the seeds of hope that are being planted and nurtured by these immigrants both in their own lives and in the lives of their adopted communities on account of their faith.

To be sure, Christian immigrants from the Global South have intensified the nature and profile of Christianity as a world religion, as their churches and congregations are fertile grounds for articulating a vision of a religious community across different national boundaries. At the same time, their experience also shows us the importance of further theological reflection on diversity and on the positive experiences that the creation of congregations in which, for instance, multilingual prayers, songs, and other forms of culturally embedded spirituality can be lived so that difference becomes a source of enrichment and openness for dialogue.

What is also clear is that Christianity is being reshaped in its universal (missionary and transnational) and particular (ethnic, folk, and lay-

---

[59] Philip Jenkins, *The Next Christendom: The Coming of Global Christianity* (Oxford: Oxford University Press, 2003). The most recent version (third edition) was published in 2011.

[60] These are Philip Jenkins, *The New Faces of Christianity: Believing the Bible in the Global South (Oxford: Oxford University Press, 2008);* and Philip Jenkins, *God's Continent: Christianity, Islam, and Europe's Religious Crisis (*Oxford: Oxford University Press, 2007).

oriented) dimensions by immigrant Christians from the Global South. For instance, the shift in the face of the missionary and missionizing practices, such as those among African immigrants in Europe on a mission to bring Christianity back to its former heartland, contribute to new layers of religious and transnational complexity. In fact, at no other point in its history has Christianity been a transnational civil society agent with a global network than it is at present in the hands of southern Christian immigrants who embrace their religion as their portable homeland. For Christian churches, particularly in Europe, it offers the opportunity to reflect on the place of mission and evangelism within the church, rather than with affiliated missionary agencies, and to rediscover the significance of evangelism as central to Christian witness as a whole. At the same time, the critical role of laypeople in the life of Christian communities among immigrants from the Global South, whether as founders, financiers, volunteers, and missionaries, cannot be underestimated. This and the hundreds of faith communities that continue to be founded and led by these lay Christians, including women, point to an increasing de-centering of power and authority in Christianity from the center (European, male, ordained, elite) to the margins (southern, male and female, nonordained, poor). Responses to these changes and other questions that arise from a dialogue with the experience of southern Christian immigrants are crucial in securing the future of Christianity.

Part II

World Christianity and
New Ways of Doing Theology

6

READING THE BIBLE IN THE *NEW* CHRISTIANITY: A CONTEXTUAL BIBLICAL HERMENEUTICS

vanThanh Nguyen

Reading and interpreting the signs of the times are important tasks for all believers, especially for theologians. In the New Testament, Jesus sternly rebuked the leaders of his time for their failure to interpret the signs of the times, saying, "When you see a cloud rising in the west, you immediately say, 'It is going to rain'; and so it happens. And when you see the south wind blowing, you say, 'There will be scorching heat'; and it happens. You hypocrites! You know how to interpret the appearance of earth and sky, but why do you not know how to interpret the present time?" (Luke 12:54–56). For the Word of God to have contemporary relevance for people across the globe, a contextual biblical hermeneutics that takes into consideration the social location of the reader is essential. As the map of Christianity continues to shift, one important question that needs to be addressed is how the Bible is read in global context in a manner that takes into consideration all perspectives and locations.

To demonstrate the usefulness of this approach for reading and interpreting the Bible in a global context, this essay examines a controversial and enigmatic saying of Jesus. A closed reading of Jesus's difficult saying, "Let the dead bury their own dead" (Luke 9:60), will show that Jesus neither stands in opposition to family ties nor disregards the cultural principles of filial piety, which are key values that are widely accepted and upheld by first-century hearers and today's Asians worldwide. Consequently, the excursus will help restore an authentic Asian face of Jesus.

The New Face of Christianity

The map of Christianity is rapidly changing, and so are its faces. Peter Phan, while acknowledging the unreliability of statistical projections of religious membership, is confident of the "surging growth" in southern Christianity in the next fifty years,[1] arguing that this demographic shift also provides new prospects for Christianity.[2] With Christianity growing at a phenomenal pace in the Global South, there is an increased likelihood that in the near future most Christian scholars will also be concentrated in the southern continents. Consequently, the shift in Christianity's center of gravity from the Global North to the Global South is not only demographic but also theological.[3] The result of this shift will have a seismic affect by doing theology that is moving away from the *center* to the *periphery*. This movement toward the *margin* will definitely impact the way people read and interpret the Bible. While there is a possibility that literalist or fundamentalist readings of the Bible might be the trend or norm of the southern tradition,[4] this interpretive prediction remains speculative.[5]

Philip Jenkins observes that in "the growing churches of the global South, the Bible speaks to everyday, real-world issues of poverty and debt, famine and urban crisis, racial and gender oppression, state brutality and persecution."[6] He suggests that this development "will push theologians to address the faith to poverty and social injustices, to political violence, corruption, and the meltdown of law and order; and to Christianity's witness amidst religious plurality," thereby bringing about "a freshness and authenticity that adds vastly to its credibility as an authoritative source and a guide for daily living."[7]

More importantly, the shifting Christian demographics are giving rise to a new way of conceiving, reading, and interpreting the Bible to address the reality, challenges, and hopes of women and men of all ethnic backgrounds, races, classes, and gender, especially those on the margins, and enabling their

---

[1] Peter Phan, "A New Christianity, but What Kind?" in *Landmark Essays in Mission and World Christianity*, ed. Robert L. Gallagher and Paul Hertig (Maryknoll, NY: Orbis Books, 2009), 204.

[2] For how it might look like in Asia, see Phan, "A New Christianity," 201–18.

[3] Priscilla Pope-Levison and John R. Levison, *Jesus in Global Contexts* (Louisville, KY: Westminster/John Knox Press, 1992), 12.

[4] Philip Jenkins, *New Faces of Christianity: Believing the Bible in the Global South* (Oxford: Oxford University Press, 2006), 2.

[5] See Phan, "A New Christianity," 204–5.

[6] Jenkins, *New Faces*, 5.

[7] Ibid.

voices to be heard. The continental shifts will challenge the *monocentric* (for example Eurocentric) perspectives to embrace a more *polycentric* perspective. What this means is that the old model of biblical interpretation, namely, the historical–critical method inherited from the Enlightenment period that has dominated European and North American biblical scholarship for over two centuries, is now being called into question as the *indispensable* approach of biblical interpretation.

Reading the Bible in Global Contexts

In the preface of their edited book, Walter Dietrich and Ulrich Luz concede, "In our own northern and western European context we experience especially that 'the older ways of understanding' the Bible 'no longer seem to work.'"[8] However, this is not the case in Africa, South America, and Asia.[9] A large part of the reason is that Western biblical interpretation lacked real context and thus remained abstract and unappealing to the ordinary reader. Dietrich and Luz write,

> It seems to us that Western biblical scholarship suffers most from being "without context." It is carried out abstractly and therefore leads to abstract results and truths, which are not related to any context. "Abstract" is not only understood in the usual sense as being opposed to "concrete." "Abstract" also means: unattached to the life and reading of "ordinary" people, far away from their questions, developed from the present and from its problems, concerned only with the reconstruction of a past with all its problems. Finally, another way of scholarly, "abstract" reading that is disconnected from the real concerns of present-day readers is to flee into an imaginary "text world"—imaginary, because it is entirely created by scholars. "Abstract" in the widest sense means: without context. All this does not contribute to understanding, which is related to our own context.[10]

The historical–critical method is primarily concerned with the diachronic processes that gave rise to the ancient writings. Its aim is to achieve a *scientific objectivity* and a *single meaning* of an ancient text. Further-

---

[8] Walter Dietrich and Ulrich Luz, eds., *The Bible in a World Context: An Experiment in Contextual Hermeneutics* (Grand Rapids, MI: Wm. B. Eerdmans, 2002), vii.

[9] Ibid., viii–ix.

[10] Ibid., ix–x.

more, since historical–critical studies do not essentially deal with the *actualization* or *appropriation* of the struggles of everyday life of the community, the church, or the world,[11] its methods have been a disappointment for many scholars, pastors, and believers. Kathleen O'Connor expresses her disenchantment with the emphasis of the historical–critical approach on the past as follows: "Historical criticism explicitly kept ancient meaning at a distance, more or less sealed off from the modern world and the lives of interpreters, readers, believers."[12] Recognizing that no interpretation is "objective" or "context-free," O'Connor concedes, "Scientific objectivity, in the sense that historical-criticism attempted it, is not achievable. The shift toward reader-response and reception theories within biblical studies expresses the change of focus from the past of the text to the present of the reader."[13]

As a narrative told from many viewpoints and situations, the art of reading and interpreting the Bible in the new Christianity must seriously take into consideration the context of the reader or interpreter. Teresa Okure hits the mark when she states, "A reading of the Bible that is not directly related to the social location of the reader is almost considered out of fashion."[14]

Toward a Contextual Biblical Hermeneutics

Priscilla Pope-Levison and John Levison explain that all theologies are contextually conditioned: "All theologies are influenced by and committed to a specific context, just as all theologians are shaped by their social location."[15] Consequently, we must acknowledge that there is no universal theology that is applicable in all contexts. Stephen Bevans, for example, has been insisting that doing theology contextually is not an option but really "a theological imperative."[16] Bevans continues to emphasize, "There is no 'theology' as such—no 'universal theology'—there are only contextual

---

[11] This aspect of hermeneutics deals with the *so what* question of exegesis.

[12] Kathleen O'Connor, "Crossing Borders: Biblical Studies in a Trans-cultural World," in *Teaching the Bible: The Discourses and Politics of Biblical Pedagogy*, ed. Fernando F. Segovia and Mary Ann Tolbert (Maryknoll, NY: Orbis Books, 1998), at 323.

[13] Ibid., 324.

[14] Teresa Okure, "Reading from This Place: Some Problems and Prospects," in *Reading From This Place: Social Location and Biblical Interpretation in Global Perspective*, vol. 2, ed. Fernando F. Segovia and Mary Ann Tolbert (Minneapolis: Fortress Press, 1995), at 54.

[15] Pope-Levison and Levison, *Jesus in Global Contexts*, 17.

[16] Stephen B. Bevans, *Models of Contextual Theology*, rev. and expanded ed. (Maryknoll, NY: Orbis Books, 2007), 3.

theologies."[17] Subsequently, Bevans asserts that doing theology contextually is the only way to do theology.[18] Recognizing that the *center of gravity* of Christianity has already shifted from the Global North to the Global South, where theology is currently flourishing, Bevans writes, "Theology today, I firmly believe, must be done in this global perspective. It *must* be contextual; but it must also be in dialogue, open to the other, ready to change, ready to challenge, ready to enrich and be enriched."[19]

As Christianity shifts beyond its European and North American moorings, Christian biblical scholars from Latin America, Africa, and Asia are consciously using their own context in conversation with the Bible and the Christian tradition. So much development has taken place around the globe that it is practically impossible to keep up with the vast literature emerging from these scholars and their perspectives.[20] This changing face of the world church is creating a paradigm shift of *globalization of biblical interpretation*. Because of this, contextual biblical hermeneutics is needed for scholarship to remain relevant in the new Christianity.

The task of biblical hermeneutics or interpretation is to closely examine an ancient text to ascertain the intended meaning of the text for its first hearers and furthermore to draw out the implications of that meaning for contemporary readers and hearers. Since context is the starting point of theological reflection, biblical interpretation should also begin with one's location—the here and now of the present situation. Starting with one's context rather than with the text itself will guarantee the hermeneutical relevancy of the biblical text. To demonstrate the usefulness of contextual biblical hermeneutics in the global contexts, let us examine a controversial and enigmatic saying of Jesus.

---

[17] Stephen B. Bevans, *An Introduction to Theology in Global Perspective* (Maryknoll, NY: Orbis Books, 2009), 4.

[18] Ibid.,167.

[19] Ibid., 5.

[20] See O'Connor, "Crossing Borders," 326–27. Some significant edited collections include Fernando F. Segovia and Mary Ann Tolbert, eds., *Reading from This Place: Social Location and Biblical Interpretation in Global Perspective*, vol. 2 (Minneapolis: Fortress Press, 1995); Daniel Patte, ed., *Global Bible Commentary* (Nashville: Abingdon Press, 2004); R. S. Sugirtharajah, ed., *Voices from the Margin: Interpreting the Bible in the Third World*, rev. and expanded 3rd ed. (Maryknoll, NY: Orbis Books, 2006); D. N. Premnath, ed., *Border Crossings: Cross-Cultural Hermeneutics* (Maryknoll, NY: Orbis Books, 2007); Randall C. Bailey, Tat-siong Benny Liew and Fernando F. Segovia, eds., *They Were All Together in One Place? Toward Minority Biblical Criticism* (Atlanta: Society of Biblical Literature, 2009); Roland Boer and Fernando F. Segovia, eds., *The Future of the Biblical Past: Envisioning Biblical Studies on a Global Key* (Atlanta: Society of Biblical Literature, 2012).

Jesus's Difficult Saying in Luke 9:60

As a Vietnamese who deeply values the practice of filial piety, I have grappled with the challenge of interpreting Jesus's stern instruction in Luke 9:60: "Let the dead bury their own dead!" Likewise to the ears of first-century hearers, Jesus's harsh saying must have not only been insensitive and unsympathetic but also a blatant transgression of law and tradition. Given the importance of the sacred obligation and cultural expectation to bury one's parents, several pressing questions arise: How should we interpret this difficult and mysterious saying of Jesus? Could Jesus really teach us to completely sever our family ties? Is the commitment to follow Jesus so radical that we have to transgress our own cultural values and obligation of filial piety? Jesus's remark, if taken out of its appropriate contexts, could pose a huge obstacle to evangelization and missionary endeavors in a culture that pays great honor to the dead. The saying seems to stand in opposition to family ties and disregards the cultural principles of filial piety, which are values that are widely accepted and upheld by Asian communities worldwide. As such, the aim of this excursus is to provide the appropriate contexts for interpreting this controversial and enigmatic saying of Jesus. To understand how difficult it is for many Asians to accept Jesus's embarrassing statement, let me begin by briefly examining Confucius's teaching on filial piety.[21]

Filial Piety in Confucianism

The Confucian tradition has greatly influenced the social and cultural norms in China and its many neighbors, including Vietnam. For Confucius (551–479 BCE), the central focus of one's life is cultivating virtues. While humaneness, etiquette, and loyalty are core virtues, filial piety (*hiếu thảo* in Vietnamese or *xiao* in Chinese) is "the foundation and root of all virtues."[22] Since filial piety is one of the founding pillars of Confucianism and a cardinal virtue in Confucian ethics and tradition, it shapes people's mind-set, ethical behaviors, and lifestyle. Daniel Qin writes,

---

[21] What follows is a condensed and revised version of an article that was previously published: vanThanh Nguyen, SVD, "'Let the Dead Bury Their Dead' (Lk 9:60): A New Perspective," *New Theology Review* 27/2 (2015): 14–22.

[22] Peter C. Phan, *Christianity with an Asian Face: Asian American Theology in the Making* (Maryknoll, NY: Orbis Books, 2003), 131; see also Heidi M. Szpek, "Filial Piety in Jewish Epitaphs," *International Journal of the Humanities* 8/4 (2010): 183–201.

[Filial piety] emphasizes the affection and duty of the children in parent-child relationships. Children are obliged to obey, support, and honor their parents. Filial piety is both a recognized virtue and a cultural norm. In other words, it is both an inward virtue that children should follow with sincere hearts and an outward etiquette toward their parents.[23]

Right or honorable relationship between parents and children, in particular between the father and the eldest son, is greatly esteemed in the Confucian cultural system and quite distinct from Western cultures. Guo Qiyong states, "Feeling for one's family members constitutes the most sincere, most beautiful, and most important form of the various human feelings . . . Loving our own family members is the basis for loving other people in society."[24] Consequently, a son who fulfills his filial obligation is regarded as the ideal person in society and is considered a real "gentleman."[25] In fulfilling filial responsibilities, he exercises the virtues of humaneness, kindness, or goodness and thus contributes to the public welfare. Carrying out filial obligation is so important that it even takes precedence over public service. His patriotism is never questioned since being loyal to the family is considered being loyal to the state or country.[26] As such, filial responsibility should take precedence over all other duties, "including obligations to emperor, Heaven, or any other source of temporal or divine authority."[27]

Nurturing or caring for one's father and mother while they are still alive is only one of the many expressions of filial piety. When asked about the meaning of filial piety, Confucius himself explains: "Serve your parents in their lifetime according to *li* [the rites]; when they die, bury them according to *li*; make sacrificial offerings to them according to *li*" (*Analects* 2:5).[28]

---

[23] Daniel Qin, "Confucian Filial Piety and the Fifth Commandment: A Fulfillment Approach," *Asian Journal of Pentecostal Studies* 16/2 (2013): 140.

[24] Guo Qiyong, "Filial Piety, Three Years Mourning, and Love," *Contemporary Chinese Thought* 42/4 (2011): 19.

[25] Phan, *Christianity*, 129. The literal translation of the Chinese (*junzi*) or Vietnamese (*quân tử*) word for *gentleman/noble person* is *lord's son*. It is a description of the ideal man.

[26] See Phan, *Christianity*, 131; and Guo, "Filial Piety," 19.

[27] Mary Yeo Carpenter, "Familism and Ancestor Veneration: A Look at Chinese Funeral Rites," *Missiology: An International Review* 24/4 (1996): 505.

[28] This passage is translated by R. Eno whose translation of the *Analects of Confucius* is made available online: http://www.indiana.edu/~p374/Analects_of_Confucius_%28Eno-2012%29.pdf.

Consequently, Peter Phan notes, "A good son also wants to be near his parents so that at their death he may be able to come back and perform the rites of mourning."[29] Phan's observation comes directly from the *Analects of Confucius* where it states, "While father and mother are alive, a good son does not wander far afield; or if he does so, goes only where he has said he was going."[30]

Mencius (372–289 BCE) emphasized funeral ceremonies for sending off the dead, saying, "It is reasonable that filial sons and benevolent men should bury the remains of their parents."[31] Mencius believed that "funeral and mourning rituals represented an inevitable and natural development of human nature and human feelings."[32] Since mourning is an important expression of filial piety, Peter Phan notes that children should not be stingy in burying their parents and must observe a three-year period of mourning. During the period of mourning, their grief must be seen to be sincere by carefully avoiding any show of joy or happiness. For example, if he eats sweets, he does not relish them, or if he hears music, he does not enjoy it.[33] During the period of mourning, family members wear special mourning garb. The children of the deceased parent normally wear coarse gauze turbans and tunics. The daughters and daughters-in-law of the deceased also wear a white muslin veil covering most of the body. Relatives of the deceased wear white headbands.

Filial Piety in the Bible

Confucius was not the only person in ancient times who taught the importance of honoring one's parents. The ancient Israelites also valued the human virtue of filial piety since they, too, considered it as the basis for all

---

[29] Phan, *Christianity*, 131.

[30] *Analects* 4:19; quoted in Phan, *Christianity*, 131.

[31] Mencius 3A5, quoted in Guo, "Filial Piety," 27. Not burying one's parent could have tragic consequences. Mencius warns, "Now in the past ages, there were those who did not bury their parents. When their parents died, they took them and abandoned them in a ditch. The next day they passed by them, and foxes were eating them, bugs were sucking on them. Sweat broke out [on the survivors'] foreheads. They turned away and did not look. Now, as for the sweat, it was not for the sake of others that they sweated. What was inside their hearts broke through to their countenances. So, they went home and, returning with baskets and shovels, covered them. If covering them was really right, then when filial sons and benevolent people cover their parents, it must also be part of the Way" (Mencius, 3A5).

[32] Guo, "Filial Piety," 27.

[33] Phan, *Christianity*, 133.

human relationships. While the term *filial piety* is not found in the Bible per se, many passages emphasize the importance of this virtue. Among them, the fourth commandment bears the most significance because it is a fundamental divine commandment.[34] In Exodus 20:12, God says, "Honor your father and your mother, so that your days may be long in the land that the LORD your God is giving you."[35] This commandment is repeated in Deuteronomy 5:16, reinforcing that it is the Lord God who commands it. According to the Jewish Torah, children are expected to treat their parents with deep respect and reverence (Lev. 19:3). They ought to hear and obey the instruction and teaching of their parents (Prov. 6:20) and must do everything possible to avoid causing them shame and dishonor (Prov. 30:17).

The book of Proverbs reinforces the importance of keeping the fourth commandment by giving many helpful counsels concerning child–parent relationships. Several notable quotations are worth highlighting:

Hear, my child, your father's instruction, and do not reject your mother's teaching; for they are a fair garland for your head, and pendants for your neck. (Prov. 1:8–9)

A wise child loves discipline, but a scoffer does not listen to rebuke. (Prov. 13:1)

Listen to your father who begot you, and do not despise your mother when she is old. (Prov. 23:22)

While children who honor their parents are rewarded with longevity and blessings (Exod. 20:12), disobedient and rebellious children are cursed (Deut. 27:16) and shall even be put to death (Deut. 21:18–21). The author of Leviticus gives a very stern warning saying, "All who curse father or mother shall be put to death; having cursed father or mother, their blood is upon them" (20:9). The author of Proverbs also admonishes, "If you curse father or mother, your lamp will go out in utter darkness" (20:20). Proverbs depicts a horrific death for children who disobey their parents saying, "The eye that mocks a father and scorns to obey a mother will be pecked out by the ravens of the valley and eaten by the vultures" (30:17).

The Hebrew Bible records many passages emphasizing the importance of one's obligation to bury the dead (Gen. 47:29–31; Deut. 28:26, 34:6; Jer.

---

[34] This commandment is generally regarded in Protestant and Jewish traditions as the fifth commandment; however, in the Catholic tradition, it is the fourth commandment.

[35] All scripture citations are cited from the NRSV unless otherwise noted.

7:33, 8:1–2; Ezek. 6:5, 29:5, 39:17; Ps. 4:19).[36] One notable example comes from the book of Tobit. In this Jewish folktale, Tobit's piety is demonstrated by his faithfulness in burying the dead (Tob. 1:16–20), and his son Tobias is praised and remembered because he takes seriously his filial duty to bury both his father and mother (Tob. 4:3, 6:15). Since burying one's parents was an act of piety that derived from the fourth commandment, neglecting to do so was shameful and liable of harsh punishment (Deut. 28:26; Jer. 7:33; Ezek. 6:5; 2 Macc. 5:10, 9:15).[37] Both prerabbinic and rabbinic sources took for granted the burial of the dead, especially one's parents, as a "*halakhic* duty" and a "*fortiori.*"[38] According to the Talmud, burial of one's family superseded all other commandments, "He who is confronted by a dead relative is freed from reciting the Shema, from the Eighteen Benedictions, and from all the commandments stated in the Torah."[39] Even Gentile authors from the Greco–Roman period, for example Josephus and Suetonius, saw the burial of one's family member or friend as an act of piety and esteemed virtue.[40]

Jesus as Obedient Son

As a faithful Jew and an obedient son, Jesus of Nazareth knew the importance of keeping the commandment of *honoring your father and your mother*. Jesus actually referred to this divine commandment many times in his teaching and expected everyone to observe it (Matt. 15:4, 19:19; Mark 7:10, 10:19; Luke 18:20). The gospel writers also show that Jesus makes a

---

[36] Other biblical passages that refer to burial, often father by son, are as follows: Gen. 49:29–32, 50:5, 25; 2 Sam. 21:10–14; Tob. 1:17–18, 4:3–4, 6:14–15, 12:12–13, 14:10.

[37] Other passages are Jer. 8:1–2, 16:4, 25:33; Ezek. 29:5; 1 Enoch 98:13. In the Old Testament there are two exceptions to the expectation that a son will take care of his parents' burial. The high priest (according to Lev. 21:11) and the Nazirite (according to Num. 6:6–8) are both prohibited from involvement in the care of the dead, even of their close relatives.

[38] Markus Bockmuehl, "'Let the Dead Bury Their Dead' (Matt. 8:22/Luke 9:60): Jesus and the Halakhah," *Journal of Theological Studies* 49/2 (1998): 554. *Halakhah* is the entire body of Jewish law and tradition comprising the laws of the Bible, the oral law as transcribed in the legal portion of the Talmud, and subsequent legal codes amending or modifying traditional precepts to conform to contemporary conditions.

[39] Berakoth 3.1a, quoted in Martin Hengel, *The Charismatic Leader and His Followers*, trans. J. C. G. Greig (Edinburg: T&T Clark, 1981), 9.

[40] See Josephus, *Jewish Wars* 2.465 and Suetonius, *Vespasian* 2.3, quoted in Warren Carter, *Matthew and the Margins: A Sociopolitical and Religious Reading* (Maryknoll, NY: Orbis Books, 2000), 208.

great effort to observe this commandment. The Evangelist Luke says that Jesus was submissive to his parents (2:51). The Evangelist John shows that Jesus was obedient to his mother at the wedding in Cana (2:1–12) and fulfilled his filial duty before dying on the cross (19:25–27). These two stories serve as bookends, one at the beginning and other at the end of his ministry, to highlight the theme of filial piety in the Fourth Gospel. The Evangelist John repeatedly portrays Jesus as the obedient son who came to fulfill the Father's will (5:30, 10:17–18, 12:49–50, 14:31, 17:1–26). In the Synoptic Gospels, Jesus calls God in a very endearing and unusual way, namely, "Abba Father" (Mark 14:36). In his prayer and in his parables, Jesus often referred to God as his Father (Luke 15:11–32; Matt. 11:25–27). As an obedient son, he seeks to do the Father's will, even to death on the cross (Luke 22:42). Similarly, Saint Paul taught the new believers at Philippi that Jesus was an obedient son who emptied himself and took the form of a slave to the point of death—even death on a cross (Phil. 2:8–11). In a similar vein, the author of the letter to the Hebrews wrote, "Although he was a Son, he learned obedience through what he suffered" (5:8). It is clear that many New Testament writers take pains to show that Jesus fully observed the fourth commandment by the way he fulfilled his filial duty to both his earthly parents and his heavenly Father.[41] Since the fourth commandment is the perfect expression of filial piety, it corresponds with Confucian filial piety. As a result, Daniel Qin concludes, "Jesus came, by his words and deeds as the fulfiller of both the [fourth] commandment and Confucian filial piety."[42]

As a culturally sensitive Jew, who knew the importance of honoring one's parents, one would think that Jesus would fully understand the request of the would-be disciple who says, "Lord, let me first go and bury my father" (Luke 9:59). Since burying one's parent is a fulfillment of the fourth commandment and of the filial piety, such a request is quite reasonable according to conventional Jewish customs.[43] The problem, however, is that

---

[41] Other New Testament writers also stress the importance of fulfilling the filial obligation. The author of Colossians writes, "Children, obey your parents in every-thing, for this is your acceptable duty in the Lord" (3:20). The letter to the Ephesians states, "Children, obey your parents in the Lord, for this is right. Honor your father and mother—this is the first commandment with a promise: so that it may be well with you and you may live long on the earth" (6:1–3).

[42] Qin, "Confucian Filial Piety," 160.

[43] W. D. Davies and Dale C. Allison, *A Critical and Exegetical Commentary on the Gospel According to Saint Matthew*, vol. 2: *Matthew VIII–XVIII* (Edinburgh: T&T Clark, 1991), 53; see also Luke T. Johnson, *The Gospel of Luke*, Sacra Pagina Series

at the request of the would-be disciple, the response that Jesus gave, "Let the dead bury their own dead," apparently contradicts the divine command to honor and respect one's parents and also departs from conventional Jewish tradition. Based on all the ancient sources that are available concerning the duty to bury the dead, especially one's father or mother, Jesus's statement is not only shocking but also scandalous.[44]

Jesus's Shocking Statement in Context

Jesus's hard saying, "Let the dead bury their own dead," which is found in Luke 9:60 and Matthew 8:22, derives from the "Q" Source.[45] Both Luke and Matthew preserved this apparently authentic saying of Jesus from "Q"[46] and appropriated it into their gospels along with other independent sayings of Jesus to emphasize the nature of discipleship. Unfortunately, the original context of this specific saying is unknown.[47] It is reasonable to conclude that Luke took this saying and grouped it together with two other similar sayings about the cost of discipleship to form one unit of three episodes with three sayings of Jesus addressed to three would-be followers (9:57–62). As Jesus was going along the road, the first would-be follower comes up to him and makes an enthusiastic promise of unconditional commitment saying, "I will follow you wherever you go." Jesus responds, "Foxes have holes, and birds of the air have nests; but the Son of Man has nowhere to lay his head." Contrasting with the first man who eagerly volunteers to follow Jesus, the second would-be follower is invited by Jesus himself. The man is more than willing to accept Jesus's invitation to discipleship, but he requests a brief

---

(Collegeville, MN: Liturgical Press, 1991), 163–64; and Joseph A. Fitzmyer, *The Gospel According to Luke (I–IX)*, Anchor Bible (Garden City, NY: Doubleday, 1981), 834–37.

[44] For Warren Carter, Jesus's response is "stunningly iconoclastic" (*Matthew*, 208).

[45] "Q" or *Quelle* in German is a hypothetical source that contains materials only found in both Matthew and Luke.

[46] There is almost a unanimous agreement among scholars in attributing this logion to the historical Jesus. See John Nolland, *Luke 9:21–18:34*, Word Biblical Commentary, vol. 35B (Dallas, TX: Word Books Publisher, 1993), 540. Fitzmyer, for example, says that the harshness and obscurity of the saying are a guarantee for its authenticity (*Luke [I–IX]*, 835). The saying also passes the criterion of dissimilarity; see Byron R. McCane, "Let the Dead Bury Their Own Dead: Secondary Burial and Matt 8:21–22," *Harvard Theological Review* 83/1 (1990): 41.

[47] Fitzmyer suggests that this saying along with the other two sayings found in Luke 9:57–62 may have come "from entirely independent contexts in the ministry of Jesus" (*Luke [I–IX]*, 834).

delay with enough time to bury his father in order to fulfill his filial duty dictated in the Torah and conformed to cultural expectations. Nevertheless, Jesus responds to the man saying, "Let the dead bury their own dead; but as for you, go and proclaim the kingdom of God." The third would-be follower, who is similar to the first man, also spontaneously offers to follow Jesus; however, like the second man, he too makes a condition saying, "I will follow you, Lord; but let me first say farewell to those at my home."[48] Jesus responds to him saying, "No one who puts a hand to the plow and looks back is fit for the kingdom of God."

Interestingly, while the first and second sayings found in Luke 9:57–60 are closely paralleled by Matthew 8:18–22, the third saying is found nowhere else in the gospel tradition except in Luke. Whether it is a purely Lukan composition drawn from his special source ("L") or whether it is the case of Matthew's omission from the "Q" Source, we cannot really know with certainty. In any case, Luke took these independent sayings of Jesus and grouped them together to form a concentric unit, with Luke 9:60 as the central piece emphasizing the motif of discipleship that transcends even personal security (as in the case of the first saying), filial piety (as in the case of the second saying), and family affection and ties (as in the case of the third saying). Furthermore, by placing the three sayings before the sending of the seventy-two disciples on their mission (10:1–16) and within the traveling narrative from Galilee to Jerusalem (9:51—19:27),[49] Luke not only reconstructs the narrative context but even supplies the motif for interpreting Jesus's most shocking statement, "Let the dead bury their own dead" (9:60).

Consequently, the Lukan narrative context has led many biblical scholars to misinterpret the saying as part of the call to radical discipleship that requires a complete break with the Torah or family ties by taking precedence over the care for one's parent (living or dead).[50] One scholar proposes

---

[48] The man's request to bid farewell to his family echoes Elisha's found in 1 Kings 19:19–21. Unlike Elijah, Jesus's response seems to indicate the unconditional demand of the call to discipleship that does not even allow bidding farewell to one's family.

[49] It is interesting to note that while Luke places the triple-sayings in the context of Jesus's journey from Galilee to Jerusalem, Matthew's double-sayings are situated within the section of Jesus's miraculous works (8:1–9:35). Furthermore, while in Luke the sayings serve as the context for the sending of the seventy-two on their mission (10:1–16), Matthew's sayings serve as the introduction of the miraculous stilling of the storm on Jesus's journey by boat to the other side of the Sea of Galilee (8:23–27).

[50] For an interpretation that emphasizes a break with law and custom, see Hengel, *Charismatic Leader*, 3–15. For a reading that focuses on Jesus's redefinition of God's

that the saying indicates that Jesus took the Nazirite vow and therefore encouraged his followers to practice it.[51] Moreover, since Jesus's demand is so uncharacteristically stringent, some scholars have sought to interpret it as a Semitic hyperbole or metaphor that is not meant to be taken literally.[52] Unfortunately, none of the above proposals adequately resolves the mystery of this difficult saying simply because its social context has not been appropriately considered.

Secondary Burial Custom

The key to solving the riddle of Jesus's hard saying lies with a burial custom, known as secondary burial, that was practiced by Jews in first-century Palestine, especially among the elites living in Jerusalem.[53] In his seminal work on Jewish death rituals in early Roman Palestine, McCane correctly points out that biblical interpreters have *incorrectly* assumed that "the saying presupposes the ritual of primary burial, that is, the initial interment of the body at the time of death."[54] Jews in first-century Palestine promptly buried the dead within the same day. During the first few days after burial, family members of the deceased were expected to observe the mourning ritual and to remain at home to receive the condolences of relatives and friends.[55] Under such circumstances, it would not be possible—without violating the cultural script and custom of the time—for the would-be disciple to be out and about conversing with an itinerant preacher when his father either had just died or recently been buried. Consequently,

---

family in which blood ties are relativized by obedience to the will of God because of the urgency of the eschaton, see Fletcher-Louis, "'Leave the Dead,'" 39–68.

[51] Bockmuehl, "'Let the Dead,'" 553–81. Nazirites were regarded as uniquely dedicated to God, for example, Samson (Judg. 13:7) and Samuel (1:11, 22). According to Bockmuehl, the Torah prescribes two exceptions prohibiting both High Priests (Lev. 21:11–12) and Nazarites (Num. 6:6) to contract corpse impurity even in the case of close relatives or parents. As such, Jesus's saying is not a deliberate attack on the Torah as suggested by Martin Hengel; rather his religious duty as a Nazarite took precedence over even the basic family obligation of burying one's parent.

[52] Culpepper, 216; Carter, *Matthew,* 209.

[53] McCane, *Roll Back the Stone: Death and Burial in the Time of Jesus* (Harrisburg, PA: Trinity Press, 2003), 9–14. See also McCane, "'Let the Dead,'" 31–43.

[54] McCane, *Roll Back,* 74.

[55] The portrayal of Martha and Mary staying home to mourn for their dead brother Lazarus in John 11 reflects the mourning ritual and custom of Jews in Palestine. See also the story of Jesus's raising the young girl in Mark 5:35–43. For rabbinic sources confirming this common practice, see McCane, *Roll Back,* 74–75.

the most plausible social context of Jesus's hard saying is not the ritual of the primary burial but the secondary burial.[56]

The ritual of secondary burial takes place a year after death and has two main purposes. First, it is the closing act of mourning for the family members of the deceased. Second, and more importantly, it is a ritual that symbolically enacts the transferring of the deceased to a permanent residence in the world of the dead. In other words, after the body has decomposed, the bones were collected and placed with those of other members of the family. This ritual possibly reflects the ancient biblical practice known as "to be gathered to their ancestors" repeatedly referred to in the Old Testament (Judg. 2:10; 2 Sam. 21:12–14; 2 Chron. 34:28).[57] However, sometime during the Greco–Roman period (from third century to first century BCE), Jews in Palestine discontinued the gathering of bones of their loved ones en masse or into a communal familial depository.[58] Rather, the remains were now placed into a separate box or ossuary highlighting the individuality of the person. Furthermore, by the second half of the first century BCE, many of the elite class of Jerusalem, including the high priests, embraced the Hellenistic culture. The practice of gathering bones into ossuaries, according to Jodi Magness, "is one aspect of the adoption of Hellenistic and Roman fashions by Jerusalem's elite during Herod's reign."[59] Magness provides further clarification stating,

---

[56] Brink is correct to point out that understanding the practices of burials in the ancient world provides another lens with which to interpret this and other passages in the Bible concerning death and burial. See Laurie Brink, "'Let the Dead Bury the Dead': Using Archaeology to Understand the Bible," *Bible Today* 49/5 (2011): 191–96. See also McCane, "'Let the Dead,'" 40.

[57] Other references alluding to the practice of gathering of the bones to be with the ancestors are found in the burial of Abraham (Gen. 25:8), Moses (Deut. 32:50), David and Solomon (1 Kgs. 11:21, 43) and Josiah (2 Kgs. 22:20).

[58] Brink, "'Let the Dead,'" 294.

[59] Jodi Magness, "Ossuaries and the Burials of Jesus and James," *Journal of Biblical Literature* 124/1 (2005): 122. Magness provides archaeological evidence for Jewish tombs and burial customs in the late Second Temple period, focusing on Jerusalem. From her findings, she attributed the appearance of ossuaries to the influence of Roman cinerary urns. In other words, in the late first century BCE and first century CE, cremation was the prevailing burial rite among the Romans. The ashes of the deceased were placed in small stone containers called *cineraria* (cinerary urns). Since the Jewish law prohibited cremating their dead, Jews in Jerusalem could only adopt the external trappings of cremation by depositing the bones of the deceased in ossuaries (urns) instead of their ashes.

The appearance of ossuaries and other aspects of Romanization in Jerusalem should be understood in the context of the close contacts and interactions between Augustus and his family, on the one hand, and Herod and his family, on the other. It is not surprising that beginning around 20 BCE, the style of life—and death—of Jerusalem's elite was heavily influenced by Roman culture.[60]

Archaeological evidence shows that the practice of secondary burial, namely, the gathering of decomposed remains (bones) into ossuaries primarily served as a fashion statement to enhance the social status of the wealthy class residing primarily in Jerusalem.

Since ossuaries were mainly used in rock-cut tombs, and since rock-cut tombs were only available for the wealthy, the practice was not for the masses but primarily for the wealthier members of the Jewish society. In contrast, the poorer classes were buried in simple individual trench graves dug into the ground. Perhaps Magness's assessment is correct in concluding that the practice of secondary burial, along with its numerous features and trappings, "has little or nothing to do with religious beliefs in the afterlife and everything to do with social status."[61]

Renunciation of Elite Social Status as Criterion for Discipleship

Against the background of secondary burial, Jesus's hard saying, "Let the dead bury their own dead," is given a new perspective for interpretation. The social context shows that the would-be disciple is asking for a temporary postponement to perform the Roman secondary burial practice of depositing decomposed remains into an ossuary. The ossuary is then placed in a

---

[60] Magness, "Ossuaries," 140.

[61] Ibid., 135. Magness convincingly argues that the use of ossuaries was not connected with the concept of the individual, physical resurrection of the dead; rather, it was greatly influenced by Roman cinerary urns. Magness writes, "If the use of ossuaries was connected with the concept of the individual, physical resurrection of the dead, they should have become even more popular after 70 C.E., when this belief became normative in Judaism. In fact, the opposite is true. After 70 C.E., ossuaries disappeared from Jerusalem. This is because the Jewish elites who used the rock-cut tombs were now dead or dispersed. The appearance of cruder ossuaries in Galilee after 70 is probably connected with the emigration or displacement of some of Jerusalem's elite to that region after the First Revolt. By the mid-to-late third century, the custom of ossilegium died out" ("Ossuaries," 136).

family rock-cut tomb. The request reveals that the would-be disciple, who probably came from an elite class and had assimilated into the Hellenistic and Roman culture and lifestyle, needed to fulfill a Roman burial ritual to maintain his and the family's status. Consequently, Jesus's response directly and uncompromisingly challenged the would-be disciple to renounce all forms of wealth and prestige that promoted a privileged social status. Furthermore, our context indicates that Jesus's reply does not necessarily imply a complete renunciation of family ties as a criterion for discipleship. Scholars usually justify this harsh and antifamily hostility to Jesus's imminent eschatological worldview. In other words, the reason Jesus required a radical commitment and allegiance that transcended and even abandoned family ties is because of his conviction of the imminent arrival of the end-time.[62] Contrary to this popular interpretation, I propose that the saying is not about the subordination of family ties or about the opposition of filial piety; rather, with this saying Jesus severely opposed the Roman burial practice that had little or no religious significance, but rather promoted a practice that preserved the social status of an elite wealthy class. For Jesus, authentic discipleship demands a complete renunciation of the security of such status.

Conclusion

This essay begins by briefly acknowledging the anticipated demographic shift of Christianity in the next fifty years. Intriguingly, the shift in Christianity's center of gravity from the Global North to the Global South is not only demographic but also theological. Its shifts present enormous challenges and at the same time provide new prospects. While it is uncertain what the *new Christianity* might look like, the demographic and theological shifts will surely affect how people do theology and impact the way people read and interpret the Bible. As a narrative told from many viewpoints and locations, reading and interpreting the Bible in the new Christianity must

---

[62] See Stephen C. Barton, *Discipleship and Family Ties in Mark and Matthew* (Cambridge: Cambridge University Press, 1994), 140–55. Barton correctly points out that this logion in Matthew does not oppose filial piety or promote antifamily sentiments; however, similar to other scholars, Barton has no other explanation for its harshness other than to blame it on the eschatological motif. Likewise, McCane concludes that this saying is "anti-family" because it is shaped by "unusually intense eschatological convictions" (*Roll Back the Stone*, 83). For similar conclusions, see also Carter, *Matthew*, 209; Fitzmyer, *Luke (I–IX)*, 836; and Nolland, *Luke 9:21–18:34*, 540.

take into consideration the contexts of the reader. Furthermore, it is contextual biblical hermeneutics that is most needed to remain relevant on the global stage. To demonstrate the usefulness of contextual biblical hermeneutics, a closed reading of Jesus's difficult and controversial saying found in Luke 9:60, "Let the dead bury their own dead," illustrated that Jesus neither opposes the renunciation of family ties nor disregards the cultural principles of filial piety. Consequently, the contextual approach provides a new lens and perspective to correctly interpret and understand one of Jesus's most problematic and enigmatic sayings and at the same time reveals a genuine Asian feature and portrait of Jesus.

7

WORLD CHRISTIANITY AND THE GLOBAL CHRISTIAN MISSION

William R. Burrows

In the pages that follow, I reflect on how Christians in today's globalized world can live up to the challenge (1) to embody, witness to, and proclaim Jesus as the Christ; and (2) to honor insights into the world's radical multi-religious and multicultural reality and what Langdon Gilkey noted thirty years ago about the *rough parity* that Western culture has had to recognize between itself and other cultures in the years since World War II. We are faced even more now than when Gilkey wrote—with a difference. Today the ambiguity of religion is much more front and center, especially the ambiguities revealed in the growth of radical Islam and secularists' conviction that Christianity and all religions need to retreat from the public square.

Always in the background in what follows is an insight I received when I read the following words of Sri Lankan Jesuit Aloysius Pieris:

> The "core" of any religion is the *liberative* experience that gave birth to that religion and continues to be available to successive genera-tions of humankind. It is this primordial experience that functions as the *core* of a religion, at any time, in any given place, in the sense that it continuously re-creates the *psychological mood* proper to that particular religion, imparting at the same time its own pecu-liar character to the *socio-cultural manifestation* of that religion. It is precisely through recourse to this primordial experience that a religion revolves its recurrent crises and regenerates itself in the face of new challenges. In fact, the vitality of any given religion depends on its capacity to put each successive generation in touch with that core-experience of liberation.[1]

---

[1] Aloysius Pieris, "The Buddha and the Christ: Mediators of Liberation," in *The*

Pieris is writing about issues involved in a genuine dialogue between Christianity and Buddhism, not about Christian mission. Without using the word—probably because of its colonial overtones in South Asia—Pieris puts his finger on what makes a religious tradition vital. When a tradition loses the capacity to enliven the inward parts of a human being, it becomes dry, arid, and barren. The conversion I speak of is not primarily conversion from Christianity, for example, to Islam, or from Melanesian traditional religions to Christianity. Rather it is conversion from ordinary, plodding, day-to-day existence to a heightened level of awareness, purpose, and meaning mediated by the rites, scriptures, teaching, and practices of *any* religion.

What draws together the various strands of the essay that follows is exactly this dimension of passage—conversion—from, if you will, ordinary life devoid of a deep *participation* in the *sacred* dimension of life to living in that holy, sacred dimension. The work of Bernard Lonergan is the source of the perspective that animates this piece.[2] I draw attention to Lonergan whose articulation of the *conversion* process moving to a new basic perspective on what life is and where it is going in religions such as Christianity, Islam, Hinduism, and Buddhism. Lonergan's fifth functional specialty in theology is called *foundations*, not because he seeks a foundational spot from which one can deduce truth and its consequences, but because

By conversion is understood a transformation of the subject and his world . . . it is not just a development or even a series of developments. Rather it is a resultant change of course and direction. It is as if one's eyes were opened and one's former world faded and fell away. There emerges something new that fructifies inter-locking, cumulative sequences of developments on all levels and in all departments of human living.

Conversion is existential, intensely personal, utterly intimate. But it is not so private as to be solitary. It can happen to many, and they can form a community to sustain one another in their

Myth of Christian Uniqueness: Toward a Pluralistic Theology of Religions, ed. Paul F. Knitter and John Hick (Maryknoll, NY: Orbis Books, 1987), at 162.

   [2] In addition to his *capolavoro, Insight* (New York: Philosophical Library, 1957), Bernard Lonergan's *Method in Theology* (New York: Herder, 1972) places great emphasis on the necessity of the internal transformation that underlies moral, intellectual, and religious conversion. See Frederick E. Crowe, *Lonergan and the Level of Our Time*, ed. Michael Vertin (Toronto: University of Toronto Press, 2010) for an excellent appreciation of the significance of Lonergan's thought.

self-transformation . . . Finally what can become communal, can become historical. It can pass from generation to generation. It can spread from one cultural milieu to another. It can adapt to changing circumstances, confront new situations, survive into a different age, flourish in another period or epoch.[3]

For many centuries, Christendom in its Catholic and Protestant forms occupied a privileged position in North Atlantic cultures. How many of Christendom's adherents went through a conversion experience in the sense Lonergan gives that word? It is, of course, impossible to know, but it is equally clear that a change in culture has deprived Christianity of its privileged position, and only conversion in the sense we use it here can bring it back to life. It is the process to interiority not as some individual mystical experience as it is passage to a personal participation in the transcendence of life and the possibility of living it more deeply and authentically.

If one applies a philosophic and historical lens to Christianity and the Western culture that nurtured the forms of Christianity exported since the beginning of the modern missionary movement (which, for our purposes, I date as 1492), it is impossible not to recognize the truth of what Langdon Gilkey says: "The ultimacy and finality is . . . drained from Christian revelation, the Jewish law, the Qur'an, the Four Noble Truths, and so on; and *a fortiori* theology is reduced to an in-house exercise."[4]

In this context, Christian mission—long rooted in an assumption of the superiority of both Christianity and its Western cultural husk—is in crisis, and it seems inevitable that this crisis will spread to other religious traditions. For they, too, must eventually face up to the fact that—on historical, empirical grounds—no religious tradition can demonstrate its superiority over *other traditions*. It is, of course, impossible to do justice to this crisis in the few pages that comprise this essay.

A Key Question: What Is Universal in World Christianity?

The heart of the question about Christian mission in our globalizing era is revealed in the question, "Is there something truly important, universal, final, and decisive (or, as some would prefer, 'unsurpassable') in the person

---

[3] Lonergan, *Method*, 130–31.

[4] Langdon Gilkey, "Plurality and Its Theological Implications," in Hick and Knitter, *Myth*, at 43.

and work of Jesus?" It is exactly this that Peter Phan has so clearly enun-
ciated in the first few paragraphs of a lecture that became a major article
in *Horizons*, the journal of the College Theology Society, and in an earlier
article in the world's foremost missiological journal.[5]

In brief and in contrast to the tenor of much academic, I answer "Yes" to
Phan's question and maintain that if that yes cannot be articulated convincingly, the death of the Christian mission cannot be far behind. But—and I
say this very intentionally—this yes cuts against the grain of much contemporary theology, particularly theology as practiced in the academy, which
has become a de facto profusion of *theologies of this and that*. I am also aware
that I run the risk of playing into the hands of those who argue for strict
interpretations of two classic adages:

- "There is no other name under heaven given among mortals by
  which we must be saved" (Acts 4:12); and
- "Outside the church there is no salvation" (Cyprian of Carthage,
  Epistles 4, 4).

Overall, the claim for Christ's final and universal importance is dangerous
when used as a bludgeon that denies non-Christians access to the gates of
God's kingdom.

In terms of the mission of *World* Christianity, the only way in which we
can make sense of World Christianity is if this adjective modifies something
universal in the noun *Christianity* and if the gospel is the promise of something that is truly good news to all.

If we claim that the word *mission* reflects something essential in
Christianity,[6] we must also acknowledge that in ordinary English usage, the
word is freighted with proselytizing connotations that—again, in common
parlance—presuppose that without conversion to Christianity and entry
into the church, no one can be saved. It matters little if scholars, popes,
ecumenical councils, and movements such as Lausanne and the World

---

[5] See Peter Phan, "World Christianity: Its Implications for History, Religious
Studies, and Theology," *Horizons* 39/2 (2012): 171–73; and Peter Phan, "World
Christianity and Christian Mission: Are they Compatible?" *International Bulletin of
Missionary Research* 32/4 (2008): 193–94.

[6] This is the teaching of the Second Vatican Council in *Ad Gentes* § 2 and reit-
erated in Pope John Paul's encyclical letter *Redemptoris Missio* ("On the Permanent
Validity of the Church's Missionary Mandate"): "Proclamation [of Christ and his
gospel] is the permanent priority of mission," § 44.

Council of Churches give nuanced interpretations of the word without these restrictive connotations. That is what the world understands by it.

And, yet, although the words *mission* and *missions* enshrine key elements in Christian self-understanding and action,[7] they are *not* themselves biblical terms. Indeed, they emerge as such only when the Jesuits began using them in the sixteenth century for their members who are sent (*missi,* past plural participle of *mittere, to send*) to Asia and Latin America, as well as to Cologne and Naples. The roots of the word are in military language, no matter how often theologians say that the deeper, biblical meaning of the word rests in the Greek word *apostéllō.*

The deepest theological sense of the word *mission* is derived the *temporal sending* of the *eternal* Word and Spirit of the Trinitarian God into the world. In that context, *God* (*theos* in Greek), the one whom Jesus called Father (*abba* in Aramaic, Daddy in everyday English—translated as *patēr* in Greek) sends the Word (*ho logos*) into the world to conclude a new covenant with humankind. The Jewish tradition knew God (*Yahweh/Elohim* in Hebrew; *alaha* in Aramaic) as *One.*[8] Jews in the intertestamental period when Judaism and Christianity were trying to decide what they were in relationship to each other, were shocked, first, by actions and words of Jesus that seemed to make him *equal* to God[9] and, second, by the church ascribing that equality with God to Jesus in texts such as the prologue to the Gospel of John.[10] Controversies arose over how to reconcile the doctrine of God's unique oneness with New Testament words seeming to ascribe divinity to Jesus and the Spirit.[11] The conciliar doctrine gained acceptance with difficulty

---

[7] I refer especially to the so-called postresurrection Great Commission in Matthew 28:18–20: "And Jesus came and said to them, 'All authority in heaven and on earth has been given to me. Go therefore and make disciples of all nations, baptizing them in the name of the Father and of the Son and of the Holy Spirit, and teaching them to obey everything that I have commanded you. And remember, I am with you always, to the end of the age'"; parallel in Mark 16:16–18.

[8] I refer to the classic text of Israel's faith in Deuteronomy 6:4: "Hear, O Israel: The LORD our God, the LORD is one."

[9] See, for example, "For this reason the Jews were seeking all the more to kill him, because he was not only breaking the sabbath, but was also calling God his own Father, thereby making himself equal to God" (Matt. 20:12).

[10] "And the Word became flesh and lived among us, and we have seen his glory, the glory as of a father's only son, full of grace and truth" (John 1:14).

[11] I speak of the Councils of Nicea I (325); Constantinople I (381); Ephesus (431); Chalcedon (451); Constantinople II (553). They decreed that the best way to deal with the issue was to use formulae of there being three equally divine persons (*prosopa*) united in one divine Godhead (*theos*) of the same [divine] "stuff" (*homoousia*).

but became ascendant in antiquity only to be questioned again in the nine-teenth century. It is still controversial even today.[12]

The conciliar language was, of course, taken from philosophic discourse. To later generations was left the task of explaining the Trinity. The work of those who attempted to do this was so complicated and removed from ordinary pastoral reality that by the mid-twentieth century, Karl Rahner accurately noted that,

> for all their orthodox profession of faith in the Trinity. [Christians] are almost just "monotheist" in their actual religious existence. One might almost dare to affirm that if the doctrine of the Trinity were to be erased as false, most religious literature could be preserved almost unchanged throughout the process.[13]

The term *mission* was used to describe inter-Trinitarian *processions* as the three *prosopa* (*persons* or *re-presentations*, possibly best of all, *modes*) of the one Godhead were related to humanity. In terms made familiar by Rahner, the *economic* Trinity (God in God's relation to humanity in history) is the *immanent* Trinity (God in Godself—creator, redeemer, sustainer of all that is). Rahner's economic/immanent terminology is part of his attempt to put the Trinity at the center of our understanding of creation, soteriology, and Christology.[14] Since he wrote those words, a number of important books have taken up the task of articulating these connections,[15] and Trinitarian theology is discussed everywhere.

I rehearse all this neither to delve deeply into early conciliar or contem-porary theology. Rather, I want to make three observations:

---

[12] See, for example, Roger Haight, *Jesus Symbol of God* (Maryknoll, NY: Orbis Books, 1999), 424–66 for an excellent argument for a metaphoric, highly symbolic interpretation of these doctrines, which he judges more adequate than ontological inter-pretations.

[13] See Karl Rahner, "Remarks on the Dogmatic Treatise 'De Trinitate,'" in *Theological Investigations* (Baltimore: Helicon, 1967), 3:78.

[14] See Karl Rahner, *Trinity* (New York: Crossroad, 1970), 21–24.

[15] Among the many, I would single out books by David Coffey, *Deus Trinitas: The Doctrine of the Trinity* (New York: Oxford, 1999); and Catherine Mowry Lacugna, *God for Us: The Trinity and Christian Life* (San Francisco: HarperSanFrancisco, 1991); and more recently still Elizabeth Johnson's *The Quest for the Living God: Mapping Frontiers in the Theology of God* (New York: Continuum, 2007) and *Ask the Beasts: Darwin and the Love of God* (New York: Bloomsbury, 2014). Johnson's prose becomes poetry in evoking the sacred dimensions of life and the existence of a God-beyond-God, the perception of whom transforms those with ears to hear and eyes to see.

1. Conciliar theology of the first five centuries did not deal directly with the soteriological issues in relation to *other* religious traditions that confront us today; instead, it was concerned with teaching the divinity of Christ, from which principle came the authority of the church to teach and sanctify in God's name;

2. While affirming the equality of all three *prosopa* of the Trinity, the status of the Holy Spirit, especially in the West, was effectively reduced to that of providing a sort of guidance of the church's officers, a tendency especially pronounced in Roman Catholicism; and

3. The world outside the church, and to a great extent within it, is caught between studies that find great riches in all religions and countervailing tendencies to think that religion is the root of, if not all, then at least most evil.

In regard to point three, we must also contend with the fact that, at least among academic elites and those influenced by them, there is universal disdain for any religious tradition that seriously claims to accurately describe *reality* and the destiny of world process. And much of theology has bowed to that edict, so much so that, as I averted to above, to have a legitimate place in the academy, theology and exegesis are carried on almost solely as reportage of historical positions of noteworthy academics. Meanwhile, the world of those influenced by protean skepticism about any revelation of transcendent purpose in the cosmos revealed by revelation or seminal insights of sages relegates religion to the realm of subjective opinions and values, while elevating the findings of science to the realm of objective and reliable truth.

At another level, the processes collectively known as globalization also inspire resistance to secularism and to being shoe-horned into the international economic system.[16] We simply do not know if globalization will end happily or merely be the latest tower of Babel.

Let me draw this section to a close by saying that there are many aspects of Christians' mission in the world, but what unites them is their vocation to respond to God's promise in Christ by embodying the agapaic love that Jesus epitomizes. Christianity, in other words, is intrinsically *Christomorphic*, which is to say, a way of life patterned on the life and teaching of Jesus.[17]

---

[16] Resistance to the globalization of these systems is at the center of Pope Francis's two great encyclicals, *Evangelii gaudium* ["The Joy of the Gospel"] (Vatican City: Libreria Vaticana, 2014) and *Laudato si'* ["On Care for Our Common Home"] (Vatican City: Libreria Vaticana, 2015).

[17] See Richard R. Niebuhr, *Schleiermacher on Christ and Religion* (New York: Scribner's, 1964), 210–14 on Christomorphic theology.

Given the New Testament's revelation of God as Father, Son, and Spirit, and the centrality of Jesus in revealing the Trinitarian nature of God, I want to propose that—if *World* Christianity *is* a single *thing*—Christianity revolves around the mission of followers of Jesus to make manifest the reality of the Triune God's promises and the first fruits of their realization. The phrase *re-membering the dangerous memory of Jesus* highlights the Christomorphic nature of the revelation and walking in the world as one who has been given new life in the Spirit. This way of dying to self and rising with Christ rests in the experience of the Holy Spirit. St. Paul puts the issue of our faith and hope as the result of being at peace with God through Christ and the action of the Spirit:

> Since we are justified by faith, we have peace with God through our Lord Jesus Christ, through whom we have obtained access to this grace in which we stand; and we boast in our hope of sharing the glory of God. And not only that, but we also boast in our sufferings, knowing that suffering produces endurance, and endurance produces character, and character produces hope, and hope does not disappoint us, because God's love has been poured into our hearts through the Holy Spirit that has been given to us. (Rom. 5:1–5)

Without a vital connection to this dynamism of life in the Spirit, Christianity is mere words, and this may well be the reason that charismatic and Pentecostal movements are the most lively examples of living mission.

Ramifications of the Christomorphic Trinitarian Principle

Among Christians, the claim to the universality and finality of Christ has it that all that is comes from and is destined to find fulfillment in the Trinitarian Godhead. Christianity is an eschatological faith that sees in the promises embodied in God's election of and promises to Israel and in and through Jesus of Nazareth the pattern of the cosmos moving toward a single divine destiny. Yes, there are ethical obligations inherent in embracing the gospel as God's promise of forgiveness, regeneration, and salvation, but the key to Christianity is not human action to make the world a better place. Rather, the center of the Christian mission in the world is to become the living, complex body of Christ as the people to whom God has entrusted the vocation of making known the good news of God's Trinitarian reality unfolding in a cosmic process so vast as to be incomprehensible. "In [Christ] ... he [God] has made known to us the mystery of his will in accord with his favor that he set forth in him as a plan for the fullness of times, to sum up all things in Christ in heaven and on earth" (Eph. 1:7–10).

There are many texts that speak to this cosmic scope, none more explicitly than St. Paul's words in the Letter to the Romans:

> I consider that the sufferings of this present time are as nothing compared with the glory to be revealed in us. For creation awaits with eager expectation the revelation of the children of God; for creation was made subject to futility, not of its own accord but because of the one who subjected it, in hope that creation itself would be set free from slavery to corruption and share in the glorious freedom of the children of God. We know that all creation is groaning in labor pains even until now; and not only that, but we ourselves, who have the first fruits of the Spirit, we also groan within ourselves as we wait for adoption, the redemption of our bodies. For in hope we were saved. Now hope that sees for itself is not hope. For who hopes for what one sees? But if we hope for what we do not see, we wait with endurance.
>
> In the same way, the Spirit, too, comes to the aid of our weakness; for we do not know how to pray as we ought, but the Spirit itself intercedes with inexpressible groanings. And the one who searches hearts knows what is the intention of the Spirit, because it intercedes for the holy ones according to God's will. (Rom. 8:18–27)

Paul is notoriously hard to decipher. I put myself in the hands of N. T. Wright whose work seeks to retrieve Paul and his message as the translation into Greek of a message often given in parabolic form in Aramaic by Jesus.[18] Wright's Paul is obsessed with explaining Jesus and the promise of his gospel as being in continuity with and the fulfillment of God's covenants with Israel, a context set in Genesis 12:1–3, where Israel is constituted as a

---

[18] For those wishing to go more deeply, I commend N. T. Wright's multivolume series, *Christian Origins and the Question of God,* which includes vol. 1, *The New Testament People of God* (Minneapolis: Fortress Press, 1992); vol. 2, *Jesus and the Victory of God* (Minneapolis: Fortress Press, 1997); vol. 3, *The Resurrection of the Son of God* (Minneapolis: Fortress Press, 2003); *and* the two-volume *Paul and the Faithfulness of God* (Minneapolis: Fortress Press, 2013).

blessing to the nations that respect her and a curse to those who do not. In a Christian reading of the history of Israel, that nation has moments of glory when its life corresponds to Torah. But the larger story is one not unlike the history of Christianity, one in which the many give notional assent to what is asked of them, and a few see its downfall to be the result of not comprehending what Deuteronomy in the seventh century knows is what God truly desires:

> Hear O Israel! The Lord is our God, the Lord alone! Therefore you shall love the Lord your God, with all your heart, and with all your soul, and with all your strength. Take to heart these words which I enjoin on you today. Drill them into your children. Speak of them at home and abroad, whether you are busy or at rest. (Deut. 6:4–7)

In response to the self-justifying questions of the Sadducees, Jesus in Matthew 22:34–40 puts himself firmly in the camp of those trying to implement the Deuteronomic reforms. What God wants, in this view, is not the sacrifice of bulls and oxen but the love and devotion of a puri-fied heart.[19] And insofar as he preaches ethical obligations, the parables of Matthew 25 speak (1) of the mysteriousness of the coming of the kingdom (vv. 1–13); (2) of the terrifying justice that will be administered to those afraid to take risks for the sake of the kingdom (vv. 14–30); and (3) of the fate of the unmerciful (vv. 31–46) when the kingdom comes. Alfred Loisy (1857–1940) gives us the famous quip, "Jesus foretold the kingdom, and it was the Church that came."[20] In reality, what came before the church is the advent of the Holy Spirit, as portrayed in Luke-Acts, a theme magisterially developed by David Stanley.[21] According to Stanley, the advent of the Spirit in Acts 2 leads to the realization on the part of the Eleven that the "messi-anic times have been inaugurated by the descent of the Spirit and not by the Lord's second coming" to restore sovereignty to Israel.[22] I find the develop-ment of this theme and its implications for missiology in Stephen Bevans's and Roger Schroeder's *Constants in Context* to be the best text to read on

---

[19] See Psalm 51:12–19, especially verses 18–19: "For you are not pleased with sacrifices; should I offer a holocaust, you would not accept it. My sacrifice, O God, is a contrite spirit; a heart contrite and humbled, you will not spurn."

[20] Alfred Loisy, *The Gospel and the Church*, trans., Christopher Home (Philadel-phia: Fortress Press, 1976; orig. ed. 1903), 166.

[21] David M. Stanley, "From Kingdom to Church: The Structural Development of the Church in Apostolic Christianity," *Theological Studies* 16/1 (1955): 1–29.

[22] Ibid., 5.

this subject.[23] Bevans and Schroeder draw out the complex development of the self-consciousness of the Jerusalem community to the recognition at Antioch that the gospel is to be proclaimed to all peoples.

Before entering into my reflections on the Christian mission in the context of World Christianity in a globalizing world, however, I wish to draw attention to the issue of the Holy Spirit and conversion in the sense given it in my citations of Bernard Lonergan above.

First one must realize that the Pauline corpus (certainly in the indisputably Pauline authored letters, but also in the Deutero-Pauline "letters" written under his influence), antedates both Luke-Acts and the other two Synoptic Gospels and the Gospel of John. For Paul, as for Luke in the Luke-Acts tradition, the Spirit leads men and women to faith in the Messiahship of Jesus and to experience the reality of God's forgiveness of (i.e., not counting as debts requiring payment) acts committed (1) under the conditions of *hamartia* (blindness to the true nature of the self and its obligations to God and our fellow humans), on the one hand, and (2) in the state of *anomia* (rebellion against our creaturely state), on the other.[24]

Paul's teaching is that freedom ensues when one accepts the paradox that life is gained by death to self, following the pattern of Christ (1 Cor. 2), and this pattern finds its fulfillment in the purification of the heart and the renewal of the self as Christ is *formed* in the Christian (Gal. 4:19). This theme is taken up in verses 12–16 of Galatians 4: "For we who live are constantly being given up to death for the sake of Jesus, so that the life of Jesus may be manifested in our mortal flesh . . . although our outer self is wasting way, our inner self is being renewed day by day."

Paul is teaching that the mode of God's presence and activity today is in the power of the Holy Spirit showing us in our hearts the paradox of God's wisdom revealed in the Cross (1 Cor. 2:6–12—"this God has revealed to us through the Spirit" [v. 11]).

The intertestamental and apostolic church internalized the message of and about Jesus not as a new ethical code (for there is little in Jesus's moral teaching that one cannot find in the prophets and the rabbis of his age). Instead, the kerygma was about who Jesus is in relation to God and the new life made available to those who trusted the interior movements of the Spirit. It was not a mere private reception of a message but an experience of the Spirit's power, and here we come to the reason why the permanent priority of mission is

---

[23] See Stephen B. Bevans and Roger P. Schroeder, *Constants in Context: A Theology of Mission for Today* (Maryknoll, NY: Orbis Books, 2004), 10–31.

[24] See Galatians 3–6.

proclamation of who Jesus is. Knowing that Jesus is equal to God in all ways—and that he is one with us—opens up the realization that life on this earth is anchored in the eternal reality and plan of God for the universe.

The threefold pattern of the parables of Matthew 25 that we spoke of above constitutes, to be sure, moral lessons about the kind of behavior that is compatible with life in the kingdom, but please note that neither above nor here have I said anything about election to, and promises of, salvation that are rewards for good behavior. Nor have I spoken of *salvation* that is not available to persons following other religious traditions. The construal of Christianity as the sole path to salvation of the soul after death has, however, been central to what mission has been based on, and it has scriptural backing texts such as Acts 4:12 and the puzzling juxtaposition of universal blessing and curse in John 3:1–21. It does us no good to deny it. From the practice of ransoming pagan babies and baptizing them so they can be saved from perdition to fulminations about the evils of paganism, Christians have seen themselves as privileged by having been given access to salvation denied to those who do not convert to Christianity.

Embarrassment in the face of such teachings has led many to abandon the Christology of scripture as clarified in the early councils. They have come to construe Christian mission as a form of aid given to the less fortunate, turning away from the eschatological–Christomorphic dimensions of biblical faith. This is due in no measure to a veritable *deus ex machina* soteriology enshrined in purely forensic interpretations of the epistles of Paul, culminating in the death and resurrection of Jesus—a form of cosmic child abuse followed by a miraculous rescue. The doctrine of redemption is then derived from ahistorical use of St. Anselm's (c. 1033–1109) satisfaction theory in *Cur Deus homo*, according to which only a divine person could satisfy the offense given to God by rebellious humanity. Anselm's theory made sense in his own day but needs careful handling in today's world. Yet his soteriology was at the heart of Christian proclamation of who Christ was and what he did for many generations. When it is rejected, we are faced with the question, if not this, what are we proclaiming?

What Are We Really Proclaiming in *World* Christianity?

At the beginning of the twentieth century, the great philosopher, physician, organist, medical missionary, and theologian Albert Schweitzer (1875–1965) set out to reconcile the conflict between Reformed, Lutheran, and Catholic theology (rooted in the language of scripture and St. Anselm), on the one hand, and the minimalist results of the first modern historical–critical search for a reliable historical portrait of Jesus, on the other hand. He published his findings in *The Quest of the Historical Jesus* (translated by William Montgomery and published in 1910).[25]

Schweitzer concluded that the image of Jesus delivered by the first quest for Jesus reflected the philosophical and theological proclivities of the exegete rather more than what Jesus could possibly have imagined himself to be or to be teaching. Schweitzer concluded that Jesus's life and thought were part and parcel with late and intertestamental Jewish eschatology and pretty much discredited the first quest. This paved the way for the neo-orthodox of figures such as Karl Barth to articulate the kerygma in the life and message of Jesus in more satisfactory ways. After being eclipsed for a generation by the second quest for the historical Jesus, Barth is enjoying a renaissance once again, and, as David Bosch once quipped, "the eschatological office" was once again open.[26] However, I am getting ahead of myself.

According to Schweitzer, Jesus must have thought that his work and teaching would bring about the end of history; the historical Jesus, in other words, was an eschatological figure in Schweitzer's theological judgment, which was confirmed in his subsequent books on St. Paul. They show that Paul had reinterpreted the idea of an imminent return of Jesus into the notion that human beings were called to die and rise with Christ. I find Schweitzer's insights into the foibles of the first quest equally applicable, *mutatis mutandis*, with both second quest (by Rudolf Bultmann et al.) and for the more recent third quest (exemplified by exegetes such as John Dominic Crossan and the so-called Jesus Seminar). I am not going to enter into a detailed critique of the Jesus Seminar, not least because it is beyond my competence, nor will I attempt to update Schweitzer by enlisting the impressive work of N. T. Wright to which I have referred above. What I do wish to say is that the eschatological dimensions of the life, death, and teaching of Jesus—as related to the center of that teaching on God's kingdom—have a great deal to say about the mission of the church in an era of globalization and World Christianity. I summarize these dimensions in five points:

---

[25] A significantly revised edition was published in German in 1913 but not published in English until 2000 by SCM Press in London.

[26] David Bosch, *Transforming Mission: Paradigm Shifts in the Theology of Mission* (Maryknoll, NY: Orbis Books, 1991), 498–501.

1. Both the New and Old Testaments mean to teach the divine origins and destiny of the cosmos.

2. The pattern both testaments seek to reveal is the importance of responding to God's promises and living in harmony with God's designs.

3. The Christian gospel revolves around and reveals the Trinitarian nature of God and the manner in which humanity is invited to participate in God's saving presence within and transcendent to world process.

4. To reduce Jesus to the role of teacher is to ignore these patterns in the scriptures; and since the revelation of the Trinitarian pattern of creation, redemption, and salvation is the point of the New Testament as a whole, one either has to say a trusting "yes" or admit that the Christ-event and the Bible that witnesses to it are deceptive.

5. The testimony of the promise of the gospel is witnessed to by the Holy Spirit in deeds of power and healing and/or revealed by an inner resonance of one's heart with that Spirit are crucial; it finds fruition in a resonance described by St. Paul as a "hope that does not disappoint, because the love of God has been poured out into our hearts through the holy Spirit that has been given to us" (Rom 5:5).

When Pope St. John Paul II says in his encyclical on the permanent validity of Christian mission that, "Proclamation is the permanent priority of mission,"[27] the pope is pointing to this pattern of saying "Yes" to testimony about Jesus as the Christ. And if one reads carefully John Paul's encyclical on the Holy Spirit, *Dominum et Vivificantem* (DeV), it is clear that the pope believes the Spirit is active outside visible Christianity. The Trinitarian God of Christians, John Paul maintains, is not sectarian:

> [We] cannot limit ourselves to the two thousand years which have passed since the birth of Christ. We need to go further back, to embrace the whole of the action of the Holy Spirit even before Christ-from the beginning, throughout the world, and especially in the economy of the Old Covenant. For this action has been exercised, in every place and at every time, indeed in every individual, according to the eternal plan of salvation, whereby this action was to be closely linked with the mystery of the Incarnation and

---

[27] Pope St. John Paul II, *Redemptoris missio* (1990), no. 44.

Redemption, which in its turn exercised its influence on those who believed in the future coming of Christ. This is attested to especially in the Letter to the Ephesians 1:3–14.[28]

Is the pope teaching relativism? No. If one reads the entirety of Part II of his encyclical on the Holy Spirit ("The Spirit Who Convinces the World of Sin," §§ 27–48), it becomes clear that the role of the Spirit is not merely one of mediating some sort of fuzzy love on the part of God for humanity. Instead.

> This convincing is in permanent reference to "righteousness": that is to say to definitive salvation in God, to the fulfillment of the economy that has as its center the crucified and glorified Christ. And this salvific economy of God in a certain sense removes man from "judgment," that is from the damnation which has been inflicted on the Sill or Satan, "the prince of this world," the one who because of his sin has become "the ruler of this world of darkness." (Eph. 6:12).[29]

In John Paul's explication of mission, then, human beings do not live in a neutral environment but one in which "we find ourselves at the very center of what could be called the 'anti-Word,' that is to say the 'anti-truth.' For the truth about man becomes falsified: who man is and what are the impassable limits of his being and freedom."[30]

Meanwhile, those who have been critical of the demythologizers and have preferred the narrative language of the scriptures or the philosophical language of the Councils of Nicea (325) and Chalcedon (450) were thought to be unenlightened. The difference between the views of the *enlightened* and the *unenlightened* are not without significance for the mission of the church.

We cannot hope to resolve these issues here, but it is important to realize, first, that one's view of who Jesus *is* has consequences and not just for Western Christianity. Those in the Global South must also find ways to answer that question in terms of their own cultures. Second, it is important to realize that applying the terms *mission* and *missions* to the work of Christians who went out to work among persons of other faiths and cultures

---

[28] Pope St. John Paul II, *Dominum et vivificantem*, 1987, no. 53.

[29] Ibid. no. 28.

[30] Ibid. no. 37. "Man" as third person pronoun is in the official translation."

as *missionaries*—with a view to converting them to Christianity—is at the beginning of the twenty-first century highly ambiguous. Mission and proselytism are inexorably linked in the popular imagination and this despite efforts that are epitomized in the words of the Anglican bishop, missionary, and scholar Stephen Neill (1900–84) who wrote, "The age of missions is at an end; the age of mission has begun."[31] This change, Neill said, expressed the Christian mission as action to minister to the world in the Spirit of the Gospel, while overcoming what had become the negative legacy of mission in the colonial era. I am not so sure.

We are now clearly in not just a postcolonial era but even in an anti–neo-colonial era. I see little evidence that the word *mission*—in popular culture—has lost its connotation as an unwarranted proselytic activity.

In all that follows, several questions must be kept in mind. First, when one important component of the worldwide Christian communion holds the term *mission* in high regard, what do they understand by it? Why do other, equally sincere and committed members of the church and morally sensitive non-Christians condemn it? Is the term redeemable from complicity in the colonial-era presupposition that the West had the right to colonize the lands and minds of the rest of the world? Can one be, in Peter Phan's terminology, "religious 'interreligiously'" and still have a robust sense of the Christian gospel as something to be shared with all peoples?

This is not the place to settle such arguments. What is fruitful is to point to emerging understandings that hold promise that Christians who occupy various places on the continuum between extremes can find common ground. Chapter 12 of David Bosch's *Transforming Mission* ("Elements of an Emerging Ecumenical Missionary Paradigm") has achieved magisterial status among scholars of mission on all sides of the theological division. Stephen Bevans and Roger Schroeder refine and focus Bosch's thirteen elements in the light of subsequent discussions.[32] Synthesizing their position and the thought of Pope John Paul II, is it possible to envision a viewpoint on Christian mission that sees *mission as evangelization ("gospeling") and evangelization as a complex reality.* Evangelization along such lines involves

1. participating in the *mission of God*, presenting Jesus as way, truth, and life, inviting all interested peoples to consider following Jesus in faith, and founding new churches for those who wish to follow him;

---

[31] Stephen Neill, *A History of Christian Missions* (New York: Penguin Books, 1964), 572.

[32] See Bevans and Schroeder, *Constants in Context*, 281–398.

2. *contextualizing* or *inculturating* the church and translating the gospel into the languages of all peoples, while entering into what Bevans and Schroeder call prophetic dialogue;

3. promoting justice, peace, and the integrity of creation;

4. developing and practicing modes of liturgy, prayer, study, and contemplation that enable people to enter more deeply and intentionally into unity with God and to realize their rightful place in the cosmic order;

5. enhancing intercultural and interreligious understanding through conversation, academic study, and dialogue, always in a spirit of prophetic dialogue that not only shares Christ but is prepared to learn from others;

6. striving to reconcile estranged peoples, religious, political, and social traditions, as well as humanity and God.

It goes without saying that persons who identify most with one or the other of these points will emphasize that point and put more weight on it. Christian mission is, when all is said and action begins, a multifaceted, pluralistic enterprise. What bears underlining is that Christians today are about one-third of the world's population, and the most vital sectors of the church are no longer in the West and North. Indeed, the numerical center of Christian gravity has moved south to Africa and Latin America. In Asia, the numbers are not as significant as in Africa and Latin America, but the phrase *Pentecost in Asia* is not without meaning.

While northern and western churches hold the preponderance of material resources to carry on the mission summarized in the six points listed above, the sense of participating in God's mission seems liveliest in the so-called Global South. Christian Indonesians *in mission* among their fellow Indonesians, for example, are working with friends and neighbors. The tenor of their evangelizing efforts differs from that of foreign missionaries in the classical era of modern mission. Their work is *missio inter gentes* (mission *among* and not just *to* the nations). They and counterparts in Korea and Colombia, for example, are also increasing their work among other peoples abroad.

I conclude with a reminder of what I said above in reference to the necessity of *conversion* on the part of the Christian. In an age made suspicious of marketing and the hidden hand of powerful global interests, the authenticity of the evangelizing agent is the *sine quā non* of a dialogue that is both prophetic and respectful, able to assert one's own belief and learn from that of others, aware that there is a deep and mutual complementarity and asymmetry within and between the world's religions.[33] We all await the convergence of all in God in the eschaton.

At the practical level, it is important to realize that conversion, both as a fundamental shift from one tradition to another or a gradual deepening and maturation within one's Christian faith, takes place *within psychological, cultural,* and *historical conditions.* The conversion of a Melanesian villager living in Timbunke along the Sepik River is going to be quite different from that of an EU official with a doctorate in economics working in Brussels. Just how different those conversions are is something we need to understand far better.

It is evident that the way in which an individual is led to faith by the Spirit determines the scope of that individual's mission within his or her situation. A woman working in the highest levels of the European Union has a chance to bring her conversion to bear on issues of war, peace, and economic justice at an international level. A Melanesian villager brings his conversion to bear on a situation where a woman is scapegoated as a witch and accused of sorcery. In this vein, churches in Timbunke and Brussels will bring their corporate ministries to bear in different way. Each must have means of building up national, regional, and global ecclesial responses to diverse needs in a globalizing world.

Only when we realize that the authenticity and depth of conversion—as a shift in consciousness to a Christomorphic horizon—will Christians have the impact God desires at local, regional, national, and international levels. Here words written by Alfred Loisy well over a century ago are well worth contemplating today.

> Jesus foretold the kingdom, and it was the church that came; she came, enlarging the form of the gospel, which it was impossible to preserve as it was, as the Passion closed the ministry of Jesus. There is no institution on the earth or in history whose status and value may not be questioned if the principle is established that nothing may exist except in its original form. Such a principle is contrary to the law of life, which is movement and a continual effort of adaptation to conditions always new and perpetually changing.[34]

---

[33] "Asymmetrical complementarity" is a key concept in Jacques Dupuis's *Christianity and the Religions: From Confrontation to Dialogue* (Maryknoll, NY: Orbis Books, 2002), 133–37, 255–59.

[34] Loisy, *Gospel and Church*, 166.

Loisy wrote these words a hundred years ago and could hardly have envisaged the dawn of Christianity as a world religion in a globalizing word. He may have had rationalistic tendencies that were rightly criticized, but he had his finger on a dynamic we ignore at our peril in the twenty-first century.

8

MODELS OF CONTEXTUAL
THEOLOGIZING IN WORLD CHRISTIANITY

Stephen Bevans

Among the giants in the development of theologizing in the context of World Christianity has been Peter Phan. His groundbreaking book on Alexandre de Rhodes, *Mission and Catechesis*, demonstrated the thoughtfulness, creativity, and cultural sensitivity, within the context of his times, of this great Jesuit pioneer in Vietnam.[1] His many lectures on inculturation, interreligious dialogue, and Asian theologies have been collected in the invaluable trilogy with the titles *Christianity with an Asian Face*, *In Our Own Tongues*, and *Being Religious Interreligiously*.[2] He has also edited two important series of theological reflection—"Theology in Global Perspective" published by Orbis Books and "Christianities of the World," published by Palgrave Macmillan.[3] These are only a few examples of Peter's prolific publishing in this area and what seems to be his indefatigable ability to travel throughout the world to teach and lecture.

As Peter has expressed it in a landmark article on doing theology with the relatively new consciousness of World Christianity, what is key to understanding the task of theologizing today is a recognition of the shift that has taken place in the center of gravity of Christianity, and the discovery of Christianity's essential and continuing non-Western nature. Such recognition has

---

[1] Peter C. Phan, *Mission and Catechesis: Alexandre de Rhodes and Inculturation in Seventeenth-Century Vietnam* (Maryknoll, NY: Orbis Books, 1998).

[2] Peter C. Phan, *Christianity with an Asian Face: Asian American Theology in the Making* (Maryknoll, NY: Orbis Books, 2003); Peter C. Phan, *In Our Own Tongues: Perspectives from Asia on Mission and Inculturation* (Maryknoll, NY: Orbis Books, 2003); and Peter C. Phan, *Being Religious Interreligiously: Asian Perspectives on Interfaith Dialogue* (Maryknoll, NY: Orbis Books, 2004).

[3] The series "Theology in Global Perspective" contains some twelve volumes already published; the "Christianities of the World" series, which Peter Phan has edited with Dale T. Irvin, has published nine volumes to date.

resulted in major methodological shifts.[4] Peter lays some of these out, and what I would like to do in this essay is to lay out several more. I would like to do this by proposing four models of how Christian women and men are doing and can do theology with a World Christianity consciousness today. These are (1) the *Contextual Theology* Model; (2) the *Neglected Themes* Model; (3) the *Global Perspective* Model; and (4) the *Comparative Theology* Model.

Before I begin, however, let me explain briefly my use of *models* in this essay. To express it negatively, *models* here does not mean the same as my use of the term in my 1992/2002 work *Models of Contextual Theology*.[5] In that work I referred to models in the more technical sense as, in Avery Dulles's words, "relatively simple, artificially constructed" cases that are "found to be useful and illuminating for dealing with realities that are more complex and differentiated."[6] As I will explain below, I proposed six *models* that offered methodological options of and for doing contextual theology across a wide spectrum of theological perspectives, all of which are valid and useful depending on the context in which they are used. In this essay, I see this sixfold approach to doing contextual theology as *one way* of doing theology in the context of World Christianity. I am using the term *model* here, therefore, in a wider, less technical sense, perhaps more along the lines of an *approach* to theologizing. Compared to my use of *models* in the first approach presented in this essay, this understanding is more analogical than literal.

The Contextual Theology Model

A first way that theology is being done today within World Christianity is with the Contextual Theology Model. The basic idea of this model of doing theology is to focus on a particular context—a personal or social experience, social location, a culture, or social change, as I have explained it[7]—and put this focus in a mutually critical dialogue with the Christian scriptures and the Christian tradition.

Of course, while all theology is contextual, not all contextual theologizing is done in the context of World Christianity. For example, a North

---

[4] Peter C. Phan, "Doing Theology in World Christianity: Different Resources and New Methods," *Journal of World Christianity* 1/1 (2008): 29.

[5] Stephen B. Bevans, *Models of Contextual Theology* (Maryknoll, NY: Orbis Books, 2002).

[6] Ibid., 29, quoting Avery Dulles, *Models of Revelation* (New York: Doubleday, 1983), 30.

[7] Ibid., 5–7.

American feminist theologian focusing on her own particular context may be using many of the resources of a more Western, classical theology in her theologizing, and she may well privilege the North American or Western experience of women. However, the Contextual Theology Model within World Christianity focuses on the particular resources in places and within social groups that have not ordinarily been considered as *proper* theological resources. Just as important as Western sources, in other words, for theologizing within World Christianity—and in this context more important—are resources that are proper to Latin America, Africa, Oceania, or Asia, or to marginalized groups in Western contexts.

Peter Phan and Doing Theology in World Christianity

In Peter Phan's article in the *Journal of World Christianity* to which I referred earlier, for example, Peter has recourse to the Federation of Asian Bishops' Conferences (FABC) Office of Theological Concerns document on Asian Theological Method.[8] This document relates how Asian theology uses specifically *Asian* resources "in correlation with the Bible and the Tradition of the Church," and notes how the "use of these resources implies a tremendous change in theological methodology."[9] It goes on to name these resources as

> the cultures of peoples, the history of their struggles, their religions, their religious scriptures, oral traditions, popular religiosity, economic and political realities and world events, historical personages, stories of oppressed people crying out for justice, freedom, dignity, life, and solidarity . . . The totality of life is the raw material of theology. . . . This implies theologically that one is using "context" (or contextual realities in a new way).[10]

Peter goes on to unpack these sentences, focusing on Asian resources, but also opening up to other places and contexts not usually included in more classical theology. He names a first resource as "ordinary people themselves, both Christian and non-Christian, with their stories of joy and suffering, hope and despair, love and hatred, freedom

---

[8] Office of Theological Concerns, *Methodology: Asian Christian Theology: Doing Theology in Asia Today*. FABC Papers no. 96 (Hong Kong: FABC, 2000).

[9] Ibid., 29.

[10] Ibid.

and oppression."[11] These are stories that will not be found in standard, Western history books, but stories that are rather "kept alive in the 'dangerous memory' (Johann Baptist Metz) of the 'underside of history' (Gustavo Gutiérrez)."[12] A second resource, Peter notes, is these stories in the memories and from the lips of women and girls. Peter cites Korean theologian Chung Hyun Kyun's powerful description of "women's truth" as "generated by their *epistemology from the broken body*."[13] Third, Peter points out the resources present in sacred texts and religious practices and traditions beyond Christianity, all of which "convey the people's sense of the sacred and their quest for salvation."[14] Third and fourth are cited local philosophies and spiritualities, often, as in Asia, rooted in monastic traditions,[15] together with a sixth resource of "stories, myths, folklore, symbols, poetry, songs, visual arts, architecture, music, and dance."[16] To these we might add particular issues in people's experience in the Global South, like contending with the AIDS crisis, seeking reconciliation after the fall of violent regimes or devastating civil wars, struggling with the effects on the environment of mining or the destruction of forests, or recovering from natural disasters like earthquakes or tsunamis. Any of these experiences, when correlated with scripture and tradition, are ways that the Contextual Theology Model is employed in World Christianity.

Models of Contextual Theology

Just *how* the correlation takes place as this model is employed, however, as I have outlined in *Models of Contextual Theology*, depends on the particular context in which theological reflection is carried out and on the particular theological perspective out of which that reflecting comes. Accordingly, they might employ a *translation model* that adapts or translates a concrete experience to a more traditional theological doctrine or scripture text. Or they might *pull theology out* of their experience by working out of an *anthropological model*. Their theological reflection might alternatively

---

[11] Phan, "Doing Theology in World Christianity," 37.

[12] Ibid., 37.

[13] Ibid., quoting Chung Hyun Kyun, *Struggle to Be Sun Again: Introducing Asian Women's Theology* (Maryknoll, NY: Orbis Books, 1990), 104.

[14] Phan, "Doing Theology in World Christianity," 38.

[15] Ibid., 38–39.

[16] Ibid., 39.

arise from a commitment to a particular practice that yields new theological understanding (the *praxis model*). A dialogue between their own experience and their own authentic faith (the *transcendental model*) might yield deep theological understandings, or a radical critique of their situation might be the result of using the *countercultural model*. In any case, the result of the critical correlation of experience with the traditional Christian theological sources results in a theologizing that is rooted in a particular context in a particular situation in the world, and so can truly be said to be theologizing in a World Christian context.

The Neglected Themes Model

A somewhat similar approach to theologizing in the context of World Christianity, but one that I see as still rather distinct, is to do theology out of a particular theme that has been heretofore neglected in *mainstream* theologizing, and yet is a vital one in the wider world, particularly among the peoples of or from the Global South. I offer two examples here of how this particular model can be employed.

Amos Yong and Renewal Theology

In a fascinating review of the 2010 *Cambridge Dictionary of Christianity* (CDC), originally delivered as part of a panel at the American Academy of Religion in 2010,[17] Chinese American Pentecostal theologian Amos Yong reflects on how the then newly published CDC deals with Pentecostal–charismatic Christianity in its pages. Yong begins by expressing his appreciation of the fact that, to some degree, the CDC is sensitive to the fact that Pentecostal–charismatic–renewal Christianity "is literally exploding across the global South, and the most vibrant forms of Christian growth are occurring among renewal type churches and movements."[18] He goes on to list a number of articles that deal with world Pentecostalism in general, in particular parts of the world (e.g., in Eastern, Southern, and Western Africa, Asia, Australasia, Brazil, and Chile), in specific articles like *Pentecostal worship*, and in *many other entries* that "call attention to the role of Pentecostal and charismatic Christianity across the global landscape."[19]

---

[17] Daniel Patte, "Foreword: The Making of the *Cambridge Dictionary of Christianity*," *Journal of World Christianity* 4/1 (2011): 1.

[18] Amos Yong, "The Emerging Field of World Christianity: A Renewal Reading of the *Cambridge Dictionary of Christianity*," *Journal of World Christianity*, 4/1 (2011): 33.

[19] Ibid., 35.

But then Yong presses beyond. Given the reality of the growth of renewal churches today, he suggests that any scholarship on World Christianity in our time will have to have some expertise in the area of Pentecostalism. More than this, however, such a Pentecostal perspective will be able to read the history of Christianity and the Christian doctrinal tradition in a way that it will be able to recognize renewal movements at every stage of that history and tradition, despite efforts of the institution to suppress them. This is why Yong critiques the CDC's articles on the Acts of the Apostles and the Gospel of Luke. As eminent as are the authors of these articles, they do not include a Pentecostal perspective in them, and "given the paradigm opened up by the CDC,"[20] they should have. In addition, Pentecostal perspectives should have been offered on articles dealing with topics like *deliverance*, *visions*, and *dreams*, and Yong suggests as well that Pentecostal perspectives should be covered in other more general articles and perhaps written by Pentecostal theologians themselves.

In 2014, Yong himself published a complete systematic theology inspired by and from the perspective of Pentecostal–charismatic–renewal studies, a work endorsed, incidentally, by Peter Phan. Yong's hope, he says, even though he admits that his survey is in no way exhaustive, is to offer "to renewalists and other Christians . . . a helpful primer on how to think theologically in the twenty-first-century global Christian context."[21]

The text is extraordinary on several counts. First, Yong makes many efforts throughout the book to focus on issues and interests that would arise in the world church. In this regard, not only does he refer to various examples and implications throughout the chapters but also builds a reflection from the perspective of World Christianity into the basic method of his theologizing.[22] Second, Yong uses the World Fellowship of the Assemblies of God Statement of Faith as his outline. Because he wagers, however, that a renewalist perspective should begin with the doctrine of the Holy Spirit, which is ultimately a perspective of eschatology, Yong reverses the order of the Statement of Faith in his treatment, beginning with eschatology, then moving to the gifts of the Spirit, baptism of the Spirit, etc. In this way, he hopes to treat systematic theology from the perspective of how Christians—particularly renewalist Christians in the Global South—actually come to, and appropriate, their faith. Third, the book is presented with

---

[20] Ibid., 41.

[21] Amos Yong, with Jonathan A. Anderson, *Renewing Christian Theology: Systematics for a Global Christianity* (Waco, TX: Baylor University Press, 2014), xxiii. See also ibid., 11 and 22–23.

[22] Ibid., 24.

color plates and reflections by art professor Jonathan A. Andrews of Biola University. In several places within each chapter, Andrews offers a short reflection on a particular piece of art—usually a painting but sometimes a sculpture. Many of these are from the Western tradition, but included as well are pieces of art from India, Indonesia, Japan, Mozambique, Peru, and several from Orthodox and Coptic sources. As Yong expresses it, the text "is now also informed by the artwork, even as the artwork is complemented by the text."[23] Yong's book, I suggest, is a major contribution to the doing of theology in the context of World Christianity.

Jehu Hanciles and Migration

Another book and theme that might be mentioned in light of the Neglected Themes Model of theologizing in World Christianity is Jehu Hanciles's *Beyond Christendom: Globalization, African Migration, and the Transformation of the West.*[24] The book is lengthy and complex, using methods of the social sciences, history, biblical studies, and missiology. Its basic thesis, however, is that the massive migrations of our day from the "new heartlands of the faith"[25] in Africa, Asia, and Latin America are not only transforming the face of the churches of the West but are changing the understanding of Christian mission as such. These migrations, Hanciles, argues, in fact, are not simply "crucial to the unfolding of the divine plan of salvation, but also [furnish] the basis for a biblical critique of global cultural hegemony."[26]

Up until now, missiological thinking (indeed, theological thinking as well) has been little impacted by international migrations. But the potential for such thinking is immense. Hanciles quotes Timothy Smith's observation that "migration [is] often a theologizing experience."[27] He outlines some of the missiological and ecclesiological implications of migrant communities, especially in the United States, as a result of this theologizing in several points. He emphasizes the missiological impact of their very presence, the fact that they represent a movement more from the margins than from the

---

[23] Ibid., 20.

[24] Jehu J. Hanciles, *Beyond Christendom: Globalization, African Migration, and the Transformation of the West* (Maryknoll, NY: Orbis Books, 2008).

[25] Ibid., 3.

[26] Ibid., 4.

[27] Ibid., 4, quoting Timothy L. Smith, "Religion and Ethnicity in America," *American Historical Review*, 83/5 (1978): 1174–75.

center, their impact on the secularized society around them, their acceptance of religious plurality, and their commitment to change and innovation.[28] But, he says, these implications are not only theological. He argues that "not only is immigration central to the emergence, character, and development of the American nation, but it is also crucial to its future."

As other authors have also pointed out, theologizing out of the often-neglected theme that is so crucial in World Christianity has many other theological and practical implications. Peter Phan himself, together with Elaine Padilla, has edited and contributed to a volume on migration and theology, as have Daniel Groody and Gioacchino Campese (in which Peter has a chapter). Important dissertations on theology and migration, representing important theologizing in the World Christian perspective, have been written by Gaetano Parolin and Gioacchino Campese.[29] Theologizing out of these and other neglected themes represent, to my mind, a major contribution to doing theology in the context of World Christianity.

The Global Perspective Model

A number of books have been written in the last several years that survey a particular topic in theology from various contexts in both the Global North and Global South, resulting in a kind of theologizing from a broader, global perspective. Kirsteen Kim's *The Holy Spirit in the World*, is one example of this kind of global theologizing, as is—to a certain extent, at least—Elizabeth Johnson's beautiful work, *Quest for the Living God*, and Veli-Matti Kärkkäinen's works on the Trinity, Christology, and pneumatology.[30] In some ways, these books make use of what I am calling here the

---

[28] Hanciles, *Beyond Christendon*, 297–302.

[29] Elaine Padilla and Peter C. Phan, ed., *Contemporary Issues of Migration and Theology* (New York: Palgrave Macmillan, 2013); Daniel G. Groody and Gioacchino Campese, eds., *A Promised Land, A Perilous Journey: Theological Perspectives on Migration* (Notre Dame, IN: University of Notre Dame Press, 2008); Gaetano Parolin, *Chiesa Postconciliare e Migrazioni: Quale Teologia per la Missione con I Migranti* (Rome: Editrice Pontificia Università Gregoriana, 2010); Gioacchino Campese, "Una Chiesa Missionaria nell'Era delle Migrazioni" (Ph.D. diss., Pontifical Urbaniana University, Rome, November, 2014). Peter Phan's chapter in his edited volume with Elaine Padilla is "The Experience of Migration as Source of Intercultural Theology," 179–209; in the Groody and Campese, eds. volume, it is "Migration in the Patristic Era: History and Theology," 35–61.

[30] Kirsteen Kim, *The Holy Spirit in the World: A Global Conversation* (Maryknoll, NY: Orbis Books, 2007); Elizabeth A. Johnson, *Quest for the Living God: Mapping*

Global Perspective Model of theologizing within World Christianity, but these works, as I have said, only provide a survey from various perspectives. A richer employment of the Global Perspective Model develops a broader dialogue between traditional approaches and various approaches that have emerged in more subaltern places and among subaltern groups.

At the outset of this essay, I referred to the fact that Peter Phan has served as the editor of a series of theology entitled "Theology in Global Perspective," published by Orbis Books. At the beginning of every volume in the series there appears a kind of *statement of purpose*, certainly written by Peter himself, which outlines the method envisioned for the series. Peter writes that the series "responds to the challenge to re-examine the foundational and doctrinal themes of Christianity in the light of the new global reality." This will be done by taking "account of the insights and experience of churches in Africa, Asia, Latin America, and Oceania," in a way that will be equal to the insights and experience of theologians and theology as it has been traditionally done in the West. In addition, the series hopes to incorporate insights as well from science, technology, and ecology. The idea, in other words, is to construct systematic theologies in ways that use perspectives, sources, and theologians from the entire Christian world.[31]

Kenan Osborne on Orders and Ministry

The first book in the series, written by Franciscan scholar Kenan Osborne on orders and ministry in the church, reflects on the topic from the perspectives of contemporary movements of globalization and the contemporary emphasis on cultural identity. The first chapter in the book is a sustained reflection on the meaning of both perspectives, and presents a history of the inculturation of the faith that highlights the Semitic culture of Jesus, the development of Hellenistic Christianity in its first centuries, the important *Germanization* of Christianity in the early Middle Ages, and the efforts in our own day of taking culture seriously in Christian life and theologizing.[32]

Frontiers in the Theology of God (New York: Continuum, 2007); Veli-Matti Kärkkäinen, *The Trinity: Global Perspectives* (Louisville, KY: Westminster John Knox Press, 2007); Veli-Matti Kärkkäinen, *Christology: A Global Introduction* (Grand Rapids, MI: Baker Academic, 2003); Veli-Matti Kärkkäinen, *Pneumatology: The Holy Spirit in Ecumenical, International, and Contextual Perspective* (Grand Rapids, MI: Baker Academic, 2002).

[31] See the statement, for example, in the first of the series to appear: Kenan B. Osborne, *Orders and Ministry: Leadership in the World Church* (Maryknoll, NY: Orbis Books, 2006), ii.

[32] Ibid., 11–39.

The themes of globalization and culture appear throughout the book and, in their light, there arises a need for "honest dialogue and conversation about Church order," that will entail a change in the policy of ordination (ordaining married men), reconsideration of the role of women in church order, and an honest conversation on racism and white privilege.[33] Osborne is aware of the delicate nature of these issues, and of current teaching of the magisterium regarding celibacy and women's ordination, but his point is that the global nature of Christianity today and the importance of cultural identity make it imperative to rethink and restructure the church for the sake of its pastoral and evangelizing mission. Theologizing in global perspective brings these and other issues like styles of liturgical celebration and the proper autonomy of the local church.

Richard Gaillardetz's Ecclesiology

A second example of the Global Perspective Model employed in Phan's series is the volume on ecclesiology by Richard R. Gaillardetz.[34] Although he begins his reflection quite traditionally (at least after Vatican II's breakthrough from a hierarchical understanding of the church to an understanding of the church as the People of God) with a reflection on the church's communal nature, his second chapter reflects on the church's catholicity as a major component of the church's understanding today. In this chapter, Gaillardetz engages the thinking about global Christianity proposed by Lamin Sanneh and Andrew Walls, reflects on catholicity in the light of contemporary challenges of interreligious dialogue, and has recourse to the documents of the FABC and its commitment to the triple dialogue with culture, religions, and the poor.[35] Gaillardetz enriches his ecclesiology by tapping into the life of the church in various parts of the Global South. To give a few examples, reflecting on the church as communion, he uses as an example the African understanding of the church as the family of God, understandings of ministry in the African and Latin American context, and tops off a discussion on the episcopate by offering the examples of Bishop Samuel Ruiz of Mexico and Francisco Claver of the Philippines.[36]

---

[33] Ibid., 139–56.
[34] Richard R. Gaillardetz, *Ecclesiology for a Global Church: A People Called and Sent* (Maryknoll, NY: Orbis Books, 2008).
[35] Ibid., 35–84.
[36] Ibid., 126–30, 154–62, 278–81.

Stephen Bevans's Introduction to Theology
in Global Perspective

My own volume in Peter Phan's series is an "introduction to doing Catholic systematic theology in global perspective," as I describe it in the Introduction.[37] The first two chapters in the book on revelation and faith are fairly traditional, very much inspired by the theology of Karl Rahner, and define theology with Anselm of Canterbury's classic definition: "faith seeking understanding." As the book progresses, however, that definition is expanded in several ways. In Chapter 3, I offer eight *variations* on this classical theme in a reflection on how theology is faith seeking understanding in a global church. Among these variations, I propose that theology is not necessarily an academic endeavor, but one that arises from ordinary, common Christian experience, particularly those at the margins of society. I also propose that theology is not so much a content but an activity, an idea that I develop later in the book when I write about the method of liberation theology. Theology as well, I propose, is essentially a contextual activity and not necessarily done discursively. These are all themes that come out of a more global consciousness and from theologians doing theology in the Global South. The entire second part of the book—entitled "Faith Seeking Together: The Ecclesial Nature of Theology"—comes out of my own wrestling with a more communal consciousness that I discovered in my years as a missionary and theology teacher in the Philippines (1972–81). It is in the context of the communal nature of theologizing that I locate the more traditional reflections on tradition and magisterium. To give one more example of how I employ the Global Perspective Model in the book, the final section on the history of theology is an attempt to sketch the history of theology from a thoroughly global perspective, including areas like North African and East Syrian theology in the early church, dialogue with Islam from the seventh century into the Middle Ages, and efforts of theologizing in Asia during the years of European expansion in the sixteenth century.

My own sense is that the Global Perspective Model is one that has great promise for theology today. Indeed, I would argue that any theology done today should employ this model to some extent.

---

[37] Stephen B. Bevans, *An Introduction to Theology in Global Perspective* (Maryknoll, NY: Orbis Books, 2009), 1.

The Comparative Theology Model

A final model highlighted in this essay that theologizes in the context and from the perspective of World Christianity is what I would call the Comparative Theology Model.

The Comparative Theology Model and World Religions

The Comparative Theology Model has been employed as a relatively new way of doing theology in response to today's consciousness of religious diversity in the world today,[38] and has been pioneered in particular by Harvard scholar Francis X. Clooney. In a world of many religions, any theologizing done in World Christianity has to take this dazzling diversity into account, take up its challenges, and be enriched by it. In his important introduction to the comparative theological method, Clooney names theologians like David Tracy, Robert Neville, Raimon Panikkar, and James Fredericks as pioneers in this area,[39] and in an edited volume published in the same year introduced several comparative theologians from the *next generation*, two among whom are women.[40]

Clooney distinguishes clearly between comparative theologizing, which he understands as a proper theological discipline marked by a firm faith commitment on the part of the comparative theologian, and the disciplines of the comparative study of religions and the theology of religions, and even from the practice of interreligious dialogue.[41] He outlines a fairly detailed method for engaging in comparative theologizing,[42] but it might be summarized by stating that it consists particularly in the *intelligent reading* of a particular text from a religious tradition other than Christianity. Such a reading, of course, involves expertise in the particular language of the text, a broad knowledge of the tradition being studied, and a wide reading of the available and relevant commentaries. The result of such reading is that "as we learn another tradition in some depth, we will then begin also to re-read our own in light of that other. In the end, because we are theologians, we must

---

[38] Francis X. Clooney, *Comparative Theology: Deep Learning across Religious Borders* (Malden, MA: Wiley-Blackwell, 2010), 8.

[39] Ibid., 42–53.

[40] Francis X. Clooney, SJ, ed., *The New Comparative Theology: Interreligious Insights from the Next Generation* (New York: T. & T. Clark, 2010).

[41] Clooney, *Comparative Theology*, 9–16.

[42] Ibid., 57–68.

also put the whole together, so as to be able to communicate our learning to wider academic and faith communities."[43]

Clooney's own practice of intelligent reading is of Hindu texts, particularly the Vedanta tradition. James Fredericks specializes in Buddhist texts, and one of the authors in the edited book on the *new* comparative theology reflects on a text of the Mishna.[44] Clooney admits that his own approach might be rather "elitist," but he acknowledges as well that "other versions of comparative learning are possible." Indeed, "if imaginative theologians can also draw on other materials and weave together comparative theological narratives, all the better."[45] In any case, the comparative theological method that he and others have proposed seem to me a significant way of doing Christian theology in the context of World Christianity. Not only can such a patient and respectful approach lead to new friendships and relationships, as Fredericks especially advocates, it can lead as well to new and perhaps startling ways of understanding our twenty-first century Christian faith.

An Intercontextual *Approach*

I would like to propose, however, that the Comparative Theology Model might also be used beyond the reading of texts and practices of other religious traditions, and employed in a mutually critical dialogue between contexts. The Contextual Theology Model, as I outlined earlier in this essay, engages a particular context (experience, social location, culture, change) in a mutually critical dialogue with the wider Christian tradition. What I am proposing here, however—in a way analogous to the method of comparative theology proposed by Clooney and others—is that a *particular* contextual theology be put in dialogue with *another* contextual theology. In other words, I'm suggesting that one contextual theology be taken as a *text* to be *read* by another contextual theology so that the *reader* might be enlightened, challenged, or enriched by that reading.

---

[43] Ibid., 60.

[44] See, for example, Francis X. Clooney, SJ, *Theology after Vedanta: An Experiment in Comparative Theology* (Albany, NY: State University of New York Press, 1993); and Francis X. Clooney, SJ, *Divine Mother, Blessed Mother: Hindu Godesses and the Virgin Mary* (New York: Oxford University Press, 2005); James Fredericks, *Buddhists and Christians: Through Comparative Theology to Solidarity* (Maryknoll, NY: Orbis Books, 2004); Daniel Joslyn-Siemiatkoski, "Comparative Theology and the Status of Judaism: Hegemony and Reversals," in Clooney, *The New Comparative Theology*, 89–108.

[45] Clooney, *Comparative Theology*, 67.

Such *readings* have been already done in a world Christian context, with considerable success. I am thinking of the dialogue that took place in the late 1960s in the dialogue between US black liberation theology, particularly that developed by James Cone, and the black theologies of liberation that began to emerge in South Africa in the time of Apartheid.[46] There has also been a dialogue between Latin American liberation theology and US Latino/a theology in which while the latter, while acknowledging the former's influence in its earlier years, has ultimately gone its own way in a dialogue with US Latino/a culture and popular religiosity.[47] As Jonathan Tan documents in his introduction to Asian American theologies, the dialogue between Asian theologies and Asian contextual realities has been a rich source for Asian American theologians as well, Peter Phan certainly among them.[48]

While these intercontextual dialogues are extremely important, what I would like to further propose has, to my mind, something that has not yet been done, or done very little. Here in the United States, there has been dialogue between black theologians and Latino/a theologians, particularly at the annual conventions of the Catholic Theological Society of America. But, as far as I know, there has not been a real mutually critical intercontextual dialogue between contextual theologies that have more or fewer affinities with one another. For example, I would wonder what might come out of a dialogue between theologies emerging from African traditional religions and Latin American popular religious practices. What might be the results of a mutually critical dialogue between themes in Filipino theology and the same themes in Indonesian theology? How might a New Zealand Maori theology profit from a dialogue with Australian Aboriginal theology? What might be the yield of a dialogue between the texts of the FABC and the Conference of Latin American Bishops? I think these are intriguing questions, and their answers may indeed hold out a future for theologizing from the perspective of World Christianity.

---

[46] See Mikgethi Motlhabi, "The History of Black Theology in South Africa," in *The Cambridge Companion to Black Theology*, ed. Dwight N. Hopkins and Edward P. Antonio, (Cambridge: Cambridge University Press, 2012), 224. Motlhabi cites in particular Basil Scott Moore, "Black Theology in the Beginning," *Journal for the Study of Religion*, 4/2 (1991): 25.

[47] See, for example, Roberto S. Goizueta, "Third World Theologies in the First World: Hispanic," in *Dictionary of Third World Theologies*, ed. Virginia Fabella and R. S. Sugirtharajah (Maryknoll, NY: Orbis Books, 2000), 212–14.

[48] Jonathan Y. Tan, *Introducing Asian American Theologies* (Maryknoll, NY: Orbis Books, 2008). See ibid., 105–6 for a mention of Peter Phan.

Conclusion

I have offered here four models of contextual theologizing in the context of World Christianity. Unlike the six models operative within the Contextual Theology Model, which I believe are methodologically exhaustive, there may be many more models of theologizing in World Christianity, both already being practiced and still to be developed. My hope is that what I have delineated here might be helpful as theologians who do theology with a consciousness of the reality of World Christianity discern ways of making that theology both more relevant and more challenging to today's Christians of all kinds and in all parts of the world. Peter Phan has certainly been a leader in this kind of discernment and a model in its practice. May his example inspire many others to follow in his very large footprints.

9

Exploring New Horizons in Trinitarian Theology: World Christianity in Interreligious Encounters

Ruben L. F. Habito

In his widely celebrated (and for some controversial) book *Being Religious Interreligiously: Asian Perspectives on Interfaith Dialogue*,[1] Peter Phan describes features of our postmodern world, and the challenges it thereby brings to Christian faith and theology, suggesting possible Asian contributions for addressing these challenges. Wherever we may be living in our contemporary multifaith global society, it is no longer possible to take on the tasks of Christian theology responsibly for the Christian community without reference to the fact of the presence of, and without regard to, the truth claims of Religious Others among us.[2] This essay explores how interreligious encounters are opening new horizons in thinking about, appreciating, and appropriating the central Christian doctrine of the Trinity in the context of an emerging World Christianity.

Recent years have seen the publication of a good number of creative theological works on this theme of the Trinity and the world's religions.[3] We

---

I am deeply indebted to my esteemed senior colleague, Charles M. Wood, Emeritus Lehman Professor of Christian Doctrine at Perkins School of Theology, Southern Methodist University, for carefully going over an initial draft and making valuable suggestions I was able to incorporate in the final version.

[1] Peter Phan, *Being Religious Interreligiously: Asian Perspectives on Interfaith Dialogue* (Maryknoll, NY: Orbis Books, 2004).

[2] See David Lochhead, *The Dialogical Imperative* (Maryknoll, NY: Orbis Books, 1988).

[3] I use this term *the world's religions* with an awareness of the critical perspectives presented by Tomoko Mazusawa in her *The Invention of World Religions: Or, How European Universalism Was Preserved in the Language of Pluralism* (Chicago: University of Chicago Press, 2005).

can distinguish two approaches in this regard. One is a turn to Trinitarian theology for providing a hermeneutical framework in proposing or developing a particular position in the Christian theology of religions. A second approach is the exploration of specific themes or notions found in the other traditions to shed new light on, or open the way to, a deeper understanding, enhanced appropriation, and effective articulation of the central Christian doctrine of the Trinity.

Christian Theology of Religions in Light of the Trinity

Theology of religions is an area and discipline in Christian systematic theology that addresses the question of the nature and role of the many religious traditions of the world in light of the revelation and message of salvation given in and through the mystery of Jesus Christ and the church as the bearer of that revelation and message of salvation. As Christians come to encounter people of other faith traditions and interact with them as fellow human beings, their faith seeking understanding brings up questions such as, "How are Christians to take the differing truth claims in other religions?" and "Can their adherents attain ultimate salvation as Christians understand it, and if so, how?"

Alan Race, in his noted work *Christians and Religious Pluralism,* sets forth the classic threefold typology of Christian approaches to the Religious Other, naming these as exclusivism, inclusivism, and pluralism.[4] A Christian seeking to be faithful to one's own tradition who actively engages in dialogue and in cooperative ventures with members of other faith traditions with an open heart, and enters into bonds of friendship and spiritual solidarity with them, comes to recognize the inadequacy of the models outlined above as frameworks for creative and constructive encounters with Religious Others. Amos Yong pointedly remarks,

> Christian thinking about the religions can no longer be done in an *a priori* manner, from the theological armchair, as it were. Rather,

---

[4] Alan Race, *Christians and Religious Pluralism: Patterns in the Christian Theology of Religions* (Maryknoll, NY: Orbis Books, 1983). To this threefold categorization, a fourfold typology has been proposed by Paul Knitter in *Introducing Theologies of Religions* (Maryknoll, NY: Orbis Books, 2002) renaming the three above and calling them the Replacement ("Only One True Religion," i.e., the Christian), Mutuality ("Many True Religions Called to Dialogue"), and Fulfillment ("The One, [i.e., Christianity] Fulfills the Many") models, respectively, to which he adds a fourth, the Acceptance ("Many True Religions: So Be It") model.

theologizing about the religions requires engaging them . . . In short, a Christian theology of religions needs to emerge out of a genuine dialogue with the religions. Such a dialogue, of course, needs to steer clear between the Scylla of a monologistic, *aprioristic*, and colonialistic/imperialistic defining of religious others on the one hand, and the Charybdis of a syncretistic (simply) empiricistic, and relativistic attitude on the other.[5]

In this regard, some theologians have suggested a moratorium on theorizing about Religious Others, and recommend active engagement with Religious Others as a basis and resource for formulating a Christian theology of religions, instead of making the latter a prelude to or requirement for such engagement.[6] The move taking Trinitarian doctrine as a framework in considering other religions comes from taking up this challenge and invitation that Religious Others present to Christian faith.

Raimundo (Raimon) Panikkar (1918–2010) had been taking on this theological task of relating the Trinity and the world's religions since the middle of the last century, and stood a pioneer in forging paths in this direction, an intellectual and spiritual giant whose erudite and densely written works continue to provoke and inspire many new insights among thinkers.[7] His biological origins (son of a Spanish/Catalán Roman Catholic mother and an Indian Hindu father) led him to delve deeply into the religious heritage of both parents, and after ordination as a Catholic priest, he went to his father's native country to study Indian religion and philosophy. His early work *The Unknown Christ of Hinduism*[8] developed the theme of the Triune God at work in all the religions, and pointed to the presence of Christ, the Logos, in the sacred scriptures of the Hindu tradition. This was followed up in his *Trinity and the Religious Experience of Man*,[9] wherein he proposes

---

[5] Amos Yong, *Beyond the Impasse: Toward a Pneumatological Theology of Religions* (Grand Rapids, MI: Baker Academic, 2003), 19–20.

[6] See Knitter, *Introducing Theologies of Religions*, 203–4, referring specifically to the work of Francis Clooney and James Fredericks.

[7] See Joseph Prabhu, ed., *The Intercultural Challenge of Raimon Panikkar* (Maryknoll, NY: Orbis Books, 1996); and Raimon Panikkar and Joseph Prabhu, *Raimon Panikkar: Selected Writings—Modern Spiritual Masters* (Maryknoll, NY: Orbis Books, 2015).

[8] Raimundo Panikkar, *The Unknown Christ of Hinduism* (London: Darton, Longman & Todd, 1964; rev. ed., Maryknoll, NY: Orbis Books, 1981).

[9] Raimundo Panikkar, *The Trinity and the Religious Experience of Man: Icon-Person-Mystery* (Maryknoll, NY: Orbis Books; London: Darton, Longman & Todd, 1973) (also known as *The Trinity and the World Religions*).

that the notion of the Trinity is not unique to Christianity but that similar themes can be found in other religions, taking varying forms.

Panikkar's key insight about the *theandric* (that is, an integral and nondual vision of the divine and the human) nature of reality, which he develops further and expounds in great detail in his later works (revising his terminology as he goes along, settling on *cosmotheandric*), takes him from an inclusivistic position (as reflected in the first edition of his *The Unknown Christ of Hinduism* (1964) to a decidedly pluralistic stance, already evident in the revised edition of the same book (1981). However, his is not a pluralism that would simplistically regard the many religions as *different paths to the same mountain peak*, but rather would celebrate and affirm the diversity found in these many traditions, in and through which one is able to discern the work of the Triune God.

His empathetic, open-hearted approach to other religions can be discerned in his often-quoted statement, "I left Europe [for India] as a Christian, discovered myself a Hindu, and returned as a Buddhist without having ceased to be a Christian."[10] An underlying theme of Panikkar's entire life work can perhaps be summed up as a contemplation of a Trinitarian vision seen in the light of the world's religions. I will offer further reflections on this aspect of his work in the second section of this essay.

Jacques Dupuis (1923–2004) was a Belgian Jesuit priest who spent many years in India studying Hindu philosophy and religion, and teaching Catholic theology at a Jesuit college in Delhi, and later at the Gregorian University in Rome. His deep familiarity with Hindu religion and culture and his thorough grounding in the Catholic tradition bear fruit in his magnum opus, *Toward a Christian Theology of Religious Pluralism*, published in 1997.[11] This volume brings in the intricacies in the dynamics of Trinitarian interrelations in considering the question of other religions and their status in God's universal plan of salvation.

It is important not to be misled by the title, and quickly assume that Dupuis is taking a *pluralist* stance in his theology of religions. A careful reading will make it clear that the author stands firmly in Catholic Christian tradition that affirms the uniqueness and universal efficacy of salvation in Jesus Christ, and thereby has not *crossed the (theological) Rubicon* with pluralists (who have abandoned that stance in favor of *equal parity for*

---

[10] Raimundo Panikkar, *The Intrareligious Dialogue* (New York: Paulist Press, 1978), 2.

[11] Jacques Dupuis, *Toward a Christian Theology of Religious Pluralism* (Maryknoll, NY: Orbis Books, 1997).

all religions). The question that he addresses for Christians to consider is whether the de facto reality of religious pluralism (some would prefer to use the term *plurality* in this sense) in the world today is a matter needing to be lamented and overcome, and therefore that all Christians should keep praying and working hard in evangelizing others so we may all come to belong to one fold, *or* "whether theology is able to assign to the plurality of religious traditions a positive meaning in God's overall design for humankind."[12] The theological implication is that, if so, Christians are then called to welcome this reality of religious pluralism *in principle (de jure)* and (re)consider the mission of the church in its light. Dupuis lays out his position affirming that "God spoke in many and various ways" (Heb. 1:1), not limiting this to the covenant with Israel: "Religious pluralism in principle rests on the immensity of a God who is love."[13]

Yet it is important to note that Dupuis continues to emphasize the person of Jesus Christ and the Christ event as *constitutive* for the salvation for all of humanity. The Trinitarian Christology model that he develops in this volume opens the way for Christians to discover God's truth and grace found in savior figures of other religious traditions, not simply as *seeds* or *stepping-stones* to the Christ event, and that would thereby be superseded or later abrogated by the latter, but as *relational* to it. "The truth to which Christianity witnesses is neither exclusive nor inclusive of all other truth; it is *related* to all that is true in other religions."[14]

What the above theses imply then is that engaging with Religious Others in interfaith dialogue (and mutual cooperation in our earthly tasks) is an imperative and an inherent feature of the Christian task of contributing in bringing about the Reign of God toward its eschatological fullness, as the "common final achievement of Christianity and the other religions."[15] The role of the church is to be at the service of the coming of this Reign of God, affirming what has been laid down in *Lumen gentium* (20): "The church is the sacrament of salvation for all humankind, and her activity is not limited only to those who accept her message. She is a dynamic force in humankind's

---

[12] Ibid., 386.

[13] Ibid., 387.

[14] Emphasis added. Ibid., 388, citing Claude Geffré, "La singularité de Christianisme à l'age du pluralisme religieux," in *Penser la foi: Recherces en théologie auhourd'hui: Melanges offerts à Joseph Moingt,* eds. J. Doré et C. Theobald (Paris: Cerf-Assas 1993), 358; see also Joseph O'Leary, *La verité chrétienne à l'âge du pluralisme religieux* (Paris: Cerf, 1994), 279–80.

[15] Dupuis, *Christian Theology of Religious Pluralism,* 390.

journey toward the eschatological Kingdom, and is the sign and promoter of Kingdom values."[16]

Dupuis critically evaluates previous approaches in theology of religions, emphasizing and firmly maintaining a balanced, "both/and" position with regard to three areas of opposition where other writers on the theme may favor one or the other: the opposition between Christ and God (*Christo-centrism vs. Theocentrism*), the opposition between the Reign of God and salvation as the norm for evaluating religions (regnocentrism vs. soteriocentrism), and the opposition between the Son and the Spirit in the work of the economic Trinity (Christocentrism vs. Pneumatocentrism).[17]

In sum, Jacques Dupuis's Trinitarian approach offers a highly nuanced, well thought out, and very engaging proposal for grounding faithful Christian engagement in interreligious dialogue. It is an approach that does not water down the central Christian claims of the uniqueness and universally salvific efficacy of the person and work of Jesus Christ, while at the same time welcoming and relating to Religious Others with an openness to learning from them, with full respect for their differences and with due acknowledgment of their respective contributions toward our common realization of our shared eschatological destiny in the Triune God.[18]

---

[16] Ibid., 340.

[17] See Veli-Matti Kärkäinen, *Trinity and Religious Pluralism: The Doctrine of Trinity in Christian Theology of Religions* (Burlington, VT: Ashgate, 2004), 50–52. In this connection, I find Keith E. Johnson's characterization (and critique) of Dupuis, that the latter "uses trinitarian claims to undermine Christian teaching regarding the person and work of Christ," (see Keith E. Johnson, *Rethinking the Trinity and Religious Pluralism: An Augustinian Assessment* [Downer's Grove, IL: IVP Academic, 2011], 205), or that he errs in "employing deficient accounts of the relations among the Father, Son, and Holy Spirit" (ibid., 102), to be based on Johnson's own failure to appreciate the intricate nuances of Dupuis's masterful work.

[18] It is unfortunate that Jacques Dupuis's work was subjected to scrutiny by the Congregation for the Doctrine of the Faith of the Vatican, based on gross misinterpretation of his works, and blatant misunderstandings of his positions. (Documentations of this exchange with the Vatican office are publicly available online.) In all this, Dupuis maintained an attitude of humility and obedience, seeking dialogue with Vatican officials to clarify his positions. He passed away in 2004, bearing the toll that this inquisition caused upon his work and his person, but his work characterized by creativity and originality together with fidelity to the Catholic tradition took the conversations in Christian theology of religions a significant step forward. For Dupuis's response to the Vatican's critique of his writings, see William R. Burrows, *Jacques Dupuis Faces the Inquisition: Two Essays by Jacques Dupuis on Dominus Iesus and the Roman Investigation of His Work* (Eugene, OR: Pickwick Publications, 2012).

Dupuis's vision of human ultimate destiny culminates in the "eschato-logical fullness of the Reign of God (that) is the common final achievement of Christianity and the other religions."[19] In clear contrast with this, S. Mark Heim, arguing for a genuine respect of the differences in the world's religious traditions concerning their understanding of human ultimate destiny, proposes a vision that admits to a diversity of religious ends that is based on the diversity in the Triune God.[20] This genuine respect for diversity is a crucial point that undergirds Heim's entire project, as he seeks to find a way of situating this diversity within an intelligible framework that is in accord with Christian claims to ultimate truth and human destiny. The key Heim offers is the Trinity.

Heim acknowledges indebtedness among others to Raimundo Panik-kar's distinction of three spiritualities in the human religious quest (iconic, personal, and mystical),[21] and also specifically to a work of Smart and Konstantine that describes human ultimate destiny as communion in three dimensions of divine life.[22] The first dimension is the "infinity of the divine life as it circulates through the three persons," the second is "the plurality of the persons themselves and their relations with each other," and the third is "the common will or the collective 'I' of the Trinity, according to which God acts with perfect unity of purpose."[23] Building on these dimensions, Heim envisions different modes of communion with God, which are (1) *nonrela-tional* or impersonal, (2) interactive and personal, and (3) communal, in a "mutual indwelling, in which the distinct persons are not confused or iden-tified, but are enriched by their participation in each other's inner life."[24] Thus, the descriptions of human ultimate destiny given in (1) Theravāda Buddhism or Advaita Vedanta, (2) Islam or *bhakti* Hinduism or other forms of devotional theism, and (3) Christianity, with their differences, can each be accounted for with their respective complexities, in the depth and rich-ness of the Triune God.

In considering Heim's, and in fact any other proposal about divine reali-ties and ultimate destiny, we need to heed a point Heim himself makes in

---

[19] Dupuis, *Christian Theology of Religious Pluralism,* 390.

[20] S. Mark Heim, *The Depth of the Riches: A Trinitarian Theology of Religious Ends* (Grand Rapids, MI: Wm. B. Eerdmans Publishing), 2001.

[21] The three forms of spirituality are indicated in the title of Panikkar's work, *The Trinity in the Religious Experience of Man*: icon, person, mystery.

[22] Ninian Smart and Stephen Konstantine, *Christian Systematic Theology in World Context* (Minneapolis: Fortress Press, 1991).

[23] Heim, *The Depths of the Riches*, 157.

[24] Ibid., 196.

his introduction, which tends to be overlooked in our theological discourse (God-talk), namely, that we are dealing with a human activity that "must trade heavily in speculation."[25] It is an endeavor driven by the exigency of faith seeking understanding, with the full recognition that at best we can only *see through a glass, darkly*. This does not mean that theological speculation is entirely useless or fruitless, but as Heim suggests, can be pursued in a way that would hold "that theological interpretation to be convincing which can show the way in which its eschatological visions reflect realities we can already see in some measure now, and which can show how such eschatological visions actually clarify these realities themselves."[26]

Gavin D'Costa offers a proposal for a Trinitarian theology of religions within the framework of Roman Catholic theology in a seminal essay written in 1990, summed up in five theses.[27] First, affirming God's continuing self-revelation throughout history through the work of the Holy Spirit (assuring the openness of Christians to revelation and salvation beyond the boundaries of the historical church), he also emphasizes the particularity and the normativity of the historical revelation through Jesus Christ. Second, the Holy Spirit who is God's self-disclosure in history is also the Spirit of Christ: this connects the particularity of Christ to the universality of God's salvific work. Third, loving communion within the Triune God is the primary mode of being, and thus it is imperative for Christians to love their neighbor, excluding no one, and concretely, include adherents of other religions. Fourth, the self-giving love embodied in Jesus Christ crucified grounds a stance of openness and dialogue in relating to Religious Others. Fifth, the church, the community of believers in God's self-revelation in Jesus Christ, stands under the judgment of God the Holy Spirit, making it imperative for Christians to be open and faithful to the Holy Spirit as manifested in and through other religions. In sum, D'Costa's stance seeks to avoid the extremes of particularistic exclusivism, on the one hand, and of relativistic pluralism, on the other, declaring a committed openness to other religions in dialogical encounters as an implication of the church's fidelity to the Triune God.

D'Costa follows up on this essay with a volume addressing the same theme, published ten years later.[28] The first part of the book critiques

---

[25] Ibid., 10.

[26] Ibid.

[27] Gavin D'Costa, "Christ, the Trinity, and Religious Plurality," in *Christian Uniqueness Reconsidered: The Myth of a Pluralistic Theology of Religions*, ed. Gavin D'Costa (Maryknoll, NY: Orbis Books, 1990), 16–29.

[28] Gavin D'Costa, *The Meeting of Religions and the Trinity* (Maryknoll, NY: Orbis Books, 2000).

various types of pluralism,[29] while the second lays out his proposal for a Trinitarian theology of religions in greater detail, with a declaration of his approach being "unashamedly Roman Catholic in method, orientation, and accountability."[30] D'Costa weaves a convincing argument for what he calls "a Trinitarian orientation to the question of other religions," which he claims is "neither pluralist nor inclusivist, but both open to others and yet faithfully committed to its tradition-specific (Roman Catholic) way of narrating the world."[31] D'Costa's Trinitarian theology of religions is clear in its emphasis on the *imperative* for Christians and for the church as a community to engage adherents of other religions in dialogue and cooperation in ways characterized by openness, tolerance, and equality, for the following reason:

> Since we have seen that the Holy Spirit may be active within other religions, if the church is closed to other religions, then the church will be guilty of being inattentive to the promptings of God which may lead it to greater holiness, truth, and goodness. Being inattentive to other religions is a form of idolatry.[32]

Amos Yong considers the Triune God in relation to the world's religions with a pneumatological focus coming out of the Pentecostalist tradition wherein he finds his ecclesial home. His *Discerning the Spirit(s): A Pentecostal-Charismatic Contribution to Christian Theology of Religions,*[33] followed by *Beyond the Impasse: Toward a Pneumatological Theology of Religions*, already cited above (note 5), receive inspiration from George Khodr, who in 1971 suggested a shift from a Christological to a pneumatological framework in understanding the world religions.[34] Khodr cites an expression from

---

[29] D'Costa names Paul Knitter and John Hick as Christian representatives, and Dan Cohn-Sherbock, Sarvepalli Radhakrishna, and the Dalai Lama as Jewish, Hindu, and Buddhist representatives, respectively, and critiques their positions in the first three chapters. See D'Costa, *Meeting of Religions*, 19–95.

[30] Ibid., 99.

[31] Ibid., 138. This side remark of his (that his proposal is neither pluralist nor inclusivist), which stands in contrast with his earlier essay wherein he describes his own approach explicitly as inclusivist, is not to be construed as a reversal to an exclusivist standpoint, given his positive and open attitude toward interreligious encounters.

[32] Ibid., 133.

[33] Amos Yong, *Discerning the Spirit(s): A Pentecostal-Charismatic Contribution to Christian Theology of Religions* (Sheffield, UK: Sheffield Academic Press, 2000).

[34] George Khodr, in an address to the Central Committee of the World Council of Churches held at Addis Ababa, published as "Christianity in a Pluralistic World—The Economy of the Holy Spirit," *Ecumenical Review* 23/2 (1971): 118–28.

second-century Bishop Irenaeus of Lyons, referring to the Son and the Spirit
as the "two hands of the Father" (*Adversus haereses* 4, Preface, 4).

Yong makes his position clear as an evangelical theologian in launching
his project, declaring his commitment to "the authority of Scripture, to the
importance of a personal relationship with Jesus (as mediated by the Spirit,
of course), and to the task of Christian mission and evangelism."[35] He places
his work as a proposal in contemporary Trinitarian (systematic) theology,
as well as in the theology of mission (missiology) that will "enable a more
genuine and effective engagement with the post-Christian and postmodern
cultures of the twenty-first century,"[36] including Christian engagement
with adherents of the world's religions in ways that would not fall into the
colonialistic/imperialistic mind-set that he has already cautioned about
(paragraph referring to note 5, above). He puts forth his thesis in three
axioms, namely, that (1) "God is universally present and active in the Spirit,"
(2) "God's Spirit is the life-breath of the *imago Dei* in every human being
and the presupposition of all relationships and communities," and (3) "the
religions of the world, like everything else that exists, are providentially
sustained by the Spirit of God for divine purposes."[37]

Yong's work is important in that he considers his primary audience
to be his fellow Pentecostal–charismatic, and more widely, evangelical
Christians, whose numbers are said to be increasing exponentially in
different parts of the world and who are a major force in the development
of the emerging World Christianity.[38] Yong's work has been subjected to
critiques by some evangelical theologians, who point out some facets in his
proposal with which they are not able to concur,[39] but he is also celebrated

---

[35] Yong, *Beyond the Impasse*, 32.

[36] Ibid., 35.

[37] Ibid., 44–46.

[38] See Philip Jenkins, *The Next Christendom: The Coming of the Global South*, 3rd
ed. (New York: Oxford University Press, 2011); and Philip Jenkins, *The New Faces of
Christianity: Believing the Bible in the Global South* (New York: Oxford University
Press, 2008).

[39] Gerald R. McDermott and Harold A. Netland, *A Trinitarian Theology of
Religions: An Evangelical Proposal* (New York: Oxford University Press, 2014), while
critiquing some aspects of Yong's proposal, commend him "for pushing evangelicals to
consider the possibility that the Holy Spirit might be at work among those whose religions have been traditionally dismissed as merely demonic" (ibid., 75), and affirms that
he is "also right to encourage evangelicals to be more Trinitarian and not simply Chris-
tomonist, with Christ in effect wholly replacing the Trinity" (ibid.). Keith E. Johnson,
in note 17, above, also critiques Yong for, among other things, "severing the two hands

and welcomed as a fresh voice among Pentecostal–charismatic and evangelical Christians.

Writing from an evangelical perspective, Veli-Matti Kärkkäinen has evaluated various proposals made in Christian theology of religions that pertain to Trinitarian doctrine since Barth up to recent works.[40] In a chapter surveying Roman Catholic Trinitarian theology in Christian–Muslim encounters, he briefly addresses the inevitable challenging question, "Is the Christian (Triune) God the same as the Muslim God?"[41] In his concluding chapter, Kärkkäinen describes his own position picking up elements from other theologians whose views he has described earlier in the book, resonating in many ways with the views of D'Costa (see below). He also critiques the kind of pluralism that levels off all religions from an elevated standpoint, emphasizing that each religion must be taken seriously for its own claims that its quest for ultimate truth be honored. This emphasis comes with a call for an engagement with, and serious study of, other religious traditions on the part of the Christian theologian.

Kärkkäinen is critical of theological attempts to overplay distinctions between Father and Son, and between Son and Spirit, and highlights the need to see these precisely in integral Trinitarian relations. He places importance on this integral connection between (though not identification of) the church and the kingdom as the presence of the Triune God in the world, and is thereby critical of theological moves to downplay the role of the church in favor of a *kingdom-centered* approach. While disclaiming the salvific efficacy of other religions as such, he sees their role as enabling the church to encounter more deeply the divine mystery and encourages Christians toward a stance of openness to the gifts of other religions, discerning the presence of the Holy Spirit in them.[42] Kärkkäinen's theological stance has been acclaimed as one that "charts the directions in which evangelical

---

of the Father" (*Rethinking the Trinity and Religious Pluralism*, 121), that is, separating the economy of the word with the economy of the Spirit in Trinitarian life.

[40] Veli-Matti Kärkkäinen, *Trinity and Religious Pluralism: The Doctrine of the Trinity in Christian Theology of Religions* (Bloomington, VT: Ashgate, 2004).

[41] Kärkkäinen reviews the doctoral dissertation of Risto Jukko (approved in 2001, University of Helsinki), later published as a book entitled *Trinity in Unity in Christian-Muslim Relations: The Work of the Pontifical Council for Interreligious Dialogue* (Leiden: Brill, 2007), 155–63. Needless to say, this is another major issue that itself calls for ongoing dialogue and theological reflection but is beyond the purview of this essay. See also David Burrell, "Trinity in Judaism and Islam," in *The Cambridge Companion to the Trinity,* ed. Peter Phan (New York: Cambridge University Press, 2011), 344–62.

[42] Kärkkäinen, *Trinity and Religious Pluralism*, 164–84.

Trinitarian theologies of the religions must proceed" and is thus given a highly positive appraisal by his evangelical colleagues.[43]

One significant feature that is common in the various proposals for a Trinitarian approach to Christian theology of religions is this—they are inspired and informed by their authors' active engagement with other religions, whether through a sustained study of the texts, doctrines, rituals, and other relevant sources of the traditions concerned, or through a combination of this kind of study hand in hand with interreligious encounters through dialogue and mutual cooperative ventures. It is this actual engagement that opens these authors to a heightened sensitivity and respectful stance vis-à-vis their dialogue partners, leading in many cases to associations and friendships that make them no longer capable of relegating Religious Others to a mere objective category or label or class of people in a detached and impersonal way, but as flesh-and-blood human beings full of good will also intent on asking similar questions about truth and human ultimate destiny as they. Many faithful Christians have found such friendships to be truly transformative, leading them to chart new paths in their own theological vision and spiritual lives.[44]

Above I have summarized some of the notable contributions on the question of how Trinitarian theology can shed light on the formulation of a viable Christian theology of religions. There are a number of others that we can only list in passing.[45] As we can see, over the last two decades especially, interest in this theme of Trinity and the world's religions has come to the fore among Christian theologians, such that a section devoted to this topic is now found in many treatments of recent developments in Trinitarian theology proper.[46] This is reflective of the growing consensus that

---

[43] McDermott and Netland, *A Trinitarian Theology of Religions*, 82.

[44] See James Fredericks and Tracy Sayuki Tiemeier, eds., *Interreligious Friendship after Nostra Aetate* (New York: Palgrave MacMillan, 2015).

[45] I. P. Grave, *Trinity and Interfaith Dialogue: Plenitude and Plurality* (Oxford: Peter Lang, 2003); Keith E. Johnson, *Rethinking the Trinity and Religious Pluralism: An Augustinian Assessment* (Downers Grove, Il., IVP Academic, 2011); Veli-Matti Kärkäinen, *Trinity and Religious Pluralism* (Bloomington, VT: Ashgate, 2004); Kevin J. Vanhoozer, *The Trinity in a Pluralistic Age: Theological Essays on Culture and Religion* (Grand Rapids, MI: Wm. B. Eerdmans Publishing, 1997).

[46] See, for example, Anne Hunt, *Trinity: Nexus of the Mysteries of the Christian Faith* (Maryknoll, NY: Orbis Books, 2005); Peter Phan, ed., *The Cambridge Companion to the Trinity* (New York: Cambridge University Press, 2011); Declan Marmion and Rik Van Niewenhove, *An Introduction to the Trinity* (Cambridge: Cambridge University Press, 2005); Veli-Matti Kärkäinen, *Trinity and Revelation, A Constructive Christian Theology for the Pluralistic World* (Grand Rapids, MI: Wm. B. Eerdmans Publishing 2014), ; and Anselm Min, *Paths to the Triune God: An*

Christian theology can no longer be effectively undertaken in the light of today's global realities without understanding, taking account of, and engaging Religious Others in dialogical encounters. The next section will now examine some fruits of these interreligious encounters for Trinitarian theology in an emerging World Christianity.

Trinity in Light of the World's Religions

Dialogical engagement with other religions in ways that may shed light on Christian understanding is called comparative theology, a specific area of study and reflection in Christian systematic theology.[47] This is usually understood as a discipline among specialists who have also been trained in a religious tradition other than their own, engaging this other tradition in order to see one's own in fresh light, or vice versa, engaging one's own tradition as a way of shedding new light on the other. Francis Clooney describes key features of a "faithful and reasonable theology in a pluralistic world" as (1) interreligious, (2) comparative, (3) dialogical, and (4) confessional.[48] I join those who argue that engagement with other religions need not, and should not, be confined to specialists in other religions as such, but needs to be a feature of any and all areas of Christian theological endeavor, that is, the pursuit of faith seeking understanding, with the four features Clooney lays out. In this essay, I will confine my scope to contributions based on dialogical encounters with Asian traditions.[49]

A pioneer in this venture is nineteenth-century Indian theologian Brahmabhandav Upadhyaya, a convert to Christianity from Hinduism.

Encounter between Aquinas and Recent Theologies (Notre Dame, IN: University of Notre Dame Press, 2005), among others.

[47] See Francis Clooney, *Comparative Theology: Deep Learning across Borders* (West Sussex, UK: Wiley Blackwell, 2010) for the methodological features and thematic developments in this groundbreaking area of theological work. See also Clooney's many other works beginning with his *Theology after Vedanta* (Albany, NY: SUNY Press, 1993).

[48] Francis Clooney, *Hindu God, Christian God: How Reason Helps Break Down the Boundaries between Religions* (New York: Oxford University Press, 2001), 163–83.

[49] For a more comprehensive panoramic view of Trinitarian theology in the context of World Christianity, see Veli-Matti Kärkkäinen, *The Trinity: Global Perspectives* (Louisville, KY: Westminster John Knox Press), 2007. See also Ninian Smart and Steven Konstantine, *Christian Systematic Theology in a World Context* (Minneapolis: Fortress Press, 1991), which offers an articulated version of the Christian faith "written against the background of the modern, religiously plural world" (ibid., 9) that addresses the Trinitarian question in this light.

Timothy Tennent calls attention to the work of Upadhyaya, who, inspired by Thomas Aquinas's use of Aristotelian philosophy as infrastructure for his construction of Christian theology, turns to Hindu religious thought to build the foundations of a Christianity that would flourish on Indian soil.[50] Among his tasks was the reformulation of the doctrine of the Trinity, taking the Hindu notion of *sacchidānanda* (=*sat*, Truth; *cit*, Consciousness; *ānanda*, Bliss), the threefold attributes of *Brahman* (Supreme Ultimate Reality) as basic components.[51]

Without going into the merits or demerits of Upadhyaya's particular proposal in Trinitarian theology, what I would like to highlight is the significance of his move of turning to Hindu religious thought that could serve as *building blocks* for Christian theology.[52] He found his rationale in the fact that Western Christianity was also built on an infrastructure informed by Greek philosophy. In short, this is an intentional step of seeking expressions of Christian faith outside the parameters of the Greco–Roman and medieval European cultural context, through which much of Western Christianity has hitherto been transmitted. What would this mean for people of the widely diverse cultural matrices living in different parts of the world?

In surveying the terrain already covered since the last century up to recent years in this area of Trinitarian thought seen in the light of other religions, the work of Raimundo Panikkar, briefly noted in the first section, looms large on the horizon. In *The Trinity and the Religious Experience of Man: Icon-Person-Mystery*, Panikkar describes three forms of human spirituality, corresponding to the three items in his subtitle.[53] These reflect the three yogas, or ways to union with the divine in the Hindu tradition: the way of

---

[50] Timothy Tennent, *Building Christianity on Indian Foundations* (Delhi: ISPCK, 2000).

[51] Timothy Tennent, "Trinity and *Sacchidānanda* in the Writings of Brahmabhandav Upadhyaya," *Dharma Deepika*, 7/1 (2003): 61–75, excerpted in David R. Brockman and Ruben L. F. Habito, eds., *The Gospel among Religions* (Maryknoll, NY: Orbis, 2010), 182–93.

[52] For a historical overview of attempts at finding comparisons or correlations with the Christian Trinity in Hindu religious worldview, with an incisive critical evaluation of these attempts, see Francis Clooney, "Trinity and Hinduism," in Phan, *The Cambridge Companion to the Trinity*, 309–24, See also Veli-Matti Kärkkäinen, "Brahman and the Trinitarian God," in *Trinity and Revelation, Vol. 2 of A Constructive Christian Theology for the Pluralistic World* (Grand Rapids, MI: Wm. B. Eerdmans Publishing, 2014), 386–405.

[53] Raimundo Panikkar, *The Trinity and the Religious Experience of Man: Icon-Person-Mystery* (Maryknoll, NY: Orbis Books, 1973).

worship/ritual action (*karmamārga*), the way of devotion (*bhaktimārga*), and the way of intuitive knowledge (*jñānamārga*). These three forms are also found in other religious traditions in various modes and patterns. Panikkar then correlates these with the Father, the Son, and the Holy Spirit, respectively, suggesting that the Trinity "may be considered as a junction where the authentic spiritual dimensions of all the religions meet."[54] In the last chapter, he introduces the notion that was to become central in his entire lifework, that of *theandrism*, by which he means "a spirituality which combines in an authentic synthesis the three dimensions of our life on earth as in heaven."[55] His engagement into other religious traditions leads him to the claim that "this is not a concept inherent in and introduced by Christian faith alone but that it is already present as the end towards which the religious consciousness of humanity tends."[56]

Panikkar includes the *cosmic* dimension in addition to the *divine* and the *human*, formulating what he calls a cosmotheandric spirituality, which would unite the many different levels of dualistic separation that lie at the root of the woundedness of the human condition, and that would heal "the chasm between the material and the spiritual, and with this, between the secular and the sacred, the inner and the outer, the temporal and the eternal."[57] In his final work published just before his death in 2010, *The Rhythm of Being*, this cosmotheandric vision of reality is laid out further in great detail and in highly dense poetic prose that invites the reader to a spiritual experience in the course of the reading.[58]

It is preposterous to assume that one could sum up Panikkar's monumental lifework in a few paragraphs as we are doing here. Several volumes have already been published with varying laudatory, as well as critical, appraisals of one who is considered an intellectual and spiritual giant of our time.[59] Suffice to say at this point that his own spiritual and intellectual journey as a Christian has forged new paths across the terrain of Hindu,

---

[54] Ibid., 42.

[55] Ibid., 82.

[56] Ibid., 66.

[57] Raimon Panikkar, *The Cosmotheandric Experience: Emerging Religious Consciousness*, edited, with an introduction by Scott Eastham (Maryknoll, NY: Orbis Books, 1993).

[58] Raimon Panikkar, *The Rhythm of Being: The Gifford Lectures* (Maryknoll, NY: Orbis Books, 2010).

[59] One worth mentioning here is Joseph Prabhu, ed., *The Intercultural Challenge of Raimon Panikkar* (Maryknoll, NY: Orbis Books, 1996), featuring essays by well-known theologians and religious scholars.

Buddhist, and other religious traditions, taking on a multireligious way of being in his own person.[60] He thus embodies a radical way of being truly *catholic*, *kat'holos* ("according to the whole").[61] He extends an invitation to all, and how far other Christians are able to follow him in his spiritual and theological vision remains an open question.

Elements of the religious vision as found in the Buddhist traditions also reveal resonances to, and shed light on, Trinitarian doctrine. In a collection entitled *Buddhist Emptiness and Christian Trinity*, Christian theologians engage Buddhist philosopher Masao Abe in addressing the theme of the volume.[62] In separate essays in this volume, Michael von Brück and Paul Ingram examine the Buddhist notion of *śūnyatā*, conventionally translated as *emptiness*, as an existential insight into the relational nature of ultimate reality, which, seen in tandem with David Bohm's holistic paradigm, provides an inroad for understanding the nature of the Triune God in their inner relations as well as in relation to creation.[63] Providing another Buddhist perspective, Donald Mitchell examines Hua-yen's cosmological vision of the interconnectedness of all reality, a Chinese development of the Mahāyāna notion of *śūnyatā*, as finding resonance in the Trinitarian life of communion.[64] Another Buddhist notion that appears to have resonances with Trinitarian doctrine is that of *trikāya*, or the three bodies of the Buddha. Closer examination, however, shows only surface-level similarities but would bring to light different structural approaches to the nature of ultimate reality.[65] I will revisit Buddhist

---

[60] The lifework and writings of Swami Abhishiktananda (1910–73), born Henry Le Saux, and of Dom Bede Griffiths (1903–93), born Allan Richard Griffiths and known later in life as Swami Dayananda, Christian monks whose lifestyles and vision came to be thoroughly seeped in Hindu spirituality, and wherein we may also find insights that shed light on Trinitarian understanding, deserve mention here.

[61] See his section on "The Catholic Moment," in Panikkar, *Cosmotheandric Experience*, 46–53.

[62] Paul Knitter and Roger Corless, eds., *Buddhist Emptiness and Christian Trinity*, (Mahwah, NJ: Paulist Press, 1990).

[63] Michael von Brück, "Buddhist Śūnyatā and Christian Trinity: The Emerging Holistic Paradigm," in Knitter and Corless, *Buddhist Emptiness and Christian Trinity*, 44–66; Paul Ingram, "A Response to Michael von Brück," in Knitter and Corless, *Buddhist Emptiness and Christian Trinity*, 67–74.

[64] Donald Mitchell, "Trinity and Buddhist Cosmology," in *Buddhist Christian Studies* 18 (1998): 169–80.

[65] See J. S. Cleary, "Trikāya and Trinity: The Mediation of the Absolute," *Buddhist Christian Studies* 16 (1986): 63–78; and Ruben L. F. Habito, "The Trikāya Doctrine in Buddhism," *Buddhist Christian Studies* 16 (1986): 52–62, for different approaches

perspectives and the possibilities they open for Trinitarian theology in the concluding section of this essay.

Jung Young Lee (1935–96), a Korean-born theologian who studied and taught in the United States, proposes an alternative view of the Trinity taking key concepts in East Asian thought for its philosophical infrastructure.[66] He takes the yin–yang symbol, a well-known feature of East Asian views of reality, examining its duality-in-nonduality, and nonduality-in-duality, as a key for elucidating Christian understanding of the Trinity, as well as embodying the Trinity in our own individual Christian life, in our prayer, in family life, church life, and life in society as a whole. Lee presents his proposals fully aware of the inherent limitations of his work as a theologian face to face with divine mystery. What he offers are mere "re-imaginations of the divine mystery from an Asian perspective," recalling the cautionary note from the *Tao Te Ching (Daodejing)*: "The tao that can be told is not the eternal Tao; the name that can be named is not the eternal Name."[67] This stance of awe before the mystery is what the theologian (i.e., one who engages in *God-talk*) needs to maintain while engaging in one's tasks, so as not to be carried away by the dazzling ideas and enticing words that come out of our speculative minds.

Making an exception to our self-imposed limitations confining our scope to Asian traditions, here I include two recent works of North American authors emerging out of their engagement with currents of philosophical and scientific thought that seek to enrich Christian approaches to Trinitarian doctrine. One is *The Holy Trinity and the Law of Three: Discovering the Radical Truth at the Heart of Christianity,* by Cynthia Bourgeault, Episcopal priest and spiritual writer.[68] Inspired by the work of G. I. Gurdjieff (1866–1949), she explores the latter's thought on *laws of world creation and world maintenance*, and highlights what is called the Law of Three, deriving from this her key proposals for a reconfiguration of our Christian understanding of Trinity as a living dynamic reality that can reinvigorate our way

to the subject. See also James L. Fredericks, "Primordial Vow: Reflections on the Holy Trinity in Light of Dialogue with Pure Land Buddhism," in Phan, *The Cambridge Companion to the Trinity*, 325–43.

[66] Jung Young Lee, *The Trinity in Asian Perspective* (Nashville: Abingdon Press, 1996).

[67] Lee, *The Trinity in Asian Perspective*, 212. See also Heup Young Kim, "The Tao in Confucianism and Taoism: the Trinity in East Asian Perspective," in Phan, *The Cambridge Companion to the Trinity*, 293–308.

[68] Cynthia Bourgeault, *The Holy Trinity and the Law of Three: Discovering the Radical Truth at the Heart of Christianity* (Boston: Shambala, 2013).

of living our Christian faith, in a way that is attuned to the compassionate power at work at the heart of the universe.

The World in the Trinity: Open-Ended Systems in Science and Religion, by Joseph Bracken, a noted process philosopher/theologian, is another work that invites a closer look.[69] Bracken has written several other important works addressing the Trinitarian theme from a process perspective, and this latest incorporates many of the ideas developed in his earlier writings.[70] Bracken's work seeks to integrate the insights of process thought, systems theory, and the discoveries of contemporary science with Trinitarian doctrine, opening up new avenues in rethinking traditional Catholic notions in the light of a new cosmological and ecological vision. The works of Bourgeault and Bracken deserve closer examination and evaluation for their contribution toward a broader and deeper appreciation of the Triune mystery in the midst of our fragmented, broken earthly existence, leading those of us who would listen toward ways of healing and into deeper communion.

Inconclusive Reflections:
Exploring New Horizons in Trinitarian Theology

The early community of believers who gathered together as church (*ekklesia* = assembly) sought ways to articulate the ineffable mystery that they encountered in and through the person of Jesus Christ, propelled on by power of the Spirit unleashed at Pentecost. Jesus Christ is the Beloved Son sent by that undisclosed mystery that he called Father, who is the creator of the universe, from whom proceeds the Spirit that enlightened their minds and set their hearts on fire with divine love. God is One, and God is Three. The Father is God, Jesus Christ is God, the Holy Spirit is God. Jesus Christ is fully God, and fully human. The Father, the Son, and the Holy Spirit are not the same. Yet all the same, God is One.[71]

The articulations of the faith that the Christian community agreed on in formal councils, which became the creedal statements of Christian tradi-

---

[69] Joseph Bracken, *The World in the Trinity: Open-Ended Systems in Science and Religion* (Minneapolis: Fortress Press, 2014).

[70] See also Marc A. Pugliese, *The One, the Many and the Trinity: Joseph Bracken and the Challenge of Process Metaphysics* (Washington, DC: Catholic University of America Press, 2011) for a book-length critical assessment of Bracken's work.

[71] See Stephen Bullivant, *The Trinity: How Not to Be a Heretic* (New York, Paulist Press, 2014) for a remarkably lucid exposition of orthodox Christian Trinitarian doctrine.

tion handed down to us, were derived from the Hellenistic cultural matrix and the Greek philosophical thought framework, which became underpinnings of Western cultures. Now that the ever-growing numbers of the Christian population are from a widely diverse variety of cultures beyond the Western, the question of how to articulate their faith in ways consonant with their own diverse cultures comes to the fore as a vital task in an emerging World Christianity. And as the diversification of the expressions of Christian faith in various cultures becomes an accepted reality in a veritable *World* Christianity, these new and diverse expressions may serve to enhance, renew, and deepen the way Christians throughout the world understand and appreciate key doctrines of creation, incarnation, Trinity, eschatology, etc., in a way that extends beyond the particularities of the cultures from which they originate. The various attempts at articulating the Triune mystery in the light of encounters with the world's religions (as well as philosophical traditions and scientific thought) surveyed above are initial examples of how this enhancement, renewal, and deepening might happen.

In concluding this essay, reflecting on the first section, I would like to suggest a way of addressing the dilemma that serves as the initial impetus for the enterprise of the Christian theology of religions: how can we fully and wholeheartedly affirm (Axiom A) the uniqueness and universality of the revelatory message and the salvific grace brought to humankind in Jesus Christ, and *at the same time* (Axiom B) fully and wholeheartedly maintain an openness to accepting and welcoming other religions and their adherents in their Otherness (eschewing colonial/imperialistic attitudes and proselytizing intent), in a way that grants the possibility of authentic revelatory truth and salvific grace in them, thus making it imperative for Christians to engage them in dialogue and cooperative ventures for mutual learning and benefit? My suggestion, inspired by Trinitarian doctrine, is what I would like to call a Nicene–Chalcedonian proposal, taking off *in an analogous way* from the pronouncements of two early councils. In short, the Council of Nicaea proclaimed that God is One and *at the same time* Three, without mitigating the significance of *one* or of *three*. The Council of Chalcedon proclaimed that Jesus Christ is the same person who is fully divine and fully human, without mitigating the significance of *divine* or of *human*. In an analogous way, we can fully and wholeheartedly accept Axiom A and Axiom B, without mitigating the significance of either, and without falling into the inherent pitfalls of exclusivism, inclusivism, and pluralism.

With regard to the second section, seeking to contribute in this direction, I would like to lay down the bare outlines of a theological project I intend to follow up in greater detail in the future, taking Zen Buddhist practice as my launching pad.[72] I have already described elsewhere the contours of the path of Zen practice, which entail (1) stopping the discursive mind in its tracks and being enveloped in ineffable mystery, (2) a return to immediate and intimate experience of the fullness of the *here and now* wherein the barrier between *self* and *not self* is overcome, and (3) an opening of the heart and mind to an infinite ocean of compassion for all beings. This is a threefold movement that I refer to as an experiential entry into a Triune mystery.[73] Does this, and if so how does all this, relate and refer to the experience of the ineffable mystery in Jesus Christ through the spirit of love articulated in the creedal statements of the worldwide Christian community? This is the theological task I intend to pursue, taking hints from Mahāyāna Buddhist dialectics as a possible way of articulating the ineffable.

For this task, I intend to stand on the shoulders of two (still largely unheralded) philosophical and theological giants, whose works continue to provide an inspiration and a challenge. One is John P. Keenan, who remarks,

> Just as Plato did for the Fathers of the early church and Aristotle for
> Aquinas, Mahāyāna opens avenues of thought and questioning for
> contemporary theologians that will gift our cultures with new theo-
> logical insight into the meaning of Christ's presence to and among
> human beings.[74]

Another is Joseph O'Leary, who has written a trilogy of volumes that lay out how theological language may be validly and effectively used to convey the realm of the ineffable in ways that direct us right back to the experience of mystery, learning from the deconstructive axe of Mahāyāna Buddhist

---

[72] Ruben L. F. Habito, *Healing Breath: Zen for Christians and Buddhists in a Wounded World* (Boston: Wisdom Publications, 2006).

[73] Ruben L. F. Habito, "Zen Experience of the Triune Mystery," in *Living Zen, Loving God* (Boston: Wisdom Publications, 2004), 103–10.

[74] John P. Keenan, "A Mahāyāna Theology of the Real Presence of Christ in the Eucharist," *Buddhist Christian Studies* 24/1 (2004): 89–100, excerpted in David R. Brockman and Ruben L. F. Habito, eds., *The Gospel among Religions* (Maryknoll, NY: Orbis Books, 2010), 194. See also John P. Keenan, the *Meaning of Christ: A Mahāyāna Theology* (Maryknoll, NY: Orbis Books, 1989); John P. Keenan and Linda K. Keenan, *I am/No Self: A Christian Commentary on the Heart Sutra* (Grand Rapids, MI: Wm. B. Eerdmans Publishing, 2011); and John P. Keenan, *The Emptied Christ of Philippians: Mahāyāna Meditations* (Eugene, OR: Wipf and Stock, forthcoming).

philosophy and its teaching on the two levels of (conventional and ultimate) truth as reference points.[75]

Theology, *God-talk*, seeks to articulate that which by its very nature is beyond the reach of the discursive mind but is directly and unmistakably given in the human experience of ineffable mystery. Yes, ineffable, and yet articulate we must, using our clumsy words, prodded on by faith seeking understanding. At best its outcome can be likened to the proverbial finger pointing to the moon, pointing, that is, beyond itself toward that shining brilliance illuminating the darkness, pointing us beyond our often ineffectual and fumbling words and the concepts we use as we try to name that which cannot be named, and usher us toward an ever deeper experiential encounter with this divine mystery ever beyond reach, yet always in our midst, "more intimate to me than I am to myself."[76]

---

[75] Joseph O'Leary, *Questioning Back: The Overcoming of Metaphysics in the Christian Tradition* (Minneapolis: Winston Seabury, 1985); Joseph O'Leary, *Religious Pluralism and Christian Truth* (Edinburgh: Edinburgh University Press, 1996); Joseph O'Leary, *Conventional and Ultimate Truth: A Key for Fundamental Theology* (Notre Dame, IN: University of Notre Dame Press, 2015).

[76] Augustine, *Confessions*, bk. 3, chap. 6.

10

JESUS BEYOND THE WEST: CHRISTOLOGICAL CONVERSATIONS IN THE AGE OF WORLD CHRISTIANITY

Anh Q. Tran

The New Contextual Christologies

More than two millennia after his birth, Jesus of Nazareth continues to spark imagination across generational and geographical lines. Various portraits of Jesus Christ, biblically, theologically, historically, and culturally, have been offered as responses to the question Jesus posed to his disciples: "Who do you say that I am?" (Mark 8:29).[1] From New Testament descriptions to the confessions in the fourth and fifth centuries and contemporary expressions, the many reflections on the person, life, and work of Jesus have been formulated into many Christolo*gies*. If Christology is the experience of Jesus seeking understanding, we can speak of Christology in a plural sense. Diverse understandings and interpretations of Christ, hence Christolo*gies*, are attempts to make Jesus Christ meaningful and relevant for committed Christians and other people of goodwill in the midst of different contexts while trying to maintain fidelity to tradition.

Prior to the historical critical studies of the life of Jesus beginning in the eighteenth century, it was generally assumed that there is but one Christology in Western theology—that which is derived from the Chalcedonian confession: *true God and true man*. This approach, called *Christology from Above*, was the dominant orientation of the meaning of the Christ event (i.e., his life, death, and resurrection). Viewed from the confession of faith in Jesus as Lord and Savior, the New Testament was believed to offer a unified representation of Christ. The differences between the gospels were harmonized into one coherent narrative of Jesus Christ, as evidenced in many

---

[1] The classic survey on the subject remains Jaroslav Pelikan, *Jesus through Centuries: His Place in the History of Culture* (New Haven, CT: Yale University Press, 1999).

popular *lives* of Jesus. This was also reflected in the Christological controversies in the early church, and eventually culminated in the pronouncements from Nicea to Chalcedon regarding the person and nature of Christ and his relationship with God the Father. For the next thousand years, Christological treatises were more or less expositions and commentaries on this basic orientation and understanding of Christ.[2]

Since the Enlightenment, however, there began another approach to Christ, eventually known as *Christology from Below*. Biblical scholars and theologians investigated the data from the gospel accounts and creedal confessions to see if they were compatible with the history of Jesus. The so-called quests of the historical Jesus are attempts to go beyond the traditional confessions to ascertain the validity of the New Testament witnesses. Rather than identifying a single Christology, multiple portraits of Jesus are studied in their own right. Each gospel offers a legitimate theological interpretation of the Christ event.[3] Even the letters of Paul and other New Testament writings (such as Hebrews) present their Christological perspectives. The Jewishness of Jesus is duly noted, and studies on the apocryphal gospels continue to bring out fresh, often sensational, interpretations of Jesus.

A sound historical basis for Christological beliefs is thought to give believers and critics alike a fair and accurate account of Jesus Christ. The main aim is to focus on the human person of Jesus, how he lived, and what he did, rather than on the divine Christ confessed by the church. The task of Christology, therefore, is to offer a rational and historical support for the doctrine of Christ. In the end, one does not have to choose between these approaches. The Jesus of history need not be separated from the Christ of faith as theologians of recent times have argued. A high Christology informs us of the faith in Christ; a low Christology deals with the context(s) from which faith arises. Both approaches are valid and complementary to each other. One emphasizes the *sameness* of Jesus and the other *differences* in our understanding of Jesus. Jesus has been studied in his own context and the contexts of believers—thus, contextual Christolog*ies*.

---

[2] Of course, one should be reminded that Chalcedon itself was an attempt to bridge the divide between Alexandrian and Antiochene Christologies. It was not entirely successful, because (1) it did not resolve differences in the church, and (2) it was not able to explain just who the *person* was—a problem that plagued most of the Middle Ages theological debates.

[3] For example, the Suffering Messiah in Mark, the King of the Jews in Matthew, the Compassionate Savior in Luke-Acts, or the Word of Life in John.

The creative interactions between the biblical text and the contemporary context(s) allow the inquirer to engage the New Testament with specific questions arising from his or her contemporary context. The result is a fusion of two worlds—the biblical world and the contemporary social, cultural, and religious realities. A contextual Christology can be seen as an interpretive dance between text and context. Although the biblical text is fixed (i.e., canonized), the context remains changing, allowing for multiple interpretations. Since no interpreter stands in a neutral location, their interpretation of Jesus's life and work would bear the imprint of social, historical, economic, political, religious, and other life contexts of the interpreter. The goal of contextual Christology is not simply to uncover the meaning of Christ but also to make him accessible and relevant for the contemporary audience.

The contextual approach to Christology is a method often favored by theologians from the *Majority World* or *Global South*. Following the postcolonial trends in the 1950s and 1960s, these theologians began to explore questions related to their Christological concerns. The Christ that many Majority World Christians received from the missionaries was too Eurocentric, and became less relevant in their new indigenization and social movements. New theological voices began to be heard around the globe, from Latin America to Africa and Asia. In Latin America, liberation theologians tried to understand Jesus from the reality of social economic inequality: Christ is a friend and a liberator of the poor.[4] African theologians concentrated on viewing Christ from a cultural and familial lens: Christ is the life-giver, mediator, and leader par excellence.[5] Working within diverse cultural and religious backgrounds, Asian theologians tried to make sense of the uniqueness of Christ in relationship to the other world religious

---

[4] See Juan Miguez Bonino, *Faces of Jesus: Latin American Christologies* (Maryknoll, NY: Orbis Books, 1984); Donald E. Waltermire, *The Liberation Christologies of Leonardo Boff and Jon Sobrino: Latin American Contributions to Contemporary Christology* (Lanham, MD: University Press of America, 1993); Carlos R. Piar, *Jesus and Liberation: A Critical Analysis of the Christology of Latin American Liberation Theology* (New York: Peter Lang, 1994).

[5] See J. N. K. Mugambi and Laurenti Magesa, eds., *Jesus in African Christianity: Experimentation and Diversity in African Christology* (Nairobi, Kenya: Initiatives, 1989); Robert Schreiter, ed., *Faces of Jesus in Africa* (Maryknoll, NY: Orbis Books, 1991); Kawame Bediako, *Jesus and the Gospel in Africa: History and Experience* (Maryknoll, NY: Orbis Books, 2004); Diane B. Stinton, *Jesus of Africa: Voice of Contemporary African Christology* (Maryknoll, NY: Orbis Books, 2004); Clifton R. Clarke, *African Christology: Jesus in Post-Missionary African Christianity* (Eugene, OR: Wipf & Stock, 2011).

figures and founders (e.g., Buddha, Krishna, Confucius, or Muhammad): Christ amid other Asian ways, truths, and lights.[6] In these conversations, even the non-Christians joined in: there are visual and textual portraits of Jesus from Buddhist, Hindu, Muslim and Jewish perspectives.[7]

Due to the diversity of these Majority World Christologies, it is beyond the scope of this survey to evaluate adequately every individual proposal.[8] Instead, I would acknowledge the shared interests, cross-conversations, and mutual influences between Christologies generated from Latin America, Africa, and Asia that have reached beyond their geographical origins and are significant to understand and interpret World Christianity today. By presenting Jesus Christ from three perspectives of liberation, inculturation, and interreligious, I pay tribute to the *triple dialogue* with the poor, the cultures, and the religions of Asia—a theological approach advocated by the Federation of Asian Bishops' Conferences and a favorite method of Peter C. Phan for the past two decades.

Liberation Christologies

Liberation theologies originated in social movements in Latin America where theologians reflected on socioeconomic and political concerns. In his classic work, *A Theology of Liberation*, Gustavo Gutierrez sees salvation as liberation: from economic and political oppression, from dehumanization, and from sin (both personal and structural).[9] In other parts of the world, liberation theology addresses other situations of oppression and exclusion, for example, feminist theologians denounce sexism and patriarchy, black theologians target racism, Korean Minjung theologians fight for political inclusion, and Indian Dalit theologians oppose caste.

---

[6] For example, R. S. Sugirtharajah, ed. *Asian Faces of Jesus* (Maryknoll, NY: Orbis Books, 1993); Michael Amaladoss, *The Asian Jesus* (Maryknoll, NY: Orbis Books, 2006); John Parratt, *The Other Jesus: Christology in Asian Perspective* (Frankfurt am Main, Germany: Peter Lang, 2012).

[7] Gregory A. Barker, *Jesus in the World's Faiths* (Maryknoll, NY: Orbis Books, 2005).

[8] Interested readers can consult, for example, Volker Kuster, *The Many Faces of Jesus Christ: Intercultural Christology* (London: SCM Press; Maryknoll, NY: Orbis Books, 2001); Martien E. Brinkman, *The Non-Western Jesus: Jesus as Bodhisattava, Avatara, Guru, Prophet, Ancestor of Healer?* (London: Equinox, 2009); Gene L. Green, Stephen T. Pardue, and K. K. Yeo, eds., *Jesus without Borders* (Grand Rapids, MI: Wm. B. Eerdmans Publishing, 2014).

[9] Gustavo Gutierrez, *A Theology of Liberation* (Maryknoll, NY: Orbis Books, 1988).

Liberation Christologies focus on the words and deeds of Jesus as reported in the Synoptic Gospels. Jesus is seen as the advocate for the voiceless, the friend of the socially marginalized, the healer and reconciler, champion of equality and social justice. Jesus as the liberator ushers in the Reign of God—a new reality and social order—with fulfillment taking place in history and in the eschatological future.

Jesus as Companion of the Oppressed and the Marginalized

In the gospel narratives, wherever Jesus found social exclusion and marginalization by religious leaders and institutions, he denounced oppressive practices. He insisted that the application of the Torah should not be burdensome to the poor, and he frequently performed acts of mercy (through healing) on the Sabbath. His view of table fellowship is that of inclusion: everyone should be welcome into the banquet of God—the blind, the lame, the unclean, the prostitute and tax collector, and even non-Jews. The healing of the leper (Mark 1:40–45), the demoniac (Mark 5:1–20), or the hemorrhagic woman (Mark 5:24–34) are Jesus's acts of reintegration of marginalized individuals into their social and religious world.

Feminist theologians are pioneers in claiming that Jesus not only challenged the social institutions but also the oppressive underlying beliefs of these institutions. Jesus's rejection of divorce, his association with marginalized women (e.g., the Samaritan woman of John 4, the unnamed sinner of Luke 7), and the inclusion of woman disciples are cited as example of Jesus's liberation of sexism. In addition, women in the developing countries are identified with the poor and marginalized in a unique way: poor women are often at the bottom of the social scale and suffer multiple level of oppression. Sexism heightens the effect of poverty since many girls and women, especially in rural areas, have little education. Many are illiterate and have no job skills that can advance them in society. Thus, liberation theology from a woman's perspective also demands that actions are taken to advance the cause of woman—to liberate them from the mistreatment by a patriarchal ideology. Jesus the liberator is also Jesus the social reformer.[10]

---

[10] The literature on feminist approach to theology and Christology are many. Here, in the interest of space, I refer only to recent works those from Majority World perspectives: Kwok Pui-Lan, *Introducing Asian Feminist Theology* (Sheffield, UK: Sheffield Academic Press, 2000), Kwok Pui-Lan, ed., *Hope Abundant: Third World and Indigenous Women's Theology* (Maryknoll, NY: Orbis Books, 2010); María Pilar Aquino and María José Rosado Nunes, eds., *Feminist Intercultural Theology: Latina Explorations for a Just World* (Maryknoll, NY: Orbis Books, 2007).

Social transformation is a frequent theme in liberation Christologies: Jesus's fellowship with the marginalized and social outcast finds strong resonance, not only among poor Latin Americans, but also among Africans and Asians with their deep roots in communal cultures. The suffering of the poor and oppressed is felt collectively in the case of a whole people or social class, resulting in grassroot movements representing the consciousness of a group of people who are deprived, persecuted, and marginalized—whether political, economic, social, religious, or gender based. Two particular Asian liberation theologies have had a considerable impact on local social transformation: Minjung theology in Korea and Dalit theology in India. Because they are responses to specific factors within their marginalization, these theologies are much more contextual and localized. Nevertheless, the lessons from these specific cases can be extended to other situations where political actions warrant.

Jesus of the Multitude

Minjung theology (Korean: *minjung sinhak*) emerged in South Korea in the early 1970s as a Christian response to social injustice. It claims to represent those on the margin of society, hence the name *theology of the common people*.[11] Although its roots can be traced to the oppression and colonization by the Chinese and Japanese, Minjung theology attracted attention because of its sociopolitical stand during the military regime of Park Chung-hee (1962–79).

Central to Minjung theology is the experience of *han*, the prevalent mood of resentment, repressed anger, and helplessness, which propels desire for a better future. *Han* is the people's lived experience of oppression and defeat. It was felt individually and collectively when Korea experienced rapid economic growth, while facing massive injustice and oppression by the government in the 1970s. This was the context in which Korean theologians read the Bible.

Elements of a Minjung Christology can be found in the 1973 *Theological Declaration of Korean Christians*. Led by the biblical scholar Ahn

---

[11] Minjung is a difficult concept to render in European languages. It combines of two Chinese characters *Min* (民, *min*, people) and *Jung* (衆, *zhong*, crowd, mass). Taking together, it means the majority, ordinary people. The early writings of Minjung theology can be found in Committee on Theological Concerns of the Christian Conference of Asia (CCA), *Minjung Theology: People as the Subjects of History* (Maryknoll, NY: Orbis Books, 1983). The movement gained currency in the 1980s and the 1990s, but in recent years, it has been quite down.

Byung-mu, Korean theologians presented Jesus as the messiah, a defender and champion of the poor and oppressed people. Because of his confrontation of political structure, he suffered a violent death. Nevertheless, his resurrection can transform and liberate the people. The authors of this declaration called on Christians to follow the example of Jesus, living in solidarity with the poor and oppressed, working for transformation of society through political action.[12] Ahn Byung-mu takes the mass (*ochlos*), the unorganized crowd around Jesus, differentiated from the disciples, religious leaders, or the ruling class, as the subject of Jesus's ministry.[13] He sees an explicit relationship between the multitude and Jesus, that of suffering. For Ahn, Jesus is not merely representing the Minjung, "he identifies himself with the Minjung. He exists for no other than for the Minjung."[14]

Minjung Christology sees Jesus as the embodiment of the suffering of the masses, and his death and resurrection as symbols of *Minjung*'s political suffering and striving for justice.[15] The life and action of Jesus is interpreted as manifestation of God's solidarity with the people, especially the underdogs. Salvation history is found within the historical struggle of the ordinary people. Like other liberation theologians, Minjung proponents see the Reign of God as a historical reality, one that can be attained by social transformation.

Jesus of the Outcastes

Similarly in India, Dalit theology arose as a theology of the outcastes. The term *dalit*, derived from a Sanskrit term meaning *crushed* or *suppressed*,

---

[12] The full text says in part, "Jesus the Messiah, our Lord, lived and dwelt among the oppressed, poverty-stricken and sick in Judaea. He boldly confronted Pontius Pilate, a representative of the Roman Empire, and he was crucified while witnessing to the truth. He had risen from the dead, releasing power to transform and set the people free. We resolve that we will follow the footsteps of our Lord, living among our oppressed and poor people, standing against political oppression, and participation in the transformation of history, for this is the only way to the Messianic kingdom." Quoted in Parratt, *The Other Jesus*, 110.

[13] Ahn Byung-mu, "Jesus and the Minjung in the Gospel of Mark," in CCA, *Minjung Theology*, 138–52; Ahn Byung-mu, "Jesus and People (Minjung), in Sugirth-arajah, *Asian Faces of Jesus Asian Faces of Jesus*, 163–72.

[14] Ahn, "Jesus and People," 169.

[15] As other Minjung theologians have claimed. See Jin-Kwan Kwon, "The Minjung (Multitude), Historical Symbol of Jesus Christ," *Asian Journal of Theology* 24/1 (2010): 153–71; Yong-Bok Kim, "Minjung Social Biography and Theology," *Asian Journal of Theology* 1/2 (1987): 523–30.

has been adopted as a self-designation by those who were formerly considered *untouchable* according to the Hindu caste system.[16] These people were considered ritually impure, often taking menial jobs, and banned from social participation in traditional Indian society. Discrimination against and subjugation by the majority Hindus prompted many to convert to Buddhism, Sikhism, and Christianity.[17]

Notwithstanding Christian rhetoric of equality, Dalit Christians continue to experience social discrimination and unequal treatment within churches, especially in rural areas. They have not been able to escape the caste system altogether. Christian leaders do not endorse the system, but they accept and tolerate the status quo. The double oppression that many Dalits feel—both inside and outside of the church—prompts them to look for social–cultural change, followed by economic development and political participation. Drawing from their history, myth, folklore, poetry, and song, Dalit's theological reflections on the experience of suffering have resulted in creating a Dalit consciousness and subsequently a Dalit theology.

Dalit thinkers link the gospel message to the history of socioreligious revolutionary movements in India. Many prominent non-Christian Indians, including Mahatma Gandhi and B. R. Ambedkar, were inspired by Jesus's words, actions, and life in their own struggles for freedom from foreign oppression. Several Dalit theologians have made important contributions by claiming that Jesus is relevant, not only for Indian Christianity but also the Indian society at large, in their struggles to build an equitable, new humanity. Arvin P. Nirmal claims not only that Jesus is on the side the Dalits; he is the *Dalit* God, the servant God.[18] M. E. Prabhakar sees his suffering on the cross as the appropriate symbol for *dalitness* of the divine–human relation.[19] Sebastian Kappen highlights the relevance of the gospel message as a critique of

---

[16] These people, constituting about 16 percent of the Indian population, are called by various names: officially scheduled castes by the Indian government, formerly, *harijans* (children of God) by Gandhi, or *avarna* (no caste). The term also encompasses other ethnic minorities groups called scheduled tribes.

[17] On Dalit history and its involvement with Christianity, see James Massey, *A Concise History of the Dalits* (Delhi: ISPCK, 1989); James Massey, ed., *Indigenous People, Dalits* (Dehli: ISPCK, 1990); John Webster, *The Christian Dalits: A History* (Delhi: ISPCK, 1994).

[18] Most of the Dalit literature is not widely disseminated outside of India. Here I rely on the summary by John Parratt, "Recent Writing on Dalit Theology," *International Review of Mission* 86/329 (1994): 329–38; also see Parratt, *The Other Jesus*, 103–9, at 105–6.

[19] As summarized by Parratt, *The Other Jesus*, 107.

the Hindu worldview. Jesus's concern for the individual person rather than the social, religious, and political institution of his days can inspire all Indians to work toward a social and cultural transformation.[20] To these theologians, salvation is seen in term of humanization.

While both Minjung and Dalit theologies arose from different social economic and political contexts, they are a theology of subversion, sharing a common concern for the marginalized and oppressed people in their respective societies.[21] However, there is a tendency in both theologies to read the gospel as a political manifesto and to reduce Jesus Christ to be one of the Minjung or the Dalit. Like most liberation theologies of the 1970s and 1980s, these particularizations of the gospel message to a social agenda run the risk of making them less relevant once the social situation has improved and political rights are obtained.[22]

Inculturation Christologies

In artistic and pictorial representation, it is not uncommon to see a portrait of Jesus with features of an African, or Asian, or Native American, or member of other indigenous groups. Nevertheless, European portraits of Jesus are not yet out of favor in the Majority World. Indeed, there may be cultural wars on which is the *real* Jesus—one with European facial features and clothing disseminated by the missionaries, or one with indigenous characteristics offered by local artists.

Yet inculturation is more than remaking Jesus in the images of the local people. Theologians also focus on using categories from their social–cultural contexts to theologize about Jesus, and build up their own

---

[20] Sebastian Kappen, "Jesus and Transculturation," in Sugirtharajah, *Asian Faces of Jesus*, 173–89.

[21] For example, Jinkwan Kwon, *Towards Theology of Justice and Peace: Minjung—Dalit Theological Dialogue* (Bangalore, India: BTESSC, 2012).

[22] This might be the factor why Latin American liberation theology and Korean Minjung theology have less impact today than when they were introduced forty years ago. The case of Dalit theology is still open, but one does not know whether it is capableof transforming Indian society in the near future, especially in the backlash of Hindutva political control. Recent works on Dalit theology include Sathianathan Clarke, Deenabandhu Manchala, Philip Vinod Peacock, eds., *Dalit Theology in the Twenty-first Century: Discordant Voices, Discerning Pathways* (Oxford: Oxford University Press, 2006); Peniel Rajkumar, *Dalit Theology and Dalit Liberation: Problems, Paradigms and Possibilities* (Burlington, VT: Ashgate, 2010); Keith Hebden, *Dalit Theology and Christian Anarchism* (Burlington, VT: Ashgate, 2011).

Christology that integrates and makes meaningful the Christ event in the lives of their people. Since family and community are central to the life of many Africans, Asians, Native Americans, and other indigenous populations in Oceania, it is natural that their theologians favor Jesus as a kinship figure or a community leader. Jesus has been depicted as an ancestor, an elder brother, a chief, etc. In the following sections, I would like to offer a few portraits of these familiar images.

Jesus as Intimate Family Member: Elder Brother, Mother, Lover

A popular description of Jesus in African (and by extension Asian) context is that of an elder brother.[23] This image of Jesus flows from the role of the elder brother in the family: often as a stand-in for the father when he is absent, a mediator between younger siblings and parents and among the siblings, defender of siblings in outside quarrels, bearer of responsibility for their actions, etc. As the "first-born within a large family" (Rom. 8:29) Jesus naturally fits this familial profile as a mediator and representative. For many Africans, Jesus is the *big brother* who cares for them, protects them, and defends them; he is their model and their advocate. Like them, he also goes through the rites of passage that mark life's important moments: at birth (baptism), at puberty (bar-mitzvah), and at death (funeral). The only exception, of course, is that Jesus was not married and had no children of his own.

African feminists are drawn more toward another familial image: Jesus as a mother.[24] For many, the image of motherhood bespeaks of one who nurtures life and provides selfless giving. In the wake of many health crises (Ebola, HIV/AIDS), famines, wars, and other atrocities, motherhood stands out as the symbol of love, mercy, and compassion. The life-giving qualities of provision, protection, guidance, loving kindness, nurturing, grace, and mercy, are often associated with the ideal motherhood and, in turn, are transferred in the person of Jesus. Jesus's compassion, affection, and tenderness for people around him reflect a motherly concern. Here, Jesus is not portrayed as a female, but rather the embodiment of those qualities of mother.

Another image of Jesus popular among women is that of a loved one.[25] In some African (and traditional Asian) cultures, women have no identity of

---

[23] Stinton, *Jesus of Africa*, 146–52.

[24] Anne Nasimiyu Wasike, "Christology and an African Woman's Experience," in Mugambi and Magesa, *Jesus in African Christianity*, 123–35, discussed in Stinton, *Jesus of Africa*, 152–60.

[25] Stinton, *Jesus of Africa*, 160–64.

their own, except in relationship with a man of their life—father, husband, or son. In their disappointment in their relations with various male figures, the ideal man whom they can trust and depend on is Jesus Christ, the perfect companion, provider, and protector, who complements the biblical revelation of God as unconditional love.

Jesus as Ancestor

In traditional African and Asian societies, the family circle includes the living and the dead. Ancestors are not dead and forgotten members of the family but are *spiritualized* ones, serving as bridges between the physical and spiritual worlds. They are part of an extended community encompassing the living and the dead. Being mediators and a watchful presence over the community, ancestors still exercise influence on communal affairs.

By virtue of his death and resurrection, Jesus enters the realm of the ancestors who mediate life and give blessings upon the descendants (in this case, his followers, Christians).[26] Charles Nyamiti sees in Jesus the following characteristics of the ancestor: kinship and source of life for earthly relatives, a supernatural status acquired at death, mediation between God and humanity, a moral exemplary life, frequent communication through prayer and oblations.[27] According to the traditional view, the ancestors are a reservoir of life force, or living energy from which the living can benefit. Since the ancestors are often models of behavior for the living, Jesus's life serves to guide Christians in moral and selfless acts, confirming African values of hospitality and care for the downtrodden.

Nevertheless, since the traditional description of ancestor falls short of Jesus Christ, Bénézet Bujot considers Jesus as the proto-ancestor.[28] As the first born of all creation, Jesus's place among the ancestors is unique. He not only holds authority over other malevolent ancestors and spirits, but also transcends all human relationships enabling him to relate to people of all tribes and nations, and becomes the common life-giving spirit for all. Furthermore, as the mediator to the Father (cf. John 14:6) Jesus

---

[26] See Charles Nyamiti, *Christ as Our Ancestor: Christology From an African Perspective* (Gweru, Zimbabwe: Mambo Press, 1984); François Kabasélé, "Christ as Ancestor and Elder Brother," in Schreiter, *Faces of Jesus in Africa*, 116–27.

[27] Nyamiti, "African Christology Today," 19.

[28] Bujot uses the term *proto-ancestor* to distinguish between Jesus and the other ancestor. See Bénézet Bujo, *African Theology in Its Social Context* (Maryknoll, NY: Orbis Books, 1992), 80.

brings people, their prayers, and offerings to God, joining the human and divine together. Through the mediation of Jesus, God communicates with humanity and, by extension, to the rest of creation.

The description of Jesus as ancestor also finds resonance among many Asians, for whom ancestor worship or veneration[29] is part of their cultural social fabric. Peter C. Phan's portrait of Jesus as the eldest brother and ancestor is an attempt to situate Jesus within the Vietnamese Confucian worldview, where filial devotion is significant.[30] A mark of filial piety is performing the obligation duties of children toward parents (e.g., obedience, loving service, and care) when they are alive and after they pass away (e.g., proper burial, memorial service). Among all family members, the eldest son has a special responsibility to fulfill these duties, especially in his role as a representative of his family in worship ceremonies. In his function as the high priest, Jesus represents all of his brothers and sisters to offer sacrifices, thus fulfilling the role of a first-born Asian son. Furthermore, Phan argues that through his death and resurrection, Jesus himself also joins the world of the ancestors and becomes the ancestor par excellence.[31]

Jesus as Leader: Chief and King

This metaphor is an attempt to render the New Testament concept of Jesus as Lord (*kurios*) to its cultural equivalent. For many Africans (and Native Americans by association), the word *Lord* might recall the colonial experience of subjugation in a master–slave relationship, and thus, they prefer to use a native image that reflects their experience—that of a chief or tribal leader. Jesus is seen as a chief because he is a hero, the son and emissary of the chief, a strong man, a generous and wise leader, and the reconciling mediator.[32]

Some African theologians apply the title *king* to Jesus as an alternative for chief. This image is consistent with the biblical portraits of Jesus as a *king*

---

[29] The distinction between worship (*latria*) and veneration (*dulia*) is at the heart of the Chinese Rites Controversy (1645–1743) when Chinese (and other East Asian) Christians were dissuaded from participation in ancestral rites, seeing these rites as violation of the commandment of honor God alone. In traditional Asian cultures, such an attitude did not exist.

[30] Peter Phan, "Jesus as the Eldest Son and Ancestor," in *Christianity with an Asian Face: Asian American Theology in the Making* (Maryknoll, NY: Orbis Books, 2003), 125–45.

[31] Phan, "Jesus as the Eldest Son and Ancestor," 140–43.

[32] François Kabasélé, "Christ as Chief," in Schreiter, *Faces of Jesus in Africa*, 103–15.

of the Jews, whose kingdom is not of this world (John 18:33–37). However, in African cultures, the role of the king might encompass more than a political leader: he is supposed to be the guide, the moral example, the warrior, the master of initiation, the judge, the priest–healer, to name but a few functional images.[33] The main difficulty with this image of chief/king is that in reality, many leaders are tainted with power hungry, corruption, and often act like war lords. Few are truly servant–leaders and stand in solidarity with their people, and thus fall short of the biblical image of the kingship or lordship of Jesus. Furthermore, in the modern world, king and chief are losing their status and may carry a ceremonial role.

Jesus as Healer

Also popular among Africans and Asians is the biblical image of Jesus as a healer.[34] This reflects a world where the presence of spirits is taken for granted. Health in these cultures is holistic, encompassing spiritual, mental, and physical aspects. Aylward Shorter has compared the African medicine man and Jesus, and sees many similarities between the two.[35] Both are concerned about the total well-being of a person not a lack of physical illness. The main difference is that Jesus is the *wounded healer*, bearing the infirmities and the afflictions of his people through the pain and suffering on the cross.

In recent years, Pentecostal and charismatic movements have gained popularity in the Majority World because of their strong emphasis on healing. In presenting Jesus as the divine healer and protector against evil spirits, Pentecostal and charismatic Christians demonstrate the power of God in meeting human need. Faith in prayer and divine healing can lead to a rejection of conventional medicine, which is controversial in some cases.[36]

While the usage of images and metaphors drawn from cultural elements brings many Africans and Asians closer to Jesus, seeing him as their own flesh and blood, each of these metaphors should be understood in an analogical sense. These human figures serve as the starting points for Christological

---

[33] Stinson, *Jesus of Africa*, 178–92.

[34] Cécé Kolie, "Jesus as Healer," in Schreiter, *Faces of Jesus in Africa*, 128–50.

[35] Aylward Shorter, *Jesus and the Witchdoctor: An Approach to Healing and Wholeness* (Maryknoll, NY: Orbis Books, 1985).

[36] Of course, this is not a new phenomenon, the total reliance on the power of prayer and invocation of Jesus's name is also a practice of Christian Scientists and Jehovah's Witnesses.

discussion but not exhaustive of Jesus, who because of his universal significance could be appropriated in each and every culture. Viewing Jesus from
relational perspectives, nevertheless, appeals to the common people, whose
stories and images of Jesus often are told in poetry, song, and dance.

Interreligious Christologies

In Asia, some theologians integrate religious concepts from the many
religions of the continent of Asia. John Paul II's encyclical *Ecclesia in Asia*
acknowledges this reality:

> Asia is also the cradle of the world's major religions—Judaism,
> Christianity, Islam and Hinduism. It is the birthplace of many
> other spiritual traditions such as Buddhism, Taoism, Confu-
> cianism, Zoroastrianism, Jainism, Sikhism and Shintoism. Millions
> also espouse traditional or tribal religions, with varying degrees of
> structured ritual and formal religious teaching. The Church has the
> deepest respect for these traditions and seeks to engage in sincere
> dialogue with their followers.[37]

Dialogue with members of other religions has enriched the imagination of Christian theologians and allowed them to develop Christologies
that are inspired by the highest ideals in Asian philosophical–religious
traditions.[38] While the true divinity and humanity of Jesus Christ must
be affirmed and proclaimed as such, Jesus Christ has been introduced as
Avatar and Guru (Hindu), Bodhisattva and Buddha (Buddhist), Prophet
(Muslim), Sage (Confucian), the Way (Daoist). Indeed, one can detect this
trend in some images of Jesus described in *Ecclesia in Asia*: "The Teacher
of Wisdom, the Healer, the Liberator, the Spiritual Guide, the Enlightened
One, the Compassionate Friend of the Poor, the Good Samaritan, the Good
Shepherd, the Obedient One."[39] Most of these portraits have biblical refer-
ences, but some are drawn from Asian cultural and religious background to

---

[37] *Ecclesia in Asia*, no. 6.

[38] In many Asian religious traditions, the distinction between philosophy and religion or theology does not exist. Questions such as "Is Confucianism (or Buddhism,
Hinduism) a philosophy or religion?" become pointless and reflect a false dichotomy.
Asians tend to view their religions as a way of life, including philosophical and religious
(or theological) elements blending together.

[39] *Ecclesia in Asia*, no. 20.

make Jesus familiar with Asian people. After all, he was born in Asia. In the following sections, I will introduce a few of these Christologies drawn from interreligious encounters; some of these are still in development in relation to the Christian tradition.

Jesus, the Avatar of God

Of many titles attributed to Jesus in India, the word *avatar* deserves a special consideration because it represents the interface between the divine and the human. Avatar, literally *descent*, is used to express the nearness or manifestation of the divine within the world. In Hindu mythology, Brahman manifests itself in three personalities: Brahma (Creator), Vishnu (Protector) and Shiva (Destroyer). Only Vishnu and Shiva are worshipped in India, and their followers have slightly different understandings of the concept of avatar.

In advaitic (nondualistic) philosophy, the Absolute (*Brahman*) is self-sufficient, remote, impersonal, and beyond comprehension (*nirguna Brahman*). However, there is an immanent aspect of Brahman, called *saguna Brahman* or *ishvara*. As the revelation and personal aspect of Brahman, *ishvara* creates and is involved in the world as the guarantor of Brahman's immanence. He is the acting Brahman and yet is distinguished from Brahman in a similar way like the Logos is equal to God but distinguished from God the Father.[40] The *bhakti* (devotional) tradition considers avatars the manifestations of *ishvara* in the world. The divine comes in various forms on various occasions for various purposes, basically to reveal, to express love, and to save. According Vaishnavism, Vishnu can take on a body, becoming an avatar in special occasions of cosmic disorder.[41] In Shaivism there are also stories of divine interventions to protect devotees or to *play* with them, but the divine is too pure to get mixed up with limited humanity in bonds.[42]

The idea of Jesus being an avatar was first proposed by the Hindu thinkers of the nineteenth century when they encountered Christianity.[43]

---

[40] Raimon Pannikar, *The Unknown Christ of Hinduism: Toward an Ecumenical Christophany* (Maryknoll, NY: Orbis, 1981), 152–54.

[41] According to the Vaishnavism, there are nine avatars of Vishnu in history and another one in the future: the Fish, the Tortoise, the Boar, the Man-Lion, the Dwarf, Parasurama, Rama, Krishna, Gautama Buddha, Kalki (still awaited). The role of Krishna as avatar is told in the *Bhavagagita* (chap. 4) and other devotional literature.

[42] The mediation between humanity and the divine is achieved through the guru (spiritual master), who by their virtues and wisdom can lead people to the divine.

[43] Notably through the works of Ramakrishna Paramahamsa (1836–86) and his disciples Swami Vivekenanda (1863–1902), mentioned in Amaladoss, *The Asian Jesus*, 22–23.

A comparison between Krishna, an avatar of Vishnu, and Christ seems to indicate a similarity of function: an immanent God promoting a historical salvific process. In the concept of avatar, God has become human to make human relationship to, and experience of, the divine possible. Furthermore, the divine can be loved and served in its human form in a human way. Salvation is not merely spiritual and other-worldly—it is human and historical. Many holy people are seen as avatars by their disciples, somewhat like the idea of Christian saints.

A crucial question remains as to how the concept of avatar is understood in relation to incarnation.[44] First, since avatar is primarily understood as a theophany, can it fail to take Jesus's humanity seriously? Second, to what extent is an avatar involved in human suffering and death? Can an avatar completely be self-emptying of its divinity? And finally, in the Hindu concept, a multiple manifestation of the divine in history is possible, whereas for Christians the incarnation is unique.[45] Christians do not expect another incarnation of God in history; they are waiting for the return of Christ. Nevertheless, the concept of avatar can be useful to speak of God's desire to be with the humans in the world, and vice versa—the human desire to make God in their own image. Reflecting on this image of Jesus as an avatar can be fruitful in Hindu–Christian dialogue with regard to divine–human encounter.

Jesus as Guru

Another popular concept in the Indian spiritual tradition is that of a *guru*, or divine master/guide.[46] Like avatar, a guru occupies a special place in the divine–human encounter, but from the human side. A guru is more than a transmitter of knowledge; he is a teacher in a wider social tradition, someone who can show the way to the divine because s/he has experienced it. All religious traditions in India have gurus. In some forms of Vaishnavism, there is a tendency to consider spiritual leaders as avatars and even worship them. In Shaivism, a guru can be a special manifestation of Shiva, but more

---

[44] Noel Sheth, "Hindu Avatara and Christian Incarnation: A Comparison," *Vidyajyoti* 67/3 (2003): 181–93 and 67/4 (2003): 285–302; Amaladoss, *The Asian Jesus*, 69–85.

[45] Middle Ages Christian theologians also speculated about the multiple incarnations of Christ. Thomas Aquinas dealt with the question in ST III, q.3, art. 7. I am indebted to George Griener of the Jesuit School of Theology for this observation.

[46] Xavier Irudayaraj, "The Guru in Hinduism and Christianity," *Vidyajyoti* 39 (1975): 338–51; Amaladoss, *The Asian Jesus*, 69–85.

often s/he is mere divine instrument. Shiva can appear in a human form to relate to a disciple, or s/he can work through a human agent when the disciple is ripe.

The Jesuit missionary Robert de Nobili (1541–59) first spoke of Jesus as guru. Many Hindus also consider Jesus as their guru. Thus, to look at Jesus as guru is to consider oneself his disciple. Calling him the guru is not giving a speculative or metaphorical name to Jesus, but involves a commitment to follow him. Unlike other gurus, who merely attract disciples, Jesus actively chooses and forms them, and they are meant to constitute a tradition.

Jesus as Bodhisattva and Buddha

In most Buddhist traditions, *compassion* and *wisdom* are held as the highest values. A Buddha is one who is enlightened, that is, a person who realizes the true nature of all phenomena as transient and empty in itself. This realization or enlightenment subsequently frees the person from the suffering of clinging to self and the phenomenon world, trapping him or her in the endless cycles of birth and death (*samsara*). A bodhisattva is also one who is enlightened, but also has a compassionate heart to help other sentient beings realize the same truth and thus achieve salvation (or liberation).

Siddhartha Gautama the historical Buddha was considered one who discovered the path to liberation (*moksha*) from this phenomenon world (*samsara*). He is said to have reached the finality of all reality (*nirvana*) and in turn shows the way of liberation to other humans. Whereas in Theravada Buddhism, one needs to attain nirvana by one's own effort, in Mahayana Buddhism, one can rely on the help of other spiritual guides and protectors. In Theravada Buddhism, bodhisattva refers to Gautama in his past lives, but in Mahayana Buddhism, it denotes selfless practitioners of compassion and mercy, those who are just about to enter nirvana, but choose to stay back in samsara to be in solidarity with other unenlightened beings.

Many East Asian Buddhists would not hesitate to call Jesus a bodhisattva for his selfless sacrifice on the cross. Some Christian theologians have also explored the concept of bodhisattva in comparison with the kenosis of Christ in service to humanity.[47] Like the bodhisattva who put other's well-being before his/her own, Jesus manifests the compassionate face of God in solidarity with the poor and downtrodden. As helper on the way to final reality, Jesus points the way to the Father. The crucial differ-

---

[47] Hee-Sung Keel, "Jesus the Bodhisattva: Christology from a Buddhist Perspective," *Buddhist Christian Studies* 16 (1996): 176–92.

ence, of course, is that Christians consider Jesus *the way* as well. In a similar vein, Jesus can be seen as an Enlightened One according to Peter C. Phan.[48] Taking note that Buddha is a title applied to Siddhartha Gautama, Phan proposes that a similar title, Enlightener, can be used for Jesus. As light from Light, Jesus is not only enlightened in self-knowledge and his mission; he in turn enlightens others and brings them on the way to God as well.

Jesus as Sage and Embodied Dao

Just as Indian Christians would compare Jesus to Rama, Krishna, or Buddha, Chinese Christians cannot help but see Jesus through one of their most revered teachers, Confucius. For many Chinese, Confucius is considered a sage (聖, *sheng*),[49] the highest honor a person can attain. In the Confucian worldview, a sage is one who understands and harmonizes the three worlds of heaven, earth, and human. Etymologically, *sheng* is made up of two characters *listen* (耳, *er*) and *proclaim* (呈, *cheng*), signifying someone who is able to discern the wisdom or way of heaven and proclaim what he has heard to the rest of world. Jonathan Tan has made this connection to Jesus as one who comprehends the way of his Father and communicates that to the rest of humanity.[50] Using the term *sage* for Jesus has been done by biblical scholars in the Jewish sapiential tradition,[51] and thus there is nothing unique about claiming Jesus to be a perfect and divine sage for Chinese Christians. Being the "crucified and risen sage," however, is what sets Jesus apart.[52] The particularity of Jesus manifests in his embodiment of the Way of heaven (*tiandao*) in his life, through his death and resurrection, and inviting others to embrace and walk along this Way.

---

[48] Peter C. Phan, "Transformation and Liberation by Enlightenment: Jesus as the Enlightener and the Enlightened One," in *Being Religious Interreligiously: Asian Perspectives on Interfaith Dialogue* (Maryknoll, NY: Orbis Books, 2003) 128–36.

[49] This word is often translated in Christian circle as *saint*. But in Confucian usage it does not denote a holy person, but rather a spiritually enlightened one. Confucius never used this title for himself but applied it to the ancient divine king of the Chinese antiquity.

[50] Jonathan Y. Tan, "Jesus, the Crucified and Risen Sage: Constructing a Contemporary Confucian Christology," in *The Chinese Faces of Jesus,* vol. 3, ed. Roman Malek (Sankt Augustin, Germany: Institut Monumenta Serica, 2007), 1481–1513.

[51] Ben Witherington III, *Jesus the Sage: The Pilgrimage of Wisdom* (Minneapolis: Fortress Press, 1994).

[52] Tan, "Jesus, the Crucified and Risen Sage," 1509–12.

For many East Asians, *Dao* (道, also spelled *Tao*, literally means *path* or *speech*) has a metaphorical meaning of being the principle that guides heaven, earth, and humanity. It is the Chinese equivalent of logos and was used by early translators of the Chinese bible to render John 1:1. Heup Young Kim has utilized this concept to propose Christ as the "theanthropocosmic Tao."[53] As Dao harmonizes the three worlds of heaven, human, and earth, likewise Christ is the unifying principle of these worlds, hence the neologism *theanthropocosmic*."[54] By aligning Jesus Christ as Dao, and coining the new term *Christotao* to replace Christology, Kim is engaged in one of the most creative applications of East Asian thought to the study of theology. His goal is to reconceive Christology in terms of harmonizing and reconciling opposite tendencies. The dynamic of the Dao is animated by the yin and the yang. In the balance of yin and yang, Christ embraces all differences and brings them all into one (cf. Gal. 3:28).

Jesus as Prophet and Servant of God

In dialogue with Islam, the image of Jesus as a prophet is frequently evoked.[55] Isa, the Muslim name of Jesus, is recognized as a prophet of God in the Qur'an. The typology of Jesus being a prophet has its foundation in the Synoptic Gospels, where Jesus is frequently referred to as a prophet. Jesus is also said to have understood his mission in a prophetic way (cf. Luke 4:16–30). Nevertheless, the Muslim concept of prophet (*nabi*) is one person in a long line of prophets; each confirms the message of his predecessor, and Muhammad is considered the last and greatest prophet of all. In contrast, for Christians, Jesus is *more than a prophet* (cf. Mark 12:1–9); he is the fulfillment of Old Testament prophecy and the unique Son of God (Heb. 1:1–14)—a title frequently rejected by Islam.

Likewise, Muslims also talk about Jesus as a servant (*'abd*) of God. This term is mentioned in the Qur'an (Q 4:172, 19:30, 43:59), and it has precedent in the Bible (Isa. 42:1, 49:6). Jesus, indeed, emphasizes the fact

---

[53] Heup Young Kim, "Toward a Christotao: Christ as the Theanthropocosmic Tao," *Studies in Interreligious Dialogue* 10/1 (2000): 5–29.

[54] A composite adjective of *theos* (god) + *anthropos* (humanity) + *cosmos* (world). This neologism is also used by Raimon Pannikar in his many writings.

[55] Alexander Malik, "Confessing Christ in the Islamic Context," in Sugirtharajah, *Asian Faces of Jesus*, 75–84; Mustansir Mir, "Islamic View of Jesus," in Barker, *Jesus in the World's Faiths*, 115–24; Mona Siddiqui, "Jesus in Popular Muslim Thought," in Barker, *Jesus in the World's Faiths*, 125–31.

that he did not "come to be served, but to serve" (Mark 10:45). And yet, while Christians espoused the image of a suffering servant in Isaiah (cf. Isa. 52–53), they do not reduce Jesus to this role. Service is seen primarily as an act of self-emptying of the Son of God (Phil. 2:7). In conversations with Muslims, it is clear that these images do not make bridges between Christians and Muslims for there remains different interpretations of the person of Christ in both traditions.[56]

Jesus and the Other Religious Figures

A related question is the place of Jesus among world religious figures. This is often the contention between Christian theologians. Depending on their theology of religions—exclusivist, inclusivist, pluralist, or particularist[57]—theologians will offer different views on the significance of Jesus vis-à-vis other religious divinities and founders. A high Christology, often espoused by traditional Christians and Evangelicals, insists on the superior, unique, and absolute character of Jesus. Because of his divinity, Jesus is the supreme and unique Savior, standing above everyone else. Their positions range from a total rejection of the role of other religious figures in God's salvific scheme (the exclusivist) to a reluctant acceptance of them as *extraordinary* means of salvation while maintaining the universal character of Jesus Christ (the inclusivist).

Other theologians, however, try to reevaluate the normativity of Jesus Christ (*and* by extension Christianity) in light of religious pluralism of the modern world. Some maintain that Jesus is one among the many saviors (or avatars, or prophets) of God (the pluralist) while others drop the comparison altogether, seeing it as unproductive since there are different religious ends for different religions (the particularist).

While most Christian theologians are rightly reluctant to reduce Jesus to one among the many faces of God, it is obvious one cannot avoid the appreciation and positive evaluation of other religious founders. Long gone

---

[56] For a recent assessment on this subject, see Mark Beaumont, *Christology in Dialogue with Muslims: A Critical Analysis of Christian Presentations of Christ for Muslims from the Ninth and Twentieth Centuries* (Eugene OR: Wipf & Stock, 2011).

[57] The typology was first proposed by Alan Race in 1983. Since then, Paul Knitter has updated and expanded this threefold category into four: theology of replacement (exclusivism), fulfillment (inclusivism), mutuality (pluralism), and acceptance (particularism). See Paul Knitter, *Introducing Theologies of Religions* (Maryknoll, NY: Orbis Books, 2007).

are the days that Christians could easily dismiss the Buddha, Krishna, or Muhammad, seeing them as lesser beings. Those who would like to maintain some distinction between Jesus and other religious figures and yet do not want to insist on the absoluteness of Jesus have proposed various nuances. For example, Stanley Samartha suggests that one should speak of Jesus in terms of "relational distinctiveness."[58] Jacques Dupuis maintains that Christ's uniqueness is not absolute nor relative but "constitutive" and "relational."[59] Paul Knitter holds up Jesus as a "decisive," "representational" revelation of God.[60]

The intra-Christian debates between the pluralists and traditionalists[61] have helped theologians to clarify and update their understanding of Jesus.[62] So far, there is no comprehensive answer to an obvious tension: how to maintain the universal desire of God to save everyone *as well as* the particularity of Jesus's salvific role? In the end, it may be suggested that as a man born in a specific time and place, the historical Jesus could not have exhausted the divine Logos. Jesus is confessed to be fully God (*totus Deus*) but not the whole or totality of God (*totum Dei*). This solution seems to be reasonable since the Christian tradition has always maintained the *equality* of the Son to the Father (*homoousios*) while at the same time keeping a clear *distinction* between them. As Christians, we profess that in Jesus we have salvation, but that does not mean that God cannot use other means or ways to reach humanity. Salvation is the mysterious act of the whole Godhead, who alone knows how best to save humanity.

Jesusologies or Christologies?
An Inconclusive Conclusion

Majority World theologies have shown the cross-fertilization of Christian thoughts within the diverse economic, political, cultural, and religious

---

[58] Stanley Samartha, *One Christ, Many Religion: Toward a Revised Christology* (Maryknoll, NY: Orbis Books, 1990), 77.

[59] Jacques Dupuis, *Toward a Christian Theology of Religious Pluralism* (Maryknoll, NY: Orbis Books, 1998), 283.

[60] Paul Knitter, *Jesus and Other Names: Christian Mission and Global Responsibility* (Maryknoll, NY: Orbis Books, 1996), esp. chap. 4.

[61] I avoid the term *exclusivist*, since it carries a negative connotation of narrow-mindedness.

[62] Massimo Serreti, *The Uniqueness and Universality of Jesus Christ in Dialogue with the Religions* (Grand Rapids, MI: Wm. B. Eerdmans Publishing, 2004); Sung Wook Chung, ed., *Christ the One and Only: A Global Affirmation of the Uniqueness of Jesus Christ* (Grand Rapids, MI: Baker Academic, 2005).

landscape of Latin American, Africa, and Asia. As a result, theological conversations, including contextual Christologies, have also moved across boundaries. Using a Buddhist metaphor, Choan-Seng Song has urged Asian Christians to engage in a *third-eye* theology, seeing Christ not only through Indian, Chinese, or Japanese eyes but also through African and Latin American perspectives.[63]

A critical reader may suggest that what I have done is to present various portraits of Jesus, amounts to *Jesusologies*, the political, cultural, and religious studies of Jesus, rather than to offer proper Christologies, those that highlight the salvific role of Jesus the Nazareth as God-among-us. The dichotomy between Jesus and Christ, or between *Jesusology* and *Christology*, is a matter of emphasis. No devout Christian would deny the various titles given to Christ in the New Testament and subsequent tradition: the Messiah (*christos*), the Lord (*kurios*), the Son of God, the Incarnate Word, etc. But as important as they are, these titles serve as confessional attributions to Jesus by Christians throughout the ages. They tell less about the person whom the Christians worship and honor, but more about how he is related to them. By extending the titles to include other categories such as the liberator, the ancestor, the prophet, or even the bodhisattva, Christians and non-Christians today are appropriating Jesus for themselves, making him relevant in their lives.

Any contemporary theological reflection on the meaning and relevance of Jesus Christ is more than just repeating the creedal statements about who he is and what he has done for us; it also requires Christians to transform their beliefs in Christ into action, leading a Christ-like life in their own particular context. In a recent collection of Korean theology, one can detect a movement from a social-political concern to a cross-cultural dialogue and interfaith *dia-praxis*.[64] It is understood that dialogues are not separation from action. In a similar way, any new development in Christology today must consider both the faith in Jesus and his exemplary action together. Devotion to Jesus implies imitation of him. Only in this way can they boldly proclaim that *Christ remains the same, yesterday, today and forever.*

---

[63] Choan-Seng Song, *Third-Eye Theology: Theology in Formation in Asian Settings* (Maryknoll, NY: Orbis Books, 1979).

[64] See part II of Paul S. Chung, Veli-Matti Karkkainen, and Kim Kyoung-Jae, eds., *Asian Contextual Theology for the Third Millenium: Theology of Minjung in Fourth-Eye Formation* (Eugene, OR: Pickwick Publications, 2007).

11

THE EVER-INCULTURATING CHURCH: DOING ECCLESIOLOGY IN THE AGE OF WORLD CHRISTIANITY

Gerard Mannion

If ecclesiology is the study of the church and its stories, aspirations, trials and tribulations, self-understandings, as well as organizational, ministerial, and missionary trajectories and priorities, among other distinctive areas of focus, what lessons for ecclesiology in our times and for tomorrow can be learned from the turn toward a focus on World Christianities? Here I do not mean lessons that ecclesiology has learned exclusively thanks to the emergence of the differing waves of the methodological approach that is now called World Christianity. There have been, of course, other differing sources, methods, and existential inspirations that have helped ecclesiology develop in recent times. But it is certainly the case that the emergence of World Christianity has helped transform the way in which ecclesiology is now done and must be done in the future in multiple ways and for the better. Nor do I suggest that the flow of influence has been in one direction only. Developments in ecclesiology have also had a great influence on the emergence and development of World Christianity as an area of study in its own right too.[1]

---

[1] See discussion in Peter C. Phan, "World Christianity: Its Implications for History, Religious Studies, and Theology," *Horizons* 39/2 (2012): 171–88. Cf. the related essay, Peter C. Phan, "World Christianity and Christian Mission: Are They Compatible? Insights from the Asian Churches," *International Bulletin of Missionary Review* 32/4 (2008): 193–200; and also Peter Phan, "A New Christianity, but What Kind?" *Mission Studies* 22/1 (2005): 59–83. Examples of recent ecclesiological studies from the North American and European contexts that seek to be attentive to the understanding of Christianity as a world religion and so as a global church, while also treating ecclesiology in relation to the wider historical and methodological debates in recent times include Richard R. Gaillardetz, *Ecclesiology for a Global Church: a People Called*

In this essay, I seek to explore seven specific areas, where I think both recent and contemporary ecclesiology and World Christianity have particularly converged and collaborated in helping to transform our understanding of this faith and particularly of the church of churches with its multiple communitarian manifestations at the global and local levels alike. Here I will not seek to offer a detailed commentary on the particular direction of influence, but rather highlight some specific themes prevalent in the study of World Christianity that have and will continue to prove invaluable lessons and resources for ecclesiology going into the future. I will then offer an example of how these lessons are becoming increasingly mainstream, with a short section illustrating striking parallels between the ecclesiological visions of Peter Phan and Pope Francis.

Good News:
The Inescapability of Inculturation

Central to much of the work being done in the study of World Christianity is the concept of inculturation. It is important to stress that that inculturation is effectively a multilayered series of processes. Peter Phan offers the following definition of inculturation and the processes it entails:

> Inculturation is a two-way process of inserting the already inculturated gospel into a particular culture and this culture into the gospel, so that the resulting inculturated Christianity will be something different and new (as a dialogue between two cultures, it could also be called "interculturation" . . .). Inculturation is an integral and constitutive dimension of mission . . . The principal agents of inculturation are the local church and the native people, not the missionaries, the experts or the central authorities. . . . Inculturation embraces all aspects of church life, from theology to ethics, law, liturgy, catechesis, and spirituality.[2]

---

and Sent (Maryknoll, NY: Orbis Books, 2008), Roger Haight, *Ecclesial Existence* (New York: Continuum, 2008); and Gerard Mannion, *Ecclesiology and Postmodernity: Questions for the Church in Our Time* (Collegeville, MN: Michael Glazier, 2007).

[2] Peter C. Phan, "Inculturation of Christianity and the Gospel" in *The Cambridge Dictionary of Christianity*, ed. Daniel Patte (Cambridge: Cambridge University Press, 2010), 594. See also Phan C. Phan, *In Our Own Tongues: Perspectives from Asia on Mission and Inculturation* (Maryknoll, NY: Orbis Books, 2003), 3–12; Peter C. Phan, *Christianity with an Asian Face: Asian American Theology in the Making* (Maryknoll, NY: Orbis Books, 2003), 47–74.

It is especially important to appreciate the impact that the cultures and contexts that Christianity comes to anew have, in turn, upon the wider faith itself—the inculturated becomes the inculturator or inculturating energy at work in a much broader sphere of influence.

All of this leads us to state here one of the most fundamental lessons for ecclesiology in our times—a lesson that we see throughout the long history of the church: *Neither the faith nor the church is ever found* pure *and untouched by culture and context: every ecclesiology is a contextualized and inculturated ecclesiology bar none.*

An acknowledgment of the inescapability of inculturation is thus both an imperative for doing ecclesiology and yet equally inspiring of a virtuous disposition for ecclesiological work alike. When one does acknowledge and embrace such realities, then the possibilities for ecclesiologies with a global reach and for the very consciousness of World Christianity itself become immense. This is the first and a primary valuable lesson for doing ecclesiology in our times.

Ecclesiology without Borders— Christianity Is a Global Religion and the Church a Global Church

Karl Rahner once famously predicted that the church at the end of the twentieth century now had to face the challenge of becoming truly a global church (or otherwise face a long march into a sectarian, ghettoized form of existence).[3] The post–Vatican II church must, by necessity realize the world had become so radically different a place from that which had shaped the ecclesiological thinking up to and, still for many council fathers, throughout that council between 1962 and 1965. Rahner therefore spoke, among other priorities, of the need for a declericalized church, a church with open doors (comfortable with fluid boundaries), one that is concerned with serving, that stands up for the poor and for justice and freedom,[4] a church that offers morality without moralizing, which has "concrete directives" as well as "real" (and socially relevant and transformative) spirituality. Furthermore, it must become ever more an ecumenical church, a "Church from the Roots,"[5] a democratized church and a sociocritical church.

Rahner's vision, of course, was addressed primarily to Roman Catholicism but could equally be applicable in so many ways to many other

---

[3] Karl Rahner, *The Shape of the Church to Come* (London: SPCK, 1974), esp. 93.

[4] On the latter, see ibid., 62–63.

[5] Ibid., 108.

denominations.[6] In fact, Rahner's list of thoughts about the way forward for the church is mirrored in much of the work of Peter Phan and in multiple fruits from the study of World Christianity from so many other scholars, particularly those who work in or come from the Global South. Peter's life and work not only reflect the key shift in ecclesiology to a global focus in recent decades, but he has actively helped shape and influence many components of that shift.

The transcending of borders—methodological, ecumenical, religious, cultural, and ethnic is a constant (if perhaps at times latent) feature throughout much of Phan's work.[7] Nietzsche once said that all philosophy is thinly veiled autobiography,[8] and I have stated elsewhere that the same can often be said of much theology. Contra Nietzsche and so applying this insight here in a very positive sense, in Peter Phan's enormous corpus of work, we also see reflected his own rich biography.

And Phan helps take such a wider and transformative vision for the church so much further still, developing that great insight from Asian Christianity of the imperative to embrace a "triple dialogue"—dialogue with the cultures, with the peoples, especially the poor and with the religions of one's context.[9] Thus, he has commented frequently and often upon that great insight from liberation theology[10]—the need for a shift from an ecclesiocentric focus (where the institutional church is at the center) to a "regnocentric" focus[11] (where building the kingdom of God, of justice and righteousness is the core focus and priority, and the church only exists to serve this aim).

---

[6] See also Karl Rahner, "Towards a Fundamental Theological Interpretation of Vatican II," *Theological Studies* 40/4 (1979): 716–27, which Phan himself draws upon in Phan, *In Our Own Tongues*, 3.

[7] As an example, see Phan's masterful discussion of "Crossing the Borders," culminating in an extended mediation on "Jesus, the Border Crosser," which is hugely insightful, Phan, *In Our Own Tongues*, 130–50.

[8] "It has gradually become clear to me what every great philosophy has hitherto been: a confession on the part of its author and a kind of involuntary and unconscious memoir; moreover that the moral (or immoral) intentions in every philosophy constituted the real gem of life out of which the entire plant has grown," Friedrich Nietzsche, *Beyond Good and Evil*, trans. R. J. Hollingdale (Harmondsworth, UK: Penguin, 1990), § 6.

[9] Peter C. Phan, "Asian Christian Spirituality," in *The Oxford Handbook of Christianity in Asia*, ed. Felix Wilfred (New York: Oxford University Press, 2014), 516–17; see also Phan, *In Our Own Tongues*, 32–44.

[10] See Phan, *Christianity with an Asian Face*, 26–46, esp. 26: "Future historians of Christianity will no doubt judge liberation theology to be the most influential movement of the twentieth century, possibly even since the Reformation."

[11] See, for example, Phan, *In Our Own Tongues*, 32–44, Phan, *Christianity with an Asian Face*, 75–97.

In all, the consciousness of the global reach of Christianity, the insights World Christianity gives to our awareness and appreciation of this, alongside Peter Phan's own specific work on theology transcending borders and divisions, engaging in far-reaching dialogue that has profound moral and especially social consequences, hold an important further lesson for ecclesiology—in a global church, ecclesiology must be done *sans frontiers*. If we grasp this fact and make it a further guiding ecclesiological virtue, then there will be important positive consequences for ecumenical, interfaith, and church-world dialogue, just as there will be greater ecclesial attentiveness to the plight of the poor and marginalized. Therefore, the church's mission and the building of the kingdom will be enhanced by such borderless ecclesiology. This is a second valuable lesson for doing ecclesiology in our times and leads us directly to our next vital lesson for ecclesiology.

Evolution in the Consciousness of World Christianity

The emergence of World Christianity as a distinctive approach in its own right is well documented in chapter 1 by Dale Irvin and chapter 2 by Scott Sunquist in this volume, and in a succinct yet informative fashion in Phan's own 2011 Burke Lecture. Suffice to say here it marked a shift in focus and attention from perceiving Christianity as a Eurocentric or at best Western faith (read Euro-North America-centric) to one where it was perceived as a global religion with multiple differing manifestations as well as cultural and ethnic manifestations.

The final decades of the twentieth century have witnessed the emergence of the consciousness and so specifically systematized and oriented study of Christianity as a religion with not simply differing branches and loci in terms of historical origins, doctrines, and practices (i.e., denominational consciousness), but also one with distinctive cultural, ethnic, and regional forms and trajectories. This is not simply to reflect denominational difference but great differences within specific Christian churches, even within specific regions and sometimes the very same country.[12] These realizations, too, have fundamental implications for the doing of ecclesiology in our times and our world.

And the emergence of World Christianity has also brought about multiple contributions from methods and scholars far beyond the subdisciplines of theology alone. Charles Farhadian speaks of three paradigms in the interpretation of World Christianity. First is that which explores the expan-

---

[12] For example, cf. Phan, "Asian Christian Spirituality," 510.

sion of Western Christianity (and other Western values and cultural norms) through mission across the globe. The second, emerging in the late twentieth century, acknowledges the polycentric nature of Christianity, with multiple centers of authority. The rise of such local centers of Christianity helped move forward the postcolonial revolution. Themes such as liberation, localized and contextualized biblical interpretation, and the shift in Christianity to that of a religion predominantly of the Global South (e.g., Philip Jenkins's *The Next Christendom*)[13] with the attending rise also of more conservative theological and ethical positions among some of the new churches also featured prominently in such interpretations.[14]

The third approach, which Farhadian's own collection seeks to promote, both builds on and critiques the earlier paradigms and widens the scope of those more historical-oriented approaches to illustrate and explore the "connections between social, cultural, political, religious and historical forces and their uneven relationships with Christianity." This approach is mindful of specific resultant developments and "flows," including the emergence of distinctive forms of "citizenship, mobilization, and subjectivities," because Christianity has helped transform so many different aspects of human life.[15] It is an approach that "combines both historical breadth and social scientific depth."[16]

As indicated, there has been a two-way relationship between ecclesiology and these differing methodological waves of World Christianity. Developments in ecclesiology have both helped shape, and likewise been influenced and transformed by, each of these waves. Ecclesiology has increasingly interacted with and drawn resources from historical, philosophical, social scientific, and a range of other approaches in recent decades.[17] There

---

[13] Philip Jenkins, *The Next Christendom: The Coming of Global Christianity*, rev. and exp. ed. (Oxford: Oxford University Press, 2007). Another oft-cited key text here is Lamin Sanneh's *Whose Religion Is Christianity?: The Gospel beyond the West* (Grand Rapids, MI: Wm. B. Eerdmans Publishing, 2003), which he builds upon in his later study, Lamin Sanneh, *Disciples of All Nations: Pillars of World Christianity* (Oxford: Oxford University Press, 2008).

[14] Charles F. Farhadian, *Introducing World Christianity* (Oxford: Wiley-Blackwell, 2012), 1–2.

[15] Ibid., 2.

[16] Ibid., 3.

[17] For example, consider the range of historical, methodological, global and conceptual, thematic, and interdisciplinary approaches gathered together in Gerard Mannion and Lewis Seymour Mudge, eds., *Routledge Companion to the Christian Church* (New York: Routledge, 2008). See also the brief overview essay about developments in ecclesiology in

have been more local community or congregational and practice-oriented approaches in recent times, too.[18]

So this next vital lesson for doing ecclesiology in our times is to be mindful of the *evolving* nature of our consciousness of Christianity as a world religion and therefore of the differing methods, milestones, and contributions that have collectively helped bring this new area of study into being as a distinctive realm of academic enquiry in its own right. Ecclesiology should dialogue and collaborate with scholars working in World Christianity, and the reverse is equally true—scholars in World Christianity should also be attentive to the dynamics of investigation in contemporary ecclesiology and seek to engage such in their own ongoing work.

'Twas Ever Thus:
Fourth Vital Lesson for Ecclesiology

Christianity has enjoyed such diverse forms of existence from the earliest times. There are four gospels and multiple epistles in the New Testament reflective of differing communities with differing interpretations of the faith and practices pertaining to it as well as of shared beliefs and practices, too.

Lest we forget (and too often people *do* forget), Christianity did not originate in Europe but in West Asia and, from very early times, spread far and wide. Within a few centuries, it moved into Central Asia and beyond, including India, it is believed, in the first century CE, as well as into Africa, also from the very first century CE. Its spread continued, across the Mediterranean and various outposts of Europe, including the westernmost part, Ireland, reaching China in the seventh century. In each place this new faith, which emerged as a renewal movement in the much older Jewish religion, found itself, by necessity it took on inculturated forms and practices. How could it have been otherwise? As two of the other leading figures in the present wave of studies in World Christianity state,

> Christianity was not a European religion that spread to other parts of the world for the first time after the year 1500, as it has often been portrayed. Christianity was born at the juncture of three continents and within its first century had become deeply established on each

---

Gerard Mannion, "The Point of Ecclesiology," in Sune Fahlgren and Jonas Ideström, eds., *Ecclesiology in the Trenches: Theory and Method under Construction* (Eugene, OR: Wipf and Stock, 2015) ix–xiv.

[18] See, for example, the range of contributions to Fahlgren and Ideström, *Ecclesiology in the Trenches*.

of them. By the year 1500 it was already something of a world religion. It had also become the dominant and established religion in western Europe, as it continued to be in the East Roman (or Byzantine) empire that had Constantinople as its capital.[19]

With the age of exploration, the faith spreads

in regions on earth where they had not previously been located, most notably in the hemisphere that came to be called South and North America. While in most cases these communities of faith continued to be related in both character and expression to churches in western Europe, they were never only duplicates of them. In a number of places across Asia and Africa, Christians from western Europe also encountered indigenous Christian communities of various Orthodox traditions that had lived in these places for over a millennium. The results of these encounters were significant for both parties.[20]

These experiences subsequently made a lasting impact on Christianity back in Europe, also, which was already undergoing momentous change itself.

These vital historical reminders are underscored by a further valuable lesson that other theologians have helped to emphasize in various ways and forms throughout much of the story of the church, but especially in modern and contemporary times: not only is the church never to be considered separated from the world, but nor can it ever transcend history and the forces and energies of historical change either. We know that many suffered gravely for their statement and expanded articulations of this fact, for example, those scholars pejoratively labeled *Catholic Modernists* at the outset of the twentieth century.

One of the founding fathers of World Christianity as a disciplinary area in its own right, Andrew Walls, helps further emphasize the importance of this fact for the study of World Christianity. In his words, "In Christian belief, salvation is a historical process. . . . salvation comes not only *in* history but *through* history; history is, as it were, the stuff, the material in which salvation takes place."[21]

---

[19] Dale T. Irvin and Scott W. Sunquist, "Modern Christianity from 1454–1800," in *History of the World Christian Movement* (Maryknoll, NY: Orbis Books, 2012), 2:xi–xii.

[20] Ibid., 2:xii.

[21] Andrew Walls, "Globalization and the Study of Christian History," in *Global-*

It is another vital lesson for ecclesiology to acknowledge and embrace that salvation history and world history are not two separate entities—as those, such as Karl Rahner, to the first-wave theologians of liberation have reminded us—history is one and the same. All too often, including in recent times and to this very day, we come across Christians of various persuasions and outlook who yet continue to try and divorce the church from both the world and from history—from the personal and distorted views of individual Christians to the ahistorical and world-renouncing perspectives of church leaders and even official teaching documents.

This is both bound up with and returns us to our earlier key lesson and ecclesiological virtuous disposition for ecclesiology, that Christianity is never found in a form cut off from context—that all Christianity and so all forms of being church and thus of understanding and articulating what it is to be church must, by necessity, be inculturated. All of these key lessons together are perhaps particularly well illustrated in one of the many places in which Peter Phan, himself, defines *World Christianity*, and where he tells us that we must resist tendencies toward perceiving the term as facilitating a revival of the notion of Christendom and be wary of overtly Western and normative drives toward a homogenous church unity alike. Rather,

> the expression refers to the historical, sociological, cultural and theological diversity and multiplicity of Christianity, from its very beginning, throughout its two-millennia history, and arguably more so in the future. The legitimate concern for the unity of the church, especially after the emergence of heresies and schisms and, for the Catholic Church, during the centuries-long concentration of ecclesiastical power in the papacy, has masked this diversity and multiplicity in favour of an imagined and often enforced uniformity. There is not, nor has there ever been, one Christianity; rather there exist Christianities (in the plural), all over the world and all the time.[22]

This further underscores that religion is always and has always been found in inculturated forms—that is to say—that a particular faith by neces-

---

izing Theology: Belief and Practice in an Era of World Christianity (Nottingham, UK: Apollos, 2007), 70.

[22] Phan, "World Christianity: Its Implications for History, Religious Studies, and Theology," 175. See also Phan, *In Our Own Tongues*, 3: "Though the term *inculturation* is a neologism to describe this way of performing the church's mission, it has been the church's modus operandi, with varying degrees of success, since its very beginning, as it moved out of its Jewish matrix into the Graeco-Roman, then Franco-Germanic worlds."

sity becomes refracted through and in turn is changed and developed by the cultural milieu in which it is lived out and how there is a profound two-way relationship of influence between religion and the cultures in which it is practiced. This has immense implications for religion in differing communities in our world as well as for the relations between differing branches of the same faith, including Christianity today. Therefore, there are multiple implications for the practice of ecclesiology.

Expanding the Explicit Consciousness of World Christianity

The two-way processes of interaction between the faith, and the cultures and peoples in which it flourished, was a vital feature of Christianity from the very outset. The manner in which this faith spread through the remaining centuries of the first millennium continued thus.

In fact, further reiterating our earlier considerations, *wherever* this faith went, it found itself as shaped and transformed as much by its encounter with the cultures and peoples with which it was engaging as vice versa. This can also be said for the interaction between Christianity and other faiths, major as well as local in character.

In the modern era, as the two-way processes of inculturation continued apace across the global continents, Europe and North America increasingly began to be educated and influenced by movements such as liberation theology and postcolonialism, while struggles against evils such as apartheid, poverty, and exploitation have further helped gradually *de-Westernize* many of the core priorities and foci of Christianity further still. In many of these developments, the church's social consciousness and mission were expanded and transformed, perhaps one might say intensified, all the more in a fashion that in many ways took the church's priorities back to those that were more prevalent in the church's earliest times.

For example, the sense of doing theology *from the underside of history* that was developed in Latin America through liberation theology, along with the now mainstream *preferential option for the poor*, are inculturated features of Christian life, thought, and above all practice that have been shaped the through lived experiences of particular communities, lands, and regions, and that have in turn gone onto radically transform the global church in general.[23] All of this helps us to appreciate, as Farhadian states,

---

[23] See Gerard Mannion, "Liberation Ecclesiology," in Mannion and Mudge, *Routledge Companion to the Christian Church*, 425–46.

that "What is important to recognize is that world Christianity is not only dynamic but relational. . . . And studying world Christianity helps us to appreciate its translocal, interconnected nature."[24]

Discerning the World(s)
of Christianity in Our Times

The prevalence and affirmation of modern and contemporary forms of inculturation have helped turn the attention of all interested in ecclesiology toward the realities of the global forms and practices of Christianity—the rich kaleidoscope of those innumerable communities that call themselves churches cannot be ignored by ecclesiologists.

If one looks at what was, in effect, ecclesiology in the nineteenth century (even though the term did not, as such, come to hold its present meaning until further into the twentieth century), the reach and focus of how the church is understood, explored, analyzed, and critiqued is now unrecognizable from the older treatises *De Ecclesia,* with a neoscholastic and new rigid slant in Roman Catholicism from the nineteenth century onward, too. Nor can ecclesiology again ever be content to suffice with the models of understanding and shaping the church and Christian life known to the great Protestant reformers and their successors or the effectively ecclesiological writing of the great *Western* Protestant theologians of the nineteenth century down through to the second half of the twentieth century.[25]

The key lesson here for ecclesiology today builds on the earlier lessons, including the fact that Christianity is a global religion and is always found in contextualized and inculturated forms. But, in addition to this, ecclesiology today has to not only acknowledge but equally to grapple with the implications of the fact Christianity has *no* distinct center anymore, and this can and should be embraced as a good thing. It is a polycentric faith.

In order to discern those ecclesiological implications, consider some of the revealing facts from the Pew Forum study of Global Christianity from 2010 (published in December 2011).[26] These facts demand attention from

---

[24] Farhadian, *Introducing World Christianity,* 3. He acknowledges that his collection does not contain any perspectives from theologians or biblical scholars because of this intended methodological focus.

[25] Again, consider the brief overview in Mannion, "The Point of Ecclesiology," in Fahlgren and Ideström, *Ecclesiology in the Trenches: Theory and Method under Construction* ix–xiv; and the range of perspectives in Mannion and Mudge, *Routledge Companion to the Christian Church.*

[26] Available at http://www.pewforum.org. One informative recent study of the

ecclesiologists because the way in which we look at the church can never be precisely the same (nor even approximate to coming close to being such) as the ways in which people were conscious of and understood and explained the church in the past. In 2010, there were 2.18 billion Christians on the planet—almost a third of the global population of 6.9 billion. To consider how things have changed for and in the church, consider that there are four times as many Christians today as just over one hundred years ago when there were approximately 600 million (out of a global population of 1.8 billion). The proportion of the human family that identify as Christian has not actually changed that much in the intervening century—Christians constituted 35 percent of the global population in 1910; in 2010 they were 32 percent. Yet *where* we find those Christians has radically altered. In 1910, two-thirds of all Christians lived in Europe compared to just 26 percent now—from two out of every three to only one in every four. Thirty-seven percent of Christians in 2010 lived in the Americas, with 24 percent in Sub-Saharan Africa, while Asia and the Pacific was home to just 13 percent.

Hence, Christianity has firmly become much more a religion concentrated in the Global South than the Global North. This is a fact Peter Phan has commented upon on frequent occasions.[27] A staggering 60.8 percent (1,327,700,000) Christians now reside in the Global South—where they constitute just 23.5 percent of the regional population as a whole. Undoubtedly, the proportion of the global Christian family in the south will continue to grow.

Ecclesiology, then must realize that there are multiple areas of growth, decline, regrowth, and sometimes subsequent decline again that once more require scholars, ministers, practitioners, and church leaders alike to revisit their priorities and foci. It takes but one century—a blink in the eye of church history—for such monumental changes to take place around the world. Once more ecclesiologists must learn that what may have been true (i.e., factually the case) or even accurate just a relatively short time ago, will not necessarily continue to be so long into the future. Time and history has the annoying habit (for some) of not standing still for any person—and this includes popes, prelates, and professors alike.

---

demographics of world Christianity is Douglas Jacobsen, *The World's Christian: Who They Are, Where They Are and How They Got There* (Oxford: Blackwell, 2011).

[27] For example, Peter C. Phan, "The Church in an Asian Perspective," in *Routledge Companion to the Christian Church*, 275–90; see also Phan, "A New Christianity, but What Kind?" 59–83.

Catholicity Reimagined:
Ecclesiology, the Global and the Local—
A *Both/And* Range of Focus

What additional lessons might all such facts suggest about Christianity in the world—indeed the very different *worlds* Christianity has inhabited and the worlds it finds itself inhabiting anew, suggest for ecclesiology? Naturally, the need for a global perspective and attention is further underlined, but then, equally, so is the need for attention to more diverse local Christian stories, narratives, and dynamics.

More recent accounts acknowledge that it is a case of both/and—the globalizing and localizing tendencies have emerged in tandem and frequently because of one another, and we now live in an era where *globalization* is taken as a given. However, this is not simply about homogenization—there are, of course, the attendant dynamics of what is termed *glocalization*.[28]

In fact, ecclesiology must learn the lessons of the need to be attentive to both these seemingly contradictory yet actually intertwined developments of the age. Robert Schreiter's now classic study, *The New Catholicity: Theology between the Global and the Local*,[29] explored the various "global theological flows" at work in a world of globalization and went on to explore how we can go about engaging in intercultural hermeneutics. He identified, in particular, the twin challenges of finding a "renewed and expanded"[30] understanding of the term catholicity for today that does full justice to both traditional meanings that might account for the globality, on the one hand, and the fullness of faith, on the other. This is because, of course, for Christians, catholicity is the conceptualization of such interconnectedness—indeed solidarity—

---

[28] Which some also call heterogenization. Note, also, the related concept of *deterritorilization*. Glocalization, then, is the adaptation of globalizing tendencies to local particularities and contexts. One might even say it shares certain conceptual parallels with inculturation. Some particularly influential discussions of this phenomenon have been offered by Roland Robertson, including his "Glocalization: Time-Space and Homogeneity-Heterogeneity," in *Global Modernities*, ed. Mike Featherstone, Scott Lash, and Roland Robertson (London: Sage, 1995), 25–44; and Roland Robertson, "Globalisation or Glocalisation?" *Journal of International Communication* 1/1 (1994): 33–52. He discusses the evolution of the concept in Roland Robertson, "The Conceptual Promise of Glocalization: Commonality and Diversity," http://artefact.mi2.hr/_a04/lang_en/theory_robertson_en.htm.

[29] Robert Schreiter, *The New Catholicity: Theology between the Global and the Local* (Maryknoll, NY: Orbis Books, 2007).

[30] Ibid., 127–28.

understood in theological as much as geographical, social, and moral terms. Schreiter's own conclusions were as follows:

> A new catholicity can meet the challenges of our time, both as a theological vision of the Church and as a policy for intercultural communication. It will provide a way of negotiating between the global and the local, recognizing the possibilities and perils of both. To negotiate that path in theology, we must at once be aware of how our world has been changing and what skills and practices are needed to understand, communicate and act within it. . . . Living in a globalized world, where time and space have been compressed, where those who have and those who have not are driven further apart, a truly intercultural way of doing theology between the global and the local is required of us. And a vision of a new catholicity can guide us to it.[31]

Our final lesson, then, is that ecclesiology in our times must be aware that this fundamental mark of the church must be reenvisioned and expanded anew for the times, contexts, and challenges of a world at once globalized and glocalized.[32] This has implications both for the internal dynamics and priorities of churches, especially the larger denominations such as Roman Catholicism, but also for the ecumenical and interfaith priorities, strategies, and encounters of all Christians and churches at the official level, at the grassroots level, and for those more recently seeking to build bridges between the two.

New Ecclesiological Visions, New Ecclesial Priorities: From Vietnam to Argentina

Today the church stands radically transformed from that which surveyed itself and the world at the outset of the previous century. Of course, these lessons for ecclesiology are much more lessons for those doing ecclesiology in Europe and North America than they are for those seeking to make sense of the church elsewhere, for on other continents the lived reality of World Christianity is so often in the air they breathe and therefore all pervasive of

---

[31] Ibid., 133.

[32] Cf., for example, Vincent J Miller, "Where Is the Church? Globalization and Catholicity," *Theological Studies* 69 (2008): 412–32; and Gerard Mannion, "Driving the Haywain: Where Stands the Church 'Catholic' Today?" in *Ecumenical Ecclesiology: Unity, Diversity, Otherness in a Fragmented World,* ed. Gesa Thiessen (New York and London: T&T Clark, 2009), 13–34.

their experiences. The challenge in those other regions is to resist the categories, some of the epistemological strictures, and the normative ecclesiological patterns, methods, and structures that have dominated so much thinking for too long in the Euro–North American academy and ecclesia alike.

Peter Phan, himself, has echoed and expanded upon the call for a reenvisioned catholicity, with transformed ecclesial structures and priorities, which we briefly considered in our last section; and he has done so with specific reference to the emergence of World Christianity:

> All available data tend to indicate a southern shift in the Christian population. As a result, for the first time in its history Christianity is becoming a truly global or world church. This phenomenon presents tremendous challenges to its unity but also provides numerous opportunities for its growth into catholicity. The way to meet these challenges and to become truly global does not seem to lie in a return to Christendom or the Counter-Reformation but in forging communities of communion and solidarity.[33]

Phan has especially demonstrated how the inculturated churches can help transform the wider church in many ways and so, therefore, also for ecclesiology.[34] Elsewhere he summarizes further ways, speaking of the Asian Bishops' conferences' commitment to a *new way of being church in Asia*.[35] This vision of the church, this *new ecclesiology* is one constructed out of the labors of Christians who have lived out the reality of being Christian and so being church in diverse contexts—the contexts that World Christianity has helped scholars better appreciate and that ecclesiology has been seeking to better engage. Obviously, it is an ecclesiology that is very different from those of a more traditional Euro–North American character:

> This new way of being church is not concerned with structural and organizational issues but with a spirituality [so, also ecclesiology] that is appropriate to the Asian context. The focus of Asian Christian spirituality is not on *ad intra*, "churchy" issues. These have relevance only to the extent they contribute to the *ad extra* mission of witnessing to the presence and work of Christ and the Spirit in all humanity,

---

[33] Phan, "A New Christianity, but What Kind?" 81.

[34] See Phan, *Christianity with an Asian Face*, 171–83.

[35] See Phan, *In Our Own Tongues*, 14–17; and Phan, *Christianity with an Asian Face*, 176–82.

and not only in Christianity. In other words, spirituality is not geared inward, that is, toward building up the institutions of the church; rather it adopts a predominantly outward movement, toward realizing and spreading the reign of God, in oneself and in others.[36]

In all this, we see further developments in recent ecclesiologies mirroring most notably the need to move away from normative, *blueprint* ecclesiologies applied across the board and imposed *top-down* to approaches that proceed *from below* and so can be more attentive to local realities, needs, aspirations, cultures and, contexts.[37]

The further good news is that ecclesiologies that are informed by such lessons are fast becoming more prevalent;prominent; influential; and, in a number of the larger denominations, even more mainstream. And many of the theological insights that scholars such as Peter Phan have helped contribute to and develop are equally becoming more mainstream—even those aspects that were once deemed suspect or even unorthodox.

Let us consider the example of Pope Francis. He and Peter Phan have much in common. Both come from the Global South. Both are acutely attentive to the need to be mindful of the needs of particular contexts and especially of the plight of the poor and marginalized. Both know all too well the damage wreaked by colonialism, having seen its lasting effects first hand. Both know that doctrinal details are far less important than social justice and dialogue among differing churches, and both exhibit a nonhierarchical ecclesiology formed by their contexts, and both owe much to the liberationist theologies for the shaping of their ecclesiologies. The similarities do not end there. Both are incredibly grounded. If Pope Francis was the first pope to have worked as a nightclub bouncer, then Peter Phan may be unique or at least among a tiny select band of theologians to have worked as a garbage collector.

Perhaps we can say that this is the very first pope to address many of the key insights of the emergence of World Christianity as a discipline, not just to allow such to influence his, but also, in many instances, to bring such insights into church teaching and so effectively to become official church policy.

At the heart of his vision for the church, of course, is that it becomes more fully a *poor church for the poor*, which also addresses the contexts of the Global South much more directly than many alternative ecclesiological

---

[36] Phan, "Asian Christian Spirituality," 515–16.

[37] See for example, Roger Haight, *Historical Ecclesiology: Christian Community in History* (New York, 2004), 1:17–67; and Mannion, *Ecclesiology and Postmodernity*, esp. chaps. 1–4.

visions. This is clearly demonstrated in his groundbreaking apostolic exhortation, *Evangelii gaudium*.[38]

Francis's ecclesiology, his vision of church, is one that is no longer by default hierarchical—in fact, one could say the ecclesiology of *Evangelii gaudium* is very much one that prioritizes the perspective from below. Inculturation is actually endorsed in multiple parts and even stated as necessary. Outdated liturgical mentalities, the imposition of Western cultural forms, outdated wider ecclesial practices, and norms and laws are mildly chastised here, or fastidiously rejected there.

Pope Francis also deals with the issue of inculturation at the same time as he deals with questions of differing forms of interpreting and expressing the faith. He speaks of "a unity which is never uniformity but a multifaceted and inviting harmony."[39] There are profound ecumenical implications for what he communicates here. Traditionalists who reject any sense of contextual theology and practice are admonished, and by logical implication so is the perspective that would impose a rigidly uniform liturgy across the world when Francis states,

> We would not do justice to the logic of the incarnation if we thought of Christianity as monocultural and monotonous. While it is true that some cultures have been closely associated with the preaching of the Gospel and the development of Christian thought, the revealed message is not identified with any of them; its content is transcultural. Hence in the evangelization of new cultures, or cultures which have not received the Christian message, it is not essential to impose a specific cultural form, no matter how beautiful or ancient it may be, together with the Gospel. The message that we proclaim always has a certain cultural dress, but we in the Church can sometimes fall into a needless hallowing of our own culture, and thus show more fanaticism than true evangelizing zeal.[40]

Elsewhere in the document, we are told that pluralism is deemed to be the work of the Holy Spirit (no. 131), even when encountering difference can prove challenging. Francis takes care to stress the importance of freedom in all this and acknowledges that

---

[38] Pope Francis, *Evangelii gaudium* (November 2013), no. 49.
[39] Ibid., no. 117.
[40] Ibid.

for those who long for a monolithic body of doctrine guarded by all and leaving no room for nuance, this might appear as undesirable and leading to confusion. But in fact such variety serves to bring out and develop different facets of the inexhaustible riches of the Gospel.[41]

It is thus that Francis enshrines the goodness and even necessity of theological and doctrinal pluralism for the faith: "we need to listen to and complement one another in our partial reception of reality and the Gospel."[42] Again, this runs very much counter to the official ecclesial vision of his immediate predecessor for whom pluralism and relativism were effectively one and the same thing, and therefore to be resisted by the church.

It further appears, both in his frequent citing of teaching documents from national and regional episcopal conferences—something repeated with even more intensity in his June 2015 encyclical *Laudato si'*, but, much more importantly, in the substantive statements he makes of his own in other parts of the document—that Francis is stressing the importance of, perhaps one might say even priority of the local church and emphasizing the need for decentralization.[43] For example, consider *Evangelii gaudium* no. 30, "It is the Church incarnate in a certain place, equipped with all the means of salvation bestowed by Christ, but with local features."

As if directly addressing the debates and issues we have been considering throughout this essay and the transformation of ecclesiology that the era of World Christianity demands, he states that "Christianity does not have simply one cultural expression," indeed, "In the diversity of peoples who experience the gift of God, each in accordance with its own culture, the Church expresses her genuine catholicity."[44] This reflects the new understanding of catholicity emergent from the fruits of the World Christianity discipline, which, in turn, of course, are the fruits of the lived experiences of the diverse Christian communities around the globe: "The whole is greater than the part, but it is also greater than the sum of its parts. There is no need, then, to be overly obsessed with limited and particular questions. We constantly have to broaden our horizons and see the greater good which will benefit us all."[45]

---

[41] Ibid., no. 40.

[42] Ibid., no. 40, note 44.

[43] Francis actually *begins* this document by declaring that decentralization in the church is to be a key priority for his pontificate (ibid., no.16).

[44] Ibid., no. 116.

[45] Ibid., no. 235.

Conclusion

In this discussion on doing ecclesiology for our times, we have explored some of the main lessons those doing ecclesiology in these times can learn from embracing the inescapability of inculturation, acknowledging the global reach of the church, affirming the world in so doing, and helping to both understand and further develop the consciousness of World Christianity itself. Furthermore, we have considered the implications of the fact that the sense of the church as enjoying a wide range of diverse and inculturated local manifestations is nothing new and the two-way inculturative processes we hear ecclesiologists and scholars of World Christianity discussing today have equally always been with the church. This is good news.

We have also explored the developing consciousness of World Christianity and of Christianity as a polycentric faith, alongside the need to reenvision and expand our understanding of catholicity in the light of the twin phenomena of globalization and glocalization. These lessons for ecclesiology are primarily for the Euro–North American church and academy because in other continents the lived reality reflects the truth of these lessons on a daily basis. Therefore, we can learn much about new ways of being church (and so of understanding church, that is, doing ecclesiology) from the Global South and other contexts. In particular, solidarity and social justice rightly come more to the missionary fore in such visions, just as ecumenical and interreligious dialogue are more openly and enthusiastically embraced. In all, we come to appreciate in new ways and in greater depth the full extent to which Christianity is a world religion that is always local and universal—an ever-inculturating church of churches.

12

RESHAPING LITURGICAL AND
SACRAMENTAL LIFE IN A WORLD CHURCH

Kenan Osborne

Fifty years ago, the bishops at Vatican II ended the council with prayers of gratitude, hope, and humility. They were grateful for the many sessions of Vatican II and for the documents that they had promulgated. They were hopeful that the Catholic Church throughout the world would be blessed by the changes they had expressed in their documents. They humbly asked the members of the Roman Catholic Church to make the bishops' suggestions a part of their belief in God.

It is well known, however, that the conciliar documents were proposed and developed by a council of bishops that was clearly divided. In a subtle way, Pope John Paul II, in his apostolic letter, *"Tertio millennio adveniente,"* described the situation as follows:

> The Second Vatican Council is often considered as the beginning of a new era in the life of the Church. This is true, but at the same time it is difficult to overlook the fact that the Council drew much from the experiences and reflections of the immediate past.... The "new" grows out of the "old and the "old" finds a fuller expression in the "new."[1]

The liturgical renewal had already begun long before Vatican II. From 1830 to 1903 there was a *monastic phase* of liturgical renewal under the leadership of the Benedictine, Prosper Guéranger (1805–75),[2] and there was an apostolic or *pastoral phase* under the Benedictine, Lambert Beauduin

---

[1] John Paul II, *Tertio millennio adveniente*, no. 18.
[2] Prosper Guéranger, however, followed the Roman liturgical prescriptions in a strict way. Nonetheless, he involved the Benedictine monks in a more active liturgical framework.

(1873–1960).[3] In the same period of time, other liturgical leaders were also renewing sacramental liturgy, such as Odo Casel and Romano Guardini in Germany,[4] Pius Parsch in Austria,[5] and Virgil Michel in the United States.[6] These liturgical reformers paved the way for the interest in the liturgy exhibited by Pius XII. Thomas O'Meara describes Pius XII in the following way:

> Pius adopted a moderate attitude toward modernity's relationship to the Church; he approved a limited use of the historical-critical method for biblical studies (*Divino Afflante Spiritu*, 1943); a modest beginning for the liturgical movement (*Mediator Dei*, 1947); and a theology of the Church that promoted positive relationships with nonbelievers (*Mystici Corporis*, 1950).[7]

From the pontificate of Pius XII down to the opening session of the Second Vatican Council on October 11, 1962, many Catholic scholars had centered their research on the history and theology of the church's sacramental and liturgical life. As a result, many of the conciliar bishops came to Rome with a strong background in the history and theology of the Christian sacraments. Because of this background, the bishops were able to promulgate *Sacrosanctum concilium* as their first official constitution, on December 4, 1963.

From the second half of the eighteenth century down to today's fiftieth year after Vatican Council, several major issues have seriously restructured Catholic sacramental theology and sacramental liturgy.

1. *Over the past one hundred years, the history of each sacrament has been researched in detail.* From 1896 down to today, the history of each sacrament has been studied, analyzed, and formulated. Never before did the Christian community have such a detailed history

---

[3] See Keith F. Pecklers, "Liturgical Theology," in *The New Westminster Dictionary of Liturgy and Worship,* ed. Paul Bradshaw (Louisville, KY: Westminster John Knox Press, 2002), 285.

[4] For the liturgical leadership of Odo Casel, see John Schanz, *Introduction to the Sacraments* (New York: Pueblo Publishing, 1983), 136–42. For Romano Guardini, see Nathan Mitchell, *Meeting Mystery* (Maryknoll, NY: Orbis Books, 2006), 249–50.

[5] Pecklers, 285.

[6] See Kenan Osborne, *Community, Eucharist, and Spirituality* (Liguori, MO: Liguori Publications, 2007), 93–94.

[7] Thomas O'Meara, "Pius XII," in the *Harper-Collins Encyclopedia of Catholicism* (New York: HarperCollins Publishers, 1995), 1006.

of each sacrament, and by the end of the twentieth century, this historical research had raised serious challenges to the teaching of the church that all seven sacraments were instituted by Christ.

2. *The sevenfold number of the sacraments has been theologically reconsidered on the basis that either Jesus's humanity or the church itself is the Ursakrament.* From 1960 onward, major theologians have presented the humanity of Christ as the foundational sacrament or *Ursakrament*. In the same period of time, other major theologians have presented the church as the foundational sacrament, the *Ursakrament*. Moreover, the documents of Vatican II explicitly state seven times that the church is a sacrament. Contemporary theologians have used the term, *Ursakrament*, to emphasize that either the sacramentality of the human nature of Jesus or the sacramentality of the church itself is the foundational sacrament from which the seven ritual sacraments obtain their respective theological and liturgical meanings. Both of these positions present a major theological change vis-à-vis the church's teaching on the sacraments.

3. *The current participation of Catholic clergy and scholars in interreligious dialogues has raised the question of an infinite God.* From the middle of the twentieth century, the leadership of the Catholic Church has slowly but surely endorsed the participation of Catholic clergy and scholars in the major ecumenical meetings such as the World Council of Churches. However, after Vatican II, church leadership has strengthened its endorsement of Catholic participation in major interreligious dialogues. In the interreligious discussions, church leaders have begun to include other world religions within the framework of the kingdom of God. Today's interreligious conferences have not yet considered in any detail the infinity of God. However, if God is truly infinite, no denominational church or religion can claim that their God is the one and only true God.

Over the Past One Hundred Years the History of Each Sacrament Has Been Researched in Great Detail

In 1896, Henry Charles Lea published his volume, *A History of Auricular Confession and Indulgences in the Latin Church*.[8] This volume was strongly anti-Catholic. A French Catholic canon lawyer, Auguste

---

[8] H. C. Lea, *A History of Auricular Confession and Indulgences in the Latin Church* (Philadelphia: Lea Brothers, 1896).

Boudinhon, was one of the first Catholic authors who wrote an article, refuting several major positions that Lea maintained, but Boudinhon's article was historically insufficient to contradict many aspects of Lea's presentation on the sacrament of penance. In the next decades, more scholarly and detailed studies were written by Catholic authors such as Francis Xavier von Funk, Elphège-Florent Vacandard, and P. A. Kirsch.[9]

Lea's three-volume book engendered a strong interest in the history not only of penance but also an interest in the history of all seven sacraments. A large number of these historical studies on the seven sacraments offered in a detailed way a new appreciation of each sacrament. These historical studies of each sacrament by reputable Catholic scholars also challenged the standard church teaching on Catholic sacramental life. These works have seriously called into question the sensitive issue that Jesus, during his lifetime, instituted all seven sacraments.

Today, we can say that baptism and Eucharist have their historical roots in the life of Jesus. However, the histories of the other five sacraments *qua sacramenta* do not have a sacramental beginning in the New Testament writings. The first instance of a *sacrament* of reconciliation is found in the writings of Hermas (c. 140) who in a brief way describes that there is a penitential rite for serious sin after baptism, but this penitential ritual could only be received once in a person's lifetime. Prior to this statement by Hermas, we have no other text that focuses on a sacramental rite of reconciliation. There are many references to a forgiving God, but the brief historical reference by Hermas is the first sacramental reference to a forgiving God.

In the *Apostolic Tradition* (c. 215), we have the first extant reference to a sacramental ordination ritual that was apparently taking place in the region of Rome at least for some decades. As there is no other third-century reference to a sacrament of ordination, it would appear that the ritual that the *Apostolic Tradition* described could only be seen as a local or regional sacramental rite.[10]

---

[9] Francis Xavier von Funk, "Zur altchristlichen Bussdisciplin," in *Kirchengeschichtliche abhandlungen und untersuchungen*, vol. 1 (Paderborn, Germany: F. Schoningh, 1896), 144-209; Elphège-Florent Vacandard, *La pènitence publique dans l'Eglise primitive* (Paris: Bloud, 1903); and P. A Kirsch, *Zur geschichte der Katholischen beichte* (Würzburg, Germany: Gobel & Scherer, 1902).

[10] See Kenan Osborne, *Priesthood: A History of Ordained Ministry in the Roman Catholic Church* (New York: Paulist Press, 1988). In chapters 4 and 5, I present in detail the historical development of sacramental ordination. There is a detailed analysis of the *Apostolic Tradition*. We have to wait several centuries after the *Apostolic Tradition* before we find clear data on the sacrament of ordination.

In the *Apostolic Tradition*, we have the first clear indication of sacred oil for the sick. In the early church, Catholic women and men would bring a vial of oil to the church to have it blessed and then take it home, where they anointed a sick child, or a sick relative, or even an anointing of themselves. In the latter part of the tenth and eleventh centuries, some theologians began to unite the sacrament of anointing with the forgiveness of sin. Slowly but surely, since the forgiveness of sin was involved, only those who were priests were officially legislated as the only administers of this sacrament.

The history of the sacrament of confirmation has engendered serious problems. I have presented this situation in detail in my book, *The Christian Sacraments of Initiation*.[11] In the fourth and fifth century, there were instances when the bishops would come to a village church and *confirm* those who had been baptized. At first, this *confirmation-anointing* was related to the earlier baptism. It confirmed that an individual was not baptized into a small parish community. Rather, one was baptized by the major leader, the *episcopus*, into a larger diocesan community. In the Eastern churches, down to the present, the anointing with oil is a major part of baptism and administered by priests, and this anointing is confirming the baptism. In the Rite of Christian Initiation of Adults, today, priests also confirm at the same time that they baptize. As cited above, the sacrament of confirmation presents us today with a number of major issues. One of the main issues is its separation from baptism.

In 1150, Peter Lombard "determined that there are seven 'sacraments' of the New Law."[12] We have seen that the sacraments of reconciliation and confirmation have histories that do not go back to the New Testament. The sacrament of marriage is also a development with the Catholic Church. Theodore Mackin has published three volumes of major research on Catholic marriage: *What Is Marriage in the Catholic Church?*, *Divorce and Remarriage in the Catholic Church*, and *The Marital Sacrament*.[13] In his

---

[11] See Kenan Osborne, *The Christian Sacraments of Initiation* (New York: Paulist Press, 1987), 107–37. In these pages, I cite Sigisbert Regli, Louis Ligier, Hans Küng, Gregory Dix, and many others. Sometime in the eleventh century, we find in the West—and only in the West—a celebration of confirmation separated from baptism.

[12] See Kevin Irwin, "Sacrament," in *The New Dictionary of Theology* (Wilmington, DE: Michael Glazier, 1987), 914. Irwin's article is rather lengthy—c. 12 pages—and he is presenting the common position that Peter Lombard's *Sententiae* is the first theological source that states that there are seven sacraments.

[13] Theodore Mackin, *What Is Marriage in the Catholic Church?* (New York: Paulist Press, 1982); Theodore Mackin, *Divorce and Remarriage* (New York: Paulist Press, 1984); and Theodore Mackin, *The Marital Sacrament* (New York: Paulist Press, 1989).

volumes as well as in other Catholic writers, marriage seems to have been accepted as a sacrament in the twelfth century.

In the early church, both the terms—*mystery* and *sacrament*—were often used for liturgical celebrations. Dennis O'Callaghan, in his article, "Christ, Sacrament of God," states the following:

> The original usage of mystery-sacrament was much more flex-
> ible—it was applied not only to the Mass, the seven sacraments
> and various liturgical acts, but to Christian doctrine, Church disci-
> pline and the whole Christian religion. In particular, it [the term
> sacrament] was used to denote the divine plan of salvation and
> the mysteries of Christ's life (*sacramentum passionis, incarnationis,
> paschatis*)—here sacrament means a truth or incident which has a
> hidden divine salvific meaning and content.[14]

From 1150 onward, the major medieval theologians, such as Peter Lombard, Alexander of Hales, Thomas Aquinas, Bonaventure, and John Duns Scotus, developed lengthy *theologies* of the seven sacraments, but these authors did not have the historical data to verify when each sacrament first appeared. Thus, they assumed that they were all instituted by Jesus himself.

In the Protestant Reformation of the sixteenth century, leaders, such as Martin Luther, John Calvin, and Ulrich Zwingli, maintained that in the sacred scriptures, only baptism and Eucharist were presented as sacraments. Roman Catholics, from the sixteenth century onward, have maintained over and over again that all seven sacraments were instituted by Christ.

In the *Revised Catechism of the Catholic Church*, there are only a few paragraphs that deal with the history of the sacraments, and the authors do not indicate the ways in which this sacramental history has reshaped the neoscholastic approach to the seven sacraments as presented in the *Catechism*.[15] The authors of this section of the *Catechism* (nos. 1210–1266),

---

[14] Dennis O'Callaghan, "Christ, Sacrament of God," in *Sacraments: The Gestures of Christ* (New York: Sheed and Ward, 1964), 25.

[15] In the *Catechism of the Catholic Church*, the presentation of the sacrament of penance offers a historical note in no. 1447. In the early centuries of the church only those who committed certain grave sins had to enter the process of reconciliation. From other sources, we know that the grave sins were publicly known murder, publicly known apostasy, and publicly known adultery. The authors then add, "To this order of penitents (which concerned only certain grave sins), one was only rarely admitted and in certain regions only once in a lifetime." The authors make no mention of the many Christians who did not commit the above *grave sins* and during their entire lifetime they

which deals with the seven sacraments, use the title *Section Two: The Seven Sacraments of the Church*. In these pages, there are only a few references to the history of the sacraments, and these references are all in small type, which indicates "observations of an historical or apologetic nature, or supplementary doctrinal explanations." The authors do not present any detailed history of each sacrament.[16] One might say that these authors have simply ignored the historical studies on each sacrament that took place in the twentieth century.

In general, one can conclude that in the official Roman Catholic Church today the history of the individual sacraments has not modified the sacramental rituals in any overarching way. On the other hand, one can state that Catholic liturgical and sacramental theologians for the most part carefully present a full picture of sacramental history, and the results of their historical analyses call into question the historical institution of the seven sacraments by Jesus.

Since 1960 Five New Sacramental Theologies Have Been Accepted by the Catholic Church

From 1960 to 1997, five new theological presentations on the Christian sacraments have changed the Tridentine teaching on the sacraments in a radical way. In this period of time, a number of Catholic theologians began to present a wider theological understanding of sacrament. Not only have they theologically presented the humanity of Jesus as a primordial sacrament, an *Ursakrament*, but they have presented the church itself as an *Ursakrament* (in the documents of Vatican II, the bishops on seven occasions state that the church itself is a sacrament). The *Catechism of the Catholic Church* includes a restatement of the neoscholastic approach to the seven sacraments, but there is a second theology of the Christian sacraments found there that is new but also official. This new sacramental theology is

---

never received the sacrament of reconciliation. Their sins were forgiven in and through their prayers and their reception of the Eucharist. This historical situation lasted many centuries, and therefore during these centuries the majority of Christians never went to confession. The history of each sacrament offers us new and different insights that complicate any simple statement that the seven sacraments were instituted by Christ in a way that has never been essentially changed. The historical material on each of the seven sacraments presents us with major changes. For the history of baptism in the *Catechism*, see nos. 1229–1233; for confirmation, see nos. 1290–1292; for Eucharist, anointing of the sick, ordination, and marriage, historical explanations are minimal.

[16] *Catechism of the Catholic Church*, no. 20, p. 11.

entitled "The Liturgy—Work of the Holy Trinity." In this part of the *Cate-chism*, the term *liturgy* includes sacramental liturgy, see Section One, nos. 1076–1112. As a result, contemporary theology of the Catholic sacraments is no longer limited to the seven sacraments. Let us consider in some detail, each of these different approaches to sacramental theology. Each of them has its own validity, and none of them have been rejected by the Vatican curia.

The Human Nature of Jesus Is a Sacrament of God

One of the most important and influential authors, who focused on the sacramentality of Jesus's human nature, was Edward Schillebeeckx. In 1960, he published a book entitled, *Christus: Sacrament van de Godsont-moeting* (English translation: *Christ the Sacrament of the Encounter with God*, 1963).[17] In 1963, Karl Rahner published a similar book, *Kirche und sakrament* (English translation: *The Church and the Sacraments*, 1963).[18] Both authors were widely read by Catholic scholars and by many bishops, and as a result both writings influenced many bishops and theologians who were officially present at Vatican II. In the documents of Vatican II, Jesus as primordial sacrament is not mentioned, but the openness to sacramentality beyond the seven sacraments is clearly evident in the documents of Vatican II, as we shall see in the third approach.

The Church Itself Is the Ursakrament, The Foundational Sacrament

In 1963, Otto Semmelroth published a volume entitled *Vom Sinn der sakramente* (English translation: *Church and Sacrament*, 1965).[19] In this volume, Semmelroth describes the church as a sacrament over and over again. He writes,

---

[17] Edward Schillebeeckx, *Christus: Sacrament van de Godsonmoeting* (Bilthoven, the Netherlands: H. Nelissen, 1960); and an English translation by C. Ernst, *Christ the Sacrament of the Encounter with God* (New York: Sheed and Ward, 1963).

[18] Karl Rahner, *Kirche und sakrament* (Freiburg: Herder, 1961); and an English translation by W. J. O'Hara, *The Church and the Sacraments* (New York: Herder and Herder, 1963).

[19] Otto Semmelroth, *Vom sinn der sakramente* (Frankfurt: Verlag Josef Knecht, 1960); and an English translation by Emily Schossberger, *Church and Sacrament* (Notre Dame, IN: Fides Publishers, 1965).

This leads to the central theme . . . an explanation of the visible Church as a sacramental sign.[20]

The church as sacramental sign.[21]

The sacramental Church joins itself to a person in the individual sacraments and holds him/her in itself, which is in the Church as fundamental sacrament, just as a person carries something in physical closeness within the clasp of one's arms.[22]

Karl Rahner, in his essay, "Zur theologie des symbols," goes even further describing the church as the primordial sacrament, *Ursakrament*. He writes.

The teaching on the sacraments is—from the standpoint of Catholic theology—the classical place in which a theology of symbols is truly presented. The ritual sacraments are concretized and actualized by the symbolic reality of the church as *Ursakrament*.[23]

Rahner was a peritus at the Second Vatican Council, and his understanding of the church as sacrament undoubtedly helped many bishops on this issue. Prior to the council, there were theologians, such as Semmelroth, Schillebeeckx, and Rahner who presented the church as a basic sacrament. The bishops at the council did not endorse any of these preconciliar theologies of the church as a sacrament. They used the phrase *the church is a sacrament*, but they gave no distinct theology of this terminology. However, the conciliar bishops certainly approved the phrase: *the church is a sacrament*.

---

[20] *Church and Sacrament,* 13.

[21] Ibid., 28.

[22] Ibid., 85.

[23] Karl Rahner, "Zur theologie des symbols," in *Schriften zur theologie* (Zürich: Benziger Verlag, 1962), 4:299: "Die Sakramentenlehre ist der klassische Ort, in dem in der katholischen Theologie eine Theologie des Symbols überhaupt vorgetragen wird." "Die Sakramente konkretisieren und aktualisieren die Symbolwirklichkeit der Kirche als des Ursakramentes auf das Leben des einzelnen hin und setzen schon darum, entsprechend dem Wesen dieser Kirche, eine Symbolwirklichkeit." In John Schanz, *Introduction to the Sacraments* (New York: Pueblo Publishing, 1983), 41, he also describes the church as a sacrament and states that such a view is part of patristic theology.

*In The Documents of Vatican II, The Phrase,
The Church Is a Sacrament, Appears Seven Times*

In the aftermath of the Second Vatican Council, many Catholic theologians have focused on the conciliar use of the term *sacrament* as a description of the church. It appears three times in the Dogmatic Constitution on the Church, *Lumen gentium*, chapter 1, no. 1; chapter 2, no. 9; and chapter 7, no. 48. It appears once in the pastoral constitution, *Gaudium et spes*, chapter 4, no. 45. It appears twice in the liturgical constitution, *Sacrosanctum concilium*, chapter 1, no. 8 and no. 26. It also appears in the decree, *Ad gentes divinitus*, chapter 1, no. 8.

The meaning of sacrament in these citations is not specified; the word, sacrament, simply appears in the text. Some scholars claim that in the opening paragraph of *Lumen gentium*, the bishops used the term *sacrament* only in a descriptive way, since in the opening paragraph the text reads: "Cum autem Ecclesia sit in Christo veluti sacramentum." The Latin term *veluti* does not mean that the church is simply a kind of sacrament. There is no basis for such an interpretation. Rather, the term *sacrament* in these instances is similar in intent to the many other times when the bishops referred to the church as a sacrament. The Latin word *veluti* can be translated as *for example*, or *for instance*. The Vatican II documents, therefore, permit us to consider the church as a basic sacrament. This is clearly a new *officially approved* designation of the church itself.[24]

*The Updated Neoscholastic Theology of the
Sacraments in the Catechism of the Catholic Church*

In the *Catechism of the Catholic Church*, there is a lengthy section regarding the seven sacraments (nos. 1210–1666). The title reads *Section Two: The Seven Sacraments of the Church*. Each sacrament is presented

---

[24] For a detailed presentation of these conciliar statements on the church as sacrament, see Kenan Osborne, *Sacramental Theology: 50 Years after Vatican II* (Hobe Sound, FL: Lectio Publishing, 2014), 9–15. In these pages I give the Latin text and the official English translation for each citation of the church as sacrament. In *Lumen gentium*, the opening paragraph reads, "Ecclesia sit in Christo veluti sacramentum seu signum et instrumentum." Several contemporary theologians translate *veluti* by such phrases as *similar to* or *akin to*, but *veluti* in the Latin language has a variety of meanings: *just as, even as*, etc. *Veluti* is used only once; the other six instances simply use the word *sacramentum*. It is very clear that the bishops wanted to state that the church itself is a sacrament, and *veluti* is to be understood as follows: "The church is in Christ as a sacrament and sign."

in a way that clearly resembles the neoscholastic approach to the seven sacraments.[25] I would like to indicate the format that the *Catechism of the Catholic Church* uses by presenting the manner in which only one sacrament, namely, baptism, is theologically described. The reader will notice that in this explanation, there is a similarity with the pre–Vatican II catechisms of the Catholic Church. The section on baptism is divided by the following five headings. I have summarized the main point for each section.

1. *What is this sacrament called?* It is called baptism since a person is immersed into the water or the water is poured over a person's head, signifying a washing of regeneration, and also an in-depth enlightenment on the meaning of Jesus and his message.

2. *Baptism in the economy of salvation.* The authors explain how baptism is prefigured in the Old Testament through the creation of water, the flooding at the time of Noah, the crossing of the Red Sea at the time of Moses, and the crossing of the Jordan River by the People of God when they moved into the promised land.

3. *How is the sacrament of baptism celebrated?* The authors explain the liturgy of baptism and its symbolization through the use of water as well as the anointing with holy oil, the investing of the newly baptized in a white garment, and the lighting of a baptismal candle.

4. *Who can receive baptism?* The authors focus on both the baptism of adults and the baptism of infants. For adults, the women and men must accept at least the beginnings of faith, which they will then develop as their life moves on. For infants and children, faith is a part of life that they must develop through the encouragement and teaching of parents, catechists, etc.

5. *Who can baptize?* The authors state that the ordinary ministers are bishops, priests, and deacons, but in cases of necessity, anyone can baptize if they have the correct intention.

6. *The necessity of baptism.* The authors state that baptism is necessary for salvation, but they also consider that the martyrdom of an

---

[25] The neoscholastic approach is clearly found in theological textbooks prior to Vatican II. It begins with a definition of sacraments, namely, a sacrament is a sensible sign, instituted by Christ to give grace. Each sacrament has its own matter and form. Each sacrament has it legitimate minister. The one who receives the sacrament must be in proper standing with God and the church. Each sacrament has its own effect. In this section of the *Catechism*, the explanation of the seven sacraments is clearly based on the neoscholastic view of the sacraments.

unbaptized person who believes in God and Jesus, that the death of an infant prior to baptism, and that the death of catechumens prior to their baptism are also saved.

7. *The grace of baptism.* The authors state that in baptism all sins are forgiven, that is, original sin and personal sin. A baptized person is a *new creature* and is *incorporated into the church*. Baptism—as well as confirmation and holy orders—effects an indelible sign on the baptized.

I have spent time on this theology of baptism, since it indicates that an updated form of neoscholastic theology of baptism is still an acceptable baptismal theology in the Roman Catholic Church.[26] In this section of the *Catechism*, a neoscholastic theology of the sacraments remains an acceptable theology of all seven sacraments.

Sacramental Liturgy: The Work of the Holy Trinity

However—and this is a major however—in the *Catechism* there is an earlier presentation of a theology of sacraments based on the work of the Holy Trinity. This new way is found in part two, section one, just prior to section two, which presents the neoscholastic form of sacramental theology.

In the sacramental textbooks written before Vatican II, one will never find a presentation of "Sacramental Liturgy—Work of the Holy Trinity." When I first read this section of the *Catechism*, I was deeply touched. In all my research into the Catholic sacraments, I have never found this approach to a theology of sacraments. If sacramental liturgy is the work of the Holy Trinity, then this understanding of sacramental life should be in first place. We are not looking at what the ministers of sacraments are doing, or what the recipients of sacraments are doing, or what are the matter and form of the sacrament, or what are the effects of the sacraments. Rather, we are starting with God not with anyone or anything created. In this short section,

---

[26] It is obvious that the authors of the *Catechism*, as well as Pope John Paul II, have continued to endorse neoscholastic theology. In the opening citations of the apostolic letter, *Laetamur magnopere*, as well as the apostolic constitution, *Fidei depositum*, we find a validation of a neoscholastic theology of the sacraments. In *Laetamur magnopere* one reads, "The Church now has at her disposal this new, authoritative exposition of the one and perennial apostolic faith, and it will serve as a 'valid and legitimate instrument' for ecclesial communion." This does not mean that it is the only *theology* of the sacraments, but it does mean that the neoscholastic approach to the sacraments remains theologically acceptable.

there is an amazing way of understanding sacramental theology and liturgy. Sacramental liturgy is the work of the Holy Trinity.

In the section entitled "The Father—Source and Goal of the Liturgy," two words are used to explain the work of God the Father. The first word is *blessing*. It occurs twenty-one times. On three occasions, we are blessing God the Father for his benevolence. On eighteen occasions, God the Father in the sacraments is blessing each one of us. The second word is *gift* or *grace freely bestowed*. It occurs twelve times. Eight times it is God the Father who gives his grace to each one of us. On three occasions, we are giving our thanks—thanksgiving—to God the Father in response to his goodness to us.

What is the work of God the Father in the sacramental liturgies? The answer is clear. God the Father is *blessing* us and *giving* his grace to us in baptism, in confirmation, in the Eucharist, in reconciliation, in the anointing of the sick, in marriage and in ordination. The blessing and giving of God the Father to all of us is the most important aspect of sacramental life. God the Father freely blesses us and freely gives us his grace in all seven sacraments. Our reply can only be a response of thanksgiving to God. The blessing and giving of God the Father in each of the sacraments is the most important aspect of sacramental theology. Issues such as matter and form, the eligibility of the recipient, and the minister are secondary issues. In the sacraments, we celebrate what God is doing not what we are doing.

Second, what is the work of Christ in the liturgy? The authors present us with two full pages, explaining what Jesus does in the sacraments. The key issue is Jesus's sending of the Holy Spirit. The authors use a chronological format in which there are four stages in which Jesus sends the Spirit of God to the ecclesial community.

Stage one: After Jesus's life, death, and resurrection, he ascends to the Father and is seated at the right hand of the Father. He then fulfills his promise: he pours out the Holy Spirit on his body which is the church.

Stage two: Jesus sends the Holy Spirit in a special way to his disciples who are gathered in the upper room. He sent the Spirit so that his disciples might preach the gospel to every creature.

Stage three: Jesus is present in the church's liturgical celebrations. Jesus is present in every sacramental celebration. The presence of Jesus in every sacramental liturgy is likewise more important than any focus on matter and form, and the eligibility of recipient and minister.

Stage four: In every sacramental liturgy, we share in a foretaste of that heavenly liturgy in which the angels and saints are now celebrating. In every sacramental liturgy, we are already drawn to the liturgy of heaven.

What Jesus is doing in our sacramental celebrations is his presence in each sacramental rite and his sending of the Spirit not only to the recipient and to the minister but to all who are present at these sacramental celebrations. Just as the work of God the Father is paramount in our understanding of sacramental life, so too the work of Jesus is equally paramount in our appreciation of each and every sacramental liturgy.

Third, what is the work of the Holy Spirit in the sacramental liturgies? As already mentioned, the work of the Father covers a page and a half. The work of Jesus covers two full pages. The work of the Holy Spirit is explained in four and a half pages. The authors of this part of the *Catechism* are over-expressive of the work of the Holy Spirit. In order to see what the Holy Spirit does, one should trace from paragraph to paragraph the verbs that the authors use to explain the work of the Holy Spirit: the Holy Spirit teaches us the faith; works in common with the church, prepares us for the coming of the Lord, makes Christ manifest to the assembly; makes the mystery of Christ present here and now, and unites the church to the life and mission of Christ. In the above statements of the work of the Holy Spirit, I have only covered two paragraphs and we have three pages to go. In my judgement, "Sacramental Liturgy—The Work of the Holy Trinity," should be the primary and main way in which today we explain the seven sacraments. Only after this explanation, should we consider such issues as matter, form, minister, and recipient.

The above section on Christian sacraments centers on a marvelous vision of the work of the Trinitarian God. In 2011, Peter Phan edited a book on the Trinity, namely, *The Cambridge Companion to the Trinity*.[27] Many theologians presented aspects of Trinitarian theology, covering the New Testament, the early Greek and Latin Fathers, the medieval theologians, the theologians of the Protestant Reformation and also the Trinity in the works of many contemporary scholars, Protestant, Catholic, and Orthodox, male and female, scholars from Korea, Finland, Australia, and Vietnam. He himself wrote a lengthy introduction and also a chapter on the Trinity in the writings of Karl Rahner.

Today, scholars are considering the theology of the Trinitarian God from the standpoint of theological history, from the standpoint of multicultural religions, and from the standpoint of contemporary physics. Peter Phan's book on the Trinity is clearly a breath of fresh air, when one realizes the many contemporary and multicultural efforts have been made so that

---

[27] Peter Phan, *The Cambridge Companion to the Trinity* (New York: Cambridge University Press, 2011).

one can see that liturgy is the work of a multirelational, that is, a Trinitarian God. The Christian sacraments are the work of this multirelational God. A theology of a Trinitarian God is a theology of an interrelational God. The Father, Son, and Holy Spirit are the traditional names, but today one might say the God is a trirelational unity.

The Current Participation of Catholic Clergy and Scholars in Interreligious Dialogues Has Raised the Question of an Infinite God

The Constitution on the Sacred Liturgy, *Sacrosanctum concilium*, is a remarkable document. In *Sacrosanctum concilium*, there is a lengthy section on "The Reform of the Sacred Liturgy" and in these reforms the bishops focused on the many cultures in today's world. They knew that adaptations of the liturgy to various cultures could not be set to one side. They also realized that the then-current Catholic liturgical services were one-sidedly Euro-American. The Catholic population, however, was increasing in the southern hemisphere and decreasing in the northern hemisphere. The majority of bishops were fully aware that the adaption of the liturgy to cultural temperaments and traditions could not be set to one side.

In the section entitled "Norms for Adapting the Liturgy to the Temperament and Traditions of Peoples" (nos. 37–40), the bishops focused on cultural changes in celebrating the liturgy, which clearly involved an inculturation of the sacraments. In the opening paragraphs (nos. 37–38), they call for "legitimate variations and adaptations to different groups, regions and people, especially in mission countries." The adaptations will change the celebration of the individual sacraments, the use of sacramentals, liturgical processions, liturgical language, sacred music and the arts. In no. 40, the bishops focus on "even more radical adaptations of the liturgy." These radical revisions of the liturgy should be made in racially different regions beyond the current Euro-American cultures. The bishops were very clear in stating their focus. They wrote, "In some places and circumstances, however, an even more radical adaptation of the liturgy is needed and this entails greater difficulties."[28]

The regional conferences of bishops are called on to take the first step. Many of these local bishops are themselves culturally related to the Christian communities, and therefore they understand the nuances of languages and the significance of cultural art, music, corporeal positions, etc. The first task

---

[28] The Constitution on the Sacred Liturgy, *Sacrosanctum Concilium*, no. 40.

of these bishops is to meet as a group to discuss radical liturgical changes. They were also asked to obtain the views of cultural experts within their dioceses. Only then, when the local Christian leadership and scholarship has drawn up the changes in the sacramental liturgies, should the bishops send their newly constructed rituals to the Apostolic See. The bishops should urge the Vatican leaders to grant permission for the local ecclesiastical authority "to permit and to direct the necessary preliminary experiments over a determined period of time."[29] In a careful but clearly stated way, the conciliar bishops wanted liturgical changes, even radical changes, which were more in keeping with local cultures.[30]

Today, we can ask this question: has the liturgy for the sacraments of the Catholic Church been revised, even radically revised vis-à-vis culture, in the aftermath of the council? The answer is yes and no. The sacramental rituals have been translated from Latin into a multitude of languages, and this was certainly a major change. In the Asian churches, the Federation of Asian Bishops' Conferences (FABC) has moved into cultural changes in a strong way. Indeed, in many parts of the world, the Catholic Church itself has changed. Postconciliar church life includes a high intensity of cultural differentiation. The solution of Europeanizing or Americanizing non-Western cultures is no longer acceptable. Today, the entire human race lives in a highly interrelational and intercultural way. Sacramental life, unfortunately, continues to be intraecclesial. The translation of liturgical texts into differing languages is, by itself, only a first step toward a multicultural liturgy.

The Asian FABC has provided us with an example of its own outward movement.[31] As a church it retains the seven sacraments, but the Asian

---

[29] Ibid., no. 55.

[30] In the years following Vatican II, there were a fairly large number of African theologians and bishops who were moving in the direction of a *more radical adaptation of the liturgy*, which also meant a radical adaptation of theology. Paul VI, in an address to the African bishops, urged them to bring about an *Église Africaine*. Such a development moves far beyond translating European documents into a native language. Such a development needs to embrace cultural forms of expression through songs, dances, bowing, standing, sitting, kneeling, etc. Inculturation does not have as its goal an overarching and all-inclusive framework; rather, inculturation has as its goal a deep respect for each and every given culture. After the council, the bishops returned to their home base. For a few bishops, *home base* was the Vatican Curia, and these bishops by and large were very conservative. Undoubtedly, they deliberately stalled the process as long as they could.

[31] See Abraham Kadalyil, *Toward a Relational Spirit Ecclesiology in Asia* (Saarbrücken, Germany: Verlag Dr. Müller Aktiengesselschaft, 2009). In this volume, Kadalyil centers his attention in a detailed way on the FABC. See also Peter Phan,

churches exist in a non-Christian world. Asian Christians can stay within their limited environment, or they can move outward into a non-Christian environment. One of the major steps in this outward movement was a nonfocusing on church and a refocusing on kingdom. The kingdom of God is much larger and more important than the Christian church. The Asian churches have taken to heart what some recent popes have stated.

In his apostolic exhortation, *Evangelii nuntiandi*, Paul VI states the following: The kingdom of God is to be considered as the absolute good, so that everything else is subordinate to it (8); only the kingdom is absolute and it makes everything else relative (8). Christ proclaims salvation as the outstanding element and, as it were, the central point of his good news (9). This kingdom and this salvation—these words may be regarded as the key to a full understanding of evangelization of Jesus Christ (10).

In chapter two of his encyclical, *Redemptoris missio*, John Paul II writes as follows: The church is not an end unto herself (19); the church is effectively and concretely at the service of the kingdom (20); the church is ordered toward the kingdom of God (18); the church is distinct from Christ and the kingdom of God (18); the church is indissolubly united to both (18).[32]

The centering on the kingdom rather than on the church helps us today, since many Roman Catholics are beginning to be part of interreligious conferences. These contemporary interreligious conferences began in the latter part of the nineteenth century, and they have continued down to the present. As the years went by, these interreligious conferences became more focused and more effective. Some of the major meetings are as follows:

1893 The *World's Parliament of Religions* was held in Chicago. Other major ecumenical events began to take place after this meeting, and these sectarian meetings focused more on individual religions rather than on interreligious dialogues.

"'Reception' or 'Subversion' of Vatican II by the Asian Churches?" in *Vatican II: Forty Years Later*, ed. William Madges (Maryknoll, NY: Orbis Books. 2005), 26–54. Phan has provided us with a detailed description of the postconciliar Asian churches. See also Julius-Kei Kato, *How Immigrant Christians Living in Mixed Cultures Interpret Their Religion* (Lewiston, NY: Edwin Mellen Press, 2012).

[32] There are other similar citations in *Redemptoris missio* from Pope John Paul II: "This proclamation [of the kingdom of God] is relevant also for immense sections of the human race who profess non-Christian religions in which the spiritual life of innumerable human communities find valid expression" (no. 53). "These religions, possessing as they do, a splendid patrimony of religious writings, have taught generations of men how to pray" (no. 53).

1895 The *World Student Christian Federation* held its opening session in Vadstena, Sweden.

1910 The *World Missionary Conference* held its opening session in Edinburgh.

1920 The encyclical from the *Orthodox Synod* in Constantinople suggested an ongoing fellowship of churches.

1948 The *World Council of Churches* (WCC) was officially inaugurated at Canberra, Australia. Members from 147 national churches were the initial participants.

1961 Pope John XXIII established the Secretariat for Promoting Christian Unity, and he appointed *official observers* to the 1960 general assembly of the WCC in New Delhi.

1962 The *Second Vatican Council* began, and during its sessions several ecumenical and world-religion documents were developed such as the decree on ecumenism, *Unitatis reintegratio* (1964), the decree on the Catholic Eastern Churches, *Orientalium ecclesiarum* (1965), and the declaration of the relation of the church to other religions, *Nostra aetate* (1965).

1964 The first edition of the *Journal of Ecumenical Studies* appeared. In 2015, the fiftieth volume of the journal was published. In this issue of the journal, scholars from all over the world describe what Leonard Swidler and his wife had accomplished from 1964 to 2015. The essays of these men and women indicate how in depth and how widespread today's ecumenical and interreligious meetings truly are.[33]

1965 Paul VI approved Catholic participation in a joint working group, which was considered as an official forum with the WCC. Today, Catholic participants are active in the WCC, but they do so as nonofficial members of the WCC.

The separation of kingdom and church in Roman Catholic theology has helped to develop a way in which Catholics are now able to view the ways in which the kingdom of God exists in other religions. Churches and major religions may remain divided, but the kingdom of God is coextensive with the human race in varying degrees. Consequently, the kingdom of God unites the members of world religions in an intricate way.

---

[33] See, *Journal of Ecumenical Studies: A Festschrift in Honor of Leonard Swidler* 50/1 (2015). This is a major source for an understanding of how widespread interreligious dialogue has become in the past fifty years.

However, there is one more item that the interreligious conferences need to consider, and that issue is the infinity of God. To date, interreligious conferences have not focused on the infinity of God. This is a theme that has interested me over many years.[34] Neither the Old Testament nor the New Testament uses the terms infinity and infinite. In the writings of the Greek and Latin Fathers of the church, the words *infinitum, infinitas,* ἀόριστον, and ἄπειρον are used here and there, but in their writings there is no lengthy theological discussion on the infinity of God.[35] In the *Sententiae* of Peter Lombard, the term *infinite* is not used. In the thirteenth century, Alexander of Hales, Albert the Great, Thomas Aquinas, Bonaventure, and John Duns Scotus wrote lengthy passages on the infinity of God. They centered their questioning on the infinity of God either as an attribute of God or as an essential part of nature. Scotus, more than any of the others, wrote page after page on the infinity of God, which for him was not an attribute of God. Rather, infinity is an essential trait of God's nature.

Since the Middle Ages, Catholic theologians usually presented the Thomistic view of God's infinity, but from the Reformation and the Council of Trent onward, the infinity of God was never again center stage. From the Reformation down to the first half of the twentieth century, the main theological focus of the Roman Catholic Church, the Anglican Church, the Lutheran Church, and the Calvinist Church centered on ecclesiology. Each church taught that their church alone is the one true church. The infinity of God was mentioned in their theological writings only in a brief way; and at times it was simply presupposed.

Today, however, various leaders and scholars from world religions come together either for theological discussion or for pastoral and ministerial discussion. Most of these religions center on the existence of *their God.* Nontheistic religions center on a transcendent reality. In a given meeting Christians believe in a Trinitarian God; Muslims believe in Allah; religious Jews believe in YHWH. There is no univocal God; rather there are totally different understandings of God.

---

[34] I recently completed a volume, *The Infinity of God and a Finite World*, scheduled for publication in late 2015 by Franciscan Institute Publications. In this volume, I have explained in detail the ways in which the infinity of God indicates that all religions are finite and therefore limited. Each religion, however, reflects something beautiful and overwhelming of the infinite God, but no religion can reflect the totality of the infinite God.

[35] Gregory of Nyssa was the first Christian theologian who developed in detail the infinity of God. See Wolfgang Achtner, "Infinity as a Transformative Concept in Science and Theology," in *Infinity: New Research Frontier* (New York: Cambridge University Press, 2011), 27–33.

If God is infinite, then no religion can maintain that their members alone believe in the one true God, since no human mind can grasp the reality of an infinite God. Each religion, whether theistic or nontheistic, provides us with wonderful aspects of the infinite God, but no human being can ever fathom the nature of an infinite and loving God. If leaders and scholars in these interreligious gatherings continue to believe in a monotheistic God that is *their God*, then interreligious gatherings can only be focused on ministerial and social cooperation. This includes the transcendent reality of nontheistic religions. An infinite transcendent reality in a way similar to the God of many religions can never be fully understood.

Allow me to end this article in and through the writings of Peter Phan. In Asia, the number of Catholics represents only 2.9 percent of the nearly 3.5 billion Asians. Moreover, well over 50 percent of all Asian Catholics are found in one country—the Philippines. Thus, if one excludes the Philippines, Asia is only about 1 percent Catholic. In his volume, *Being Religious Interreligiously*, Phan makes the following statement:

> The attitude that behooves Christians when speaking of God to Asians must therefore be one of deepest respect and humility, Indeed, the first act of our Christian God-talk in Asia is, paradoxically, not to talk but to be silent, not to preach but to listen, not to teach but to learn. This behavior is not merely a polite thing to do, part of the social etiquette that a guest must observe in the host's home. Rather, it is steeped in the conviction that Asian cultures and religions, and the Asian people themselves, especially the poorest among them and even those whom Christians label heathens, have doctrines and practices that in certain respects are no less true and noble than, or even superior to, those of Christianity.[36]

---

[36] Peter Phan, *Being Religious Interreligiously: Asian Perspectives on Interfaith Dialogue* (Maryknoll, NY: Orbis Books, 2004), 118.

13

THEOLOGICAL BIOETHICS: FEMINIST, LIBERATIONIST, AND GLOBAL PERSPECTIVES

Christina A. Astorga

The academic discipline of theological bioethics is founded on the Christian theological commitment to social justice, a commitment that shapes public policy and social practices in bioethics, posing a critique to the ethos of exclusion, privilege, and profit in the health care system. In her groundbreaking book, *Theological Bioethics,* Lisa Cahill writes that the principles of the preferential option for the poor, the common good, distributive justice, and solidarity must challenge the fundamental inequities in health care.[1] She calls theologians to participate in the public discourse on bioethical issues, and to pose an alternative vision to the dominant themes of science, market, and liberalism, using theological principles and values.[2] Cahill is critical of the disproportionate valuing of autonomy and individual choice without social conscience, and of the promotion of the medicalization and technologization of human life at exorbitant costs, serving only the needs of the few, while millions are left dying of common treatable and curable diseases.[3] Cahill asserts that theological bioethics must be a participatory theological bioethics as it moves beyond the theoretical discourse to active alignment with networks of solidarity at the grassroots to effect social change.[4]

To that end, I propose the use of a tripartite perspective on theological bioethics—feminist, liberationist, and global. Reading bioethics from a feminist perspective is reading it from the viewpoint of gender inequity

---

[1] Lisa Sowle Cahill, *Theological Bioethics: Participation, Justice, Change* (Washington, DC: Georgetown University Press, 2005), 4.

[2] Ibid., 16–23.

[3] Ibid., 70–73.

[4] Ibid., 43–69.

and injustice in a patriarchal culture. In this culture, women have only instrumental value with reference to men, whose needs and desires they are socially expected to fulfill. Women, under the power of sexual domination, are disempowered in their self-determination relative to their domestic and social roles. Interlocked with the feminist perspective is the liberationist perspective. When understood in a more general way, the liberationist perspective is inclusive of the feminist perspective, for it sees the world from the side of all oppressed groups. To differentiate it from the feminist perspective, I use the liberationist perspective beyond specifically the issues of women to include that of all who are at the margins, who are deprived, disenfranchised, and disempowered. The recognition of their collective human misery is the context of liberation theology. Finally, the global perspective sees the world as shrinking into one global village. We are all interconnected. We can no longer see the world through a narrow prism, because while our lives are interlocked, in the sense that what happens to one of us affects us all, we remain diverse and plural. Aware of and sensitive to particularities of peoples and cultures, and yet with a global worldview, we experience ourselves as many and yet one, with one future and one destiny.

I will present here selected bioethical issues from the tripartite perspective, not always using all three together for every issue but always seeing the issues in the context of these perspectives. The specific bioethical issues I address in this essay are artificial reproductive technology, genomic technology, end-of-life issues, and AIDS.

Artificial Reproductive Technology (ART)

Modern medicine has developed many new techniques to enhance the freedom and choice of women and couples in the first world who want to become parents. These techniques substitute for natural processes in an effort to have children. There is a plurality of positions regarding the use of ART. Those who are against it uphold the inseparable unity of conjugal love and sex, procreation, and responsible parenthood. They are also against any procedure that puts the embryo at disproportionate risk, exposing it to manipulation and mutilation, and treating human life like a disposable biological matter.[5] Those who negotiate the middle ground assign central importance to the affective and relational rather than to the physical and

---

[5] Congregation for the Doctrine of the Faith, "Instruction on Respect for Human Life in Its Origin and on the Dignity of Procreation Replies to Certain Questions of the Day" (February 22, 1987), 1–23, at 8–10.

biological. Cynthia Cohen holds that "the loving conjugal bond between infertile couples can be as strong and real when they cooperate in using the IVF to bypass physical obstacles to having children as it would be were they able to have children coitally."[6] The love of a couple for a child is paramount, however that child has come into the world. Those who have crossed the boundaries are engaged in third-party reproduction in which more than two people collaborate to have a baby: the egg donor, the sperm donor, the surrogate, and middlepersons who broker the egg and sale. For instance, an enterprise known as reproductive outsourcing is a new but rapidly prosperous business in India. Commercial surrogacy, which is banned in some countries, is legal in India. Rich foreigners are able to *rent* the wombs of poor Indian women.[7] Some European countries, such as Belgium, where the infertility industry is virtually uncontrolled by law, attract foreigners who are unable to access desired services in their own countries. Reproductive *tourism* caters to clients in search of egg donors, donors for women past menopause, insemination with a brother's sperm, insemination with the sperm of a deceased husband, preimplantation diagnosis for sex selection,

---

[6] Cynthia B. Cohen and Mary R. Anderlik, "Creating and Shaping Future Children" in *A Christian Response to the New Genetics: Religious, Ethical, and Social Issues,* ed. David H. Smith and Cynthia B. Cohen (Lanham, MD: Rowman &Littlefield, 2003), 75–103, at 90. Lisa Sowle Cahill is critical of deriving moral norms too simply from the observable or physical structure of human reproduction without sufficient regard for its affective, cognitive, and volitional characters. See Lisa Sowle Cahill, "What Is the 'Nature' of the Unity of Sex, Love, and Procreation?" in *Gift of Life: Catholic Scholars Respond to the Vatican Instruction* ed. Edmund D. Pellegrino, John Collins Harvey, and John Langan (Washington, DC: Georgetown University Press, 1990), 137–48. Jean Porter does not regard it as "either possible or desirable to identify clear-cut, absolute prohibitions in the areas of sexual and reproductive morality, given the central importance of the affective and relational for this dimension of human life." See Jean Porter, "Human Need and Natural Law," in *Infertility: A Crossroad of Faith, Medicine, and Technology* ed. Kevin Wm. Wildes (Dordrecht, the Netherlands: Kluwer, 1997), 105.

[7] See Amelia Gentleman, "India Nurtures Business of Surrogate Motherhood," *New York Times,* March 10, 2008, 1–4. See also Julia Tao Lai Po-Wah, "Right Making and Wrong-Making in Surrogate Motherhood: A Confucian Feminist Perspective," in *Linking Visions: Feminist Bioethics, Human Rights, and the Developing World,* ed. Rosemarie Tong, Anne Donchin, and Susan Dodds (Lanham, MD: Rowman & Littlefield, 2004), 157–79: "Unlike some feminist objections to surrogate motherhood in the West, the main objection raised by Confucian feminists to this arrangement is not based on its creation of inequality among women . . . Rather, the major Confucian feminist objection to surrogate motherhood is based on violation of the moral norms of care and commitment in family relationships created by surrogacy" (ibid., 176).

surrogate mothers, and so on.[8] Mark Repensak raises questions regarding the human values at stake in the commodification of ART: "Does third party involvement cheapen and degrade human reproduction and result in the commercialization of baby making and the exploitation of potential donors? Is it wise to separate the components of parenting—genetic, gestational, and social? Ought we to be spending our money on IVF when the basic needs of so many go unmet?"[9] Faced with the invasion of technology in our lives, we ask the question: can technologism take over our lives, including the most sacred act of procreation?

Feminists stand against the coercive effects of ART on women. The burdens fall disproportionately on women, whether these are burdens associated with egg harvesting, with the actual intervention, with carrying and delivering the embryo, or with raising any resulting children. "And the emotional and physical tolls are high; infertility therapies require intrusive and rigorous regimen of drugs, medical procedures, and scheduled sex that can throw lives into chaos and put relationships under stress."[10] The fertility industry is feeding on the gender norms that link women's identity with marriage and that ties their fulfillment with maternity. Although mother-hood is a profoundly meaningful experience, it is not one that exhausts all of life's meaning. I agree with Maura Ryan who writes, "that as a dimen-sion of human flourishing, the opportunity to conceive or bear a child of one's own can be called basic without being necessary, central without being essential."[11] While it may seem that technology is providing women more control and choice that is at the heart of procreative liberty, they are actually being instrumentalized to serving the ends of the profit-driven infertility industry. The reproduction industry does not put on its highest value pursuits of the welfare of women, the good of resulting children, or the integrity of the familial and social roles. Women can succumb to the allure of procreative liberty, notwithstanding the values that are critically put at risk. Elizabeth Brinkman offers the alternative life of generativity and loving service to others, either through adoption or other life-giving social commit-

---

[8] See G. Pennings, "Reproductive Tourism as Moral Pluralism in Motion," in *Reproductive Technologies: A Reader,* ed. Thomas A. Shannon (Lanham, MD: Rowman and Littlefield, 2004), 99–112.

[9] Mark Repenshek, "Reproductive Technology and the Quest for Offspring," in *Health Care Ethics,* ed. Michael R. Panicola, David M. Belde, John Paul Slosar, and Mark K. Repenshak (Winona, MN: Anselm Academic, 2007), 156–190, at 161.

[10] Cahill, *Theological Bioethics,* 197.

[11] Maura A. Ryan, *The Ethics and Economics of Assisted Reproduction: The Cost of Longing* (Washington, DC: Georgetown University Press, 2001), 172.

ment to overcome the social norm of motherhood that denigrates infertility as a diminishment of one's womanliness.[12]

From a liberationist perspective, while infertility causes profound suffering and requires a compassionate response, the right to advanced fertility services is not defensible if it compromises the access of others to basic health needs and if it maintains the privilege of some to the disadvantage of others. ART must be put within the framework of common good against procreative liberty in an individualistic culture. In in vitro fertilization, fertilizing a woman's own eggs runs from $12,500 to $25,000, while donor eggs can cost up to $35,000.[13] Between brokers, legal and medical expenses, and surrogate fees, a successful fertility process can cost a prospective couple a huge fortune. But with a 66 percent failure rate, Lisa Cahill can justly conclude that individuals and couples are actually supporting the infertility industry rather than relieving infertility.[14] Deborah Blake writes that "a fundamental moral concern surrounding the use of complex reproductive technologies is the lack of solidarity with the poor and personal complicity with the unjust structure. The use of such technologies cannot be exempted from their "social, economic, and political context" or from "responsibility for the common good."[15] Against the ethos of individualism and consumerism, adoption is offered as an alternative practice. From a theological perspective, not only does adoption offer an option of hope to women suffering infertility, it also testifies to the Christian idea that *family* is inclusive and expansive across lines of religion, race, and culture.[16] To experience pregnancy and childbirth is a good and natural desire, as it is to have children with one's spouse. Infertility, which is a dysfunction that frustrates this good and natural desire, is a medical problem that seeks a medical response. However, the recourse to artificial reproduction poses problems. Exorbitant costs that yield low success rates, in the face of other medical needs and the availability of other solutions, should evoke some serious ethical pause about ART.

From a global perspective, theologians are taking up the cause of women in less privileged contexts. Here, the issues and concerns are the rights of

---

[12] Elisabeth Brinkman, *Embracing the Deficient Body: Alternative Responses to Infertility* (Ann Arbor, MI: UMI Dissertation Services, 2001), 159.

[13] Gina Kolata, "The Heart's Desire," *New York Times*, May 11, 2004, D1.

[14] Cahill, *Theological Bioethics*, 210.

[15] Deborah D. Blake, "Infertile Couples: Psychological Needs, Social Responsibilities," in Wildes, *Infertility*, 154–55, at 163.

[16] See Stephen G. Post, *More Lasting Unions: Christianity, the Family and Society* (Grand Rapids, MI: Wm. B. Eerdmans Publishing, 2000), 119–50.

women to bear children, and to be given prenatal, maternal, and childcare, as well as to be able to raise their children with access to basic necessities of adequate nutrition and clean water as well as education. When the issues surrounding early human life are put in a global context, the needs of the poor pose an urgent social agenda. While ART feeds on the profitability and marketability of first world consumers, in the global context, overpopulation is a much greater problem than infertility, and other problems as pressing that accompany it such as prenatal care, maternal and infant mortality in childbirth, and deaths from early childhood diseases. These problems are more widespread and urgent than replacing natural conception. There are problems that arise from some parts of the globe, however, that pose a unique ethical concern, such as sex selection, which is used in many traditional societies to eliminate female fetuses or to select sperm or embryos that will result in the births of boys. In these cultures, the social status of women, and sometimes even their lives hinge on their ability to bear male heirs. Sex selection perpetuates sexist attitudes toward social denigration of women.[17]

Genomic Technologies

The Human Genome Project, began in 1990 and completed at the cost of $2.7 billion after 12.5 years, was called "the search for the holy grail of biology," "a quest for humanity's blueprint," and uncovering the "book of life."[18] Its goal was to understand the genetic basis of human diseases and to eventually eradicate genetic anomalies. Such genetic research is revolutionary as it offers hope for those ailing from diseases such as cancer, cardiovascular disease, dementia, and cystic fibrosis. Equally revolutionary is the possibility of stopping the passing on of genetic diseases to children and of enhancing the characteristics of those of future generations, which opens new vistas for a disease-free life.

---

[17] Cahill, *Theological Bioethics*, 207. See Julie M. Zilberberg, "A Boy or Girl: Is Any Choice Moral? The Ethics of Sex Selection and Sex Preselection in Context," in Tong, Donchin, and Dodds, *Linking Visions*, 147–56. The premise of the author is that the significance of sex selection depends on geographical location and social situation. In her article, she compares and contrasts sex-selection practices in the United States and India.

[18] See Lily E. Kay, "A Book of Life? How a Genetic Code Became a Language," in *Controlling Our Destinies*, ed. Philip Sloan (Notre Dame, IN: University of Notre Dame Press, 2000), 99–124. See also C. Ben Mitchell, Edmund D. Pellegrino, Jean Bethke Elstain, John F. Kilner, and Scott B. Rae, *Biotechnology and the Human Good* (Washington, DC: Georgetown University Press, 2007).

The current limits of genetic technology are at genetic testing, which involves the examination of a person's chromosomes, the protein product of a gene, or DNA. Genetic technology is used to predict risks of disease, screen newborns for diseases, identify carriers of genetic disease, establish prenatal or clinical diagnoses or prognoses, and direct clinical care. Two forms of genetic testing are diagnostic testing and predictive testing. The disease or condition in an affected individual is diagnosed and confirmed through diagnostic testing. The course of a disease can be determined by diagnostic testing as well as the options of best treatment. The probability that an individual might develop a certain genetic disorder that comes from his or her family history is determined by predictive testing. (For example, mutations of BRAC1, BRCA2, or both, genes are associated with increased risk of breast and ovarian cancer.) The detection of a mutated gene through predictive testing provides an individual with his or her chances of developing a genetic disorder, but it offers no certitude that this would be so.[19]

Beyond genetic testing, new therapies that have emerged include gene therapy and germ line therapy. Gene therapy is the technique of reversing, reducing, or eliminating genetic bases by correcting defective genes that are responsible for the development of the disease. Germ line therapy is the technique of modifying genes within the reproductive system so that both the individual and his or her entire family line will have the same altered gene. Genetic enhancement is defined as improving human traits that, without any alteration, would be considered as normal, or improving beyond what is needed to maintain or restore good health. The primary areas that would be open to genetic enhancement include physical size; reducing the need for sleep; slowing the aging process; increasing memory and cognitive ability in general; and, to some extent, modifying aggressive behavior.[20]

On the one hand, gene-based research and discoveries hold out promise for miraculous new ways to treat diseases and even to enhance normal human functioning. On the other hand, they threaten to exacerbate

---

[19] John Paul Slosar, "Current and Future Applications of Genomic Technologies," in *Health Care Ethics*, ed. Michael R. Panicola et al, 217–44. See also David H. Smith and Cynthia B. Cohen, eds., *A Christian Response to the New Genetics: Religious, Ethical, and Social Issues* (Lanham, MD: Rowman & Littlefield, 2003); James C. Petersen, *Genetic Turning Points: The Ethics of Human Genetic Intervention* (Grand Rapids, MI: Wm. B. Eerdmans Publishing, 2001); and John F. Kilner, C. Christopher Hook, and Diann B. Uustal, *Cutting-Edge Bioethics: A Christian Exploration of Technologies and Trends* (Grand Rapids, MI: Wm. B. Eerdmanns Publishing, 2002).

[20] See Slosar, "Current and Future Applications of Genomic Technologies," 229–28.

worldwide disparities in health, longevity, and social advantage. It is not enough to look at gene-based interventions in their own right, as if their morality could be determined apart from the social relations they enable. The use of genetic technology could further divide the *haves* and the *have nots* within an already unjust health care system. For example, if diagnosis can lead to prevention through presymptomatic predisposition profiling, those who can afford such profiling (either personally or through their health coverage) would be at a significant advantage insofar as they could have access to therapies or cures. Those who could afford genetic enhancement, if that becomes part of medicine, could reap significant advantages in terms of physical size, less need for sleep, slowed aging, and intellect and personality disposition enhanced.

Privilege vs. social equity relative to access to genomic technology is a central ethical question. One of the most pressing ethical issues of the new genomics research is the just use of genetic knowledge in an era of economic globalization. In the context of US law and policy, justice is defined in terms of individual rights and civil liberties. Under this justice framework, freedom and self-determination is prioritized over common good. This focus on individual rights neglects the social impact of choices made by scientists, businesses, and consumers, who would operate under the protection of laws and policies that themselves need to be reexamined in the light of social equity.[21]

From a global point of view, while North Americans and Europeans seek answers to cancer and other enigmatic diseases, millions die around the world from treatable diseases such as malaria, anemia, and tuberculosis. In the context of the United States, the common good is not served when genetic treatments are provided for the privileged while so many go uninsured. Neither does it serve the common good in the global context when billions are invested into new genetic inventions while millions do not have access to the most basic needs, such as food, housing, and clean water, leaving them to die early deaths. The market demands determine the direction of genetic research. The World Health Organization reports that pneumonia, diarrhea, tuberculosis, and malaria, which account for over 20 percent of the world's diseases, receive less than 1 percent of the total public and private health research funds.[22] The cost of genetic interventions is only within the reach of those with purchasing power, and, thus, genetic research

---

[21] Cahill, *Theological Bioethics,* 214.

[22] World Health Organization Advisory Committee on Health Research, *Genomics and World Health: Summary* (Geneva: World Health Organization, 2002), 17.

is fueled by their needs and not those of millions outside of the enclave of privilege and wealth. A great deal of investment of genetic therapies will go into the most profitable applications and not into those that affect the most people or cause the most suffering. While profit is the negotiating factor of genomic technology, clean water, food, basic health care, prenatal care, and the AIDS pandemic are of life or death concern in many parts of the world.[23]

Feminist theologians have spoken their concerns about social justice issues regarding the reach of genetic advances. African American theologian Emilie Townes, speaking from a womanist point of view, writes that genetic miracles do not offer solutions to the health problems of people who live in poverty.[24] Breast cancer risk is increased by genetic factors, but the fact that many more black women who are less hit by this disease compared to white women die of it is not due to genetics. It is due to lack of access to the resources of cure. Black women have less access than white women to mammograms, early intervention, and treatment.[25] Theologian Susan DeCrane writes that "the reality of the survival rate of black women from breast cancer demands a commitment from the community to pursue *aggressively* the underlying causes of the disparity."[26] These causes are more social than genetic. But just how relevant is genetic testing for those who do not even have access to basic care or those who suffer bias and discrimination when seeking this type of testing? African Americans and others who have been victims of racial or ethnic discrimination are wary about genetic tests and treatments that not only do not serve their welfare but would also contribute to the creation of exclusionary policies and institutions. Scientific racism is a reality for them.[27]

Another part of the moral scenario of genomic technology is the sizeable profits gained by the biotech investments. Maria Angell accuses drug companies of causing shortages of drugs and vaccines for conditions such as prematurity, hemophilia, cardiac arrest, flu, pneumonia, diphtheria, tetanus,

---

[23] Cahill, *Theological Bioethics,* 215.

[24] See Emilie Townes, *Breaking the Fine Rain of Death: African American Health Issues and a Womanist Ethic of Care* (New York: Continuum, 1998), 62–68, 151.

[25] Cahill, *Theological Bioethics,* 223.

[26] Susanne M. DeCrane, *Aquinas, Feminism and the Common Good* (Washington, DC: Georgetown University Press, 2004), 150. Also see Susan Brooks Thistlethwaite, "The Chemistry of Community," in *Adam, Eve, and Genome: The Human Genome Project and Theology,* ed. Susan Brooks Thistlewaite (Minneapolis: Fortress Press, 2003), 165–67.

[27] Cahill, *Theological Bioethics,* 223.

whooping cough, measles, mumps, and chicken pox by abandoning those products that are deemed unprofitable despite medical need.[28] She further brings to notice how *big pharma* markets control the results of researchers they hire, bribe doctors, make use of huge lobby money to influence Congress, and finance the political campaign of their supporters.[29]

As major benefactors of medical schools, the drug industry's sphere of influence extends to the academic institutions eroding the objectivity and independence of research and its commitment to the common good. Sheldon Krimsky claims that the demise of public interest science was brought about by the "unholy alliance" between the pharmaceutical companies and scientists.[30] Rather than be directed by research agendas that seek solutions to social problems and provide objective and critical assessment of new technologies, scientists are pursuing priorities dictated by market and commercial forces, protecting their personal stake or the stake of institutions to which they are beholden. Rather than contributing to the common good by their work for a humane, holistic approach to health, illness, suffering, finitude, scarcity, and social interdependence, they are on the lookout for profits.[31]

An example illustrates the profit-driven practices of *big pharma*. Marcio Fabri cites a case in which a US corporation sold DNA samples from members of an African coastal tribe to a German pharmaceutical company for $70 million, claiming that it had found a cure for asthma. None of this huge financial gain was paid as remuneration to the DNA donors. Fabri writes, "The little example shows that genetics has become a field of economic and political endeavor that national and international policies cannot ignore."[32] Transnational corporations seek profit around the world,

---

[28] Marcia Angell, *The Truth about Drug Companies, How They Deceive Us and What to Do about It* (New York: Random House, 2004), 91–92. See also Mary J. McDonough, *Can a Health Care Market be Moral?: A Catholic Vision* (Washington, DC: Georgetown University Press, 2007). This book addresses the issues at the intersection of social ethics, economics, and health care. Also see David M. Craig, *Health Care as a Social Good: Religious Values and American Democracy* (Washington, DC: Georgetown University Press, 2014). This book provides an expert and comprehensive analysis of the US health care and the reform debate. Its premise is founded on justice and common good, the hallmark values of Catholic social ethics.

[29] Angell, *Truth about Drug Companies*, 200.

[30] Sheldon Krimsky, *Science in the Private Interest: Has the Lure of Profits Corrupted Biomedical Research?* (Lanham, MD: Rowman & Littlefield, 2003), 20.

[31] Ibid., 178–79.

[32] Marcio Fabri, "Power, Ethics, and the Poor," in *The Ethics of Genetic Engineering*, ed. Maureen Junker-Kenny and Lisa Sowle Cahill (London: SCM; Maryknoll, NY: Orbis, 1998), at 74.

unaccountable to any one governing authority. Genomic research is largely driven by the market on a global scale.

Profit itself is not evil. Rather, profit without social conscience constitutes social evil. Entrepreneurial biomedical research with its accompanying market investment is a legal and ethical means of making a living. Building a name and status in the scientific field is also a worthwhile pursuit. But all this, legal or ethical as they may be, must be subject to moral restraint. They should come under regulatory limits to protect not only individual rights but also the common good. John Paul II urged "the responsible international bodies to commit themselves to drawing up effective legal guarantees to ensure that the health of those who do not have a voice will also be promoted in its entirety and that the world of health care will be imbued with the logic of solidarity and charity rather than with the dynamics of profit."[33]

End of Life

For decades the controversy over legalizing physician-assisted suicide has dominated much of the US bioethical scene regarding the end-of-life care and decision making. The issue of physician-assisted suicide is in parallel with the issue of keeping seriously ill patients on life support as long as possible. On the surface, these two issues appear completely contrary, but on a fundamental level they are have much in common.

Both those who advocate physician-assisted suicide and those who advocate keeping patients indefinitely on artificial nutrition and hydration reflect an overly technological and overly individualistic approach to decline and death. They focus the moral question on the individual patient rather than on his or her relationships. They view illness and dying primarily in the medical and technological context. They have in common an excessive focus on what they consider to be individual patient rights.[34] Cited in Cahill's chapter on "Decline and Dying" is a four-year study of the end-of-life care in the United States, which estimated that half of all death occur in hospitals," surrounded by the technologies of medicine, embedded in a highly specialized sophisticated setting."[35] The seriously ill,

---

[33] John Paul II, "Health Development Based on Equity, Solidarity, and Charity" (November 1997).

[34] Cahill, *Theological Bioethics*, 70.

[35] The Study to Understand Prognosis and Preferences for Outcomes and Risks of Treatment (SUPPORT) began in 1989, lasted four years, and was supported by a grant from the Robert Wood Johnson Foundation. For a discussion, see Ellen H. Moskowitz

the aged, and their families seek refuge in hospitals in the face of decline and death but only to find themselves in a situation where medicine and technology cannot fill in their human need for care and companionship at a boundary time where life and death meet. Timothy Quill writes, "Medicine and technology have taken an increasing role in providing meaning and ritual at the end of people's lives. In some circumstances, medicine has almost become a religion, and prolonging life at all cost by using medical technology is its primary objective."[36]

While dying and death are highly medicalized and technologized for those with purchasing power, poverty is at the root of many of the health disparities and higher rates of death experienced by the disadvantaged racial and ethnic groups. This disparity puts a heavy weight on the elderly. The feminization of poverty is exemplified in women being much poorer than men within these groups. Poor housing, inadequate nutrition, and lack of access to health care constitute what it means to live in poverty. Poverty rates for older African American couples are three to four times higher than for white couples. The risk of poverty increases with age, and this is especially true for women.[37] Across all populations, the gender factor is aligned with greater poverty and lesser health status. Women compared to men receive less retirement incomes, and this is more acutely true for older African American and Hispanic women.[38]

The face of poverty in death shows that fewer people of color than white will need respirators in old age, because most likely more minorities than white would die at a much earlier age, because of both physical and social causes. For black males and Hispanic males, homicide, HIV infection, and unintentional injuries are among the leading causes of death, while suicide is among the ten leading causes of death for American Indians, Alaska natives, and Asian or Pacific Islander women. Congenital abnormalities would most likely be the cause of death of white infants while black infants would most

---

and James Lindemann Nelson, "The Best Laid Plans," *Hastings Center Report* 25/6 (1995): S3.

[36] Timothy E. Quill, *Death and Dignity: Making Choices and Taking Charge* (New York: W. W. Norton, 1993), 49. See Diana Fritz Cates and Paul Lauritzen, eds. *Medicine and the Ethics of Care* (Washington, DC: Georgetown University Press, 2001); Stanley Hauerwas, *God, Medicine, and Suffering* (Grand Rapids, MI: Wm. B. Eerdmans Publishing, 1990).

[37] Robert C. Atchley, *Social Forces and Aging: Improving Care at the End of Life* (Washington, DC: National Academy Press, 1997), 445.

[38] Townes, "Breaking the Fine Rain of Death," 451.

likely die of complications from short gestation and low birth weight.[39] It is striking to see how the face of poverty meets the face of death in ways where poverty determines not only how one lives but also how one dies.

Cahill writes that "most of the cases considered by Quill, Farley, and others who ask for reconsideration of exceptional euthanasia as well as those mandating artificial nutrition for PVS [persistent vegetative state] patients and those resisting euthanasia in favor of palliative/comfort care involve patients with access to medical resources, therapies when possible, and palliative care when not."[40] Poverty changes the entire landscape of decline and dying. It is bad enough to suffer illness and decline, but there is no human situation far worse than to be both ill and poor. On both counts, millions are so disadvantaged that death would seem to be the only option. Moreover, this option might be a far less remote one for the elderly and the debilitated, especially when resources are so limited that the welfare of one should give way to the needs of the family.

Cahill gives an example from the Philippines to illustrate how even the most wrenching decisions about the fate of terminal patients in the United States do not take place in desperate situations that could compare to those in other parts of the world. In the Philippines, a largely Catholic country, direct killing of terminally ill patients is not an acceptable option. But decision making in the event of serious illness is done in an entirely different context from that in the United States or in Western Europe. In one case, a twenty-seven-year-old boy, Mr. C was paralyzed from the neck down in an automobile accident. This was a tragedy that struck a family that was barely meeting basic needs from what his mother earned from washing clothes and what his father eked out from his little income as a writer. Mr. C, the oldest of six children, helped supplement the family resources by selling newspapers. The family was told that the boy would have to be maintained on a respirator for the rest of his life. In a few days after hearing the news, Mr. C made the wrenching decision that the respirator be removed. Imposing an inordinate financial burden on the family, keeping him on a respirator, can be considered extraordinary from an ethical viewpoint. What is extraordinary in this case, however, would be ordinary in most cases in the United States. The case of Mr. C is an acute illustration of how an individual takes an adverse course of action not only because of the burden of illness but because of the social inequity of resources.[41]

---

[39] Institute of Medicine, *Approaching Death: Improving Care at the End of Life* (Washington, DC: National Academy Press, 1997), 57.

[40] Cahill, *Theological Bioethics,* 117–18.

[41] Ibid., 118.

AIDS

Theological bioethics addresses AIDS within the framework of the preferential option for the poor, social justice, common good, and gender equity. From the perspective of theological bioethics, AIDS is about poverty and sexism. Only by addressing these two systemic evils that lie at the heart of AIDS can the world be freed of the pandemic that has taken the lives of millions.[42]

At the time, the fifteenth International AIDS Conference was held in Bangkok in July 2004, it was reported that forty million people were infected with HIV worldwide, thirty million of whom lived in the developing world. However, just 400,000 of those with HIV in poorer countries were receiving anti-AIDS drugs.[43] "The worst affected region in the world is sub-Saharan Africa with 25.4 million people living with HIV. With only 10 percent of the global population, the region is home to over 60 percent of all persons living with HIV. Africa is home to the largest number of people living with HIV/AIDS in the world.[44] AIDS has not only wiped out a generation of men and women, it has also afflicted millions of children. By mid-2005, twelve million children in Africa had been orphaned by AIDS, along with three million on other continents. AIDS as a justice issue concerns the relations of power and vulnerability that are at the base of its causes and spread—relations that are in violation of equity, common good, and the preferential option for the poor.[45]

AIDS is proliferated in different ways in different cultures. Gender discrimination stands as one of the key factors in the transmission of AIDS. In Africa, as in many cultures, women are often trapped in relationships where men wield power over their lives. Having fewer opportunities to make a living, they are dependent on men for their economic survival. Under such dependence, women are subservient to men in other areas of their lives and much more so in their sexual relationships. Without power over their sexual lives, they have little control over occasions of infection. In cultures where they are forced into marriages against their will, coerced into sexual rela-

---

[42] See Maria Cimperman, *When God's People Have HIV/AIDS: Ann Approach to Ethics* (Maryknoll, NY: Orbis Books, 2005), 19–27. See James F. Kennan, *Catholic Ethicists on HIV/AIDS Prevention* (Quezon City, Philippines: Claretian Publications, 2001). This book is a comprehensive and powerful collection of essays that evokes rigorous discourse and sensitive reflections on AIDS as a global scourge.

[43] BBC News, "Bush's AIDS Policy Faces Scrutiny," July 12, 2004, 1.

[44] UNAIDS, *Report on the Global HIV/AIDS Epidemic,* July 2004.

[45] Cahill, *Theological Bioethics,* 159.

tions with relatives of their deceased husbands, or denied the knowledge and assistance to limit their childbearing, women's health or sickness, their life or death are largely determined by their subordination to men.[46]

Since many African women live in small villages and rural areas without any access to medical education, they are at a greater risk of being infected by AIDS. Their vulnerability to the disease increases as their situation of social power decreases. A culture of ignorance, misinformation, or silence about AIDS is a primary cause for its proliferation. There is also little support for the use of condoms because it is mistakenly thought to cause rather than prevent HIV infection. Even if condoms are available, women are often powerless in persuading their husbands or male partners to engage in safe sex or in refusing sex against what traditional religion or culture require of them. When all this is combined with the lack of, or even nonexistence of, health care, women become not only victims of AIDS but also its carriers, and these women tragically transmit the disease to their newborn children.[47]

In most societies, girls and women are the most likely victims of AIDS. Women are infected at an earlier age than men, because of varied reasons, but mostly founded on the culture of male domination and female vulnerability.[48] A large proportion of new cases of HIV infection results from male perpetrated violence in workplaces, schools, and homes. Women who are trapped in oppressive and abusive marital relationships are at a high risk of contracting the disease from philandering husbands. Women are systematically targeted for sexual abuse and rape in multiple situations of military conflicts. And often, HIV-positive women are discriminated against when they seek medical care and frequently are denied the same support from family that is afforded to men.[49] In all cases, men who contract HIV/AIDS are carriers of the disease to women at disproportionate rates.

Cultural practices, such as prostitution, genital cutting, and polygamy, along with lack of education for women and the perpetuation of their submissive roles—practices that are not confined to Africa—are contributing to the global proliferation of AIDS.[50] In some cultures, victims of

---

[46] Margaret Farley, *Compassionate Respect: A Feminist Approach to Medical Ethics and Other Questions* (New York: Paulist Press, 2002), 14–15.

[47] Ibid., 15–16.

[48] *United Nations Special Session on AIDS Fact Sheet* (June 25–27, 2001), 21.

[49] Ibid., 21–22.

[50] James Olaitan Ajayi, *The HIV/AIDS Epidemic in Nigeria: Some Ethical Considerations* (Rome: Editrice Pontificia Universita Gregoriana, 2003), 74–76. See also

AIDS bear a social stigma, as they are blamed and ostracized for their illness. Women are abandoned by their husbands who infected them. They are thrown out of their marital homes and rejected by their families who fear the disgrace of AIDS would cause them social reprisal.[51] Stories abound about infected women exiled or even stoned to death, and unmarried women are raped and infected by men who believe in the myth that sex with virgins is a cure for AIDS infection.[52]

In Africa, the social consequences of rising rates of women's infection with AIDS are dire:

> As local cultures and resources disintegrate under the impact of AIDS, there are fewer and fewer women to perform their age-role of surviving in adversity and providing for community needs. Farming, which is the backbone of the social structure in traditional societies, and in which women play a key role in Africa, is on the point of collapse on that continent . . . Traditional healing arts, especially as cultivated by women, are unable to cope with the magnitude of AIDS. And there are few remaining caregivers for the millions of AIDS orphans, many of whom are already surviving on their own, or in child-headed households.[53]

From a liberationist and global perspective, one sees the connection of AIDS and poverty. Millions of people who are infected by HIV live in developing countries where they have the barest access to nutrition, health care, sanitation, and education. That poor heath is aligned with poverty needs no argument. It is a matter of fact. HIV, which attacks the immune system, feeds on conditions of poverty, where people are most vulnerable to diseases and who have no or little resources to fight them. To strike at the roots of poverty is the systemic approach to eradicating AIDS.

"If there ever was a situation in which the principle of preferential option of the poor was relevant and critical," Margaret Farley has noted, "it is difficult to think of one more dramatic than the AIDS pandemic in the South."[54] Pref-

---

Donald E. Messer, *Breaking the Conspiracy of Silence: Christian Churches and the Global AIDS Crisis* (Minneapolis: Fortress Press, 2004). The book is a call to action to the conspiracy of silence of the church and of the world in the face of Global AIDS crisis.

[51] Cahill, *Theological Bioethics*, 161.

[52] Farley, *Compassionate Respect*, 10–11.

[53] Cahill, *Theological Bioethics*, 162.

[54] Farley, *Compassionate Respect*, 18.

erential option for the poor is a moral demand to go where millions are living on the margins of society—the outcast, the exploited, the forgotten, the shamed, the sick. This is a moral demand founded on justice and inspired by compassion. There are no forces stronger than justice and compassion that could break the interlocking of poverty and AIDS. However, the world must have a new and vigorous global agenda in the fight against hunger, disease, and poverty.

Conclusion

By bringing a feminist, liberationist, and global perspective to theological bioethics, we can broaden the human contexts of bioethics. Bioethics must go beyond the framework of autonomy and individual choice, to be put within a larger frame of social justice, common good, preferential option for the poor, gender equity, and solidarity. Bioethics is social ethics. It addresses bioethical issues in their social roots and in their social consequences. The social contexts and consequences of bioethical issues burst the individual-oriented paradigm of secular bioethics, as theological bioethics argue for the need for a multidimensional sociopolitical and ethical analysis of issues and problems, which are as deep and complex as human life is in its personal, social, and global interconnectedness.

14

THE MIGRANT WITHIN:
BECOMING ICONS OF THE ETERNAL

Elaine Padilla

In many Christian liturgical traditions, the *anamnesis*, which recounts the paschal mystery of Christ's death, resurrection, and the expectation of the *parousia* or earthly return, reveals the continued trace of divine presence in our time and space. Acting like a *placeholder* between memory and longing (past and future),[1] and when performed also through social action, the *parousia* becomes the tangible substance that transfigures the now in the shape of the eternal. In particular, when considering migration, human endeavors seeking to ameliorate the deplorable conditions of the borders can put on display the divine trace inaugurated at creation continuously aiming at an *eschaton* of global well-being. The *parousia* generates the possibility for the fullness of our era, in particular, when awakened memory incites plural human reenactments of the beautiful in the world that make tangible the desire for embodying the love for God and neighbor near and far.

This essay explores the potential of the *parousia* to address the human condition at the borders by appropriating Peter C. Phan's use of the trope of the icon to recast theologies of migration through an aesthetics lens. For him, the icon is a tangible manifestation of the "betwixt and between" of boundaries and temporalities of human and cosmic realities progressively realizing their destiny of participation "in the divine life,"[2] the perichoretic

---

[1] See, for instance, St. Augustine, *Confessions*, bks. 9–11. In this essay, *parousia* is not reduced to the *second coming* of Christ only: rather this eschatological concept is inclusive of the whole of the Christian experience, which is one of expectation made visible through iconicity, a re-presencing and anamnesis of the Jesus event and the outpouring of the Spirit.

[2] Peter C. Phan, "Betwixt and Between: Doing Theology with Memory and Imagination," in *Journeys at the Margins: Toward an Autobiographical Theology in American-Asian Perspective*, ed. Peter C. Phan and Jung Young Lee (Collegeville, MN: Liturgical Press, 1999), 113–34, at 126.

Trinity, which transfigures selves partly in the form of the migrant neighbor. This process of reshaping selves and communities entails drawing near the migrant in the sense of mutually being awakened to, getting in touch with, welcoming in, and being partially transfigured in the shape of the migrant in order to embody God's love for the migrants, and in doing so to redemptively reenact migrant realities from within as icons. Preferentially opting for the migrant, by participating in the Trinitarian life and by becoming a migrant can make manifest a love of word incarnate, can encourage beauty to more fully flourish in our cities, meaning the improvement of the conditions of the arduous existence of migrants.

Another particularly relevant form of participation in the world is *accompanying* the migrants. This second principle of aesthetics of Phan's theology of migration I cross-pollinate in this essay with Latin American and US Latino/a theologians, in particular, with the aesthetic praxis of Roberto S. Goizueta. *Compañerismo* or accompaniment assumes the burden of the negative effects of globalization, the participation of everyone in a globalization system, and how through a boomerang effect, it distinctively affects Western and non-Western countries. The populations of former colonies coming to reside en masse in those territories that once exercised colonial power over them offers but one example of this rebounding effect. Here, accompaniment helps cultivate appreciation for the diversity of population that migration causes, particularly if we see the world as icon.[3] In affirming a world of beauty, this theology can also unearth the promises of multiculturalism and intersubjectivity made available in a globalized and postmodern culture.[4] After this discussion, the essay concludes with some reflections on the in-breaking kindom quality of improvisation characteristic of the theodrama of *compañerismo* in aesthetics. As a *kairos*-like event, made manifest in forms of global welfare, improvisation is a rupture between temporalities in space and has the potential to aid urban transformation. The aim of this essay is to explore the potential for a planetary theology that uses "the history of migration and the experiences of migrants as its *locus theologicus* or source."[5]

---

[3] Peter C. Phan, "Embracing, Protecting, and Loving the Stranger: A Roman Catholic Theology of Migration," in *Theology of Migration in the Abrahamic Faiths*, ed. Elaine Padilla and Peter C. Phan (New York: Palgrave MacMillan, 2014), 77–110, at 96.

[4] Peter C. Phan, *Christianity with an Asian Face: Asian American Theology in the Making* (Maryknoll, NY: Orbis Books, 2003), 54.

[5] Phan, "Embracing, Protecting, and Loving the Stranger," 94. For other works on migration and the Latino/a context as source see, among others, Daniel R. Carroll, *Chris-*

Migrant Realities of Substitution

The rapid proliferation and continuous population shifts, multiple manifestations of global migrations, origins, and destinations, and migrants of
different skill levels, age, gender, and ethnicity together can prove challenging
in exploring the topic of migration. The pursuit of better employment opportunities is only one reason why migrants embark on their lifelong and at times
perilous journeys. Migrants who seek temporary or long-term resettlement
move beyond their homelands due to other factors such as educational opportunities, marriage and other intimate partnerships, climate change, hunger,
political and religious opportunities and oppressions, upsurge in war, violence
and drug trafficking, and gender and gender orientation inequalities. What
is more, there are multiple types of backward and forward movements—
internally (as in rural–rural, rural–urban, urban–urban), nationally and
internationally—social and financial support given at the start and throughout
much of the journey and settlement, means of transportation used for migration—whether by sea or land—and qualitative differences that affect access
to such mobility. As stated in the report *Global Migration* of the Population
Division of the United Nations, "bipolar models of 'developed' and 'developing' or 'North' and 'South,' while perhaps indicative of some trends, are
essentially too static and freeze the 'underlying reality' at a point in time."[6]
As the responses of the receiving and sending nations continue to be mixed,
there will be both components of hospitality and *fortress mentality* evident
in traditional countries of immigration as much as of emigration. Hence, the
continued multiplication of experiences of migrants as they deal with hard-
ships and navigate opportunities for a better life.

Nonetheless, while it encompasses such heterogeneity, in this essay the
use of the term *migrant* pulls the theological conversation to the margins

---

tians at the Border: Immigration, the Church, and the Bible (Grand Rapids, MI: Baker
Academic, 2008); Allan Figueroa Deck, "A Christian Perspective on the Reality of Illegal
Immigration," *Social Thought* 4/4 (1978): 39–53; Miguel H. Díaz, "On Loving Strangers:
Encountering the Mystery of God in the Face of Migrants," *Word and World* 29/3 (2009):
234–42; Virgilio Elizondo, *The Galilean Journey: The Mexican-American Promise* (Maryknoll, NY: Orbis Books, 1983); Fernando Segovia, "Towards a Hermeneutics of Diaspora,"
in *Reading from This Place, Vol. 1*, ed. Fernando Segovia and Mary Ann Tolbert (Minneapolis: Fortress Press, 1993–94), 57–73; Miguel A. De La Torre, *Trails of Hope and Terror:
Testimonies on Immigration* (Maryknoll, NY: Orbis Books, 2009).

[6] Population Division of the United Nations Department of Economic and
Social Affairs, *Global Migration: Demographic Aspects and Its Relevance for Devel-
opment* (2013), http://www.un.org/esa/population/migration/documents/EGM.
Skeldon_17.12.2013.pdf.

of its global composition. It pertains particularly to the asylum seekers, refugees, stateless people, and those most vulnerable such as victims of rape and trafficking (especially women), separated and unaccompanied children, and unskilled workers. The reasons for turning our attention to this group might be apparent. Not only is there a need symbolically to narrow the definition in order to effectively theologize on this issue, but most importantly this segment of the migratory population also remains the most in need of humanitarian response and aid. According to data published by the UN High Commissioner for Refugees (UNHCR) in its report *World at War*, sixty million people are being "forcibly displaced," and are victims of "persecution, conflict, generalized violence, or human rights violations."[7] Of these, the data also show that 42 percent of them reside "in countries where the GDP per capita was below USD 5,000" and that developing regions are hosting about 86 percent of the world's refugees. While a 2013 report from the Population Division of the Department of Economic and Social Affairs of the United Nations had shown increases in international migrations originating in regions of Asia and of Latin America and the Caribbean by 44 percent and 36 percent, respectively, we can also see a considerable decrease in immigration into countries like Spain and the United States due in part "to the impact of the economic crisis."[8] As expected, by 2014 the wars and violence in the Middle East and Africa resulted in a 53 percent upsurge in asylum seekers coming from "the Syrian Arab Republic (3.88 million), Afghanistan (2.59 million), and Somalia (1.11 million)."[9]

These migrants are also unique with regard to the horror of human trafficking that many of them face. The United Nations Office on Drugs and Crime (UNODC) report shows that 79 percent of those being trafficked are sexually exploited (predominantly women and girls), with women trafficking women being the norm, 18 percent being trafficked for forced labor, and about 20 percent being children, with trafficking from parts of West Africa now being as high as 100 percent children.[10] In addition, children (those

---

[7] The UN Refugee Agency, *World at War: UNHCR Global Trends Forced Displacements in 2014*, http://unhcr.org/556725e69.html.

[8] Population Division of the United Nations Department of Economic and Social Affairs, "World Migration in Figures: A joint contribution by UN-DESA and the OECD to the United Nations High-Level Dialogue on Migration and Development, 3–4 October 2013," http://www.oecd.org/els/mig/World-Migration-in-Figures.pdf.

[9] *World at War*, 3.

[10] United Nations Office on Drugs and Crime, "UNODC Report on Human Trafficking Exposes Modern Form of Slavery" (February 12, 2009), http://www.unodc.org/unodc/en/frontpage/unodc-report-on-human-trafficking-exposes-modern-form-

below eighteen years of age) were 51 percent of the total number of refugees in 2014.[11] In the United States, the number of unaccompanied children fell from 7,176 in 2014 to "3,138 in 2015 on the U.S. side of the border with Mexico."[12]

Focusing on urban migration also becomes strategically necessary. Urban-based migrant populations continuously shift due to economic factors, time span in the host country, and factors such as the search for better environmental, social, and educational opportunities for children. The risk that migrants face can be as threatening in rural areas as in cities. Yet it is commonly known that because the majority of global flows are initially from urban to urban sectors, and migrants "are often moving towards areas of greater risk in urban areas," the urban contexts remain central to the theological task. The increase in labor that cannot be equally absorbed by the industry creates marginalization and pockets of poverty throughout cities, and this according to Juan Sepúlveda, creates a crisis of *sentido* (life-sense).[13] Such dislocation and displacement demands *a sense of solidarity* in which life for migrants can gain meaning. A *comunidad de sustitución* (substitute community) can offer uprooted and disoriented people a sense of self and humanity that empowers from within and creates a reality of homeness (even if temporary) that is transformative.[14] From within this urban situation, Gustavo Gutiérrez argues, theology can become *performative*.[15]

---

of-slavery-.html. For a theological response, see Olivia Ruiz Marrujo, "The Gender of Risk: Sexual Violence against Undocumented Women," in *A Promised Land, A Perilous Journey*, ed. Daniel Groody and Giacchino Campese (Notre Dame, IN: Notre Dame University Press, 2010), 225–42.

[11] *World at War*, 3.

[12] Washington Office on Latin America (WOLA), "Latest Border Stats Suggest Higher Family, Child Migration in 2015 than Official Projections," (April 10, 2015), http://www.wola.org/commentary/unaccompanied_children_at_the_us_mexico_border_in_the_first_half_of_2015.

[13] Juan Sepúlveda, "El crecimiento del movimiento pentecostal en América Latina," in *Pentecostalismo y liberación: Una experiencia Latimoamericana*, ed. Carmelo Alavarez (Sabanilla, Costa Rica: Departamento Ecuménico de Investigaciones/DEI, 1992), 80–81; while here Sepúlveda is speaking mostly of the urban realities in Latin America, the same can be said for the global realities at large. For an essay with content on migration and US cities, see Carmen Nanko-Fernández, "Creation: A Cosmo-politan Perspective," in *In Our Own Voices: Latino/a Renditions of Theology*, ed. Benjamin Valentín (Maryknoll, NY: Orbis Books, 2010), 41–63; and Dale T. Irvin, "Migration and Cities: Theological Reflections," in *Contemporary Issues of Migration and Theology*, ed. Elaine Padilla and Peter C. Phan, (New York: Palgrave/MacMillan, 2013), 73–94.

[14] Sepúlveda, "El crecimiento," 81.

[15] Gustavo Gutiérrez, "Poverty, Migration, and the Option for the Poor," in

In light of the above, this theology of migration assumes a "globalization of solidarity," as called for by John Paul II,[16] that offers a counterargument to the highly divisive responses emblematic of the fear that prevents our societies from offering a true humanitarian response. Militarization and the strengthening of borders fueled by and fanning anti-immigrant political sentiments have been the norm. Yet to respond using only such measures ultimately fails to address the root causes that lead to the displacement of populations such as the increase in the extraction of resources, use of cheap labor resulting in the continued impoverishment of traditional sending nations, and the conditions of climate change and violence that ravage these territories.

The humanitarian alternative to drastic counter-migratory measures is a globalized solidarity that communicates a sense of *parousia*. To achieve this, diverse communities of faith will have to cross borders. Already some road markers that point to these border-crossings have been placed along the way. For instance, the Catholic Church has addressed some of the needs of migrants by calling for care for the migrant in his/her native language, the appointment of national episcopal commissions with the specific task of providing care for the migrant. Official Catholic Church pronouncements have addressed the root causes that lead to the detriment of human dignity. It has advocated for the human rights of the migrants, condemning discrimination against them, and promulgating not only their rights to emigrate but also their responsibilities to contribute to the host countries. Likewise the magisterium has affirmed the duties of the host to welcome and integrate them into society. For example, Benedict XVI in his addresses on the 92nd and 94th World Day of Migration spoke of migration as a sign of the time—particularly noting its "feminilization" and condemning sex trafficking—and for the international convention to protect "the rights of all migrant workers and their families."[17]

Protestant traditions have offered similar performative responses. In the United States, for instance, the Southern Baptist Convention meeting in Greensboro, North Carolina (June 2006) drafted several resolutions that

---

Groody and Campese, *A Promised Land, A Perilous Journey*, 82.

[16] John Paul II, *Ecclesia in America*, 55.

[17] See Message of His Holiness Pope Benedict XVI for the World Day of Migrants and Refugees (2013), "Migrations: Pilgrimage of Faith and Hope," October 12, 2012, http://www.vatican.va; see also a good summary of various encyclicals and efforts in Phan, "Embracing, Protecting, and Loving the Stranger," 88. For more on the global response, see Elaine Padilla and Peter C. Phan, eds., *Christianities in Migration: The Global Perspective* (New York: Palgrave MacMillan, forthcoming).

honored both heavenly and earthly responsibilities, civil law as well as divine law, and that called to account the US governing administrators for their inability to enforce laws that equally protect the immigrants and prevent them from being exploited, rather than only controlling borders. They urged all Christians "to act redemptively and reach out to meet the physical, emotional, and spiritual needs of all immigrants, to start English classes on a massive scale, and to encourage them toward the path of legal status and/or citizenship."[18] Grassroots partnerships on behalf of the migrant are flourishing. These include the participation of migrants through organizations such as the Lutheran Immigration and Refugee Service, the National Hispanic Christian Leadership Conference, and the National Latino Evangelical Coalition.

In light of all this, migrating bodies can be counted among the performative components that awaken the global consciousness to the possibilities of new realities for the flourishing of all of humanity. For today's World Christianities, the thought of the lives that are lived at the borders demands of us a theological response. As we see in the work of Phan, migratory realities can be icons of the *parousia* and call for an immigrant mode of theologizing: "being 'in-between' two worlds, and as such being at the margins of the two worlds, i.e., the host country and the native country."[19] The iconicity of migrancy compels theology to "journey at the margins" and with a renewed perception of the *parousia* to gain insight "on the boundaries, betwixt and between, with memory and imagination."[20] Urban communities substituting realities that help make sense of displaced and uprooted existence are born and nurtured. Such communities have a border-crossing spirituality that redemptively performs migratory life.

Advents

In Hellenism, *parousia* as an ancient communal practice[21] meant the visit of a ruler, or "the presence of the gods" in a city.[22] In preparation for the *parousia* of a ruler, cities would undergo improvement and beautification, a

---

[18] Southern Baptist Convention, "On the Crisis of Illegal Immigration, Greensboro, NC—2006," http://www.sbc.net/resolutions/1157.

[19] Phan, "Introduction: An Asian-American Theology: Believing and Thinking at the Boundaries," in Phan and Lee, *Journeys at the Margins*, xix.

[20] Ibid., xx.

[21] See Albrecht Oerke, "parousia, pareimi," *Theological Dictionary of the New Testament*, ed. Gerhard Kittel, trans. Geoffrey W. Bromiley (Grand Rapids, MI: Wm. B. Eerdmans Publishing, 1967), 5:858–70.

[22] Ibid., 5:859.

process that would instill a sense of hope among the city dwellers. The vision included gods visiting earth, with all cosmic and earthly powers being set in motion, preceding and accompanying the one who would come. How can cities be made beautiful when populated with scores of migrants, laborers in long lines on street corners waiting to be hired? When those employed are denied full wages and benefits, or are put in endangering situations (health wise, sexually, and psychologically)? When thousands are deceived, their workplaces raided? When they are not only detained, split from their families, but also returned to where they began their journey numerous times? How can cities become beautiful when so many among us have been begging like Lazarus at the doorsteps of the wealthy nations (Luke 16:20–21)?[23]

In Christianity, and in conversation with Phan's theology of migration, *parousia* is made historically tangible in the human enactment of the accompanying Jesus: whenever the Jesus event is reenacted by means of the push and pull forces of the Spirit energizing creation's inner capacity for renewal and beauty, and wherever the flourishing of the city springs up through the cracks and fissures characteristic of these migrant realities. Urban processes are quickened by means of perichoretic participation in the accompanying and migrant Trinity that enlivens the imaginative impetus and potential for an enhanced horizontal collaboration. The divine aim imbues them with the potential for beautification, which makes possible the sketching of a future with the memory of the life, death, resurrection, and exaltation of Jesus and the outpouring of the Spirit. In anticipation of the divine *parousia*, urban communities can witness the birth of homelike hospitable spaces by setting in motion kindom principles with which to shatter structures currently shrinking territories.[24]

Compañerismo: Becoming a Divine Icon

Bringing to life intersubjective relationships with the migrant can cultivate an aesthetic performance that enhances the potential for a kindom-like well-being of the city. In Latin American and US Latino/a thought, this would be akin to *convivencia* (from the Latin *convivere*). *Convivencia,* for instance, according to Raúl Fornet-Betancourt can refer to the deepening

---

[23] Gutiérrez, "Poverty, Migration, and the Option for the Poor," 82.

[24] See also Michael Purcell who defines *parousia* in terms of a trace, that is, icons in Michael Purcell, *Mystery and Method; the Other in Rahner and Levinas* (Milwaukee, WI: Marquette University Press, 1998), esp. 106; for a philosophical overview of the concept of icon, see Jean-Luc Marion, *The Idol and Distance: Five Studies* (New York: Fordham University Press, 2001).

of relationships with "the foreign within our culture" by going beyond mere physical coexistence, and by "sharing in such a way that there is mutuality of enrichment."[25] The migrants' strangeness makes itself and respective worlds present. It enters into a "process of collective learning" whereby learning is done "together with" the migrant and as accompaniment in the sense of "positioning our own culture in relation to that of the stranger."[26] Such strangeness of the migrant incorporated into our very selves can quicken in us the desire to rebirth and transform worlds and cultures. Their more ample social or cultural integrations into those already flourishing within the receiving communities can lead to the *public* recognition of their rights, what he coins a "multicultural *convivencia.*"[27]

Roberto Goizueta describes this *strange effect* as the irruption of the bodies of the crucified yet hopeful bodies of history following in the footsteps of the world-transforming beautiful or the divine mystery. The beautiful has already taken the form as the tortured and resurrected body of Jesus that continuously irrupts in the world makes its mystery present in the form of the migrant as an anomaly. Its ugliness of global "exclusion and exploitation" subverts normative standards of beauty.[28] This paradoxical form of beauty for María Teresa Porcile entails looking beyond the sculpted bodies of Apollo, and instead seeing the children with inflated bellies, those who are orphaned, separated, and unaccompanied, and seeking a home.[29]

Porcile suggests a sense of equilibrium in the use of resources that considers the racial, gender, class, and various differences and uniqueness.[30] For this, according to Goizueta, the beauty within us (in the cosmos as a whole) draws and entices the participant into the theater of "divine glory." That beauty compels us to become in the image of the disfigured with the view of embodied resurrections via *communio.*[31] This aesthetic can be "the

---

[25] Raúl Fornet-Betancourt, "Hermeneutics and Politics of Strangers: A Philosophical Contribution on the Challenge of *Convivencia* in Multicultural Societies," in Phan and Lee, *Journeys at the Margins*, 210; for him *convivencia* is to be lived *intraculturally* and *intrasubjectively.*

[26] Fornet-Betancourt, "Hermeneutics and Politics of Strangers," 216.

[27] Ibid., 214–22.

[28] Roberto S. Goizueta, "Theo-drama as Liberative Praxis," *Cross Currents* 63/1 (2103): 63 and 74.

[29] María Teresa Porcile, "El derecho a la belleza en América Latina," in *El Rostro Femenino De La Teología*, ed. Elsa Tamez (San José, Costa Rica: Departamento de Investigaciones (DEI), 1988), 107.

[30] Ibid.

[31] Roberto S. Goizueta, *Christ Our Companion: Toward a Theological Aesthetics of Liberation* (Maryknoll, NY: Orbis Books, 2009), 109 and 117.

fullest sense of the ethical,"[32] beauty born from intersubjective relations and undergirding sociopolitical action.

The struggle for life of the migrant amid "death, war, abduction, rape and abandonment" deepens one's understanding and experience of resurrection,[33] so that with hope and faith one can say that death does not have the last word. For Luz Beatriz Arellano, we can even be joyful and celebrate this life that overcomes death through beauty, for example, as we bear the sorrows of others so that together we can transform pain into happiness and hope.[34] We eat and drink and dance together for the purpose of celebrating those things that remain to be fully expressed, Ivone Gebara intimates.[35] And as Gemma Cruz points out, to make room for celebrations among migrants (weddings, baptisms, birthdays) is a path for the cross to forge a new *ecclesiogenesis*, the starting point for "death-dealing" together with "life-giving" opportunities.[36]

In light of all of this, central to such globalized solidarities akin to iconicity is enacting a "common personhood," a planetary *compañerismo* beyond the commonly held bonds of friendship,[37] and an iconic intersubjectivity "born in and nurtured by the concrete."[38] In the case of migration, it would be a sacramental act and *spirituality* overstepping the imaginary lines of sisterhood and brotherhood that are keeping intact power grids within territorial limits. As part of the urban process, *compañerismo* dramatizes (or

---

[32] Roberto S. Goizueta, *Caminemos con Jesús* (Maryknoll, NY: Orbis Books, 1995), 128.

[33] Luz Beatriz Arellano, "Women's Experience of God in Emerging Spirituality," in *With Passion and Compassion: Third World Women doing Theology: Reflections from the Women's Commission of the Ecumenical Association of Third World Theologians*, ed. Virginia Fabella and Mercy Amba Oduyoye (Maryknoll, NY: Orbis Books, 1988), 142.

[34] Ibid., 207, referenced in María Pilar Aquino, *Our Cry for Life* (Maryknoll, NY: Orbis Books, 1993), 156. For more on the concept of "fiesta," see Otto Maduro, *Maps for a Fiesta: A Latina/o Perspective on Knowledge and the Global Crisis* (New York: Fordham University Press, 2015); Roberto S. Goizueta, "Fiesta: Life in the Subjunctive," in *From the Heart of Our People*, ed. Orlando O. Espín and Miguel H. Díaz (Maryknoll, NY: Orbis Books, 1999), 84–99.

[35] Ivone Gebara, "La Mujer Hace Theología. Un Ensayo Para La Reflexión," in Tamez, *El Rostro Femenino De La Teología*, 23.

[36] Gemma Tulud Cruz, "Expanding the Boundaries, Turning Borders into Spaces: Mission in the Context of Contemporary Migration," in *Mission after Christendom: Emergent Themes in Contemporary Mission*, ed. Ogbu U. Kalu et al. (Louisville, KY: Westminster John Knox Press, 2010), 83.

[37] Goizueta, *Caminemos con Jesús*, 207.

[38] Ibid., 210.

brings into presence through the symbolic act) a Trinity that *tents* among the poorest sectors of the cities,[39] most of which have become inhabited by migrants seeking to build their homelike existence in community.

In models that preferentially opt for the migrant poor, models such as those pioneered by Gustavo Gutiérrez, *compañerismo* would entail becoming the migrant neighbor. For Gutiérrez, for instance, it is about becoming like the Samaritan, the person who helps the one in need along the way. He describes it like this: "Being a neighbor and being a neighbor-hood is the result of specific actions and deeds. The poor [as in the migrant poor] are not those who are nearest but rather those who are distant but who become neighbors through one's commitments to them . . . a compli-cated affair precisely because theirs is a distant world."[40] *Compañerismo* enhances the human "capacity, freedom, and commitment *to pay attention to the smallest of things*,"[41] what Matthew 25:45 calls "the least of these." Love of neighbor would then mean the becoming of the neighborhood as in entire communities being neighborly so that the undocumented, the unskilled workers, and the stateless are slaves no longer, so that there is no sex trafficking, or exploitation, or oppression, so that places become hospi-table in such manner that migrants are called friends—as equals—as Jesus called his disciples (John 15:15).

Akin to these forms of *compañerismo* is Phan's concept of *paroikousia* consciousness, which we see particularly in his exploration of the urban contexts of biblical times and the patristic era. Similar to today's phenomena of migration, continuous population shifts that resulted from the war and trade that bound different civilizations together expanded and contracted the religious, political, social, and territorial reach of the local urban reali-

---

[39] In the third world, Pentecostalism has grown among the poor and down-trodden, the people at the margins, particularly the city dwellers, a phenomenon also in the United States. Litonjua states, "what may be the most significant development in twentieth-century Christianity and what is coming to be the dominant expression of Christian spirituality and piety, the Pentecostal Movement, is thriving among the poor of the world" (M. D. Litonjua, "Pentecostalism in Latin America: Scrutinizing a Sign of the Times," *Journal of Hispanic/Latino Theology* 7/4 (2000): 36). The poor are choosing the Pentecostal congregations because they are already a church where the poor are at home (ibid.). Litonjua criticizes what he calls "middle-class theologians and justice-and-peace activists" for disregarding the importance of faith in being a "bulwark against and a shelter from threatening forces" (ibid., 38). See also Sepúlveda, "El creci-miento," 84–85.

[40] Gutiérrez, "Poverty, Migration, and the Option for the Poor," 83.

[41] Ibid., 84, emphasis added.

ties. Three terms in particular describe well the character of earlier forms of intersubjective solidarity amid a globalized lack of communal sense: the stranger, the foreigner, and the sojourner.[42] Each can make present a way of being an icon of solidarity akin to intersubjective relationships. The stranger (or alien)—*zar* (Hebrew), *xenos* (Greek), *hospes* (Latin)—was a term used to describe the one who did not belong to the house or community or nation of the current residence, and who was often regarded as an enemy (Isa. 1:7; Jer. 5:19, 51:51; Ezek. 7:21, 28:7, 10; Obad. 11). The foreigner—*nokri* (Hebrew), *allotrios* (Greek), *alienus* (Latin)—was the non-Jew (i.e., a person of another race) who could be labeled an idolater; for this reason no Jew was allowed to marry a foreigner (Deut. 7:1–6). The sojourner—*ger* (Hebrew), *paroikos* (Greek), *peregrinus* (Latin)—was someone whose permanent residence was in another nation. As Phan explains, this last group was protected by the Jewish law (Exod. 22:21), along with other orphans and widows, as a population of the vulnerable worthy of divine protection (Jer. 7:6, 22:7, 29; Zech. 7:10; Mal. 3:5) and love (Deut. 10:19).

For Phan, the persistent use of this latter term *paroikos* in the writings of the Patristics suggests that a sense of being a foreigner, stranger, and sojourner in solidarity with others facing similar struggles could have been a major component of the Christian self-consciousness.[43] That these Christian communities were composed mostly of migrants "without full civic rights, [who] were subjected to discrimination and persecution" helps to strengthen his view.[44] Traces of this migrant consciousness become identifiable,[45] for example, in "The Epistle of Mathetes to Diognetus," especially its description of the manners of the Christians (chapter 5). Commenting on the letter, Phan muses how these early Christians would view themselves as *resident aliens*, and along with the Jews, perhaps potentially as being the human targets of discrimination, yet called to resist peacefully, loving those who persecuted them, as Jesus had commanded them.[46]

A *paroikousia* consciousness likewise would become tangible in the ways in which hospitality was offered as roadside inns. Phan insightfully notes that inns were "scarce, filthy, dangerous, and most often were nothing more

---

[42] Peter C. Phan, "Migration in the Patristic Era: History and Theology," in Groody and Campese, *A Promised Land, A Perilous Journey*, 48–49.

[43] Ibid., 48–58.

[44] Ibid., 49.

[45] Ibid., 51–54.

[46] Ibid., 54–58.

than brothels."[47] What were commonly known as inns were transformed into guest homes or charitable institutions (*hospotia* and *xenodochia*) for the care of strangers and the poor. Bishop Basil of Caesarea of Cappadocia and Macrina, his sister, constructed buildings "at the edge of the city to receive travelers and sick persons, especially lepers, and staffed them with qualified personnel."[48] Other examples of such welcoming places were the guest homes (*xenodochion*) built by monastics in each of their communities (like Ambrose of Milan, Paulinus of Nola, Martin of Tours, Nicetius of Lyons, and Sidonius Apollinarious of Clermont).

With these congruent ideas between the thoughts of Latin American and US Latino/a theologians and those of Phan in mind, *compañerismo* alongside a *paroikousia* consciousness can then mean the diasporic process of becoming the *paroikoi*, or the ones not *fully* at home yet offering a home in the making by means of accompaniment. Drawing from Jewish teaching, such as Abraham and Sarah having made provisions for the stranger, this would fulfill the observance of the command of hospitality to provide for the physical needs, and to secure the safety and welfare of strangers. It resembles the way of Jesus (Matt. 25:35), who described himself as a stranger, and as *ho hodos*, the Way or Journey (Acts 18:25–26, 19:23, 22:4, 24:14, 22).[49] Such examples call to mind the migratory quality of Christianity and the command for the *paroikoi* to practice *xenophilia* or love and hospitality to the stranger along the path (Matt. 25:35, 38, 43, 44; 1 Pet. 4:9; Heb. 13:2; 3 John).

Compañerismo of a *paroikousia* consciousness can then be iconic. As with yesterday's people of faith, today the becoming of *home-worldling* or *ho hodos* for a planetary home-in-the-making enacts an eschatological hope of sojourners and with the sojourners for self-transcendence and to collectively overcome *structural evils* that result in social and political alienation. By enacting love for the neighbor, by becoming neighbors, communities of faith prophetically denounce the ills of society. They can demonstrate alternatives to urban realities in terms of gender (Acts 2), social strata (Acts 4 and 5), culture (Acts 10), and religion (Acts 19).[50] The prophetic tradition of the Hebrew Bible evinced in Christ's denunciation of oppression continued

---

[47] Ibid., 51.

[48] Ibid., 53.

[49] Phan, "Embracing, Protecting, and Loving the Stranger," 77.

[50] Murray W. Demspter, "Pentecostal Social Concern and the Biblical Mandate of Social Justice," *PNEUMA: The Journal for the Society of Pentecostal Studies* 9/1 (1987): 128–53.

among writers, such as James, with similar insights and indictments against injustice being grounded in concepts of God–people and people–people relationships.

Likewise, globally minded Christians who take on the shape of the migrant—*compañerismo* of a *paroikousia* consciousness—can offer a hospitable welcome. By creating homelike hospitable spaces along the way or within and across boundaries of migrant existence, such Christians express a Jesus-like consciousness imbued with that which is yet to come, what Phan coins "migrantness."[51] People of faith, in being the least of migrants and one who also cares for all the migrants in tangible manner practice "faith, hope, and love,"[52] become signs of the *parousia*, the eternal flourishing in the now that enhances urban beauty.

A Migrant Perichoresis

The economic Trinity or God for us makes manifest God's intention in the world for the migrant and so, for Phan, the migratory nature of the immanent/transcendent Trinity.[53] The Trinitarian relations intricately bound to the realities of the migrant—insofar as their realities are related to God—can be witnessed in the world as divine intentionality and passionate insistence toward their well-being. The Trinity likewise migrates or manifests its migrantness as a migrant Trinity. We can imagine God as the primordial migrant, Jesus as the paradigmatic migrant or border-crosser, and the Spirit as the push and pull of migration. Indeed Phan does expound on concepts of human liberative praxis, as those espoused by Gutiérrez and Goizueta, which presuppose "the divine ground of all liberation."[54]

Though immanently personal and missional, the migrant Trinity makes manifest the accompanying nature of God as the outsider-ground via movements in relation with the world (the cosmos as a whole). As a family not defined by blood ties, rather by its movements toward the other or its "being-for-the-other," as Zaida Maldonado Perez, describes the Trinity,[55]

---

[51] Phan, "Migration in the Patristic Era," 57.

[52] Ibid., 55–58; See this chapter of "The Epistle of Mathetes to Diognetus" quoted in full in ibid., 55–56.

[53] See Phan, "Embracing, Protecting, and Loving the Stranger," 97–103.

[54] Goizueta, "Theo-drama," 70; for a similar model of a moving-moved Trinity, see Elaine Padilla, *Divine Enjoyment: A Theology of Passion and Exuberance* (New York: Fordham University Press, 2014).

[55] Zaida Maldonado Pérez, "The Trinity *es y son familia*," *Latina Evangelicas: A Theological Survey from the Margins*, ed. Loida I Martell-Otero and Zaida Maldonado

God gifts the divine self as ground in the peripheries of history and via movements beyond the divine self as relations—Word and Spirit—that show mutuality with the ugliness of migrant reality. Migrant life *comigrates* into the Triune God, in joining the realities of Jesus (as a fellow migrant), [56] and the Spirit. The relations, by likewise moving and drawing the migrant reality into the outsider-ground via perichoresis, partly transfigure God in the shape of the most vulnerable of migrants, an ongoing and mutual divine–human dance so that the poorest sectors in urban communities can become icons of *Dei migratoris*. Comigration leads to beauty as a result of human movements away from participation in unjust structures and toward transgressive manifestations of compassion—becoming exiled, and dwelling betwixt and between worlds.

By bringing matters of contextualization to bear upon this migratory concept of divine movements and following the paths of affirmation, negation, and of eminence, Phan posits that God as *Deus migrator* is the primordial migrant, being and not being, and being "*infinitely* a migrant."[57] The migratory God is the God who is in continuous movement within God and is therefore living continuously as the God affected by the migrant. Externally, these movements within God become evident through the divine creative acts in which God's infinity *crosses over* into form (the iconicity of the divine *parousia*) to experience among other multivaried, innate, and vulnerable actualizations of the cosmos, "the precarious, marginalized, threatened, and endangered condition of the migrant."[58] Each *crossing over* carries the potential for communal expressions of beauty and transformation reaching to the least esteemed of populations.

God is also the paradigmatic migrant who *crosses over* borders as the divine logos in the world for the fuller flourishing of material beauty (God's relation as Word). The Word, from a migration point of view, first points to creation and creativity. The divine movement that makes reality possible, a collaborative action that serves as "the culmination of that primordial border crossing by which the triune God steps out of self and eternity and crosses into the *other*, namely, the world of time and space, which brings God into existence by this very act of crossing."[59] The world becomes a

---

Perez (Eugene, OR: Cascade Books, 2013), 53; see also "The Trinity," in *Handbook of Latina/o Theologies*, ed. Edwin David Aponte and Miguel A. De La Torre (St. Louis, MO, Chalice Press, 2006), 32–39.

[56] Phan, "Embracing, Protecting, and Loving the Stranger," 106.

[57] Ibid., 98.

[58] Ibid., 99.

[59] Peter C. Phan, *In Our Own Tongues* (Maryknoll, NY: Orbis Books, 2003), 147.

manifestation of the divine love being tangibly expressed in the creative "let there be" that makes space promisingly beautiful and that infuses itself throughout the created order so that it can freely become a *good oikoumene* (world). Well-being was meant to be freely shared and nurtured, and limitlessly widespread. Second, this logos was made flesh, crossing over human existence, and in hypostatic union with the person of Jesus, transgressed the human and divine borders. The logos *tabernacled* betwixt and between two worlds—its native-heavenly country and Jesus's Jewish humanity—communicating in the flesh the human participation in God and with creation. For Phan, the historical Jesus of Nazareth as the logos/Son of God made flesh is thus "the perfect *imago Dei Migratoris,*" "the 'perfect reflection of the glory' of God the Migrant," and "the 'exact imprint of God's very being' as a migrant" (Heb. 1:3).[60]

The accompanying event of Jesus, according to the gospel message, iconizes the being and becoming of *Dei migratoris.* We can see this in the birth of Jesus (Luke 2:1–7), the escape of his parents to Egypt (Matt. 2:13–14), and in his ministry as a homeless and itinerant preacher (Luke 9:58).[61] In identifying himself with the stranger (Matt. 25:35), Jesus brings also into presence the border crossing and fluid home experiences of migrants, yet he does so redemptively by pointing to the fullness of the flourishing of material beauty. By inhabiting betwixt and between multiple borders, Jesus became the paradigmatic guest and host. Amid geographical and conventional limits, he encountered and treated with dignity women and men, rich and poor, Sadducees and Pharisees, healthy and sick, unclean and clean. Even his death, burial, and resurrection occurred generously at the boundary lines of the city (Heb. 13:12–13) between two thieves so that everyone can find a hospitable welcome. In embracing all worlds, even perpetrators are held accountable as the oppressed is heard; no one is excluded from processes of compassionate justice.[62]

Lastly, the Spirit is the redeeming push and pull of migration. It is the divine expression that turns the caustic forces of the volatile international markets that cause mass migrations into an energizing impetus for planetary well-being. Inhuman conditions that make living impossible are imbued with the life-giving source of the Spirit that entices the migrant with hope and courage. The Spirit impels the migrant to leave a homeland in search

---

[60] Phan, "Embracing, Protecting, and Loving the Stranger," 100.

[61] Ibid., 77.

[62] Phan, *In Our Own Tongues,* 148; See also Orlando E. Costas, *Christ outside the Gate: Mission beyond Christendom* (Eugene, OR: Wipf & Stock, 1982).

of a better future. The Spirit's continuous outpouring is for Phan the divine push of migrants "out of poverty and inhuman living conditions, infusing them with courage, trust, and imagination to envision a different life for themselves and their families, one that is consonant with promise of a world of justice given by the *Deus migrator*, in whose image and likeness they are."[63]

The divine immanence being made present in this Trinitarian mode in the migrant realities can be interpreted, as Phan does, as the migrant being the *imago Dei migratoris*, or the icon whose body displays components of the moving nature of the accompanying Trinity. According to Phan, the migrant partly reveals "the privileged, visible, and public face of the God who chooses, freely and out of love, to migrate from the safety of God's eternal home to the strange and risky land of the human family, in which God is a foreigner needing embrace, protection, and love."[64] The *imago Dei migratoris* makes partly visible the God who becomes an outsider to the protections of the human law and yet ontologically is the ground of the migrants' right to human dignity. Thus, in subjecting migrants to injustice, "the *Deus migrator* [becomes] subjected to the same inhuman and sinful treatment."[65] As Luis G. Pedraja argues, the Trinity is *iconoclastic*. Whenever the dominant structures come to be identified with the divine, such as the Caesars in Rome, and nineteenth-century nations claiming a divine mandate, the Trinity can serve to demolish our cultural idolatries.[66]

Hence, when considering the well-being of the city, its fuller sense of beauty, we do well to look at the human *movements* through which the divine relations are made manifest. *Dei migratoris* inhabits the boundaries of spaces and horizons of time so that urban communities can become icons of the outsider-ground moving by, beyond themselves and according to multiple belongings. In *imitatio Christi* or in imitation of the anointed Jesus, as Christians we can purposefully locate ourselves at the margins of natural and human borders,[67] and so be called *compañeros y compañeras*, the *paroikoi* who perichoretically opt for—move toward, welcome in, and become like— the migrant stranger. For as Jesus said, "I was a stranger [*xenos*] and you welcomed me" (Matt. 25:35).[68] With our sights on an indeterminate end of history, or its open-ended entelechy, or as if our vision was being drawn from

---

63 Phan, "Embracing, Protecting, and Loving the Stranger," 103.

64 Ibid., 99.

65 Ibid.

66 Luís Pedraja, "Trinity," in *Handbook of U.S. Theologies of Liberation*, ed. Miguel de la Torre (St. Louis: Chalice Press, 2004), esp. 57–58.

67 Phan, "Migration in the Patristic Era," 58.

68 Ibid.

the future, being of the Spirit is likewise *being* according to the Spirit's new frontier—never future enough—for the Spirit pulls the *paroikoi* (believing communities) toward a life where material conditions might offer migrants the possibility of "a life with dignity for all."[69] This becoming icons of an outsider-grounding reality in movement while beyond grasp and ultimately of full revelation is that which remains hoped for and always realizable in part through horizontal beautifying cooperation.

When we cooperate like this at the margins, worlds become hospitable and those who cross and dwell amid borders likewise can lead just and inclusive lives. While alienation (such as the cross) points to the defeat, failure, and sense of destruction that vulnerable migrants experience, resurrections announce hope of victory over death, of freedom from slavery. In the act of dwelling betwixt and between oppressive and marginalizing delimitations—geographically, sexually, racially, economically, politically, culturally, or religiously—a new reality of barriers becoming frontiers is announced.[70] Borders become the *placeholder*, the sites for *parousia*. Their meeting points usher the kindom of God, and turn natural and human-made limits into *hospotia* and *xenodochia*. As Phan says, "In this way, the borders of death become frontiers to life in abundance."[71]

Mixed Temporalities

Through such movements, both the divine *migrantness* and our *paroikoi* leave a trace here on earth. The Trinity crossing over into space and entering into the measurement of change (*chronos*) spurs cosmic revolutions by means of its perichoretic dance, which for Phan results in *kairos* or "moments pregnant with promise of transformation."[72] Its counterspiral motion of future time erupting in the present expands the limits of the past as it makes room for new possibilities within what "has been" and pressing toward the "full flourishing" of kindom hope in history.[73] Another way to describe it is by saying that the past is gathered up in our memory, and the future is made real in our imagination, resembling Augustine's notion of distention (past) and anticipation (future).[74]

---

[69] Phan, "Embracing, Protecting, and Loving the Stranger," 103.
[70] Phan, *In Our Own Tongues*, 148.
[71] Phan, "Embracing, Protecting, and Loving the Stranger," 102.
[72] Phan, "Betwixt and Between," 127–28.
[73] Ibid., 114.
[74] Ibid., 129.

The call to memory in anticipation of fuller forms of divine presence has been central to the embodiment of the Jesus event at each moment of celebrating the Eucharist. Intended to heal any historical amnesia and rooted in the migrant experience of remembering, the Hebrews were called to befriend the alien even when they were becoming a great and prosperous nation, for they too were once *the least of these*—aliens. For Daniel Groody, remembering where we have come from helps us to change in imitation of the Eucharistic transubstantiation. It allows us to perceive in the Eucharistic elements "the hands, the feet, the labor, the sweat of those who worked on the fields." It recalls for us the immigrant story of becoming a people of God that enacts God's goodness and that challenges "excessive nationalisms and xeno-phobic attitudes," and "the scapegoating and rejection, hostility and fear."[75]

Once endowed with its eschatological quality, the world holds the potential for being an icon of the *parousia*, a fuller unfolding of the divine kindom in its creative beauty. It "contain[s] in itself the whole material world and the fruit of humanity's noblest cultural endeavors," and it incarnates a glimpse of "the paradigm of culture-in-transfiguration."[76] The Trinitarian migratory pull is toward a history in the shape of "universal justice, perfect peace, total reconciliation, and unbounded happiness"—global well-being.[77]

As *kairos or* eschatological time enters into geographical space, and interrupts its boundaries, liberation will be in *via*, in movement, alive, an ongoing evolution. For Nancy Bedford, redemptively incarnating *the way of the migrant strangers* means being "between remembrance of things and places past and their hope for a future that cannot [be] fully realized in this 'evil age' but can be anticipated, quite concretely, in hope."[78] Being *in vi*a is for the sake of hoping against hope, of speaking a language overwhelmed by the good news, and demonstrating ways of being at home according to the divine love in motion.[79] So more like a mobile home than an occupied settlement, according to Phan, its mobility reflects the transitory enrooting

---

[75] Daniel G. Groody, "Fruit of the Vine and Work of Human Hands: Immigration and the Eucharist," in Groody and Campese, *A Promised Land, A Perilous Journey*, 303, 311.

[76] Phan, "Betwixt and Between," 126.

[77] Phan, "Embracing, Protecting, and Loving the Stranger," 103.

[78] Nancy Bedford, "Between Babylon and Anatoth: Toward a Theology of Hope in Migration," in *Compassionate Eschatology: The Future as Friend*, ed. Ted Grimsrud et al. (Eugene, OR: Cascade Books, 2011), 50.

[79] Nancy Bedford, "To Speak of God from More Than One Place: Theological Reflections from the Experiences of Migration," in *Latin American Liberation Theology: The Next Generation*, ed. Ivan Petrella (Maryknoll, NY: Orbis Books, 2005), 104–6.

of much of migratory existence.[80] And in intertwining space with time, particularly in view of eschatology, the migrant component of the divine *parousia* can showcase urban beauty that aims for that which is yet to come, namely, the *beyondness* of selves across social, cultural, religious, political, and geographical boundaries.

To the extent that we reenact the Jesus accompanying event, borders "of death" can be transformed into "valleys of life."[81] Then the gospel becomes a fulfillment in history that while not yet fully established does nonetheless usher in a new reality.[82] So the border-crossing iconicity in migrant life draws from the mixture of temporalities or "'tiempos mixtos'—premodernity, modernity, and postmodernity"[83]—turning contexts into grounds of contestation rather than synthesis. The hoped-for *parousia*, while unattainable by human effort, iconizes itself through the collective desire for a good place existent in migrants (utopia). This anticipation of planetary transformation of culture and beautification of global cities entails contemplation of the past with the hopes of reframing territories imaginatively.

With this image of full planetary flourishing in mind, being betwixt and between temporalities would entail freeing discourse on history and culture from all totalitarian powers or absolutisms (including radical messianisms). No heritage and no geographical limit can occupy center stage. Because the *paruosia* is *in* and *with*, but also *other than* all there is, it can be a gratuitous gift and the generous hope amid historical calamities with which to address economic and sociological conditions that affect all living beings (preferentially opting for the migrant near and far). It can be the offer of salvation from evil.[84] Its reconciliatory nature brings the many into unity in terms of diversity, multiplicity, and plurality. It creates a planetary well-being.

---

[80] Phan, "Betwixt and Between," 126–127.

[81] As Gutiérrez indicates, this metaphor can be extracted from the book by Daniel G. Groody, *Border of Death, Valley of Life: An Immigrant Journey of Heart and Spirit* (Lanham, MD: Rowman and Littlefield, 2002); Gutiérrez, "Poverty, Migration, and the Option for the Poor," 81.

[82] Phan, "Betwixt and Between," 127–128.

[83] Phan, *Christianity with an Asian Face*, 10. To further explore the concept of "tiempos mixtos," see Fernando Calderón, "America Latina, identidad y tiempos mixtos, o cómo ser boliviano," in *Imágenes desconocidas* (Buenos Aires: CLASCO, 1998), 225–29.

[84] Phan, *Christianity with an Asian Face*, 79–80; See also, for example, Jon Sobrino, *Chistology at the Crossroads: A Latin American Approach* (Maryknoll, NY: Orbis Books, 1982).

Material Beauty

Parousia is the placeholder betwixt and between boundaries and temporalities in which the Jesus accompanying event is continuously being reenacted through the push and pull energies of the Spirit in the communities of faith, urban sectors, and the world. Such ubiquitous yet unapparent presence is tangibly apprehended through performance. According to Hans-Georg Gadamer, representation is art overcoming its temporal distance by it being present.[85] Any work of art achieves presence in its representation, its contemporaneity.[86] It is in performance that meaning shows forth. Each performance adapts to changes in time and circumstance, with *full* presence surpassing any form of mediation through which the work is presented, in this case, the migrant Trinity being the inexhaustible reservoir of participatory performance. The presence of a work of art is presence by participation in the overflow of being,[87] what in this essay is understood as *becoming* the icons of *Dei migratoris*. As such, to be is to migrate, to welcome in, and become in the shape of the migrant neighbor. It is the performance of *compañerismo* or accompaniment with the touch of beauty.

Comparing migration to a work of art might appear to be romanticizing migration. Yet the theological trope of the icon points to the divine trace precisely because migrants, whose footsteps on earth are often ignored, become visible through the radiating inner glory of the world. The migrants are the sojourners from afar who come near and raise the question of detrimental ways of global living and exclusionary forms of border existence: the how and why, and who gets to decide about the fate of *the world* according to borders, with its varied outcomes. They remind us of our colonial heritage, the struggles between past histories that both have put in shackles and have sought to liberate the gospel.[88] And in accompanying the migrant, as Gustavo Gutiérrez challenges, one can become "conscious that poverty is the result of human agency . . . [and] not a misfortune but an injustice . . . not a destiny but a condition."[89] Furthermore, migrants' bodies serve as reminders of hope against hope, the kingdom coming on earth. Migrants, "the poor today are not only lying at the door," as with Lazarus, Gutierrez reminds us. "[T]hey are entering in search of a better, more dignified life."[90]

---

[85] Hans-Georg Gadamer, *Truth and Method*, 2nd rev. ed. (New York: Continuum, 1989), 165.

[86] Ibid., 121.

[87] Ibid., 140.

[88] Phan, *In Our Own Tongues*, 14.

[89] Gutiérrez, "Poverty, Migration, and the Option for the Poor," 78.

[90] Ibid., 76.

Migrants can awaken humanity to the "dangerous memory" (Johann B. Metz) of the "underside of history" (Gustavo Gutiérrez).[91] On this, for Phan, the context of the borders call us into accountability. In the first instance, borders help us both to cultivate a deeper appreciation for the abundance of beauty and to gain critical insight on manifestations of oppression prevalent in one's communities.[92] Acknowledgment of the internal cultural, philosophical, and even behavioral wealth accompanies confrontation of its many forms of social hierarchization and oppression. Another call to task would be that of mutual criticism and enrichment between cultures. Translation among cultures results in finding equivalents and some borrowing at some intermediate level that can lead to "confronting American culture as equals in a truly multi-ethnic and pluralistic society."[93] This would also entail the de-ghettoization of traditions and perspectives, including the ancestral now being reappropriated with an awareness of the potential resulting in solidarity with other immigrants and populations at large. It is born through seeing and listening to the stories of all migrants in order to accompany the most vulnerable among us in their struggle. Developing a keen appreciation for intercultural as well as interreligious perspectives can nurture the conditions for new ways of being Christian—ways that are neither inside nor outside usual ways of being human, and within and beyond the Catholic Church.[94] Interconnectedness of selves in a continuum of multiple perspectives grants presence to the seemingly invisible migrant.[95]

The horizons of liberation expand our present in view of the future through the outpouring of the Spirit so that we can become the icons of the divine in *via*. As icons of an inexhaustible contemporary work of art, we can continue to evolve holding in tension the migrant realities and kingdom hopes that we envision. This tension is due to how the migrant life and border existence lends itself to a type of *theodramatics* that contains a covenantal focus with a broader economy of Triune communicative action that welcomes improvisation.[96] Borrowing from Hans Urs Von Balthasar, Goizueta describes this *theodrama* as the interaction of divine and human

---

[91] Phan, "Introduction," xvi.

[92] Phan, *Christianity with an Asian Face,* 12.

[93] Ibid., 238.

[94] Ibid., 236.

[95] Phan, *In Our Own Tongues,* 195; on this insight, Phan is drawing from R. S. Sugirtharajah, *Asian Biblical Hermeneutics and Postcolonialism: Contesting the Interpretations* (Maryknoll, NY: Orbis Books, 1998), 127.

[96] For a view on the element of "improvisation" in the dramatization of the gospel, see Kevin J. Vanhouzer, *The Drama of Doctrine: A Canonical-linguistic Approach to Christian Theology* (Louisville, KY: Westminster John Knox Press, 2005).

freedoms originating in "the utterly free and gratuitous gift of love that is God's self-expression."[97]

As if vividly re-presencing *kairos* in our times or the in-breaking of the divine kindom here on earth, improvisation offers a glimpse into the creative component of mixed temporalities. Its rupture in time within space enacts the betwixt and between divine–human reality. It is an eruption of freedom from within the world that results from the continuous re-presencing of the Jesus accompanying event through the outpouring of the Spirit that is being concretized in beautification processes within cities. This divine self-expression of love in freedom interacts with the urban-migrant realities to disrupt the onslaught of the demonic harbored in social structures when as icons we choose to enact the divine praxis undertaken in solidarity with the migrant victims of rape, violence, abandonment, low wages, and lack of rights. Partly by revealing what remains to be accomplished and an initial aim of what can be, in *theodramatic* fashion we can interrupt the present impoverishing conditions of wastage, overconsumption, unfair international trades, depletion of resources, and contamination. It is a form of *parousia*, a presence of the future here and now being reflected in aspects of urban life, what Eldin Villafañe calls a presence of "living–with" in the city (*presencia de convivencia*) or a presence of salt and light in the *polis* (Matt. 5:13–16).[98]

What is more, this is a volitional act in which migrants are active participants and actors who nurture and share the good of the earth—the beautiful *oikoumene*. The border contexts that reflect the harmony between a kindom of God lifestyle and *compañerismo* (the wisdom of saints across time and space) show that migrants of today seek to regain dignity.[99] Gender, class, and racial biases along the sociopolitical, economic, and religio–cultural lines aid the migrant in identifying power structures in dire need of transformation within their spheres of limited influence. Migrants live up to their prophetic nature of transformation when in "demonstration" alongside "denunciation"[100] they display the divine love and put in place just structures, when they become multicultural and multilingual *koinonias*, and when they act as "pueblo

---

[97] Goizueta, "Theo-drama," 69.

[98] For Villafañe, presence, popular classes, and primal spirituality are the three main elements found in "Criollo" Pentecostalism (US Hispanic and Latin American forms of Pentecostalism); see Eldin Villafañe, "La fe cristiana y la calidad de vida: Hacia una teología de Shalom como clave heremenéutica de la calidad de vida," *Apuntes* 15 (1995): 100–110.

[99] Phan, "Introduction," xv.

[100] Eldin Villafañe, *The Liberating Spirit: Toward an Hispanic Pentecostal Social Ethic* (Lanham, MD: University Press of America, 1992), 217.

puente" (bridge people) for other immigrants and for second and subsequent US-born generations.[101] This urban beautifying endeavor is architectonic art in the making, the spread of life flourishing into the political, economic, social, and cultural spheres where *immigrants live* and where their worlds intersect with the host societies. And even when often prevented from participating and transforming uneven "centers of power,"[102] they become icons of redemptive *migrantness*—enacting a *compañerismo* of a *paroikousia* consciousness.

The dramatization of the accompanying event of Jesus through the continuous outpouring of the Spirit in material life lends itself to a form of spirituality that decolonizes the psychological dominations that tend to keep the migrant imprisoned.[103] The Spirit pushes and pulls the migrant into the *unrealized* dimension of the *already* work of Jesus by vivifying their human spirit and renewing their hope. *Parousia* becomes hope rooted in "Spiritual Presence" that restores courage "to hold on tenaciously even when the terrain of our pilgrimage becomes muddled and the need to escape or flee the human scene becomes most apparent."[104] This *theodrama* is a form of protest of the unconscious against the "suffocating social and economical insecurities" being manifested through "gestures, music, and joy."[105]

Overall, life viewed as a *kairos*–material beauty or "moments pregnant with promise of transformation,"[106] is sacramentally transformative. As humanity becomes a sign of the eternal being manifested in tangible and historical manner, the migratory *theodrama* makes present what for Miroslav Volf is the "materiality of salvation."[107] Rather than an exclusively inner phenomenon, the encompassing tangibility of salvation is put on display in human existence. Humanity hence comes to contribute or cooperate with the migrant Trinity in the "building of the reign of God under the conditions of history."[108] Urban expressions of faith immerse the sacred in the profane and ultimately result in a transformative paradigm—an inexhaustible contemporary artwork in-between borders.

---

[101] Ibid., 217.

[102] Phan, "Introduction," xix.

[103] Leonard Lovett, "Liberation: A Double-Edged Sword," *PNEUMA: The Journal of the Society for Pentecostal Studies* 9 (1987): 159–60.

[104] Ibid. 166.

[105] Sepúlveda, "El crecimiento del movimiento pentecostal en América Latina," 90.

[106] Phan, "Betwixt and Between," 127–28.

[107] Miroslav Volf, "Materiality of Salvation: An Investigation in the Soteriologies of Liberation and Pentecostal Theologies," *Journal of Ecumenical Studies* 26/3 (1989): 448.

[108] Ibid., 455.

A Migrant Iconicity

Transformative beauty embodied in urban communities makes manifest the accompanying event of Jesus and the push and pull forces of the Spirit (betwixt and between boundaries and temporalities), the *parousia* being partly realized through the theodramatization of the love for the neighbor in the act of becoming the migrant neighbor that transfigures the city. For Phan this also means that because I love myself, and the migrant is myself as I myself am a migrant, then the migrant is loved (Deut. 24:17–18). To become a migrant loving migrants is to be in *compañerismo* of a *paroikousia* that listens and waits patiently, retrieves memories, and helps usher in God's gift of peace and forgiveness. It is to aid in constructing a new reality with optimism and hope. It is to make space for stories of shared spirituality and common work, and even of "mutual suspicion and jealousy."[109]

Becoming in the shape of the neighbor and so the icon of the transformative love of God midwives theologies of migration.[110] When the accompaniment of becoming with the migrant is primary, no sociopolitical and economic history can remain unchallenged.[111] In this sense, a theology of migration, locates World Christianity betwixt and between boundaries, as it denounces global inequalities and promotes peace, justice, and progress. It also announces a comprehensive citizenship package with full rights and duties of the person to enjoy and to promote the well-being of the self, family life, community life, the life of nations, and the life of the planet.[112]

---

[109] Phan, *Christianity with an Asian Face*, 17.
[110] Phan, *In Our Own Tongues*, 138–43.
[111] Phan, *Christianity with an Asian Face*, 176–82. Villafañe, *The Liberating Spirit*.
[112] Phan, *In Our Own Tongues*, 21.

Part III

The Pastoral and Practical Dimensions of World Christianity

15

EMERGING PERSPECTIVES AND IDENTITY NEGOTIATIONS OF THE INDIGENOUS CHRISTIANS

Jojo M. Fung

The percentage of *indigenous Christians* in the world remains miniscule when compared with the total global Christian population, one that is estimated to comprise nearly a third of the global population. Nevertheless, it is important to map out the extent to which contemporary trends of theological reflection have pushed back the global boundaries about indigenous oral cultures and the beliefs in the spirit world. The widening theological terrain has provided greater maneuverability to offer a more nuanced explanation of the process by which the global indigenous Christians negotiate their Christian identity.

Emerging Theological Perspectives and Insights

Having engaged in the task of doing theological reflection in the Asian context of indigenous peoples in the last two decades, I believe the time has come to rethink one's theological understanding of indigenous religio–cultural traditions that would enable one to uncover their potential for shaping new theological insights and understandings. In looking at the three watershed events in 1995, 1997, and 2010, one could discern a movement of God's spirit to lead the church to generate affirming and refreshing perspectives on these indigenous traditions. These perspectives have become the vista for more life-giving reflection at the regional and global theological frontiers.

Evangelization among the Indigenous Peoples of Asia (1995)

In September 1995, the Office of Evangelization of the Federation of Asian Bishops' Conferences (FABC) organized a conference in Hua Hin,

Thailand, with the theme *Evangelization among the Indigenous Peoples of Asia*.[1] The forty-five participants, bishops, priests, religious, and laity of Asia, all of whom belonged to indigenous groups or were working with them, reflected on the theological significance of the religious heritage of the indigenous peoples and unequivocally affirmed that "over the centuries God has been speaking to indigenous peoples through their cultures."[2]

This perspective borne of Asia has specifically named the indigenous cultures as the *locus theologicus* of God's revelation. The conference delegates acknowledge that the Christian churches in Asia have unjustly treated the religious traditions and practices of the indigenous peoples and marginalized their adherents within the church. This new perspective has reversed, to a large extent, the cultural denigration on the part of the church. Today, the task of *doing mission* among the indigenous peoples calls for "collecting and studying our peoples' myths, rites, symbols, poems, and proverbs which could be used to promote a genuine prayer life and worship among indigenous peoples."[3] In other words, this new insight on the indigenous cultures confirms and elevates the relevance of the diverse cultural elements for the prayer and liturgical lives of the indigenous churches.

Because indigenous culture is revelatory of God's salvific presence, *Evangelization among the Indigenous Peoples of Asia* calls for "a new evangelization at the heart of these cultures, a profound encounter between the core values of indigenous peoples and the biblical faith."[4] It perceives the task of new evangelization as calling on the church to "support the right of indigenous peoples to exist and to be themselves" and promises to "stand with them in their struggle to live as full and equal citizens of their nations and to enter the mainstream without losing their identity."[5]

The Spirit at Work in Asia Today (1997)

In 1997, the FABC Office of Theological Concerns called for a paradigm shift in the theological understanding and perception of the

---

[1] For the final report and recommendations, see "Evangelization among the Indigenous Peoples of Asia," in *For All the Peoples of Asia, Volume 2: Federation of Asian Bishops' Conferences Documents from 1992 to 1996* (Quezon City, Philippines: Claretian Publications, 1997), 211–14.

[2] Ibid., 212.

[3] Ibid.

[4] Ibid.

[5] Ibid.

indigenous peoples in its document, *The Spirit at Work in Asia Today.*⁶ The strengths of this document are manifold.

First, *The Spirit at Work in Asia Today* makes a critical appraisal of the situation of the indigenous peoples in Asia. In many Asian societies, the adherents of the primal religions are not only numerically minorities but are often stereotyped as culturally inferior, less developed, and their traditions and customs often deemed to be of less value. Indigenous peoples are often referred to as tribals and aborigines, terms they reject as perpetuating stereotypes depicting them as backward. In various Asian countries, the adherents of primal religions are living in remote areas, isolated from the urban centers. As regard their possibilities of having access to education and participation in the economic processes, these people are marginalized and disadvantaged when compared to their urban counterparts. In most Asian countries, growing industrialization and urbanization, coupled with exploitation of the natural resources in mining and ecological destruction of local forests, seas, and wildlife, threatens the existence and livelihood of indigenous peoples who are used to traditional ways of life based on symbolic relationships with nature.⁷

Second, *The Spirit at Work in Asia Today* highlights the antiquated mission theology underlying the missionary practices that have regarded the leaders and adherents of primal religions to "have been under the influence of evil spirits rather than under the influence of the Holy Spirit," and acknowledges,

> The primal religions were often accused of propagating idolatrous and satanic practices. Their members were called people living in "darkness and far from God," because they were considered to believe in a world full of evil spirits and powers and to depend on the intercession of dubious magicians, witch-doctors, healers and exorcists. The Christian message was presented to them as the liberating force, which, with the power of the Holy Spirit, brought light into the darkness and delivered these people from an age-old oppression and slavery to religiously false ideas, which could only be called superstitious and idolatrous.⁸

---

⁶ *The Spirit at Work in Asia Today.* FABC Papers No. 81 (Hong Kong: Federation of Asian Bishops' Conferences, 1998), http://www.fabc.org/fabc%20papers/fabc_paper_81.pdf.

⁷ Ibid., 23.

⁸ Ibid., 26.

Third, *The Spirit at Work in Asia Today* calls for a rethinking of missiological approaches so that the Asian church not only "evangelizes the indigenous peoples but must be evangelized by them and learn from them new insights in areas such as ecology, community life and the celebration of life's joys and tragedies."[9] Since the cultures of the indigenous peoples have been recognized as the locus of God's self-communication, it further affirms the conclusion in *Evangelization among the Indigenous Peoples of Asia* that "much of the indigenous peoples' world view and ethos is compatible with the Christian faith."[10] To the enrichment of prayer and liturgical lives, *The Spirit at Work in Asia Today* goes a step further in stating that indigenous cultures further enrich Christian theology; "their traditional beliefs, rites, myths and symbols of indigenous peoples provide material for developing indigenous theologies and liturgical ceremonies."[11]

EATWOT 2010

In 2010, the Ecumenical Association of Third World Theologians (EATWOT) met in Antipolo, Philippines (EATWOT 2010). The final statement of the Seventh Asian Theological Conference at EATWOT 2010, "Indigenous Peoples' Struggle for Justice and Liberation in Asia,"[12] calls on the theologians to attend to the indigenous cosmic spirituality of the sacred web of interconnected relations, unpacking the implications on doing theology in Asia and in the world as follows:

> We need to make their spirituality of connectedness with nature and the land our own in our collective effort to heal the earth and promote collective well being. Their intuitiveness to the life systems and interconnectedness of all earthlings make us wonder if our current way of theologizing is inadequate if not wanting in forging a more holistic perspective in dealing with the present global crisis. We have to review the theology that has constructed our faith-vision of the cosmos, world-view and perspective of life.[13]

---

[9] Ibid.

[10] Ibid.

[11] Ibid.

[12] The full statement, "Indigenous Peoples' Struggle for Justice and Liberation in Asia," is available at http://www.eatwot-tw.org/Asia%20Region.html.

[13] Ibid.

At the same time, "Indigenous Peoples' Struggle for Justice and Liberation in Asia" also foregrounds an Asian and indigenous way of theologizing that is sensitive to the cosmic web of the unseen and seen worlds:

> The time has come to move from the rational-cognitive Western model of theologizing and expressing of our faith experiences and reclaim the intuitive, imaginative, artistic, symbolic and creative forces of Asian Indigenous Peoples. We need to reclaim our Asian manner of listening and conversing with the spirit world, our ancestors, the wonders and creativity of nature and feel the presence of the Divine in an embodied, non-dualistic and non-dominating ways. Indigenous Peoples' Wisdom and Spirituality have much to inspire us and contribute to our Asian Theology for Justice and Liberation.[14]

Likewise, the Asian Women's Meeting that met at EATWOT 2010 expressed their gendered perspective through the theme "Yearning for Running Streams: an Asian Eco-feminist Theological Perspective," challenging theologians and the churches to value the Asian cosmologies that are rooted in "ancestral/folk faith traditions."[15]

EATWOT 2010 further emphasizes the need for a "more *attentive* listening" to the experiences and struggles of the indigenous peoples that are integral to their cosmocentric spirituality. According to the conference participants, "there is a reality beyond this culturally constructed reality" that is "the arena of faith," a faith that guides the journey of the indigenous peoples in their experience of the divine and perennial struggle to create a better future.[16]

At the Theological Frontier of Asia

The refreshing perspectives and emboldened shifts have occasioned a few Asian theologians to enter the frontier, rightly the periphery of the *arena of faith*. This arena of faith deals with the oral literature and the spirit world. Limatula Longkumer, who teaches Christian ministry in the

---

[14] Ibid.

[15] The final report of the Asian Women's Meeting, "Yearning for Running Streams: an Asian Eco-feminist Theological Perspective," is available at http://www.eatwot-tw.org/Asia%20Region.html.

[16] See http://www.eatwot-tw.org/Asia%20Region.html.

Eastern Theological College of Assam in Northeast India alerts us, "today, the emphasis on written literature/text has sidelined and ignored the oral literature as non-literature or inferior to written literature" to the extent that "people do not regard it as an important literature," and "the missionaries ignored and proscribed the oral literature as heretical literature and listed them as banned books."[17] In reality, Longkumer argues, "condemning oral traditions means losing our cultural and religious values," and "we need to affirm that oral literature is authoritative literature for the tribals, the source of our culture and origin and also for theologizing process."[18]

Few Asian theologians also address the significance of the religio–cultural beliefs in the spirit world. Yangkahao Vashum, a Nagis theologian and an associate professor at Eastern Theological College, posits that indigenous peoples understand "the spirits as the mediators between God and the world" through whom "God relates to the people and world through the spirits."[19] These spirits are differentiated as "malevolent and benevolent spirits such that the malevolent spirits were associated with misfortune, calamities, and illness while the benevolent spirits such as the house spirits, fertility spirits and ancestor's spirits were known for blessing people with good health, good crops, healthy relationships between and among people, and a good family and community life."[20]

In the same vein, Pratap Chandra Gine, professor of the New Testament at the Serampore College of West Bengal, believes that the indigenous peoples "are spiritual in their own rites" due to their beliefs that "the spirit of God dwells in every human thought and expression, and word and action."[21] The indigenous communities offer sacrifices to appeal to their sacred power, not out of fear as out of reverence and love. Moreover, Gine adds, "they worship every good spirit, which they encounter in their day-to-day life like, the god of the land, the god of harvest, the god of the waters, the god of the

---

[17] Limatula Longkumer, "Hermeneutical Issues in Using Traditional Sources—Where Do We Draw Our Spiritual Sources for Our Liberation?" *Journal of Tribal Studies* 13 (2008): 39.

[18] Ibid.

[19] Yangkahao Vashum, "Jesus Christ as the Ancestor and Elder Brother: Constructing a Relevant Indigenous/Tribal Christology of North East India," *Journal of Tribal Studies* 13 (2008): 27.

[20] Ibid.

[21] Pratap Chandra Gine, "Tribalism: A New Form of Religious Fundamentalism—A Challenge for Doing Theology in Asia," *JTCA—The Journal of Theologies and Cultures in Asia* 4 (2005): 96.

animal kingdom."[22] In particular, the spirits are revered and venerated for their sacred power in creating and sustaining the earth and creation.

In most indigenous communities, the spirit world comprises the Great Spirit/creator, the ancestral and nature spirits that few scholars and theologians are able to articulate in perceptibly new rather than dogmatic ways. Philip Clayton, a scientist and theologian states, "the Spirit is set free from any metaphysical parameters and allowed to roam freely, immersing itself fully in the self-creating enterprise which is its natural birthright."[23] Anne Keary opines, "the idea of a creator god or Great Spirit" refers to the one "who had made their lands for them."[24] The Great Spirit "is a creative force in and of the land" and thus, the "creative power alive in the landscape" to the extent that "the Great Spirit made tracks on the earth; the earth, the water, and the grass speak back to the Great Spirit."[25] Native American theologians Clara S. Kidwell, Homer Noley, and George E. Tinker postulate that the Great Spirit "exists in all things in the world."[26] I believe that the Great Spirit suffuses all of creation and sustains the ancestral and nature spirits so that their presence makes creation/mother earth/nature sacred and therefore spirited. The sacredness of creation commands the reverence as well as a sense of awe and gratitude of those sensitized human beings.

In addition, a subsequent postulation of three related pneumatological principles has to be added. First, God created the life-giving benevolent spirits to serve creation and humankind. By virtue of God's creation, these benevolent spirits participate in the creative power of the omnipresent *ruach* (Jer. 23:24). This *ruach* is present in creation. Hence, the biblical authors acknowledge the Omnipresent *ruach* as the imperishable spirit that is in everything (Wisd. of Sol. 12:1).[27] This *ruach* fills the heaven and the earth (1 Kings 8:27; Amos 9:2–3), indeed the whole world (Wisd. of Sol. 1:7). By

---

[22] Ibid.

[23] Philip Clayton, *Adventures in the Spirit* (Minneapolis: Fortress Press, 2012), 11.

[24] Anne Keary, "Colonial Constructs and Cross-Cultural Interaction: Comparing Missionary/Indigenous Encounters in Northwestern America and Easter Australia," in *Beyond Conversion & Syncretism: Indigenous Encounters with Missionary Christianity, 1800–2000*, ed. David Lindenfeld and Miles Richardson (New York: Berghahn Books, 2012), 243–98, at 273.

[25] Ibid.

[26] Clara Sue Kidwell, Homer Noley, and George E.Tinker, *A Native American Theology* (Maryknoll, NY: Orbis Books, 2001), 57.

[27] Addison G. Wright, "Wisdom," in *The New Jerome Biblical Commentary,* ed. Raymond E. Brown, Joseph A. Fitzmyer, Roland E. Murphy (London: Geoffrey Chapman, 1993), 510–22, at 519.

the act of creation, the creator infused in everything, a living soul or living spirit (Wisd. of Sol. 15:11), and thus, God's *ruach* is acknowledged for its universal and life-giving activity (Job 34:14–15; Ps. 104:30) that makes creation sacred.[28] By participation in the creative *ruach*, the host of benevolent spirits, presided over by the omnipresent *ruach elohim* (Deut. 4:19–20, 10:17, 32:8–9; Ps. 82:1) enables the sustainability of life on planet earth.

Second, the abiding presence of *ruach elohim* and the benevolent spirits made creation sacred. According to Clifford and Murphy, the word *ruach* is a Hebrew word meaning "air in motion," conveying connotations of "wind," "breathe," and "spirit."[29] *Ruach* is the divine breath (1 Sam. 16:14) understood as the Spirit of God (Ps. 139:7) that makes creation and life sacred. In Genesis (1:1–2), *ruach elohim* is depicted as sweeping over the waters, transforming the primal chaos of profundity into a *cosmos* that befits all human and biospecies on earth. This is the *ruach elohim* that suffuses creation with God's sacred power and goodness (Gen. 1:4, 10, 12, 18, 21, 25, 31). Creation becomes sacramental and reflects the grandeur and splendor of God. This is the Spirit of God that sustains creation together with the benevolent spirits. Creation is therefore sacred and spirited.

Third, the benevolent spirits have oriented the lives of renowned shamans who possess moral integrity beyond self to live for the common good of the indigenous communities. The gospel injunctions—"anyone who is not against us is for us" (Mk. 9:40) and "anyone who welcomes me, welcomes the one who sent me" (Luke 9:48; cf. Matt. 8:1, 22:2–10; Luke 14:21–24)—put them as pleasing (albeit unbaptized) followers of Jesus. By inference from the universality of Jesus's Spirit, it is safe to state that the benevolent spirits that guide these renowned shamans also participate in the Spirit of Jesus. Therefore, the renowned shamans who live and act like Jesus also share in the *spirit power* of the Risen Jesus. The commitment of the renowned shamans who immerse themselves totally in the daily grind of economic poverty and political marginalization of their communities likened them to Jesus (Luke 4:18–19) in his struggle in early Palestine.[30] Their presence, knowledge, and wisdom have inspired the communities to

---

[28] Bruno Bottignolo, *"Celebrations with the Sun: An Overview of Religious Phenomena among the Badjaos* (Manila: Ateneo de Manila University Press, 1995), 38–57.

[29] Richard J. Clifford and Roland E. Murphy, "Genesis" in Brown, Fitzmyer, and Murphy, *The New Jerome Biblical Commentary*, 8–43, at 10.

[30] Pieter F. Craffert, *The Life of a Galilean Shaman: Jesus of Nazareth in Anthropological-Historical Perspective* (Eugene, OR: Wipf & Stock, 2008), 349.

share what they have, making the miracles of the fish and loaves (Mark 6:30–44, 8:1–10; Matt. 4:13–21; Luke 9:10–17; John 6:1–13) a present-day reality in the communities. Their rituals of healings for the sick, deliverance of those influenced by bad spirits, and re-creation of sacred space qualify them to be followers of Jesus.

This expanding theological space on the indigenous oral literature and spirit world prepares the stage for a more nuanced explanation of how indigenous Christians around the world negotiate their Christian identity.

Negotiation of the Religious Indigenous Identity

Most indigenous Christians living in nation-states continue to experience incessant contestation in their ancestral homelands. More often than not, the latent aim of these contestations is to pillage the resources below and above their lands. Given this political contestation, the emerging theological space needs to encourage greater consideration of the process of identity negotiation as complex, hybridized and therefore multiple, context-specific, and situational.

According to Premawardhana, "identities need not be multipled; they are multiple."[31] Jeannine Hill Fletcher concurs, "One's 'Christian' identity ought not be thought of as isolated from other communities, nor as unaffected by so-called 'non-Christian communities' (religious or cultural)."[32] This assumption presupposes that each religio–cultural tradition of the different ethnic communities is already a *crossed tradition*. The notion of a *crossed tradition* arises from Premawardhana's argument that religious traditions are "not pure origins but cross-fertilizations and hybridizations."[33] In the process of "traditioning" that Jeffery Carlson describes, traditions are already cross-fertilized/hybridized due to selective reconstruction.[34] Thus, Albertus B. Laksana summarily concludes, "local cultures with their religious components—which, in the case of Java, also include layers of Hinduism, Buddhism, and native spirituality—have become an integral part of local

---

[31] Devaka Premawardhana, "The Unremarkable Hybrid/Aloysius Pieris and the Redundancy of Multiple Religious Belonging," *Journal of Ecumenical Studies* 46/1 (2011): 77.

[32] Jeannine Hill Fletcher, *Monopoly on Salvation? A Feminist Approach to Religious Pluralism* (New York: Continuum 2005), 99.

[33] Premawardhana, "The Unremarkable Hybrid," 93.

[34] Jeffrey Carlson, "Responses," *Buddhism-Christian Studies* 23 (2003): 78–79.

Christian identity."[35] Such a mixed local Christian identity facilitates the practice of what John Berthrong calls "multiple religious participations."[36] In this sense, Premawardhana is right in postulating, "all these traditions and identities are more an "amalgam of impermanently related bits and pieces than the pristine singularities."[37]

Hybrid/Multiple Identity

As Homi Bhabha postulates, "the rearticulation, or translation, of elements that are *neither the One... nor the Other... [b]ut something else,*"[38] and "it is from this hybrid location of cultural value—the transnational as the translational—that the postcolonial intellectual attempts to elaborate a historical and literary project."[39] The notion of hybrid identities is situational in that it depends on the context and the level of understanding of the conversational interlocutor. An indigenous person may identity her/himself to an outsider who has little interaction with and knowledge of the indigenous peoples as an aboriginal person of Australia. In an international conference, an indigenous academic in a university will identify her/himself as part of the local university community and global intellectual community. At an ecumenical conference, s/he may identify her/himself as, for example, a Lakota Catholic from South Dakota, United States, a Mohawk Catholic from Alberta, Canada, or a Sami Lutheran of Lapland, Sweden. In the complex terrain of contestation, it is important to acknowledge that an indigenous Christian lives with a hybrid identity embedded in a *crossed tradition* that grounds her/his sense of personal identity. This home identity is her/his "primary cultural identification in order to survive mentally."[40] In

---

[35] Albertus B. Laksana, "Multiple Religious Belonging or Complex Identity: An Asian Way of Being Religious" in *The Oxford Handbook of Christianity in Asia,* ed. Felix Wilfred (London: Oxford University Press, 2014), 493–509, at 502.

[36] John Berthrong, *The Divine Deli: Religious Identity in the North American Cultural Mosaic* (Maryknoll, NY: Orbis Books, 1999), 35; Michae Voss Roberts, "Religious Belonging and the Multiple," *Journal of Feminist Studies in Religion* 26/1 (2010): 49.

[37] Premawardhana, "The Unremarkable Hybrid," 90; Carlson, "Responses," 78–79.

[38] Homi Bhabha, *The Location of Culture* (London: Routledge, 1994), 28.

[39] Ibid, 248.

[40] Fazal Rizvi, "International Education and the Production of Global Imagination," in *Globalization and Education: Critical Perspectives,* ed. Nicholas C. Burbules and Carlos Alberto Torres (London: Routledge, 2000), 206–26; Stuart Hall, "Introduction: Who Needs 'Identity'?" in *Questions of Cultural Identity*, ed. Stuart Hall and Paul du Gay (London: Sage, 1996), 1–17.

an age of globalization, the hybrid ethnic identity has enabled an indigenous person to navigate within the *intra* (the multiple streams of religiousness) and *inter* (lines between ethnicities and religions) boundaries of the nation-state, as well as boundaries that demarcate the local, regional, and global.

Identity Rooted in Indigenous Cosmology

There is an indigenous saying in Northern Luzon of the Philippines, among the Igorot in the Mountain Province: "You can take an Igorot out of the mountain but you can never take the mountain out of an Igorot." This idiom suggests that the sacred cosmology/spirituality is in the blood of the Igorot/indigenous communities. In other words, the Christian identity can never be dichotomized from the indigenous cosmology–spirituality. The holism of the indigenous religious beliefs is the basis to postulate that the indigenous identity is never single but multiple and therefore hybridized. In referring to Biraban and his hybridized belief, as he was a Christian of the aboriginal tribe called Awabakal, Anne Keary remarks, "Biraban remade the Christian deity as an indigenous being, incorporated him [sic] into an Awabakal cosmological and geographical order . . . and portrayed him as a special *yirriyirri* [holy] figure for Awabakal men while portraying himself the role of Jehovah's interpreter."[41] The indigenous Christians are awakening to a sense that they can be Christians and indigenous at the same time. To this end, the address of Pope John Paul II in Alice Spring was truly affirming:

> The Gospel now invites you to become, through and through, Aboriginal Christians . . . You do not have to be people divided into two parts, as though an Aboriginal had to borrow the faith and life of Christianity, like a hat or a pair of shoes, from someone else who owns them.[42]

Identity Embedded in the Spirit World

The religious cosmology of the indigenous peoples is always associated with the spirit world in which the centrality and respect of the ancestors are indispensable and integral to their religio–cultural identity. Hence, more

---

[41] Keary, "Colonial Constructs and Cross-Cultural Interaction," 282.

[42] "Address of John Paul II to the Aborigines and Torres Strait Islanders in "Blatherskite Park," Alice Spring, Australia," November 29, 1986, http://www.vatican.va.

and more indigenous Christians have become more assertive of their hybrid identity. As C. Mathews Samson urges,

> Scholars working in Mesoamerica have much to learn from the Maya worldview, which informs us that it is important not only to bring the ancestors into a new space and time but also to look for signs of balance, harmony, and equilibrium in the midst of social changes that none of us can escape.[43]

Moreover, Samson argues, in "contexts of violence and massive cultural change," the "historical memory and *testimonies* (the act of recounting the stories of individuals and peoples) augment those other discourses (religious and secular) that daily define"[44] elements that are common and particular in the religious identity construction of indigenous Christians.

These indigenous Christians need "to find a place from which to act within the world, a need to blur (and perhaps cross) boundaries in the continuing struggle to renew a sense of self and community."[45] For them, "the past is not simply left behind, and space has to be made for the ancestors who may yet speak again in unimaginable places."[46] It is not surprising that the hybridization of identity has become an undeniable reality in the life of the indigenous Christians. The richness of hybridity cannot be simplistically dismissed as religiously unacceptable/unorthodox for reasons that Samson has insightfully asserted: "Pluralism itself becomes a resource for re-enchantment rather than a threat."[47]

Conclusion

The church has awakened and recognized indigenous cultures as the revelatory locus of God. This awakening enables the church among the indigenous communities to enrich gradually her prayer life, organizational structures, worship, and theology with the cultural richness of the indigenous myths, rites, symbols, poems, proverbs, beliefs, and symbols. Besides

---

[43] C. Mathews Samson, "Conversion at the Boundaries of Religion, Identity, and Politics in Pluralicultural Guatemala," in David Lindenfeld and Miles Richardson, *Beyond Conversion & Syncretism*, 51–77, at 70.

[44] Ibid.

[45] Ibid., 72.

[46] Ibid.

[47] Ibid.

the new hermeneutical importance in the theological schools of oral literature are the theological significance of the benevolent spirits and the renowned shamans of integrity. The shamans are to be seen as motivated by the Great Spirit, the ancestral and nature spirits who participate in the power of God's Spirit and the Spirit of the Risen Lord. The emerging church operating in the contested ancestral space has to revalue hybridization of the religio–cultural identity and beliefs of the indigenous Christians/Catholics as the indigenous Christians negotiate their ethno–social–national boundaries. This is even more pronounced in their respective nation-states and the global world where contestation is part of their everyday struggle. Hybridity and pluralism that are accommodative of the complexity, differences, commonality, and particularities only enrich the multiple identities of the indigenous Christians in the world.

16

SPIRITUAL BUT NOT RELIGIOUS, MULTIPLE RELIGIOUS PRACTICE, AND TRADITIONAL CATHOLIC IDENTITIES

Joseph Cheah

The number of Catholics around the world has more than tripled in the past century, from approximately 291 million in 1910 to nearly 1.1 billion in 2010.[1] The demographic distribution of the world's Catholic population has also changed substantially: from representing about 70 percent of Catholics of the Global North (Europe and North America) in 1910 to 32 percent in 2010. Within the same period, the Catholic population in the Global South (Africa, Asia, and Latin America) has increased from about 30 percent in 1910 to at least 67 percent in 2010. Due to immigration, the Catholic population in the United States has undergone some striking demographic shifts as well: from a heavily European immigrant population in 1910 to more than 52 percent Latino/a in 2010.[2]

At the same time, in the first report of its 2014 survey concerning religious affiliation of a national sample of 35,000, the Pew Research Center finds that, on the one hand, the number of Americans in the United States who identified themselves as Christians is declining. On the other hand, the number of religiously *unaffiliated* or *nones* (agnostics, atheists, and those who are *nothing in particular*) is growing, especially among the young Millennials between the ages of eighteen and twenty-four. More importantly, the 2014 Pew report reveals that for the first time, the unaffiliated or the nones have outnumbered Catholics in the United States. As the number of Catholics in the United States has dropped from approximately 54

---

[1] For more information about the Pew Research Center and their reports that are cited in this chapter, see http://www.pewforum.org.

[2] Pew Research Center: Religion & Public Life, "The Global Catholic Population" (February 13, 2013), 1–2, http://www.pewforum.org/2013/02/13/the-global-catholic-population/.

million (23.9 percent) in 2007 to about 51 million (20.8 percent) in 2014, the unaffiliated has jumped from 16.1 percent in 2007 to 22.8 percent (56 million) in 2014. Among the combined young Millennials (ages eighteen to twenty-four) and older Millennials (ages twenty-five to thirty-three), only 16 percent said they were Catholics. The 2014 report also points out that 31.7 percent or nearly one-third of American adults indicate that they were raised Catholic, but 41 percent from this group no longer identify with Catholicism. To put this in perspective, while 12.9 percent of American adults are former Catholics, only 2 percent of American adults have converted to Catholicism from another religious tradition. Indeed, as the Pew report highlights, "no other religious group in the survey has such a lopsided ratio of losses to gains."[3]

The report underscores three factors behind the changes in Americans' religious identification. First, *generational replacement* of Catholics and mainline Protestants with Millennials who are apt to be nones, including much lower levels of affiliation with Christian churches in comparison to older generations. Among the Millennials, 36 percent of young Millennials and 34 percent of older Millennials are religiously unaffiliated. Second, the increase in the number of nones has been across the board from young Millennials to Baby Boomers (ages forty-nine to sixty-nine). About a third of older Millennials have no association with any religion, an upsurge of nine percentage points from their cohorts when the survey was taken in 2007. Nearly a quarter of Generation Xers (adults currently in their late thirties to late forties) is now unaffiliated or nones, an increase of four percentage points in seven years. In recent years, even Baby Boomers "have become slightly but noticeably more likely to identify as religious 'nones.'"[4] Third, switching religion among American adults is now a common occurrence. The group that has experienced the largest gain through religious switching is the religious nones. There is 1:4 ratio between those who are now affiliated with a religious group after having been raised unaffiliated and those who left their religious faith to become unaffiliated or nones. Because the percentage of the unaffiliated has grown significantly over the years since the 1970s, this trend of switching from a religion to a religious none appears to be ongoing rather than transitional. The group that has sustained the

---

[3] Pew Research Center: Religion & Public Life, "America's Changing Religious Landscape: Christians Decline Sharply as Share of Population; Unaffiliated and Other Faiths Continue to Grow" (May 12, 2015), 2–9, http://www.pewforum.org/2015/05/12/americas-changing-religious-landscape/.

[4] Ibid., 8.

greatest loss, as noted above, is Catholicism with 41 percent from this group switching to another religion or become unaffiliated.[5]

In this essay, I examine the ways in which the growing number of spiritual but not religious (SBNR) among those raised within the Catholic tradition have challenged the traditional notion of Catholic identity as a strict adherence to church doctrines and a faithful performance of prescribed practices. Specifically, I am interested in the implications of their rejection of institutional religion, resistance to doctrinal orthodoxy, preference for an individualized approach to spirituality, and multiple religious practice (MRP).

Spiritual but Not Religious

Pew divides the category unaffiliated or nones into three divisions: agnostics, atheists, and those who are nothing in particular. It is the last of these three that comprises the highest percentage of nones. In their follow-up questions about religious or spiritual beliefs in 2012, Pew reported that "while 42% of the unaffiliated describe themselves as neither a religious nor a spiritual person, 18% say that they are a religious person, and 37% say they are spiritual but not religious."[6] It appears that some of the unaffiliated who believe in "God or a universal spirit"[7] would not consider themselves SBNRs, while others would. From this complex, heterogeneous composition of the "unaffiliated," I will focus mainly on the SBNR group that is rapidly growing across many generations.

The terms *religious* and *spiritual* can be considered synonyms, and were used more or less interchangeably prior to the twentieth century. Over time, the word *spiritual* gradually came to be associated with an individual's private experience of the sacred or an interior cultivation of the life of faith, while the word *religious* came to be identified with one's public association with organized religion and adherence to its creeds, doctrines, and rituals. Being spiritual and being religious are not two mutually exclusive identities. Both have something to do with encountering the divine and fostering a connection or entering into a relationship with this divine figure through the practice of rituals and moral behaviors.[8]

---

[5] Ibid., 9.

[6] Pew Research Center: Religion & Public Life, "Religion and Unaffiliated: Nones on the Rise" (October 9, 2012), 1, http://www.pewforum.org/2012/10/09/nones-on-the-rise-religion/.

[7] Ibid.

[8] Robert C. Fuller, *Spiritual But Not Religious: Understanding Unchurched America* (New York: Oxford University Press, 2001), 5.

SBNRs generally do not associate themselves with absolute truth claims that characterize the self-understanding of most institutional religions. Hence, they are sometimes categorized under a religiosity of "believing without belonging."[9] However, to say that SBNRs are *anti-institutional loners* or *spiritual hermits* is not entirely accurate. Courtney Bender, professor at Columbia University, found that SBNRs engage in communal sharing not in churches or religious institutions but in yoga classes, massage clinics, drumming circles, and other nontraditional settings. One would be hard pressed, however, to find SBNRs meeting in a church or a religious setting because SBNRs are finding other outlets for community than organized religious institutions. In general, there seems to be an Orientalist tendency in the manner in which SBNRs construct their identity, beliefs, and practices. SBNR discourse tends to distinguish itself from the religious by a negation: what they are, we are not; what we are, they are not. As Bender notes, if the self-image of SBNRs "makes them think, 'I don't need history, I don't need the past'" because "I am not religious, which is about the past—I am spiritual, about the present."[10] In other words, the SBNRs' rhetoric tends to essentialize both the SBNRs and the religious, with the one depicted as the opposite of the other. For example, to say that SBNRs are more in touch with the experience of the sacred, whereas *religious people* just go through the motions without interiorizing their faith is misleading as it essentializes the term *religious*. To be sure, there are religious Catholics who overemphasize tradition to the extent of obscuring the depth of spirituality. However, there are also those who religiously follow the beliefs and practices of their Catholic tradition in order to assist them in having an experience of God and shaping their lives based on that experience—which, in essence, is what characterizes Christian spirituality.

Many SBNRs appear to have been so disenfranchised from organized religion that they manifest a strong antipathy toward the beliefs and teachings of the institutional religion. Some of the reasons for SBNRs' rejection of institutional religion include churches do not provide adequate answers

---

[9] Catherine Cornille, "Double Religious Belonging: Aspects and Questions," *Buddhist-Christian Studies* 23/1 (2003): 44. The origins of this phrase, *believing without belonging,* can be traced back to the sociologist Grace Davie who used it to describe that type of religiosity that has emerged in modern Britain. See Grace Davie, *Religion in Britain since 1945: Believing without Belonging* (Oxford: Wiley-Blackwell, 1994). See also, Catherine Cornille, *Many Mansions? Multiple Religious Belonging and Christian Identity* (Eugene, OR: Wipf and Stock Publishers, 2002), 1–6.

[10] Courtney Bender, "Examining the Growth of the 'Spiritual but Not Religious,'" *New York Times,* July 18, 2014, 3.

to people's spiritual needs; the tradition of the church is too confining; God is portrayed in an exclusively masculine image; and an exclusivistic or elitist theology that says there is only one true church and that no salvation is possible outside of a particular church or Christianity. In addition, the perception that those religious institutions, such as churches, are not supportive of cultural and social issues of importance to SBNRs: same-sex marriage, abortion, climate change, and so on. Furthermore, there is no felt need among SBNRs to adhere to the doctrinal orthodoxy of any institutional religion. They locate the source of spiritual authority within each individual rather than in the authority of the church or the magisterium. In fact, many SBNRs claim that belief is not essential in the cultivation of one's spirituality. Many distance themselves from the Christian religious tradition, and some have abandoned Western theism altogether. Overall, there is an emphasis that one ought to have the freedom to decide his/her beliefs.[11]

The tendency to minimize the importance of belief can be found within noncreedal Christianity as well. In his book, *The Future of Faith*, Harvey Cox, professor emeritus at Harvard University and a Baptist minister, distinguishes faith from belief by providing an insightful explication of faith as a "deep-seated confidence," a sort of primordial urge to hold on to what we think is true, even if we do not or no longer believe it. Cox offers an example from a short story, "Saint Manuel Bueno, Martyr," written by a Spanish writer Miguel Unamuno. In this story, a young man returns to his native village to visit his dying mother who, in the presence of a local priest, clutches her son's hand and asks him to pray for her. The son remains silent, but "as they leave the room, he tells the priest that, much as he would like to, he cannot pray for his mother because he does not believe in God. 'That's nonsense,' the priest replies, 'You don't have to believe in God to pray.'"[12] In other words, prayer, like faith, has primacy over belief. Faith is archetypal; it comes from the depths of our being. Belief, on the other hand, is related to uncertainty and opinion. Belief comes after faith and can change over time. "We can believe something to be true without it making much difference to us, but we place our faith only in something that is vital for the way we live."[13] For Cox, belief is "more like an opinion"; it is "more propositional than existential."[14] Cox's watered-down understanding of belief seems to

---

[11] Linda A. Mercadante, *Belief without Borders: Inside the Minds of the Spiritual but Not Religious* (New York: Oxford University Press, 2014), 68–70, 72–75, 97–98.

[12] Harvey Cox, *The Future of Faith* (New York: HarperCollins, 2009), 3–4.

[13] Ibid., 3.

[14] Ibid.

reflect SBNRs notion of the same. Belief is unimportant and inconsequential in one's faith and spiritual development.

While belief comes after faith and can change over time, this does not imply that belief does not hold any value at all. The first dogmatic declaration of the earliest Christians that *Jesus is Lord!* is not simply a faith confession but the central belief that distinguishes Christianity from Judaism, Islam, and other religions. It shapes the Christian understanding of the notion of the divine and the meaning and purpose of the good life. Indeed, Bernard Lonergan reminds us that belief shapes the very world in which we live.[15] Religious beliefs are crucial in the shaping of one's understanding of religion or in the ultimate meaning and purpose of life. In her qualitative research on the aspect of belief of the religiously unaffiliated, Linda Mercadante discovered that despite the dominant rhetoric of SBNRs that belief is insignificant and even potentially hostile to the development of one's spirituality, there has been a "sea change in belief" emerging from a set of principles that guide the practice of SBNRs.[16] In response to an interview in the *New York Times*, Mercadante said, "They reject heaven and hell, but they do believe in an afterlife. . . . They may like Jesus, he might be their guru, he might be one of their many bodhisattvas, but Jesus as God is not on their radar screen."[17] However, as observed above from the 2012 PEW follow-up report, this does not mean that all SBNRs reject the divinity of Jesus. Because SBNRs have less ties to the *orthodoxy* of the church, their beliefs about Jesus may not always align with traditional Christian understandings of the same.

Identity/Identities

Identity, by its very construction, is a hybrid. It employs ethnic, racial, gender, religious, and cultural descriptions. The complexity of the hybrid nature of identity construction begins to reveal itself if one considers the conflation of many problematic alignments comprising one's religious identity: ethnicity, race, gender, class, and other factors. To identify oneself as a Chinese American Catholic, for example, is to suggest a racial, ethnic, cultural, and religious identity, where one factor may predominate at any given time depending on the context in which one finds oneself. No one factor, however, can completely dominate all the others. One's Catholic

---

[15] Bernard Lonergan, *Method in Theology* (New York: Seabury, 1972), 57–60.

[16] Mercadante, *Belief without Borders*, 8–9.

[17] Bender, "Examining the Growth of the 'Spiritual but Not Religious,'" 3.

identity may predominate in a Catholic setting, but the person's religious identity does not completely replace his/her racial/ethnic, nationality, gender, and class. Each of us has many identities, and the contexts in which we find ourselves will determine which identity would predominate at a given moment. Furthermore, there are also political and theological alignments within a particular religious identity. For example, one is never just a Catholic. One can be a traditional Catholic or a Vatican II Catholic, or another sociological type of Catholic. A traditional Catholic is someone who attends Mass weekly, adheres to the teachings of the hierarchy, concerns oneself with personal salvation but has little commitment to the church's social teachings. A Vatican II Catholic is someone who participates at weekly Mass, is educated in and committed to the theology of Vatican II, is a strong supporter of this theology and the church's social teachings.[18] In other words, there has never been a singular Catholic identity in the history of the church.

Like individual identities, institutional identities are constructed within a particular social, cultural, and historical context. An institution that does not respond to new developments in the broader sociohistorical and cultural contexts will cease to exist. An institution cannot be expected to survive if it is still operating according to a set of identities and values it had thirty years ago. A healthy institutional identity is dynamic, constantly fine-tuning its identity to the changing social, economic, political, and cultural contexts.[19]

Pre–Vatican II Catholic Identities

Catholic identities from the time of the Reformation to the Second Vatican Council remained rather stable because American Catholic identities were shaped by two sources: internally from teachings and directives promulgated from Rome, influenced in part by their reactions to the Reformation, and externally in response to anti-Catholic discrimination experienced by Catholic immigrants in the United States from 1820 to 1920.[20] This was the period of massive European immigration, and there were at least forty million European immigrants, including a large number of Catholics from Ireland, France, Germany, England, Italy, Poland, and

---

[18] Arbuckle listed eleven sociological types. For other types, see Gerald A. Arbuckle, *Identity or Identities? Refounding Ministries in Chaotic Times* (Collegeville, MN: Liturgical Press, 2013), 62–65.

[19] Ibid., 6–7.

[20] Ibid., 30.

other European countries to the United States. During the nineteenth and early twentieth centuries, American Catholics suffered discrimination, persecution, and public condemnation because of their religious beliefs and practices. Within this hostile environment, the Catholic parish became a safe sanctuary for cultural preservation, ethnic reinforcement, as well as a place that prepared immigrants to make a gradual transition into the American culture. Indeed, the Catholic parish was the heart and center of Catholic immigrant communities. To protect Catholics from discrimination and the proselytizing influence of the dominant Protestant culture, ecclesiastical authorities constructed a wide range of institutions to safeguard the Catholic identities of poor immigrants: schools, hospitals, orphanages, and other facilities. Consequently, the church increasingly became inward looking, defensive, and had a fortress mentality to protect its members from external *evil* influences.

When survey was first utilized as a fact-gathering tool in the mid-twentieth century, the number of Americans who were unaffiliated or declared to have *no religion* was at the lowest with less than 2 percent of the population. This was the heyday of organized religion as it became the central feature of life in America.[21] One's religious identity was bounded by an exclusive membership in a particular religious community. As sociologist Will Herberg put it, to be American was to belong to an organized religion— mainly, Protestant, Catholic, or Jewish.[22] The 1950s were the glory years for institutional churches as Sunday liturgies were usually well attended; Catholic schools were run by priests, religious sisters, and brothers; and church authorities were generally well regarded in Catholic communities. To be a Catholic at that time was to belong to a Catholic parish, to receive a Catholic education, and Catholics were generally expected to marry other Catholics.[23] Catholic identities were formed not only from this culturally marginalized community but also from the teachings and directives of the hierarchy. Many rules and regulations connected Catholic identity to the observance of prescribed rules and expected behaviors. Catholics were not allowed to step inside a temple, mosque, or a non-Catholic worship site. Catholics were not allowed to attend a non-Catholic service without *serious reason* for fear that it would jeopardize their faith. It was a church with many

---

[21] Mercadante, *Belief without Borders*, 23.

[22] There was, of course, non-Christians in the United States in the 1950s, but their number was so small that they did not attract the attention of researchers.

[23] Christian Smith et al., *Young Catholic America: Emerging Adults In, Out of, and Gone from the Church* (New York: Oxford University Press, 2014), 10.

traditions, obsessive with a rigid performance of rituals, preoccupied with the dangers of sexual sins, and other prescribed practices. Preconciliar Catholic identity was tied not only to a strict adherence to church doctrines but also to a faithful performance of prescribed religious rituals.

Post–Vatican II Catholic Identities

The nostalgic world of the Will Herberg America of the 1950s began to unravel when the Vietnam War, civil rights movement, women's liberation, sexual revolution, and other events of the 1960s divided people intergenerationally and within the same Boomer generation itself. The Baby Boomer generation rebelled against their parents' faith and values by rejecting rampant consumerism and materialism, disparaging organized religion and institutional Christianity, and embracing Eastern and other alternative spiritualities. By the 1970s, those who described themselves as having *no religion* increased to nearly 9 percent of the population.[24] The 1960s were also the years of profound renewal within the Catholic Church as Pope John XXIII convened the Second Vatican Council on October 11, 1962. The Council (1962–1965) encouraged the Catholic Church to dialogue with the modern and non-Catholic world and brought about a period of reform within the Catholic Church emphasizing the importance of the laity, engagement with the modern world, worship in the vernacular, interreligious dialogue, human rights, religious freedom, and many other issues that are still pertinent today.[25] These were major reforms as the council moved from a highly centralized and authoritarian culture of the preconciliar church to a postconciliar church in which the world was no longer to be seen as evil in itself, and Catholics should now dialogue with adherents of other religions, including the unaffiliated.[26] It was a movement from a paternal church in which the faithful's Catholic identities could be taken for granted to a church of partnership in which the faithful must assume responsibility for constructing their own Catholic identities based on scripture and tradition. Shifting from an ecclesial culture in which Catholics were told what to believe and do to a church where they have to think for themselves has led many Catholics to confusion and chaos, resulting in many different sociological and theological understandings of Catholic identities today.[27]

---

[24] Mercadante, *Belief without Borders*, 24–25.
[25] Smith et al., *Young Catholic America*, 13.
[26] Arbuckle, *Catholic Identity or Identities*, 46.
[27] See ibid., chap. 2.

In terms of theological and canonical criteria for Catholic identity, Pope Pius XII's 1943 encyclical *Mystici corporis* identified the church of Christ with the Catholic Church. There was no distinction between the church of Christ or the kingdom of God and the Catholic Church. Such a triumphalistic notion of Catholic identity was clearly communicated to the Catholic laity—that to be a Catholic was to belong to the one true Christian church. This was supported by the 1917 Code of Canon Law, which presumed that the church of Christ and the Catholic Church share the same boundary.[28] In the Vatican II document *Lumen gentium* (LG), however, the council bishops noted that the church of Christ "constituted and organized as a society in the present world, *subsists*[29] in the Catholic Church, which is governed by the successor Peter and by the bishops in communion with him."[30] Even though the church of Christ and the Catholic Church cannot be completely separated (*Redemptoris missio* no. 18),[31] the phrase in LG, "subsists in," unambiguously acknowledges the distinction between the church of Christ and the Catholic Church and, consequently, has "the unintended effect of blurring the defining characteristics of the Catholic church as the true church."[32] In addition, Vatican II's omission of the adjective *Roman* to describe the Catholic Church added to the confusion of Catholic identities.[33]

In its attempt to dialogue with the modern and non-Christian world, Vatican II courageously and rightfully undermined the image of a pre–Vatican II triumphalistic church by clarifying that the church of Christ and the Catholic Church are not coextensive, but it also left Catholics with no clear identities, resulting in widespread confusion amongst the laity. While Vatican II instituted major reforms, it was less successful in providing adequate catechesis to its clergy and laity. Many of the significant features of reforms and the essential aspects of its teachings had not trickled down to the local level. Consequently, to many SBNRs, the Catholic Church of post–Vatican II appears hierarchical in structure and practice, patronizing in its relationship to non-Christians, and too preoccupied with tradition and orthodoxy.

---

[28] Peter C. Phan, *Being Religious Interreligiously: Asian Perspectives on Interfaith Dialogue* (Maryknoll, NY: Orbis Books, 2004), 46.

[29] Emphasis added.

[30] Austin Flannery, ed., *Vatican Council II: The Conciliar and Post Conciliar Documents* (New York: Costello Publishing, 1975), 357.

[31] John Paul II, *Redemptoris missio* [Mission of the Redeemer], (December 7, 1990).

[32] Phan, *Being Religious Interreligiously*, 50.

[33] Ibid.

Multiple Religious Practice

Multiple religious belonging (MRB) entails a deep commitment, in terms of both belief and belonging, to more than one religious tradition, whereas multiple religious practice (MRP) mainly refers to those who engage in practices from another religious tradition such as, for Christians, yoga, meditation, and other practices from primarily Eastern religions. According to Phan, MRB has little to do with the New Age syncretism of selectively choosing beliefs and practices from various religions "without regard to their truth values and mutual compatibilities,"[34] and without belonging to a community or communities from which these beliefs and practices are derived. Phan finds this form of postmodern syncretism incompatible with the Christian faith.[35]

This section deals specifically with the MRP; however, references to MRB will be made since almost all who are categorized as MRB engaged in MRP, but those who engage in MRP are not necessarily classified in the MRB group. A recent survey conducted by the Public Religion Research Institute (PRRI) indicates that 16 percent of Americans in 2014 say that they follow the teachings or practices of more than one religion. About 25 percent of non-Christian religious Americans, presumably from mostly non-Abrahamic tradition, represent the most likely groups to say they practice more than one religion. The other groups, who engage in multiple religious practices, comprise 19 percent of black Protestants, 18 percent of religious unaffiliated, 17 percent of Catholics, and 10 percent of white mainline Protestants. The PRRI survey reveals that nearly 39 percent of Americans say they meditate at least once a week, and nearly 24 percent of Americans say they explore the ideas and practices of other religious faiths.[36] Part of the increase in MRP comes from a rise of interfaith marriages. The 2012 General Social Survey found that 24 percent of marriages in the United States are among people who do not share the same religious background.[37]

Selective adoption of practices from different religious traditions, due to an increased awareness of, and, perhaps, familiarity with, the practices of other religions, is a natural consequence of living in a religiously pluralistic

---

[34] Ibid., 62.

[35] Ibid.

[36] Emily Fetsch, "Mixing and Matching: Who Practices Multiple Religions?" (April 4, 2014), http://publicreligion.org/2014/04/mixing-and-matching-a-look-at-who-practices-multiple-religions/#.Vh-0nMaFOpo.

[37] http://www.norc.org/Research/Projects/Pages/general-social-survey.aspx .

society. Buddhist meditation, for example, is appealing to many SBNRs in part because the source of spiritual authority rests within each individual rather than any anchorage in the authority of the clergy or the official body of the church. SBNRs are turned off by proscriptions and prescriptions offered by church officials with regard to the practice of certain forms of meditation because they are not of *divine origin*. Ecclesiastical officials who caution about the dangers of engaging in Eastern meditation are seldom aware that many Buddhist meditational practices in the United States have already undergone the process of demystification, that is, separating these practices from their Buddhist origins. In fact, many of us have been involved in MRP without being aware of it. Buddhist meditation without reference to its Buddhist source has been practiced by millions of Americans in schools, churches, hospitals, and businesses. Secular meditation and mindfulness exercises performed at these institutions have been so far removed from Buddhist roots that participants may not be aware that they have engaged in practices that originated in Buddhism.[38]

The word *religion* comes from the Latin root *"religio,"* which means, "to tie back," suggesting a tying back to ultimate meanings and purposes.[39] Using the meaning from the root *religio*, encountering a person of another faith and being involved in their neighbor's life or meeting them at their points of needs are, in a sense, practices of tying back to ultimate meanings and purposes of life and, therefore, can be a form of MRP. Peter Phan narrates this story about twenty-five members of his family making a nostalgic visit to their native country of Vietnam after leaving the country as refugees a quarter of a century earlier. On a visit to a Buddhist pagoda one day, Phan was shocked to see his devout Catholic mother reverently praying in front of the Buddha and, afterward, offering a donation to the maintenance of the pagoda. He asked, "How, then, could an old woman like my mother, God-loving and church-fearing, a twice-a-day churchgoer raised to believe that no one except Catholics can be saved, do what she did that day in that pagoda?"[40] Phan attributed his mother's almost instinctive and guilt-free action of praying before a Buddha figure to the "dialogue of life," which a joint 1991 document of the Congregation for the Evangelization of Peoples

---

[38] Joseph Cheah, *Race and Religion in American Buddhism: White Supremacy and Immigrant Adaptation* (New York: Oxford University Press, 2011), 70.

[39] Mary Pat Fisher, *Living Religions: Western Traditions* (Upper Saddle River, NJ: Prentice-Hall, 2003), 12.

[40] Peter C. Phan, "Praying to the Buddha: Living amid Religious Pluralism," *Commonweal*, January 2007, 11.

and the Pontifical Council for Interreligious Dialogue describes as people of different faiths living together "in an open and neighborly spirit, sharing their joys and sorrows, their human problems and preoccupations."[41] In the United States, Phan's mother lives in an apartment complex where she has bonded with two Buddhist tenants with whom she has shared the joys and problems of life as members of the same family. This experience of multiple "religious" practice—of sharing a life in common with people of another faith—is what enabled Phan's mother to open her "mind and heart to other faiths and made her reject the older view of non-Christians as 'pagans' destined to eternal damnation."[42]

MRP is not a fad; it has been part of our lives all along. Phan reminds us that double religious belonging was a part of everyday life of the earliest Christians. They were able to integrate their faith in the resurrected Jesus with the beliefs and practices of their inherited Jewish faith in a seamless manner.[43] They engaged in multiple religious practices in that they worshipped in the temple, studied the Hebrew scripture, and *broke bread* in their homes: "They went to the temple area together every day, while in their homes they broke bread" (Acts 3:46). By the time the word *catholic* (*katholikos*) and the episcopal principle first appeared and was articulated in the writings of St. Ignatius of Antioch in the last decade of the first millennium, both MRP and MRB had already been part of the Catholic identity. Today, such an integration of MRP and MRB within a Catholic identity is best seen within the Asian context.

Living in a predominantly non-Christian part of the world, Asian Catholics have centuries of experience of grappling with their Catholic identities within the inter/multireligious context of Asia. I will focus mainly on the works of the Federation of Asian Bishops' Conferences (FABC). There are already some excellent studies of FABC, including Asian American theologian Jonathan Tan's recent publication on the FABC response to the challenges of diversity and pluralism in Asia.[44] FABC is a pan-Asian voluntary association of the various Roman Catholic episcopal conferences of South Asia, Southeast Asia, Central Asia, and East Asia. The Asian bishops maintain that their knowledge of non-Christian religions is derived not

---

[41] Quoted in ibid.

[42] Ibid.

[43] Phan, *Being Religious Interreligiously*, 68.

[44] See Jonathan Y. Tan, *Christian Mission among the Peoples of Asia* (Maryknoll, NY: Orbis Books, 2014), particularly chapter 3 where he analyzes the FABC's mission theology.

simply from research but primarily from centuries of living together with non-Christians in the inter/multireligious context of Asia. Their lived experience has enabled the Asian bishops to assert that "it is an inescapable truth that God's Spirit is at work in all religious traditions."[45] It is this Spirit that invites the Asian Catholic Church to dialogue with non-Christian religions. It is this Spirit that enables the Asian Catholics to recognize that they embrace the MRB within themselves. An Asian Catholic is a Christian to be sure, but s/he is influenced by elements of Buddhism, Hinduism, Daoism, and other pertinent Eastern religions to the extent that s/he is also part cultural Buddhist, part cultural Hindu, and so on. Moreover, all Asian Catholics perform MRP whether they do Tai Chi, practice yoga, occasionally strike a few lines of calligraphy, and engage in filial piety or other *religious* expressions. This is seen by FABC as an inherent part of cultivating a truly indigenous Catholic identity. As Tan succinctly put it, "it is clear that the Asian bishops are very much at home with the diversity and pluralism of the Asian *Sitzen-im-Leben*, eschewing all forms of religious exclusivism, and seeking consistently to work within the pluralism of the Asian milieu with its diverse cultures and religions."[46]

Conclusion

The Catholic Church is diverse and differentiated not only in terms of a variety of cultures and racial/ethnic groups within its membership but also in terms of groups with different political orientations with dissimilar and, sometimes, polarized viewpoints and perspectives on their faith. One of the movements that diametrically opposed the reforms brought about by Vatican II is Catholic fundamentalism. Catholic fundamentalists want to restore the hierarchical model of the church where "Catholic identities" are to be interpreted in the singular as "Catholic identity," which means explicit "adherence to orthodoxy" or "unquestioning obedience to the hierarchy."[47] We have seen that SBNRs unequivocally reject such a model of organized church, an institution in which Catholics were told to *pray, pay,* and *obey*.

Many SBNRs maintain that beliefs are often used by institutional religion to preserve the prevailing system of hegemony over its members; that

---

[45] BIRA IV/12, art. 7, in *For All the Peoples of Asia: Federation of Asian Bishops' Conferences Documents from 1970 to 199*, vol 1, ed. Gaudencio Rosales and C. G. Arevalo, (Quezon City, Philippines: Claretian Publications, 1997), 326.

[46] Tan, *Christian Mission*, 105.

[47] Arbuckle, *Catholic Identity or Identities*, 15.

is, beliefs are employed by church authority or hierarchy as means to control its members.[48] To be sure, the Catholic Church with a history of the establishment of the Inquisition to root out heresy is not beyond reproach when it comes to the use of beliefs to control its members. A good contemporary example of an institutional religion using hegemonic control over its members concerns the manner in which Rome deals with theologians whose works do not fit the bill of doctrinal orthodoxy. While the magisterium has the right to determine the boundaries of orthodoxy, its process of discerning orthodoxy does not follow the religious and secular norms of truth, transparency, and objectivity. Arbuckle points out that Rome often resorts to "scapegoating" or "witch-hunting" as a "process of passionately searching for and eliminating agents believed to be causing harm to the cultural identity of individuals and groups, demanding that they adhere to traditional orthodox principles."[49] This procedure is a judicial process by which the Congregation for the Doctrine of the Faith (CDF) remains substantially unchanged since it was initiated in 1971: "the CDF is prosecutor, judge, and jury; the person being investigated is not told of the inquiry until stage thirteen (of eighteen stages) and may never know the identity of his or her accusers; . . . no publicity is permitted concerning the proceedings and there is no right to appeal."[50] SBNRs would find such an iron-maiden approach of maintaining orthodoxy a major reason for their rejection of institutional religion. They challenge the Catholic Church to practice what it preaches—to abide by the religious and secular norms of truth, objectivity, transparency, and to show a profound respect for the rights of the individual(s) involved.

However, not all beliefs are without justification. Every institution has the right to determine its policy of membership. This is the case with the teachings of the Catholic Church. The works of theologians Monika Hellwig and Yves Congar help us to clarify the gradation of these teachings by distinguishing Tradition (capital "T") from tradition (small "t"). Tradition (capital "T") refers to scripture, sacraments, and defined doctrines that are an essential part of the Catholic faith, while tradition (small "t") includes customs, teachings, and practices that are important but not essential. Examples of Tradition (capital "T") include the divinity of Jesus, the resurrection of Jesus, the Incarnation, and other central dogmas of the Catholic faith. Many of these essential dogmas of the church, not solemnly defined but taught as divinely revealed truths, are understood to be a part of Catholic

---

[48] Mercadante, *Belief without Borders*, 8.
[49] Arbuckle, *Catholic Identity or Identities*, 15.
[50] Ibid., 17.

identity. In fact, they are regarded with the highest solemnity in the Catholic hierarchy of dogmas. In other words, one can assume that Catholics are those who believe that Jesus is Lord, that Jesus has been resurrected, and that the second person of the blessed Trinity took on a human form by becoming one of us. SBNRs may resist doctrinal orthodoxy and traditions of the Catholic Church, but if they do not believe in any one of these central dogmas, they are not only non-Catholics but stand outside of a very broad umbrella called Christianity.

Tradition (small "t") can be used as a means of attaining hegemonic control over believers as well. Prior to the Second Vatican Council, some Catholics engaged in ritual actions by going through the motions. They assumed that if they performed certain rituals and practices for a predetermined number of times and for a certain number of days, their salvation would be guaranteed. This is an example of the Catholic principle of mediation taken to the extreme point of becoming a magical act because this practice encourages believers to bargain with God rather than establishing a genuine relationship with God. The belief that such a practice followed assiduously would guarantee salvation contributed to a lack of spiritual growth among those who engaged in it. In other words, too much tradition can lead to a formulation of Catholic identities that overemphasize the form of tradition at the expense of the substance of spirituality. However, too little tradition can result in a loss in a sense of identity. This was the problem of Vatican II when many traditional practices were abandoned with no replacement with new practices or with no application of Vatican II theology to traditional practices. This led to widespread confusion among the laity as to their identity as Catholics.

MRP and, in particular, MRB challenge the singular Catholic identity promoted by fundamentalist Catholics and many traditionalist Catholics because MRP and MRB disrupt the myth of religious purity. As noted above, Phan contends that there is no such thing as *pure* Christianity. The earliest Christians exhibited double religious belonging. For example, the earliest Eucharistic prayers recounted in the *Didache* followed the general pattern of the Jewish synagogue service. "There was the chanting of the Scriptures, the recitation of psalms, prayers, instruction, and hymns. After this instruction service ('liturgy of the word,' as we call it), there was the great prayer of 'thanksgiving' (*eucharistica* in Greek)."[51] Similarly, the message of Jesus or the gospels is filtered through a particular culture. It does

---

[51] William J. Bausch, *Pilgrim Church: A Popular History of Catholic Christianity* (Mystic, CT: Twenty-Third Publications, 1991), 67.

not exist in a vacuum or in a context-free environment. The early Christian message was expressed in the vocabulary and basic worldview of classical Greek philosophy. This union of scriptures and Greek thinking took centuries to accomplish, a process that created traditional Christianity. Phan underscores that MRB becomes a theological problem only in exclusive religions, such as Judaism, Christianity, and Islam, which "demands an absolute and exclusive commitment on the part of their adherents to their founders and/or faiths."[52] This, however, is not the case with Eastern religions where "multiple religious belonging is the rule rather than an exception, at least on the popular level."[53]

MRP is rapidly becoming the rule rather than an exception in an increasingly multireligious environment of North America. Elements of yoga, zen, vipassana, and other forms of Asian meditation are practiced by hundreds of thousands of Catholics, sometimes even unbeknownst to them, in schools, hospitals, retreat centers, and businesses across the United States. We need to acknowledge that MRP is unavoidable in an increasingly religiously pluralistic context such as that of North American society and that "Christian identities are always 'hybrid,' that is, they are created by intersecting with other categories of identity."[54] What this means is that we need to look at MRP and MRB from the lens of the Catholic principle of sacramentality, the ways in which God comes to visibility in the gathering of everyday life. The principle of sacramentality invites us to have a radical trust in the goodness of God's creation before we recognize the corruption of culture, the depravity of human beings or the sinful action of a particular individual or individuals. The sacramental principle invites us to acknowledge the working of the Spirit in the biblical tradition, in salvation history, and in realities beyond the confines of Christianity. Asian bishops declared this basic sacramental principle when they asserted that "it is an inescapable truth that God's Spirit is at work in all religious traditions."[55] Is there anything wrong when the practice of a breathing meditation (e.g., vipassana meditation) helps us to calm our frantic spirit as we recite the mantra *Jesus* instead of *Buddha* that enables us to come closer to Christ? Is there anything wrong when the practice of Eastern meditation helps us better understand and appreciate contemplative prayer or centering prayer? In other words, our

---

[52] Phan, *Being Religious Interreligiously*, 62.

[53] Ibid.

[54] Jeannine Hill Fletcher, *Monopoly on Salvation?: A Feminist Approach to Religious Pluralism* (London: Continuum International Publishing Group, 2005), 89.

[55] BIRA IV/12, art. 7, in *For All the Peoples of Asia*, 1:326.

first reaction ought not to be one of defensiveness. Recognize the goodness of God's creation first before attending to some of the dangers of a particular practice. If the practice of Eastern meditation leads us to the denial of existential reality, of self, and of God, then we have stepped outside the bounds of the orthodoxy and orthopraxis of the Catholic faith. Catholic identities are derived not only by attending to God's presence in our everyday lives but also to the God of our faith tradition. Catholic identities take shape from the Catholic worldview and the principle of sacramentality is but a lens by which Catholics use to view the world.

17

INTERCHURCH DIALOGUE: GLOBAL PERSPECTIVES

Edmund Kee-Fook Chia

Like the concept of world religions, which came into ascendancy with the West's heightened awareness of the presence of religions other than Christianity,[1] the concept of World Christianity also arose with the Western Christian's heightened awareness of the presence of Christianity in non-Western contexts. The term became popular with Dana Robert's essay "Shifting Southward: Global Christianity since 1945" (2000)[2] and Philip Jenkins's *The Next Christendom: The Coming of Global Christianity* (2002).[3] Concomitant with the embrace of World Christianity is the emergence of new ways of conceptualizing interchurch relationships and promoting interchurch dialogue. This chapter takes a closer look at the great strides that have been made over the last century in promoting interchurch dialogue and cooperation. It traces the ecumenical movement from its beginnings, focusing on the contributions of the World Council of Churches (WCC) and the progress made by the Roman Catholic Church and especially since the Second Vatican Council. It then discusses the rise of southern Christianity and points to issues that World Christianity is exploring as the agenda for interchurch dialogue for the future.

This chapter is a substantially revised version of my essay, "The Ecumenical Pilgrimage Toward World Christianity," *Theological Studies* 76/3 (2015): 503–30.

[1] Tomoko Masuzawa, *The Invention of World Religions: Or, How European Universalism Was Preserved in the Language of Pluralism* (Chicago: University of Chicago, 2005), 20.

[2] Dana L. Robert, "Shifting Southward: Global Christianity since 1945," *International Bulletin of Missionary Research* 24/2 (2000): 50–58.

[3] Charles E. Farhadian, ed., *Introducing World Christianity* (Malden, MA: Wiley-Blackwell, 2012), 3.

Nineteenth-Century Interchurch Relations

The 1910 World Missionary Conference at Edinburgh is usually regarded as the watershed for the modern ecumenical movement. However, the efforts of the nineteenth century cannot be discounted. Christian missionaries in Asia and Africa at that time found themselves cooperating across denominational lines, as they were often few in numbers and serving Christian communities that were themselves minorities in lands where other religious traditions thrive. Their experiences were officially recorded when English Baptist missionary William Carey called for an interdenominational missionary conference in Cape Town "for the pooling of missionary experience on the problems common to them all."[4]

However, from the perspective of those in the so-called mission fields, the Indian church historian T. V. Philip challenges the claim that Western missionaries initiated the ecumenical movement. He argues that interchurch dialogue was already very much alive among Asian Christians before the missionaries called for it, and was often, in fact, a response to the attitudes of the missionaries themselves:

> A study of the history of the Church in China, Japan and India will show that the real impetus for Christian unity came from the Christians in these countries and not from Western missionaries. For example, it was the protest of the Indian Christians against Western denominations and missionary paternalism that led to church unity discussions in some of the missionary conferences in India.[5]

Meantime, back in the North Atlantic there was also a host of interdenominational activities taking place especially among younger Christians. The most significant of these was the movement to address challenges posed by the radically altered social and living conditions that arose in light of the rural–urban migration following the Industrial Revolution. This informal movement eventually led to the foundation of the Young Men's Christian Association (YMCA) and the Young Women's Christian Association (YWCA) in England in the first half of the nineteenth century. These associations spread rapidly to North America, Continental Europe, and elsewhere, especially among colonies of the British Empire.

---

[4] Ninan Koshy, *A History of the Ecumenical Movement in Asia*, vol. I (Hong Kong: World Student Christian Federation, 2004), 35.

[5] T. V. Philip, *Ecumenism in Asia* (Delhi: ISPCK, 1994), 44, quoted in Koshy, *Ecumenical Movement in Asia*, 1:35–36.

The latter half of the nineteenth century saw the formation of the World Student Christian Federation (WSCF), bringing together autonomous national student Christian movements. The first impetus can actually be traced back to Asia where the first national student conference of Japan took place in Kyoto. Reflecting on the theme of "Christian Students United for World Conquest," the participants proposed that an international federation be established to assist them in connecting with other Christian youth worldwide. The proposal led to several other national gatherings in Europe and at the third international conference (Vadstena Castle, Östergötland, Sweden, 1895), the WSCF was founded.[6] Key student leaders of the WSCF, such as John Mott and Nathan Söderblom, were to become major figures at the Edinburgh 1910 conference.

Edinburgh World Missionary Conference

The 1910 Edinburgh conference had two principal aims: assist the missionaries with methods that are more effective and abate the interdenominational competition in mission fields. To be sure, the Edinburgh conference was more a missionary than an ecumenical conference. Unity, at least in the mission fields, was actually in the service of evangelism. The title of the first commission report, "Carrying the Gospel to all the Non-Christian World," highlights the evangelism motif.[7] While the impetus for interchurch dialogue was the scandal of Christian division in the colonial territories, reference was also made to the scandal of disunity in the missionaries' homelands of Europe and North America: "The Church in western lands will reap a glorious reward from its missionary labours, if the church in the mission field points the way to a healing of its divisions and to the attainment of that unity for which our Lord prayed."[8]

If for the Western missionaries, the pursuit of Christian unity was in service of evangelism, for the indigenous Christians in mission fields, it was more in the interest of nationalism and liberation. The local Christians in Asia and Africa wanted a greater voice in the management and development of their own churches. They did not like the fact that the missionaries were

---

[6] Koshy, *Ecumenical Movement in Asia*, 1:44.

[7] Edinburgh 2010, "Centenary of the 1910 World Missionary Conference," http://edinburgh2010.org. The nine volumes of the 1910 conference publications are archived on this site.

[8] *World Missionary Conference, 1910: Report of Commission VIII: Co-operation and the Promotion of Unity* (Edinburgh: Oliphant, Anderson, & Ferrier, 1910), 131.

the ones who initiated and controlled operations, while the inhabitants were expected merely to lend a hand. Local Christians longed to be treated as partners rather than subjected workers. These feelings, of course, were also shaped by the anticolonial sentiments harbored by their own compatriots in the secular world toward ruling colonial governments.

Furthermore, some local Christians were also reflecting on their experience of having served as national leaders within Christian youth movements, where relationships with missionaries were more egalitarian. This did not necessarily mean, however, that egalitarianism reigned in the international arena: of the 1,200 delegates to the Edinburgh conference only 17 came from the Global South, all invited because they were holding leadership positions in the student Christian movements (SCMs) and YMCAs of their own national chapters. One of them, V. S. Azariah of India, minced no words when addressing the assembly on the problem of the missionaries' patronizing attitudes:

> My personal observation during a period of ten years, some of which have been spent travelling in different parts of India, in mission districts worked by different Missionary societies, has revealed to me the fact that the relationship between the European missionaries and the Indian workers is far from what it ought to be, and that a certain aloofness, a lack of mutual understanding and openness, a great lack of frank intercourse and friendliness, exists throughout the country.[9]

Azariah's point was that the missionary–native problem lies in its being "a relationship of power, reflecting colonial attitudes, compounded with what we would now call racist attitudes."[10] Another delegate, Cheng Ching-yi of China, appealed to the missionaries to make an effort to appreciate what local Christians wish to happen rather than to impose their will on them. He urged that they attempt to see matters from the perspective of the Chinese, many of whom "hope to see in the near future a united Christian

---

[9] "The Problem of Co-operation between Foreign and Native Workers: The Rev. V.S. Azariah," *World Missionary Conference, 1910: Report of Commission IX: The History and Records of the Conference, Together with Addresses Delivered at the Evening Meetings* (Edinburgh: Oliphant, Anderson & Ferrier, 1910), 306–15, at 307, 311.

[10] D. Preman Niles, "Theological and Mission Concerns in the Ecumenical Movement in Asia," in *A History of the Ecumenical Movement in Asia*, vol. 2, ed. Ninan Koshy (Hong Kong: Christian Conference of Asia, 2004), 19–84, at 23.

church without denominational distinctions."[11] In the same vein, Korean statesman C. H. Yun appealed for greater consultation with local church members on where and how the distribution of money and aid should take place. Reverend President K. Ibuka of Japan "raised questions about the cumbersome Western creeds with their underlying complicated [Western] theologies that were being foisted on Japanese Christians. . . . For Japan, there had to be simpler creeds that spoke to the Japanese situation."[12] He claimed that though the natives had come up with their own simple Confession of Faith for the Church in Japan, the missionaries insisted that the Doctrinal Standards of Westminster be adopted instead. The natives, of course, "accepted, not cordially and of choice, but simply out of deference to the judgment and wishes of the missionaries."[13]

These were some of the challenges posed to Western missionaries at the Edinburgh 1910 conference. To be sure, the conference accomplished more than it had set out to, and Christian unity—interdenominational as well as intradenominational—was among these accomplishments.

World Council of Churches

Edinburgh 1910 concluded with the establishment of a continuation committee that was later to evolve into the International Missionary Council (IMC), established in London in 1921.[14] Meanwhile, Christians in Europe began supporting justice and peace projects and joint social actions especially related to the tragedies of World War I. Under the leadership of Swedish Lutheran Bishop Nathan Söderblom, the ecumenically minded Christian leaders hosted an initial gathering in Stockholm in 1925, called the Universal Christian Conference on Life and Work. On the theological front comparable efforts were also taken to explore critical issues in matters of doctrine and practice, aimed at healing ecclesial divisions. These efforts resulted in the formation of the Faith and Order (F&O) movement, which had its first international conference in Lausanne in 1927.

Aside from the above-mentioned initiatives, there was also an effort to establish a formal fellowship among the churches. This effort sprang from an idea that was actually mooted as early as 1920 when Archbishop Germanos

---

[11] Koshy, *Ecumenical Movement in Asia*, 1:54.

[12] Niles, "Theological and Mission Concerns," 24–25.

[13] "Problem of Co-operation between Foreign and Native Workers," 296.

[14] Jeffrey Gros, Eamon McManus, and Ann Riggs, *Introduction to Ecumenism* (New York: Paulist, 1998), 27.

of Thyrateira, the Ecumenical Patriarch of Constantinople, in an encyclical entitled "To the Churches of Christ Everywhere," issued a call for a League of Churches as a structure akin to the League of Nations.[15] The leadership of more than one hundred churches voted in 1937–38 to found the WCC. World War II delayed its establishment. Later, the Life and Work and the F&O movements merged in 1948 and, together with a host of mainly Protestant churches and church organizations from Europe and North America, established the WCC at its first assembly held in Amsterdam. The IMC joined the WCC in 1961, as did the World Council of Christian Education ten years later. (This latter council had its origins in the Sunday school movement of the eighteenth century.) Since these mergers, the ministries of the respective streams have continued, but now each operates under the auspices of the WCC.

The WCC was never meant to be a *world church* as such; this was clarified in response to questions that arose after its foundation and explicitly articulated in the 1950 statement "The Church, the Churches, and the World Council of Churches" adopted by the WCC Central Committee in Toronto.[16] The statement emphasized that the WCC "is not and must never become a superchurch" (III.1); it is at most to be looked upon as an instrument, albeit a privileged one, for the churches to come together to witness to the "fellowship of churches which confess the Lord Jesus Christ as God and Savior according to the scriptures, and therefore seek to fulfil together their common calling to the glory of the one God, Father, Son and Holy Spirit."[17] This statement was also the basis for membership, which was explicitly spelled out during the foundational assembly in Amsterdam. The Toronto statement also insists that the WCC "cannot and should not be based on any one particular conception of the church" (III.3). However, membership in the WCC does imply at least a recognition of and solidarity with the other member churches, even if there is divergence in understanding what it means to be church or what the WCC's overall vision is supposed to be. Such is the pervasive and inclusive nature of the WCC. And this has not been without its problems.

---

[15] Peter C. Bouteneff, "The World Council of Churches: An Orthodox Perspective," in *Celebrating a Century of Ecumenism: Exploring the Achievements of International Dialogue,* ed. John A. Radano (Geneva: World Council of Churches, 2012), 15–23, at 17.

[16] World Council of Churches, "Toronto statement" (January 1, 1970), http://www.oikoumene.org/en/resources/documents/central-committee/1950/toronto-statement.

[17] WCC, "About us," http://www.oikoumene.org/en/about-us.

To be sure, over the years, differences in understanding the WCC's vision have arisen. An extensive study on the matter, launched in 1989, culminated in a clarifying statement adopted by the Central Committee in 1997. The document, "A Common Understanding and Vision of the World Council of Churches" (CUV), suggests that the very existence of the WCC can serve as an "ecclesiological challenge" to its member churches, and that the hope it generates for Christian unity can serve "as the ecclesiological significance of *koinonia*" (3.4).[18] It elaborates on this by stating that even if there is a variety of understandings of what the WCC is meant to be, there should be an acknowledgment "that the Council is more than a mere functional association of churches set up to organize activities in areas of common interest" (3.2). This *more*, of course, refers to a variety of possibilities, including what practically all the WCC statements before and since the CUV have been emphasizing, namely, the WCC's very first objective of calling the churches to the goal of visible unity.

Faith and Order Commission

This is where the contributions of the F&O Commission come prominently into play. It is this branch of the WCC that looks specifically at theological issues dividing the one church of Jesus Christ. For this reason, it can also be referred to as the *conscience* of the WCC amid all the manifold activities it has been engaged in since its foundation.[19] The Commission on F&O meets periodically for in-depth study of questions related to Christian division and "produce texts and study documents which, while having no authority of their own over any church, are of significance and use by virtue of having been composed by a widely representative group of people from various Christian traditions."[20] The beginning years saw members of the commission engaged mainly in the task of getting to know one another and especially the variety of churches and their theologies. The comparative method was employed where beliefs and practices across denominations were listed, compared, and analyzed.

---

[18] WCC, "A Common Understanding and Vision of the WCC," (February 14, 2006), http://www.oikoumene.org/en/resources/documents/assembly/2006-porto-alegre/3-preparatory-and-background-documents/common-understanding-and-vision-of-the-wcc-cuv.

[19] Mary Tanner, "Faith and Order: Achievements of Multilateral Dialogue," in Radano, *Celebrating a Century of Ecumenism,* 24–37.

[20] WCC, "Commission on Faith and Order," http://archived.oikoumene.org/en/who-are-we/organization-structure/consultative-bodies/faith-and-order.html.

The third world conference of F&O, held in Lund in 1952, shifted dramatically to the Christological method. Here, instead of exploring the differences in ecclesiology, the focus shifted to "the reality of our fundamental unity in Jesus Christ, our common faith in Christ who is our 'given' common center."[21] The thesis of the Christological method is that when the churches are exploring how they can be more united in Christ, they will surely be growing closer to one another. Also introduced was what came to be known as the Lund principle, whereby an invitation was issued to the churches urging them to consider "[doing] together all those things which their consciences do not require them to do separately."[22] Worship and intercommunion were advances made at some interchurch gatherings. Also placed on the ecumenical agenda were so-called nontheological factors such as culture, class, race, and gender. These gave rise to contextual methodology, with serious implications on how one does ecumenical theology in general and on the Christian unity agenda in particular. Since the 1952 conference, these factors have featured prominently in WCC studies and consultations.

By the 1970s, the F&O narrowed down its study to three priority areas considered to be integral to visible unity: (1) common confession of faith, (2) common sacraments and ministry, and (3) common teaching authority.[23] The second area was attended to first or at least was the first to produce tangible results. This came in the form of a convergence document, *Baptism, Eucharist and Ministry (BEM)*, voted on in Lima in 1982. The document itself was just the first fruit of the conversations; even more impressive were the official responses to it from member churches, including most of the major denominations. More than half of the WCC member churches submitted official responses from the highest levels of authority. Combined with feedback from individual theologians and other interested parties, these responses filled six volumes of text. The *BEM* text was in its thirty-ninth printing in 2007, which at that time had "180,000 English copies in print and translations in about forty other languages."[24] Moreover, the *BEM* text, also known as the Lima document, also evolved from being simply a convergence document to a convergence instrument in that it was used to facilitate many dialogues across the spectrum of church life.

---

[21] Kuncheria Pathil, *Models in Ecumenical Dialogue* (Bangalore, India: Dharmaram, 1981), 314.

[22] Gros, McManus, and Riggs, *Introduction to Ecumenism*, 142.

[23] Tanner, "Faith and Order," 28.

[24] William Henn, "The Achievements of Faith and Order: A Catholic Perspective," in Radano, *Celebrating a Century of Ecumenism*, 38–51, at 44.

Work by the F&O on the other two priority areas met with less success. Exploration of the first concern, a common confession of the apostolic faith, resulted in the 1991 publication of the document *Confessing the One Faith: An Ecumenical Explication of the Apostolic Faith as It Is Confessed in the Nicene-Constantinopolitan Creed (381).*[25] It went largely unnoticed. Discussions on the third priority area, common ways of deciding and teaching with authority, did not realize any substantive results. Numerous other areas also received attention but, again, had little to show for the efforts. Just recently, however, another convergence document was released that might prove to be comparable in status to the *BEM* document. This document, entitled "The Church: Towards a Common Vision," was approved by the F&O standing committee at its 2012 meeting in Penang and launched at the WCC Executive Committee meeting in Bossey on March 6, 2013. Focused on "the Church's mission, unity, and its being in the Trinitarian life of God," it "addresses our growth in communion—in apostolic faith, sacramental life, and ministry—as churches called to live in and for the world."[26] The hope is that it will impel the F&O, as well as the WCC and the ecumenical movement, to meet the challenges of the twenty-first century.

Roman Catholic Church

The Roman Catholic Church is a latecomer to the modern ecumenical movement. Still reeling from the Protestant Reformation, its attitude toward ecumenism was very much shaped by an ecclesiology of *return* to the Holy Roman Catholic Church. When Anglican Bishop Charles Brent met with Pope Benedict XV in 1919 to discuss the possible participation of the Roman Catholic Church in the F&O movement, the pope declined. However, he did promise to pray for the initiative and added, "If the congress is practicable, the participants may, by God's grace, see the light and become reunited to the visible head of the church, by whom they would be received with open arms."[27] The Vatican offices similarly declined when

---

[25] *Confessing the One Faith: An Ecumenical Explication of the Apostolic Faith as It Is Confessed in the Nicene-Constantinopolitan Creed (381)*, Faith and Order Paper No. 153 (Geneva: WCC, 1991).

[26] WCC, "The Church: Towards a Common Vision," Faith and Order Paper No. 214 (March 19, 2013), http://www.oikoumene.org/en/resources/documents/commissions/faith-and-order/i-unity-the-church-and-its-mission/the-church-towards-a-common-vision.

[27] Tom F. Stransky, "Roman Catholic Church and Ecumenism," in *Dictionary of the Ecumenical Movement*, 2nd ed., ed. Nicolas Losskey et al. (Geneva: WCC, 2002), 997.

invited to send Catholic participants to the first Life and Work conference in 1925.

It is certainly not a coincidence that Pope Pius XI's encyclical *Mortalium animos* ("On Religious Unity") was promulgated shortly after the first conference of the F&O in 1927.[28] The document begins by informing Catholics about the attempts at fostering unity among Christians. It then cautions them to be wary that "beneath these enticing words and blandishments lies hid a most grave error, by which the foundations of the Catholic faith are completely destroyed" (no. 4). "This being so, it is clear that the Apostolic See cannot on any terms take part in their assemblies, nor is it anyway lawful for Catholics either to support or to work for such enterprises; for if they do so they will be giving countenance to a false Christianity, quite alien to the one Church of Christ" (no. 8). In the following decades, the Vatican blocked all attempts by Catholics to participate in the activities of the ecumenical movement. In 1948, the Vatican even issued a notice to "the Netherlands bishops to forbid [Catholics] to be present in any role, no matter how unofficial, at the WCC's founding general assembly in Amsterdam."[29]

Things miraculously took a more positive turn shortly thereafter. *Ecclesia sancta* (1949), issued by the Curia's Holy Office, looked upon the ecumenical movement with less antagonism. As Aidan Nichols remarked, the document suggested that the ecumenical movement "derived its basic impulse from the inspiration of the 'Holy Spirit' and so should constitute a 'source of holy joy' for Catholics. They were to take their efforts seriously while simultaneously insisting on the need for return to the divinely established centre of unity for the Christian world, the Petrine office."[30] Subsequently, special approval was given to some Catholic experts and theologians to engage in dialogue with their fellow Christians from other denominations. Augustinian priest George Tavard attended the Second Assembly of the WCC in 1954, albeit unofficially; later, however, he was officially appointed to serve as a Catholic observer at the F&O Commission conference in Montreal in 1963.[31] Two Jesuit priests, John Courtney Murray

[28] Pope Pius IX, *Mortalium animos* (January 16, 1928), http://w2.vatican.va/content/pius-xi/en/encyclicals/documents/hf_p-xi_enc_19280106_mortalium-animos.html.

[29] Stransky, "Roman Catholic Church," 997.

[30] Aidan Nichols, "Catholic Ecumenism," in *Catholic Thought since the Enlightenment: A Survey* (Pretoria, South Africa: Unisa, 1998), 159–63, at 160.

[31] The Assumptionists: US Region, North American Province, "Rev. George Tavard, A.A.," http://www.assumption.us/Tavard/biography.htm.

and Gustave Weigel, were also officially approved to attend the Conference on F&O in Oberlin, Ohio, in 1957. They were to become ecumenical giants within the Catholic Church and contributed significantly to the discourse on church unity especially in North America. Murray is well known for his contributions to Vatican II's *Dignitatis humanae*, Declaration on Religious Freedom, earning him the reputation of being the "key agent in making Roman Catholics safe for America, while also making America safe for Catholics."[32] Among others who played a significant role in pioneering and advancing Catholic ecumenism were theologians "such as Abbé Ferdinand Portal, C.M. (1855–1960), Dominican Yves Congar, O.P. (1904–1995), [and] Father Paul Couturier (1881–1953), [all of whose works] began to lay the groundwork that bore fruit with the Second Vatican Council."[33]

Vatican II and Interchurch Dialogue

More than any other initiative, it was the Second Vatican Council that really opened up the Roman Catholic Church to the modern ecumenical movement, producing a generation of ecumenically minded Catholics. In convoking the council, Pope John XXIII expressed his wish that Christian unity be among the primary concerns for the world's bishops to discuss. He established the Secretariat for Promoting Christian Unity in 1960 (elevated to Pontifical Council status in 1988) to identify and invite the major Orthodox, Protestant, Anglican, and Reformed Churches and Church Communions to send representatives to serve as observers of the council. Both of these moves were unprecedented in church history. By the end of 1965, nearly one hundred of these who were now called "our separated brethren"—previously known as "schismatics" and "heretics"[34]—had participated in the council.

Some of these ecumenical observers were actively involved in the WCC's F&O Commission. As the secretariat played a critical role in the preparation of "the documents on ecumenism (*Unitatis redintegratio*), on non-Christian religions (*Nostra aetate*), on religious liberty (*Dignitatis humanae*) and, together with the doctrinal commission, the dogmatic Constitution on Divine Revelation (*Dei verbum*)," the observers' influence

---

[32] J. Leon Hooper, S.J., "John Courtney Murray, S.J. (1904–67): Working with God," *Theology Today* 62 (2005): 342.

[33] Gros, McManus, and Riggs, *Introduction to Ecumenism*, 29.

[34] R. C. Sproul, "The Defense and Confirmation of the Gospel," in *The Unadjusted Gospel*, ed. Mark Dever et al. (Wheaton, IL: Crossway, 2014), 35–47, at 45.

in the council was obvious.[35] Some of their ideas naturally found their way into the Vatican documents. In fact, one can easily observe that the "Faith and Order's landmark statement on 'Scripture, Tradition and Traditions' of 1963 was contemporaneous with important developments in the way Catholics think about scripture and its relation to tradition."[36] A comparison between that F&O document and *Dei verbum* will lead one "to note the dramatic convergence that emerged."[37]

The decree *Unitatis redintegratio* (1964) was the council's official statement on Christian unity. Since then, a number of documents have been promulgated to promote the Roman Catholic Church's commitment to Christian unity. In 1967, the *Directory... concerning Ecumenical Matters, Part I* was published; Part II followed in 1970 as *Ecumenism in Higher Education*.[38] The publication in 1993 of the *Directory for the Application of Principles and Norms on Ecumenism* and Pope John Paul II's encyclical *Ut unum sint* (1995) added a major impetus to the Catholic Church's ecumenical agenda. However, the reception of Vatican II's ecumenical mandate is best discerned in the steps taken by the church at local levels. The Pontifical Council for Promoting Christian Unity (PCPCU, founded in 1960) organized a consultation in November 2004 to mark the fortieth anniversary of *Unitatis redintegratio* as well as to review and assess progress made by the church in ecumenical matters. PCPCU Secretary Bishop Brian Farrell proudly announced that "the degree of commitment to the ecumenical task at the local level throughout the Church is growing in intensity and extension."[39]

Prior to Vatican II, the Roman Catholic Church was not a member of any National Council of Churches (NCC); today about 70 of the 120 NCCs worldwide have Catholic membership.[40] Since 1968, the Vatican

---

[35] The Pontifical Council for Promoting Christian Unity, "Profile of the Dicastery," http://www.vatican.va.

[36] Henn, "Achievements of Faith and Order," 43.

[37] Gros, McManus, and Riggs, *Introduction to Ecumenism*, 144.

[38] Catholic Church, *Directory for the Application of the Decisions of the Second Ecumenical Council of the Vatican concerning Ecumenical Matters, May 14, 1967, Part I* and *Part II: Ecumenism in Higher Education* (Washington, DC: US Catholic Conference, 1967, 1970). See Gros, McManus, and Riggs, *Introduction to Ecumenism*, 40.

[39] Bishop Brian Farrell, Secretary of the Pontifical Council for Promoting Christian Unity, "Ecumenism Today, the Situation in the Catholic Church" (November 2004), http://www.vatican.va/roman_curia/pontifical_councils/chrstuni/documents/rc_pc_chrstuni_doc_20041121_farrell-ecumenismo_en.html.

[40] "Inspired by the Same Vision: Roman Catholic Participation in National and Regional Council of Churches," in *Growth in Agreement III: International Dialogue*

has been appointing about a dozen Catholic theologians to be official members of WCC's F&O Commission. It has also established a joint working group between the Catholic Church and the WCC. The PCPCU lists the following churches and world communions as partners engaged with the Catholic Church in international theological dialogues: Orthodox Churches of the Byzantine Tradition, Oriental Orthodox Churches, Assyrian Church of the East, the International Old Catholic Bishops' Conference of the Union of Utrecht, Anglican Communion, Lutheran World Federation, World Methodist Council, World Alliance of Reformed Churches, Baptist World Alliance, Disciples of Christ, Mennonite World Conference, World Evangelical Alliance, and some Pentecostal groups.

I say *some* Pentecostal groups because, while advances have been made with Pentecostals, difficulties remain. One reason is that it is not possible to identify an entity that speaks for Pentecostalism as a whole. Moreover, the international Pentecostal–Catholic dialogue has often been labeled extraordinary or improbable, as the two parties are perceived to have little in common: one regards itself as *the* church, the other as a movement; one is officially hierarchical, the other congregational; one is highly ritualized, the other more spontaneous; one has been around for millennia, the other for a mere century; and one has more than a billion adherents, the other far less, depending on how and whom you count.[41] Nevertheless, the dialogue has been ongoing for more than four decades now, even if road bumps abound. Despite the challenges, there is no doubting the Roman Catholic Church's commitment to the mandate of Christian unity.

Rise of Southern Christianity

Even if the Catholic–Pentecostal dialogue is an interesting challenge, the ecumenical movement cannot ignore it. Difficult as the dialogue is, indications are that the Pentecostal movement will be a major world player in the Christian world. They, together with the Evangelicals, and charismatics, have transformed the global ecclesial landscape. This has been well documented, the most comprehensive empirical work being done by the Center for the Study of Global Christianity of Gordon-Conwell Theolog-

---

Texts and Agreed Statements, 1998–2005, ed. Jeffrey Gros, Thomas F. Best, and Lorelei F. Fuchs (Geneva: WCC, 2007), 531–58.

[41] Cecil M. Robeck Jr., "The Achievements of the Pentecostal-Catholic International Dialogue," in Radano, *Celebrating a Century of Ecumenism*, 163–94.

ical Seminary in Boston.[42] According to its analysis, "the most significant trend within global Christianity is that, demographically, Christianity has shifted dramatically to the South."[43] This apparently began in the 1950s, accompanying the independence movement in the nations of the African continent, and continued through to the 1970s when Christianity gained significantly in numbers in many Asian countries. By 1981, the Global South had exceeded the Global North in Christian population. This is the demographic turning point into the third millennium, just as the year 923 was the turning point into the second millennium when Christians in the Global North outnumbered those in the Global South.[44] In the first millennium, Christianity was primarily a southern religion, "heavily concentrated in the Mediterranean regions, including Asia, northern Africa and southern Europe roughly centred in the Roman Empire."[45]

The blossoming of southern Christianity, however, is actually due not so much to colonialism as in spite of it. Ghanian scholar Lamin Sanneh posits that "the comprehensive decline of Christianity failed to follow the end of colonialism and of mainline missions. Instead, Christian numbers grew at a much faster rate than ever before, confounding critic and supporter alike."[46] According to Sanneh, "this expansion has taken place *after* colonialism and during the period of national awakening. Perhaps colonialism was an obstacle to the growth of Christianity, so that when colonialism ended it removed the stumbling block."[47] Typically, homegrown churches led by native missionaries are the ones that are growing by leaps and bounds. The Yoido Full Gospel Pentecostal Church in Seoul is an example. Founded by David Yonggi Cho about fifty years ago, its membership exceeds one

---

[42] World Christian Database, Gordon-Conwell Theological Seminary, Center for the Study of Global Christianity, http://www.worldchristiandatabase.org/wcd/.

[43] Todd M. Johnson and Gina A. Bellafatto, "The Demographic Status of World Christianity in the 21st Century," in *Ecumenical Visions for the 21st Century: A Reader for Theological Education*, ed. Mélisande Lorke and Dietrich Werner (Geneva: WCC, 2013), 17–26, at 19–20.

[44] John Stott and Sun Young Chung, "Christianity's Center of Gravity, AD 33–2100," in *Atlas of Global Christianity*, ed. Todd Johnson and Kenneth Ross (Edinburgh: Edinburgh University, 2009), 50–51.

[45] Wonsuk Ma, "A Millennial Shift of Global Christianity: A Brief Overview," paper presented at Global Ecumenical Theological Institute (GETI) seminar (Busan, November 1, 2013), 1, http://www.globethics.net/web/gtl/geti.

[46] Lamin Sanneh, *Whose Religion Is Christianity? The Gospel beyond the West* (Grand Rapids, MI: Wm. B. Eerdmans Publishing, 2003), 17.

[47] Ibid., 18.

million, with Sunday attendance in a single campus at more than 200,000 members, making it the largest megachurch on earth today. Homegrown movements can also be found within the mainline churches. An example from the Roman Catholic Church is the *El Shaddai* Catholic charismatic movement in the Philippines, which was born about thirty years ago. Under the leadership of Brother Mike Velarde its worldwide membership—spread primarily through Filipino migrant workers—is around ten million.[48] The Catholic Bishops' Conference of the Philippines shrewdly brought it under its official umbrella by appointing a bishop to serve as the movement's spiritual director. These are the new faces of Christianity in the world today.

The Many Faces of Christianity

The major hallmark of this new southern Christianity is that the Christian faith is expressed differently from one church to the next. The fact that it is primarily homegrown suggests that each *home* produces its own brand of Christianity. That is why it might be more accurate to speak of southern Christianity in the plural—Christianities—just as Peter Phan entitled his book *Christianities in Asia*. Christianity in Asia has to be spoken of in the plural, Phan insists, because "Christian multiformity is a function of the enormous geographical, sociopolitical, historical, cultural, and religious diversity of the continent called Asia."[49] One is reminded here of the early church, especially during the New Testament era, when the Christian communities were "diverse with different forms of ministries, patterns of organizations, and having a variety of articulations of faith and ways of worship which were spontaneously shaped by their different historical, cultural, and religious contexts."[50] Contemporary southern Christianity seems to be returning to the Christian origins of contextualized expressions of the faith. The thrust toward contextualization and localization has become the order of the day. Connie Au, the director of the Pentecostal Research Center in Hong Kong, in her discussion of Pentecostalism in Asia with an emphasis on churches spread by the indigenous and native-born missionaries, alerts us to the fact that most of these churches developed out of a "praxis derived from self-interpretation of the Bible according to its own

---

[48] José Mario C. Francisco, "The Philippines," in *Christianities in Asia*, ed. Peter C. Phan (Malden, MA: Wiley-Blackwell, 2011), 97–127.

[49] Phan, *Christianities in Asia*, 1.

[50] Kuncheria Pathil, "Theology of Ecumenism in the Asian Context: A Catholic Perspective," in *Our Pilgrimage in Hope: Proceedings of the First Three Seminars of the Asian Movement for Christian Unity* (Manila: St Paul's, 2001), 9–37, at 25.

Asian cultural and religious context and personal experience of the divine, such as the True Jesus Church and Jesus Family in China."[51]

A byproduct of the plural character of southern Christianity is that the organizational structures of the new churches are basically polycentric. If the Roman Catholic Church is identified with Rome, the WCC with Geneva, and Orthodox Christianity with Constantinople, one would be hard pressed to identify a center for the many independent, Pentecostal, and charismatic churches established in the last century. Because these churches have no centralized authority, one can imagine the length and breadth they must travel in their search for what it means to be Christian in their local contexts. It comes as no surprise then that some may espouse spiritualities that are considered eclectic or at least manifestly different from what mainline Christians are used to: "The Charismatic movement has brought a dramatic shift in Christian identities. . . . Multiple Christian identity is a reality, particularly visible in Asia where denominational boundaries are often porous."[52] The consequence is that many of these movements are not accepted or even acknowledged as Christian. Oftentimes, labels such as *sects* or *cults* are used rather unsparingly when referring to the Pentecostal, Evangelical, charismatic, and independent churches. In describing the African-initiated churches, Kirsteen Kim opines, "Because they expressed their faith in a characteristically African way, many viewed them as separatist. Because some of their practices resembled the reviled indigenous religious traditions, they were accused of syncretism." She reports that in India, compared to mainline churches, "there are at least as many Christians in indigenous churches and Pentecostal movements, plus an estimated three million who worship Christ while remaining Hindus."[53] Whatever identities these new churches and movements may embrace, it will be to the detriment of the ecumenical movement to ignore them. Kim reminds us:

> The growth of independent churches means that world Christianity—at least the half which is not part of the Catholic Church—is increasingly fragmented. The World Council of Churches is made up mainly of historic Protestant and Orthodox churches. The inde-

---

[51] Connie Ho Yan Au, "Asian Ecumenism from Pentecostal Perspective," in *Asian Handbook for Theological Education and Ecumenism,* ed. Hope Antone et al. (Oxford: Regnum, 2013), 84–93, at 84.

[52] Richard Howell, "Asian Ecumenism from Evangelical Perspective," in Antone et al., *Asian Handbook,* 80–83, at 80.

[53] Kirsteen Kim, "Mission's Changing Landscape: Global Flows and Christian Movements," *International Review of Mission* 100/2 (2011): 253.

pendent churches by their nature are not inclined to join, so that constant efforts need to be made to remember that these are the most rapidly growing churches in the world.[54]

The pluralism and fragmentation within southern or World Christianity makes the already difficult interchurch relations even more challenging. Some Pentecostal and Evangelical churches not only have no centers, they may also be anticenter as well. If the ecumenical movement is a centripetal force, drawing churches together, these Pentecostals and Evangelicals sometimes serve as centrifugal forces, pulling them away, especially from the center. At the most recent WCC assembly held in Busan, South Korea, in November 2013, hundreds of Christians were demonstrating daily outside the complex where the WCC assembly was being held. They carried banners and placards with messages such as "WCC is from the devil" and "WCC kills the church of Christ." They were members of other Korean churches who were protesting not only the assembly but also the very idea and existence of the ecumenical movement. Siga Arles, director of the Centre for Contemporary Christianity in Bangalore, puts these actions into perspective: "Historically a sense of distrust has been implanted in the minds of the 'evangelicals' about the 'ecumenicals'—as not rooted in the authority of the Bible—as not committed to evangelism and church growth and—as not promoting conversion."[55]

Challenges for the Future

It is precisely because of this distrust that some of the Pentecostal and Evangelicals are vehemently opposed to the ecumenical movement, at least in its present configuration. This makes the task of Christian unity even more demanding especially if one has to reach out to an antagonistic party or someone who sincerely believes you are working against the Christian cause. Besides the *antiecumenicals*, some other churches are also wary of the WCC and the mainline churches because the latter continue to operate along confessional lines. The wary churches are principally the independent churches that wish to remain so. Most of the newly established churches in China are of this genre. As the late Anglican Bishop K. H. Ting, who once headed the government-approved three-self patriotic movement of

---

[54] Ibid., 254.

[55] Siga Arles, "Relations between Ecumenicals and Evangelicals," in Antone et al., *Asian Handbook*, 94–106, at 94.

the Protestant Church in China, once said, "We Chinese Christians have chosen the road of post-denominational unity, not because we are better than anyone else, but because we live in our particular historical situation."[56] The three-self movement does not include self-isolation as one of its practices and so the Chinese church has no intention of shunning the worldwide Christian communion. However, these Chinese Christians are at the same time cautious:

> Since the churches re-opened in 1979, fellowship and friendship between the churches in China and worldwide have been widely established and developed. On the one hand, we appreciate very much that more and more churches overseas respect our independence and assist us sincerely in building up our churches on the basis of equality, publicity and legality. On the other hand, we always appeal to foreign churches and missionaries to "not go so far as to attempt to revive denominational feelings and loyalties, thus inviting misunderstanding and unpleasantness."[57]

As we can see from just these two profiles of the new face of World Christianity, interchurch dialogue is indeed confronted with new challenges today. Establishing a basis for engagement is already an uphill climb. Journeying together is perhaps what is needed, especially in light of the reality of Christianity's numerical southward shift and the advent of World Christianity. Emphasis should not be placed so much on the fruits as on the actual journey and ongoing dialogue. Activities are not confined to those within but extend beyond institutional boundaries, including those of other religious traditions. This is the new context within which southern Christianity is growing and invites a new vision for interchurch relations. This new vision sees ecumenism not so much as a task to be fulfilled but as a way of being and relating across church and religious lines.

---

[56] K. H. Ting, "Fourteen Points from Christians in the People's Republic of China to Christians Abroad," *A New Beginning*, Canada-China Programme of the Canadian Council of Churches (1983), 113, quoted in "The Queue—A Symbol of Emerging Christianity in China," *The Bible Society of India* (October 2013), http://www.bsind.org/Christan_China.html.

[57] Gu Mengfei, "The Post-denominational Era Chinese Churches on the Way Towards Unity," *Ecumenical Review*, July 1, 2008. See note 56 for the reference to the internal quotation.

New Vision for Christian Unity

Within Roman Catholicism, this new vision in some way correlates with the emphasis coming from Rome and the Asian bishops. From Rome, inspired by *Ut unum sint,* Cardinal Walter Kasper, long-time president of the PCPCU, introduced and promoted the method of Receptive Ecumenism.[58] Acknowledging that the ecumenical efforts of the past decades have more or less reached an impasse in what has been called an ecumenical winter, Kasper's proposal is that we continue to be committed to the conversations. What is different, however, is that instead of focusing on the gifts each church brings to the table, we now turn our attention to what each church can learn from the other communities. For the Roman Catholic Church this is called Catholic Learning.[59] The church becomes not so much an *ecclesia docens* (a teaching church) as an *ecclesia discens* (a learning church).

The Federation of Asian Bishops' Conferences, meantime, has been promoting the *triple dialogue* as a method not only for doing theology but also for being church in Asia.[60] Asian bishops use this term to invite Christians—all of them—to dialogue with the poor, the religions, and the cultures of Asia. What this means is best explained by an image used by Indian theologian Stanley Samartha, first director of WCC's subunit for Dialogue with People of Living Faiths and Ideologies, in describing the postcolonial church. He refers to the image of the bullock cart to describe what a contextualized and dialogical church entails.[61] For the bullock cart to move forward, it has to be grounded on Asian soil and interact with all the ground realities. Thus, the triple dialogue entails the church being in touch with the poor, the religions, and the cultures of Asia—not so much as preacher or teacher but as pilgrim and servant. The task and method of the new ecumenism invite Christians to be in constant engagement and dialogue with the realities of their own contexts. In today's world where the many poor, the many religions, and the many cultures are not merely confined to Asia but are very much present in the rest of the world as well,

---

[58] "May They All be One, But How? A Vision of Christian Unity for the Next Generation," *Ecumenical Trends* 40 (April 2011): 4.

[59] Ibid.

[60] Edmund Kee-Fook Chia, "Toward an Asian Theology of Dialogue," in *Edward Schillebeeckx & Interreligious Dialogue: Perspectives from Asian Theology* (Eugene, OR: Pickwick, 2012), 127–50.

[61] Stanley Samartha, *One Christ—Many Religions: Toward a Revised Christology* (Maryknoll, NY: Orbis Books, 1991), 116.

the vision of the triple dialogue applies to the entire Christian communion, including the ecumenical movement.

If Christians embrace the vision of Receptive Ecumenism and of the triple dialogue as the ecumenical methodology for the twenty-first century, they will not only be working alongside one another for the sake of God's kingdom but will be doing so together and with the poor and their neighbors of other faiths as well. Ecumenism would then be transcending the boundaries of church and Christianity and become the concern of all of humankind. The *oikoumene* would then truly represent the whole inhabited world.

Even as this might seem like an ad extra vision and involvement, it will surely help facilitate the unity of the church. Denominational and doctrinal differences would be secondary concerns when Christians of different churches can witness together to the name of Jesus and in the name of God. When Christians are able to bring to reality God's abundant life and a world of justice and peace, then the prayer of Jesus "that all of them may be one, Father, just as you are in me and I am in you" (John 17:21) will apply as much to the Christian community as to the world's human community.

18

WORLD CHRISTIANITY AND WORLD CHURCH MUSIC: SINGING THE LORD'S SONG IN A WORLD CHURCH

Lim Swee Hong

For there our captors asked us for songs,
and our tormentors asked for mirth, saying,
"Sing us one of the songs of Zion!"
How could we sing the Lord's song in a foreign land?

PSALM 137:3–4 (NRSV)

According to a 2011 Pew Forum report, Christianity has 2.18 billion adherents around the world. In 2010, this was one-third of the global population of 6.9 billion people. What was remarkable in that report was the observation that Christians were evenly located in all geographical regions such that "no single continent or region can indisputably claim to be the center of global Christianity."[1] Nonetheless, this scenario attests to a seismic shift when compared to the data of 1910. For in the span of a century, Christianity spread from its Euro-American locale to the rest of the world. Current statistics seems to indicate its highest growth region in Sub-Sahara Africa. Accompanying this growth, one would expect a phenomenal display of a multitude of tongues in worship and music making as in the days of Pentecost, where "each one heard them speaking in the native language of

---

[1] Luis Lugo and Alan Cooperman, "Global Christianity—A Report on the Size and Distribution of the World's Christian Population" (December 19, 2011), http://www.pewforum.org/2011/12/19/global-christianity-exec/.

each" (Acts 2:6b, NRSV). So is this form of music making truly occurring with various congregations around the world? What might we learn about its impact to World Christianity?

Here it is vital to declare that as an individual writing about World Christianity and the place of world church music, one is at risk of making overly broad and hyperbolical statements given the highly complex arena of sociocultural contexts and the wide spectrum of liturgical settings in World Christianity. Yet to even have a glimpse of the landscape and the music-making concerns, broad generalization is inevitable. Hence, this essay will bear witness to this approach with due cognizance of the reality that exceptions would be normative in many situations through this approach.

The world of global church music can trace its source to three fountain-heads, namely, the convening of the Second Vatican Council (1962–65) resulting in the promulgation of the *Sacrosanctum Concilium* (Constitution on the Sacred Liturgy, 1963), the purposeful contextualization of worship at the 1983 General Assembly of the World Council of Churches in Vancouver, Canada, and the Jesus People Movement of America at around 1968–71.

In Vatican II, the Roman Catholic Church crystallizes a liturgical movement that had its stirrings in 1832 through the desire of Dom Prosper Guéranger (1805–75) to recover liturgical worship practices of the church leading to Pope Pius X (1835–1914) issuing *Tra le sollecitudini,* a *motu proprio* on church music in 1903, calling for the active participation of the laity in the liturgy.[2] With *Sacrosanctum Concilium*, the door was opened for inculturation efforts in liturgical music making. Folk music Masses and even contemporary worship songs found their way into parishes of the Roman Catholic Church and Protestant churches all over the world. Congregational songs by both Catholic and non-Catholic composers, such as David Haas (b. 1957), Chris de Silva (b. 1967), Matt Maher (b. 1974), Pablo Sosa (b. 1933), and Marty Haugen (b. 1950), were equally embraced.[3] Of

---

[2] For an assessment on the impact of Vatican II, see Keith F. Pecklers, *Roman Catholic Liturgical Renewal Forty Five Years after Sacrosanctum Concilium: An Assessment,* http://ism.yale.edu/sites/default/files/files/Roman%20Catholic%20Liturgical%20 Renewal%20Forty.pdf. See also Keith F. Peckler, *The Unread Vision: The Liturgical Movement in the United States of America 1926–1955* (Collegeville, MN: Liturgical Press, 1998), in particular the chapters on "The European Roots: 1833–1925," and "The Beginnings of a Movement: Toward Full and Active Participation in the Liturgy."

[3] While both David Haas and Marty Haugen are well known, I would like to introduce readers to two emerging composers. First, writing in a much more contemporary worship music vein is Chris de Silva, a Catholic composer who originated in Singapore, currently lives in California, and is represented by GIA Publications, Inc.

course, in the arena of global church music particularly from the Caribbean, we need to keep in mind the contributions of Catholic composers Richard Holung (b. 1939) and Paschal Jordan (b. 1944) whose works have also readily crossed the Catholic–Protestant divide.[4]

In Vancouver, the liturgical shift of the worship services was rather dramatic. In his report, "The Story of an Assembly," David Gill, observed that

> Prayers were offerings to the divine mystery—not efforts to moralize at the congregation about the condition of the world and what we should be all doing to fix it. Hymns were acts of praise— not devices for extracting certain desired responses from the singers. Worship was an end in itself, not a means for achieving something else. God was worshipped, not used.[5]

Complementing Gill's observation, well-known Sri Lankan ecumenical theologian and deputy general secretary of the WCC, Wesley Ariarajah, observed,

> Music drawn from many cultures was sung in the original languages. Scripture was read in numerous languages that represented the geographical spread of the member churches. At the Lima liturgy seven persons representing different cultures and seven distinct traditions of the church stood together to break the bread. Clergy and laity, men, women and children, young and old, and persons with disabilities all participated equally in leading worship. When the Assembly ended some 650 persons had, in one way or another, participated in leading worship; over forty languages had been used. New lessons have been learnt.[6]

(see http://www.giamusic.com/search_details.cfm?title_id=15911). Second, Canadian Matt Maher is well known as a contemporary worship songwriter but lesser known as a Catholic-based artist with credible theological underpinning in his music making. An example of this is his song "Christ Is Alive" (2009), https://youtu.be/IExdrZGQVeI.

   [4] George Mulrain, "The Caribbean," in *An Introduction to Third World Theologies*, ed. John Parrett (Cambridge: Cambridge University Press, 2004), 170.

   [5] David Gill, "The Story of an Assembly," in *Gathered for Life: Official Report, Sixth Assembly of the World Council of Churches* (Geneva: World Council of Churches, 1983), 12.

   [6] Wesley Ariarajah, "Worship in the Oikoumene: The Tent and the Gym," *Ecumenical Review* 36/2 (April 1984): 150–54.

One of the new lessons learned was the emerging significance of non-Western congregational songs and their place in Christian worship through the presence of enliveners. It was in Vancouver, British Columbia, at the sixth General Assembly of the World Council of Churches (WCC) in 1983 that Pablo Sosa (Argentina), I-to Loh (Taiwan), and Patrick Matsikenyiri (b. 1937) (Zimbabwe) were invited to provide musical leadership through Rev. George Todd (b. 1925), an American Presbyterian missionary who served as director of the Office of Rural-Urban Mission in the WCC from 1972 to 1986. During that tenure, Todd had met them on separate WCC affiliated events and was impressed by them, and subsequently recommended them to the assembly worship planning committee for the Vancouver event.[7] Without a doubt, this general assembly lent credence for the enliveners to be recognized by the world church and their music-making ability being used by other international and regional Christian organizations that continue till the present. For example, in winter 2014, Patrick Matsikenyiri was featured at the Evangelical Lutheran Church of America's Global Missions Formation Program in Chicago, Illinois. While I-to Loh (b. 1935) was the Routley lecturer at the Montreat Worship and Music Conference of the Presbyterian Church (USA; PCUSA) in summer 2015, Pablo Sosa is appearing at the winter 2016 Calvin Worship Symposium, an annual worship formation event hosted by the Calvin Institute for Christian Worship, Grand Rapids, Michigan. Aside from their active enlivening work, Loh, Matsikenyiri, and Sosa have advanced the work of sharing non-Western songs in North America through the Global Praise program since 1993. S. T. Kimbrough (b. 1936), a United Methodist bureaucrat and Wesleyan scholar, sought to introduce non-Western congregational songs to North America, established this global music publishing and training entity under the auspice of the General Board of Global Ministries of the United Methodist Church. His pioneering efforts enabled many of these global songs to find their way into denominational hymnals such as *Lift up Your Hearts* (Christian Reformed Church and the Reformed Church in America [CRCNA-CRC], 2013), and *Glory to God* (PCUSA, 2013), among many others.

---

[7] Swee Hong Lim, *Giving Voice to Asian Christians: An Appraisal of the Pioneering Work of I-to Loh in the Area of Congregational Song* (Saarbrücken, Germany: Verlag Dr. Müller, 2008), "George Todd," 40–42. Todd's contribution to global church music is highly significant given that he is instrumental in introducing Loh, Matsikenyiri, and Sosa to the world's stage. An in-depth study of his relationships with these enliveners is warranted. Additional information about him can be gleaned from http://www.presbyterianmission.org.

While it may be plausible that the approach of the WCC Vancouver event came about because of Vatican II underpinnings two decades earlier, but for Loh, Matsikenyiri, and Sosa—the Protestant enliveners—their contextual efforts are likely to have arisen from their personal heightened self-awareness and their sociocultural setting.[8] From my earlier research, I know that Loh's thought on contextualization was independently shaped rather than influenced by the happenings of Vatican II as epitomized by the scholarship of Filipino Catholic liturgical scholar Anscar Chupungco (1939–2013).[9] In fact, Loh's use of the term *contextualization* rather than *inculturation* has much to do with his close association with teacher and mentor Shoki Coe (1914–88).

Aside from these two events that proffer active liturgical participation of the people in global Christianity through music making, another important contributor to global church music was the Jesus movement. Coming out of Southern California in the late 1960s, it centered around the ministry of Chuck Smith at Calvary Chapel in Costa Mesa, California. Smith's hospitality to hippies and their music subsequently took the world by storm through the offering of a new worship expression that is music driven in contrast to the ritual or preaching focused worship form.[10] This movement, morphed from a folksong style in its early years to the present popular music industry standard expression, is formidable and continues to thrive across global Christianity transcending denominational lines by marrying various local languages with its popular Western music style.[11] According to Duke University's Research Professor of Christian Worship, Lester Ruth (b. 1959), the three key catalysts to the onset of contemporary worship in the 1960s was the use of "current contemporary English" in worship and music making rather than archaic English then in use, the experimentation with "new" music-making expressions, and concerns with social issues of that era.[12]

Fueled by popular groundswell and commercialism, this genre became an impetus of the worship war that ultimately resulted in the worship band displacing the organ on Sunday morning worship and giving rise to infor-

---

[8] For more information, see C. Michael Hawn, *Gather into One: Praying and Singing Globally* (Grand Rapids, MI: Wm. B. Eerdmans Publishing, 2003).

[9] For more information, see ibid., 53–54.

[10] For more information, see Rob Redman, *The Great Worship Awakening: Singing a New Song in the Post-Modern Church* (San Francisco: Jossey-Bass, 2002); and Larry Eskridge, *God's Forever Family: The Jesus People Movement in America* (New York: Oxford University Press, 2013).

[11] An excellent summative polyglot video illustration is Chris Tomlin's *How Great Is Our God: World Edition*, presented at the 2012 Passion Conference in Atlanta, Georgia, https://youtu.be/vg5qDljEw7Q.

[12] Lester Ruth, "The History of Contemporary Worship," http://podbay.fm.

mality in worship. Within the span of forty years, the contemporary worship song has become ubiquitous and is seen as the musical solution synonymous with combating declining church attendance and the retention of youth in an otherwise staid liturgical environment. Not surprising, this naive idea is also prevalent in congregations in the Global South. In fact, the valiant effort of translating Western hymns in missional context has seen its music genre replaced with contemporary worship song! Without a doubt, contemporary worship music genre in its myriad forms of translated Western songs, and Western-nuanced local efforts has a strong presence in the global church music landscape. Yet it is only in the past decade that scholars began to critically and objectively assess its contribution to global church music. These include established and emerging scholars such as Lester Ruth, Monique Ingalls, Joshua Busman, Anna E. Nekola, Charles E. Fromm, Wen Reagan, Tanya Riches, and others.[13] Well-regarded conferences, such as the Christian Congregational Music: Local and Global Perspectives in Oxford, UK, Calvin Worship Symposium, and others, have also taken up the task of examining this musical trend in a critically thoughtful manner by their presenters.[14]

From this brief overview of the fountainheads, we see three expressions of global church music.[15] First is the translated–transplanted Western

---

[13] Lester Ruth, "Some Similarities and Differences between Historic Evangelical Hymns and Contemporary Worship Songs," *Artistic Theologian* 3 (2015): 68–86; Lester Ruth, "Divine, Human, or Devilish? The State of the Question on the Writing of History of Contemporary Worship," *Worship* 88/4 (2014): 290–310; Monique Ingalls, "Beyond Sacred and Secular: On the Ethnography of Religious Popular Music," in *Broadening Stages: Towards an Ethnomusicology of Popular Music* (Oxford: Oxford University Press, forthcoming), Monique M. Ingalls, "Awesome in This Place: Sound, Space, and Identity in Contemporary North American Evangelical Worship" (PhD diss., University of Pennsylvania, 2008); Joshua Kalin Busman, "Worshipping 'With Everything': Musical Piety Beyond Language in Contemporary Evangelicalism" (presented at the Christian Congregational Music Conference, Rippon College, Cuddesdon, Oxford, UK, 2013); Anna E. Nekola, "Between This World and the Next: The Musical 'Worship Wars' and Evangelical Ideology in the United States, 1960–2005" (PhD diss., University of Wisconsin-Madison, 2009); Charles E. Fromm, "Textual Communities and New Song in the Multimedia Age: The Routinization of Charisma in the Jesus Movement" (PhD diss., Fuller Theological Seminary: School of Intercultural Studies, 2006); Wen Reagan, "Bigger, Better, Louder: The Prosperity Gospel's Impact on Contemporary Christian Music," *Religion and American Culture: A Journal of Interpretation* 24/2 (2014): 186–230; Tanya Riches, "The Evolution of Hillsong Music: From Australian Pentecostal Congregation into Global Brand," *Australian Journal of Communication* 39/1 (2012): 17–36.

[14] See http://congregationalmusic.org/content/conference and http://worship.calvin.edu/symposium/.

[15] For a fuller description of these three expressions, refer to Swee Hong Lim,

song form. This genre features original Western songs translated to the local language and sung using the original Western music.[16] These works are originally Western hymns or contemporary worship songs. In this approach, the translated local language is juxtaposed with the Western melody. There is little effort to reconcile the tonal inflection if it was present in the local tongue such as in Khmer, Burmese, Thai, Chinese, or Nigeria's *Yoruba* languages. As a result, awkwardness of meanings is inherent in many instances due to an unfortunate distorted tonal inflection. At the same time, vernacular translation of the lyrics tends to lean toward the literal with minimal effort of contextually grounding the original text. When constrained by melodic length, the translated text may dramatically abbreviate or elongate the original text. In a recent conversation with emerging Japanese church music scholar Saya Ojiri, I learned that the entire text of the Christian classic song, "Jesus Loves Me," by Anna Bartlett Warner (1827–1915), matched a tune and refrain by William Batchelder Bradbury (1816–68). It was essentially abbreviated to "Lord Loves Me" in Japanese (see Table 1).

Table 1
English Translation of Actual Japanese Text by Saya Ojiri

English Text	Japanese Text
Jesus loves me—this I know,	Lord loves me
For the Bible tells me so;	As Lord is strong;
Little ones to Him belong—	Even if I am weak,
They are weak, but He is strong.	There is no fear.
Yes, Jesus loves me! (3 times)	My Lord Jesus
The Bible tells me so.	Loves me

Used by permission.

"Sacred Song for All God's Children: A Perspective of Post-Colonial Asian Congregational Song," in *Complex Identities in a Shifting World: One God, Many Stories,* ed. Pamela Couture, Robert Mager, Pamela McCarroll, and Natalie Wigg-Stevenson (Berlin: LIT Verlag, 2015); Swee Hong Lim, "Asian Christian Forms of Worship and Music," in *Handbook on Christianity in Asia,* ed. Felix Wilfred (New York: Oxford University Press, 2014), 524–37; and Swee Hong Lim, "Raising the Bamboo Curtain: A Visit with Asian Congregational Song," *The Hymn* 63/3 (2012): 10–21.

[16] An example of this is the video footage "Holy, Holy, Holy" in Thai as produced by Trang Church in the Seventeenth District of the Church of Christ Thailand (CCT), https://youtu.be/n9dCSguuJ_E.

At the same time, hymns bearing northern hemisphere seasonal conditions, political and ethical thoughts, or symbolic connotations are sung in southern hemisphere settings with scant regard for the receiving *in situ* setting. This disconnect is seldom addressed by churches in the Global South and inadvertently help sustain concepts of empire and reinforce the subtle dictate of meaning by powers beyond the local milieu. C. Michael Hawn elucidates when he commented on Isaac Watts's hymn, "Jesus Shall Reign:"

> By the nineteenth century Watts's free paraphrase of selected verses from Psalm 72 had come to epitomize the emerging expansion of the missionary movement. His words have shaped the thought and theology by which the Western church defined its understanding of missions during the period of its most dramatic growth. The identity of Christian missions was nurtured in the milieu of European political monarchies, and developed during a time when Christians assumed not only a relationship between the kingdom of Christ and major European kingdoms, but also the divine right of kings. "Jesus Shall Reign" gives voice to an emerging movement devoted to spreading the Good News of salvation "throughout the world which was ignorant of this knowledge of God in Jesus Christ."[17]

Clearly, meanings are imported and imposed even as the global church sings what it receives with deference and without questioning the intrinsic framing of the hymns and its social cultural context.[18] More often than not, it retains and reinforces the vestiges of power of the church (with its Western legacy) and communicates a supracultural Christian identity. Not surprising, such songs feed the yearning of the church for a tangible kingdom of God on earth, and in a way contribute to the desire for visible expression of God's power that manifests itself in signs and wonders even now captivating the imagination of Global South churches embracing the Pentecostal holiness movement in varying degrees.

Despite its obvious deficiency, this particular song form dominates the global Christianity landscape, in Africa, Asia, and Latin America. Its efficacy

---

[17] C. Michael Hawn, *Singing with the Faithful of Every Time and Place: Thoughts on Liturgical Inculturation and Cross-Cultural Liturgy*, http://ism.yale.edu/sites/default/files/files/Singing%20with%20the%20Faithful%20of%20Every%20Time%20and%20Place.pdf.

[18] For a preliminary discussion, see Michael N. Jagessar and Stephen Burns, *Christian Worship: Postcolonial Perspectives* (Oakville, CT: Equinox Publishing, 2011), 51–68.

lies in its ability to preserve a Christian tradition that was handed down and received in the previous missional context in an unadulterated manner. More often than not, this song type is used in formal ecclesial settings, that is, Sunday mornings rather than Sunday nights. Such services tend to purvey a supracultural Christian identity shaping the local faith community in that mindfulness, which essentially champions the Christian tradition that was received in a past era. It is efficacious in settings where Christianity is the minority faith tradition in an ambivalent society dominated by another faith system such as Buddhism, Hinduism, or Islam. To that end, faithful believers in that setting—where their Christian faith tradition is seemingly weak—align themselves with the Western church that seems to have a stronger projected influence. This raises the issue of commonality against cultural fault lines as loyalty divides between local and global priorities.[19] Well-known Asian church music scholar I-to Loh elucidates,

> We have paid a heavy price to be Christians. It would appear that when we choose to be reconciled with God, we become alienated from our own culture and if we choose to be culturally grounded we risk being alienated from God. Sadly, the majority of our churches appear to have this implicit attitude.[20]

The second type is the mimicked song form. Normatively speaking, this song type features local creative efforts that look to Western nuances as source. Western musical nuances serve as templates and are expressed through local parameters. In some cases, overt efforts in Western harmonic organization and rhythmic character are used to support an indigenous melody. An example of this is the Tamil Christian song, "*Thirupadham Nambi Vandhen.*"[21] However, in some Christian communities where Westernization is *de rigueur*, locally crafted congregational songs are not likely to reflect any influence from its *in situ* cultural nuances, not even in the melodic line. An example of this is the Singapore Christian song, "Unmerited Favor," produced by one of the nation's largest nondenominational congregations, New Creation Church.[22] In the process of contextualization, mimicry is an

---

[19] For detailed explanation on cultural fault lines, local and global priorities, see Lim, *Giving Voice to Asian Christians,* 194–95.

[20] I-to Loh, "Contextualized Music in Worship: My Mission," *Theology and the Church* 2/1 (1994): 132.

[21] See https://youtube.com.

[22] See ibid.

essential step for localizing church music making, as Global South Christianity is often times wary of syncretism where local expressions are perceived to adulterate orthodoxy and orthopraxis. In the mid-twentieth century, this can be seen in the church's initial hesitation to accept the electric guitar, the Argentinian church's concern about Tango, and/or the African churches' concern for drumming. As a result, global church music has had to take an alternative approach in the process of contextualization.

In the 1970s, the East Asian Christian Conference (EACC) hymnal, edited by Daniel T. Niles (1908–70) and John Milton Kelly, is an example of this compromised approach. Its four reprints (1963, 1964, 1968, 1972) for a hymnal meant for an ambivalent region serve as a testament of its widespread acceptance by local congregations in Asia. However, this popularity was paid for by the significant music dilution of Asian nuances.

In the example of an indigenous Indian song (see Figure 1), melismas that are the essence of *Marathi* music making are eliminated. In its place, Western nuanced four-part harmonic treatment is used. As a result, this song sounds Victorian English rather than South Asian. Generally speaking, mimicked song type subtly asserts its local identity and is well received by the *in situ* constituency even as it is seen to actualize the scriptural call "O sing to the LORD a new song; sing to the LORD, all the earth" (Ps. 96:1) by the churches in the Global South.

Figure 1
#144 O Kindness Wonderful (EACC Hymnal)

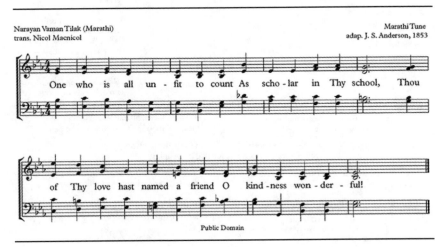

Narayan Vaman Tilak (Marathi)
trans. Nicol Macnicol

Marathi Tune
adap. J. S. Anderson, 1853

One who is all un - fit to count As scho - lar in Thy school, Thou of Thy love hast named a friend O kind - ness won - der - ful!

Public Domain

More often than not, indigenous expressed songs are better received outside than inside the local milieu. An example of this is Korean composer Geonyong Lee (b. 1947)'s *O Sosŏ* ("Come Now, O Prince of Peace") (see Figure 2).

Figure 2
O Sosŏ by Geonyong Lee

Ososŏ

Geonyong Lee, Korea

1. O - so - sŏ   o - so - sŏ,   pyŏng-hwa   ŭi   im - gŭm
1. Come now, O   God of peace, we   are   your   peo - ple;
1. Komm nun, Fürstdes   Frie - dens, ein'   uns   zu   dei-nem Lei - be,
1. Viens, viens, ô   roi de   paix   et   ras - sem - ble nous,
1. Ven,   oh Dios   de   paz pues   so - mos   tu   pue - blo;

u - ri - ga   han - mom   i - ru - ge   ha -   so - sŏ.
pour out your   spir - it   that we be   one   bod - y.
komm,Herr Jesus, komm,   ver - söh-ne dir   all   dein Volk.
viens, viens, ô   mai - tre,   ré - con - ci - lie ton peu - ple.
y   por tu Es - pí - ritu,   haz-nos un -   so - lo cuer - po.

Korean (Romanized).
2. Ososŏ ososŏ,
sarangŭi imgŭm,
uriga hanmom
iruge hasosŏ.

3. Ososŏ ososŏ,
chayuŭi imgŭm,
uriga hanmom
iruge hasosŏ.

4. Ososŏ ososŏ,
tongilŭi imgŭm,
uriga hanmom
iruge hasosŏ.

Français:

English:
2. Come now, O God of love,
we are your people;
pour out your spirit
that we be one body.

3. Come now, O God of hope,
we are your people;
pour out your spirit
that we be one body.

4. Come now, O God of joy,
are your people;
pour out your spirit
that we be one body.

Deutsch:
2. Komm nun, Gott der Liebe,
ein' uns zu deinem Leibe,
komm, Herr Jesus, komm,
versöhne dir all dein Volk.

3. Komm nun, und befrei uns,
denn du bist unser Retter,
komm, Herr Jesus, komm,
versöhne dir alle Völker.

4. Komm, erhoffte Einheit,
ein' uns zu einem Leibe,
komm, Herr Jesus, komm,
versöhne dir alle Völker.

2. Viens, viens, ô roi d'amour et rassemble-nous,   3. Viens, viens, libérateur et libère-nous,
viens, viens, ô maître, réconcilie ton peuple.   viens, viens, ô maître réconcilie ton peuple.

4. Viens, viens, source d'espoir fais de nous ton corps,
viens, viens, ô maître, réconcilie les peuples.

Español:
1. Ven, oh Dios de Paz, pues somos tu pueblo;   3. Ven , oh Dios de Gracia, somos tu pueblo;
y por tu Espíritu, haznos un solo cuerpo.   y por tu Espíritu, haznos un solo cuerpo.

2. Ven , oh Dios de Amor, pues somos tu pueblo;   4. Ven , oh Dios de Vida, somos tu pueblo;
y por tu Espíritu, haznos un solo cuerpo.   y por tu Espíritu, haznos un solo cuerpo.

Music and Korean: Geonyong Lee © 2000 Christian Conference of Asia, Hong Kong. English: © Marion Pope, 95 Prince Arthur Ave., Apt 316, Toronto, Ontario, Canada, M5R 3P6 German: Dietrich Werner and Dieter Trautwein, © Strube-Verlag, Munich. French: © Robert Faerber. Spanish: Simei Monteiro © 2005 WCC-COE, Switzerland. All rights reserved. Used by permission.

All rights reserved. Used by permission.

Composed for the 1984 WCC Conference for the Reunification of Korean Peninsula, this song is found in twelve North American hymnals, the most recent being *Glory to God* (PCUSA, 2013) and *Lift up Your Hearts* (CRCNA-CRC, 2013).[23] Yet, despite its popularity in other parts of the world, this song is not widely known to congregations in South Korea. To help address this situation, the assembly worship planning committee of the 2013 Tenth General Assembly, WCC included this song for the event held in Busan, South Korea. It is hoped that by featuring this work on the world stage, it would gain a foothold in its homeland.

To that end, the third type is the hybrid song form. This particular type keenly maintains its local nuance out of an awareness of its cultural identity and setting. An example of this is the Arabic Christian song, "Preach for the Messiah" ("*Zido Massih Tasbih*") from Egypt.[24] In this instance, the local musical characteristics are not subsumed by Western musical nuances but are aptly supported. One could say that the musical traditions are discerningly held together rather than having one dominate the other. In *Alle nasies*, the call and response that is typical of African music is matched with its Western influence harmonic treatment (see Figure 3). What is not so obvious in this printed page is that this song is typically accompanied with percussion instruments such as xylophones, rattles, etc.[25]

While hybrid songs from Africa and Latin America have gained much leeway in progressive and mainline congregations in the Global North, the same cannot be said for Asian songs, which are often perceived as being difficult in terms of their musical nuances or even the pronunciations of texts. To that end, the category of global songs is a misnomer. Often times, it denotes non-Western songs that have gained access to Western milieu through the ministry of various music-making and publishing entities such as the Wild Goose Resource Group of the Iona Community, Glasgow, the Global Praise program of the United Methodist Church, the various mainline denominations' music events like Presbyterian Association of Musicians' Montreat 2015, or the Calvin Institute for Christian Worship (Christian Reformed Church) through its annual Worship Symposium event. More often than not, these songs are accessible musically and amenable for publication and intellectual property administration. Above all, it is the West that posits this label of "global song."

---

[23] See http://www.hymnary.org.

[24] See https://youtu.be/igVwhgeBl5c.

[25] A video footage from the Tenth General Assembly of the World Council of Churches, Busan, South Korea; https://youtu.be/AZMlrIz160w.

In a recent research project, I discovered that an American publishing house is presently administering a Japanese Christian blessing song that the arranger claimed was a Japanese blessing set to a Japanese folk melody. On the contrary, Fr. Shiota Izumi (b. 1951), a Roman Catholic priest, is the

---

Figure 3
An extract of *All nasies,* a congregational song from Namibia

Reprinted under Creative Commons Attribution-NonCommercial-NoDerivatives 4.0 International Public License, 2013, Administered by World Council of Churches, Geneva.

lyricist and composer of the song. In fact, his name is clearly stated in the *Anglican Hymnal of Japan* (Tokyo, 2006) where the song was included. In my view, such misattribution does an injustice to the creator of the work. Aside from denying the rightful owner of the fair share of royalties earned from its publication in the West, such action reveals an unintentional lack of respect for non-Western composers and a sore lack of scholarship in the intellectual property management of non-Western church music materials for use in the Western church.

Indeed there is a need to address the ethical implications of singing non-Western songs. The *raison d'être* for singing is different depending on where the song is being used. Much as non-Western songs are fascinating to most Western congregations, they need to be discerningly used to avoid what liturgical scholar John Witvliet regards as "ethno-tourism" that may result in unfortunate cultural appropriation and showcasing the music without understanding its *sitz im leben*.[26] In this instance, having an informed enlivener is essential. Given the proliferation of various training opportunities in North America and elsewhere, ecclesial leadership would be prudent to encourage their appointed music leaders to participate in these programs.[27]

Here, one can take a cue from article 115 of the *Constitution on the Sacred Liturgy* that states,

> Great importance is to be attached to the teaching and practice of music in seminaries, in the novitiates and houses of studies of the religious of both sexes, and also in other Catholic institutions and schools. To impart this instruction teachers are to be carefully trained and put in charge of the teaching of sacred music.

---

[26] John D. Witvliet, "The Virtue of Liturgical Discernment," in *Music in Christian Worship,* ed. Charlotte Kroeker (Collegeville, MN: Liturgical Press, 2005), 83–97, at 95. For further discussion about global song, see S. T. Kimbrough, Jr., ed., *Music and Mission: Toward a Theology and Practice of Global Song* (New York: General Board of Global Ministries, GBGMusik, 2006); and Hawn, *Singing with the Faithful.*

[27] In Canada, Emmanuel College of Victoria University in the University of Toronto has revised its graduate sacred music program to address this concern. A short-term training program is also available through the offices of the Global Praise program of the United Methodist Church, USA; the Methodist School of Music, of the Methodist Church in Singapore; the Global Mission Formation Unit of the Evangelical Lutheran Church in America; the Global Consultation on Music and Missions in partnership with the International Council of Ethnodoxologies; and the biennial Conference on Christian Congregational Music: Local and Global Perspectives at Ripon College, Oxford, UK.

It is desirable also that higher institutes of sacred music be
established whenever possible.

Composers and singers, especially boys, must also be given a
genuine liturgical training.[28]

This same article ought to serve as an impetus for Global South congregations to nurture and embrace their God-given songs that were previously
marginalized, mindful that a theological construct on contextualization is
needed to undergird such revitalization efforts so that the hybrid song type
can truly flourish and be the heartfelt expression of the world church in its
distinctive locale. It needs to coexist in mutual respect with the other song
types and not be marginalized as it presently remains. For as United Methodist Bishop Joel Martinez is cited, "each generation must add its stanza to
the great hymn of the church." I believe this aptly applies when speaking
about the hybrid song form for it is in this song form that the global church
truly adds its voice to the world of song, reflecting diversity in the worship
of our triune God.

In conclusion, the congregational soundscape reality outside the
Euro-American region is far more conventional than what is hoped for. It
continues to be dominated by the colonially transmitted Christian religious
musical imprint to the dismay of many theologians and scholars seeking to
reverse the trend of westernization in favor of contextualized expression.
However, simply asserting indigenous alternatives at worship conferences
or publications will not bring about change when the systemic underpinnings of the social cultural context and ecclesial polity are not addressed.
Contextualization of church music is more than adopting new idiomatic
expressions, it is about revitalizing theological awareness and constructing
socially viable identity; offering the global church the necessary skill set to
creatively maneuver through an ambivalent social cultural setting where
Christianity continues to be perceived as a foreign religion.

In this essay, I described the landscape of the world church with some
attention to church music making in Asia since songs from this region appear
to be less accessible to other parts of the world and are frequently marginalized by its own people up to the present, unlike Africa or Latin America.
I proffered that there are three song types that are found in global Christianity: translated-transplanted Western song form, mimicked song, and the

---

[28] Excerpts of the *Constitution on Sacred Liturgy* are taken from http://
www.vatican.va/archive/hist_councils/ii_vatican_council/documents/vat-ii_
const_19631204_sacrosanctum-concilium_en.html.

hybrid form, and described their characteristics. It is crucial to understand the nonmusical significance of these forms and their relationship to social cultural settings. I had also commented on the need to better understand the process of contextualization of music—that it is more than changing musical nuances but forming a new identity of the church. Thereafter I posit the ethical implications in using the term *global song* and how one needs to manage this genre with discernment. I had also taken pains to highlight the injustice that exist when intellectual property rights are overlooked.

Just as the exiled people of God were asked to sing the Lord's song in captivity by their captors, Christianity in the Global South continues to struggle with this same dilemma of singing the Lord's song in the midst of an ambivalent cultural setting. Yet, the church must sing her song that fully reflects the gifts and graces that God has given in and through her cultural heritage so that she can be the light and salt of the world. I remain hopeful that the church will continue to grow in understanding her place at the margin of society and thereby play an advocacy role in offering God's way of justice and peace at this time of great uncertainty in the twenty-first century.

Part IV

Peter C. Phan's Contributions to World Christianity: Two Perspectives

19

PETER C. PHAN:
AN ACCIDENTAL THEOLOGIAN *BETWIXT*
AND BETWEEN EAST AND WEST

Julius-Kei Kato

Peter C. Phan is regarded by his peers as one of the most important Asian/Asian North American theologians today. From his roots in Asia, through the numerous uprootings and rerootings he has experienced, Phan has become one of the most recognized and respected theological voices that represent some of the most important theological reflection being currently done *from* and *on* both Asian and Asian North American Christianities. His immense output contains theological works that range from Vietnamese theology[1] to the bigger world of Asian theological topics in general.[2] It includes, more specifically, Asian North American theological reflection such as *betwixt and between* theology (arguably his preferred appellation for his own brand of Asian North American theology), interreligious dialogue, *inter-multicultural theology*, the theology of migration, and multiple religious belonging. Even without the Asian/Asian North American qualifier, Phan can very well stand on his own among the most significant theologians in the world today for his theological writings treating more universal themes in the broader world of theology.[3]

---

[1] See, for example, Peter Phan, *Mission and Catechesis: Alexandre De Rhodes and Inculturation in Seventeenth-Century Vietnam*, Faith and Cultures Series (Maryknoll, NY: Orbis Books, 1998).

[2] For example, Peter Phan, "Reception of and Trajectories for Vatican II in Asia," *Theological Studies* 74/2 (2013): 302–20; Peter Phan, "The Church in Asian Perspective" in *The Routledge Companion to the Christian Church*, ed. Gerard Mannion (Oxfordshire, UK: Routledge, 2007), 275–90.

[3] For example, Peter Phan, ed., *The Cambridge Companion to the Trinity* (Cambridge: Cambridge University Press, 2011).

On the one hand, Phan is very much also an Asian North American theologian because of his present location that has shaped a large portion of his theological output. On the other hand, he has also contextualized his work within the dynamics and wider conversations taking place today within World Christianity,[4] highlighting the diasporic dimensions of World Christianity. I have argued elsewhere[5] that Phan and many Asian North Americans have undergone what can be considered a *diasporic* experience whereby they were uprooted, rerooted, and are now positioned in what is frequently described as a liminal space between worlds. The late Korean American theologian Jung Young Lee has termed such liminal space as "in-between and in-both"[6] the worlds of Asia and North America. In particular, this liminal space exhibits characteristics arising from the realities of diaspora, hybridity, and marginality (or better perhaps, marginalization). In turn, these characteristics result in a complex of experiences—being uprooted from a homeland and moving either willingly or unwillingly to a new, often inhospitable place (hence, marginalization) where one acquires a hybrid identity over time due to one's location *in-between and in both* two (or more) cultural worlds with which one can claim *some kind of* affiliation.

In the Beginning

At the beginning of his autobiographical essay in the important 1999 book *Journeys at the Margins: Toward an Autobiographical Theology in American-Asian Perspective* entitled "Betwixt and Between: Doing Theology with Memory and Imagination,"[7] Phan looks back at the path he has trodden and reflects that there are, in reality, just a few things that one can really control in life. Most things in life are, in a sense, *accidental* happenings. Many circumstances and elements in one's makeup—such as genetic traits,

---

[4] See, for example, Peter Phan, "World Christianity, Its Implications for History, Religious Studies, and Theology," *Horizons* 39/2 (2012): 171–88.

[5] Julius-Kei Kato, *How Immigrant Christians Living in Mixed Cultures Interpret Their Religion: Asian-American Diasporic Hybridity and Its Implications for Hermeneutics* (Lewiston, NY: Edwin Mellen, 2012). The section on Phan is in chapter 5. A number of key ideas presented in this study are developed more extensively there.

[6] Jung Young Lee, *Marginality: The Key to Multicultural Theology* (Minneapolis: Fortress Press, 1995), 42, 47.

[7] Peter Phan, "Betwixt and Between: Doing Theology with Memory and Imagination," in *Journeys at the Margin: Toward an Autobiographical Theology in American-Asian Perspective*, ed. Peter Phan & Jung Young Lee (Collegeville, MN: Liturgical Press, 1999), 113–33.

race, religion, language, or culture—are the result of a "fortuitous conflu-
ence of unpredictable and uncontrollable factors."[8] With that, Phan declares
himself to be an *accidental theologian*. Theology, he muses, was something he
would probably not have chosen. It was rather *thrust upon* him. That quality
of uncontrollable destiny, Phan reflects in retrospect, characterizes his life, a
life lived—and here he introduces one of his key words to describe not only
his life but also his theology—*betwixt and between* East and West.

Phan imbibed a French education in an era when his native Vietnam
had already severed formal ties with the colonizing power. In an age of
nationalistic fervor, Phan ironically continued to be trained in the art
of becoming a good "French boy." Thus, although he was a Vietnamese
in Vietnam, he experienced early in life what it means to be alienated in
one's very own country and among one's own people.[9] Later, he pursued
philosophical studies from 1962 to 1965 in a college in Hong Kong run
by a Catholic religious congregation dedicated to the education of youth.
There in the heart of a land and culture steeped in Confucius's teachings, he
followed a program of neoscholastic philosophy (normal at the time) with
textbooks and lectures in Latin, again ironically deprived of the opportunity
to learn any Eastern philosophy and culture. Once again, he found himself
thrust into a world of cultural schizophrenia between East and West.[10]

Sent to do theological studies in Rome (1968–72), Phan found himself
yet again betwixt and between two worlds in that the Catholic Church was,
in the late 1960s and early 1970s, in a state of ferment after the earth-shat-
tering Second Vatican Council (1962–65). Phan concludes in retrospect
that living and studying in such an environment made him participate
firsthand in what can be called an interstitial experience between the preconciliar and postconciliar Catholic Church with all the euphoria, as well as the
tensions and conflicts, which that experience generated.[11] When he had to
write his thesis to obtain the licentiate in theology, he chose to work on Paul
Tillich who had forcefully put forward the so-called Protestant Principle in
his thought and work. Phan wanted the Protestant Principle of Tillich to
complement the *Catholic substance* in which he had been formed. This was
yet another instance of Phan's being poised between two worlds—Catholicism and Protestantism.[12]

---

[8] Phan, "Betwixt and Between," 115.
[9] Ibid., 116.
[10] Ibid., 117.
[11] Ibid., 118–19.
[12] Ibid., 119.

The heart of Phan's story though is how he ended up in North America, again seemingly at the mercy of circumstances totally beyond his control. He was part of the great mass of Vietnamese who were forcefully displaced by the cataclysmic conclusion of the Vietnam War. After the Fall of Saigon in 1975, he was whisked out of the country into exile in the United States with his family, through a series of chance occurrences.[13] Upon his arrival in the United States, he went through a number of experiences typical of the refugee status such as living in camps and beginning to work in a foreign land (in Phan's case, initially as garbage collector for two months). Unexpectedly, from such a state, he ended up in the world of academic theology with the initial purpose of earning a living to support his displaced family in the new and strange land.[14]

As Phan came to know better the academic world of theology, he experienced more deeply the betwixt and between state he has made a dominant leitmotiv of his theological thinking. For his doctoral dissertation, he chose to work on a Russian Orthodox theologian, Paul Evdokimov (1901–70). Phan was able to identify immediately with this thinker because Evdokimov was likewise a refugee who left his native Russia for Constantinople and eventually Paris. Moreover, Phan discovered that his engagement with Evdokimov's work, coupled with his experience of exile made him more keenly aware of the "fragility of things and the ephemeral character of time."[15] This became the crucial encounter that has led to a lifelong interest in the topic of eschatology, which he conceives of as a theme betwixt and between time and eternity.[16]

Life in North America for an academic originally from Asia brought its experiences of marginalization as well as an almost permanent difficulty of being fully integrated into the dominant White mainstream.[17] Interestingly, that produced in Phan a desire to explore in a deeper way how to "rethink certain fundamental Christian articles of belief in terms of Asian

---

[13] Ibid., 120–25.

[14] Ibid., 125.

[15] Ibid., 126.

[16] See, for example, Peter Phan, *Eternity in Time: A Study of Karl Rahner's Eschatology* (Selinsgrove, PA: Susquehanna University Press, 1988); Peter Phan, *Responses to 101 Questions on Death and Eternal Life* (New York: Paulist Press, 1998); as well as his recent work, Peter Phan, *Living into Death, Dying into Life: Death and the Afterlife* (Hobe Sound, FL: Lectio Publishing, 2014).

[17] Phan and Lee, *Journeys at the Margin*, viii.

and, in particular, Vietnamese cultural resources."[18] It drove him moreover to explore further the implications of doing theology from a metaphorical place betwixt and between Asia and America.

Recounting details from Phan's biography has been intentionally done because it makes clear that he as well as the many Asian North Americans who have had similar experiences are irrevocably marked by the traits of diaspora, hybridity, and marginalization. It is likewise obvious that Phan's contributions both to Asian and Asian North American Christian theology, as well as to World Christianity itself, are rooted and have emerged from that very Asian and Asian North American crucible of personal experience.

Location: *Betwixt and Between*

The phrase *betwixt and between* perhaps most eloquently captures Phan's distinctive way of describing his dominant life experiences and the theology that stems from them. I also think that this should be considered one of the dominant features of Asian North American Christianity (and, in a certain way, also parts of Asian Christianity as well). As Phan explains,

> To be betwixt and between is to be neither here nor there, to be neither this thing nor that. Spatially, it is to dwell at the periphery or at the boundaries. Politically, it means not residing at the centers of power of the two intersecting worlds but occupying the precarious and narrow margins where the two dominant groups meet and clash, and denied the opportunity to wield power in matters of public interest. Socially, to be betwixt and between is to be part of a minority, a member of a marginal(ized) group. Culturally, it means not being fully integrated into and accepted by either cultural system, being a *mestizo*, a person of mixed race. Linguistically, the betwixt-and-between person is bilingual but may not achieve a mastery of both languages and often speaks them with a distinct accent. Psychologically and spiritually, the person does not possess a well-defined and secure self-identity and is often marked with excessive impressionableness, rootlessness, and an inordinate desire for belonging.[19]

---

[18] Phan, "Betwixt and Between," 131.

[19] Ibid., 113. See also Peter Phan, "The Dragon and the Eagle: Toward a Vietnamese American Theology," in *Christianity with an Asian Face: Asian American Theology in the Making* (Maryknoll, NY: Orbis Books, 2003), 228–47.

Applying *betwixt and between* to his ethnic group, Phan insightfully remarks
that

> American Vietnamese will never be "American enough"; because
> of their race and culture *American* will function only as a qualifier
> for the noun *Vietnamese.* On the other hand, Vietnamese Ameri-
> cans are no longer regarded by their compatriots in Vietnam as
> authentically Vietnamese; they have "left" Vietnam and become
> Americans; *Vietnamese* functions only as a qualifier for *American.*
> In fact, Vietnamese Americans have been given a special name by
> the Vietnamese government—*Viet kieu* (Vietnamese foreigners).[20]

There is, however, also a positive side to being betwixt and between.
Phan also claims that being in such a state does not "bring total
disadvantage"[21] because, paradoxically, "being neither this nor that allows
one to be *both* this and that."[22] Since betwixt and between people belong
to both (or multiple) worlds and cultures, they are in a unique position
to act as liaison between worlds, fuse the worlds together and, utilizing
their special resources, perhaps even fashion "a new, different world."[23]
Again, "they are in a position to see more clearly and to appreciate more
objectively, both as insiders and outsiders ('emically' and 'etically'), the
strengths as well as the weaknesses of both cultures; as a result, they
are better equipped to contribute to the emergence of a new, enriched
culture."[24] One can certainly say that betwixt and between people have a
unique role to play or even "a providentially given mission and task"[25] in
bringing about "personal and societal transformation and enrichment."[26]
This is no easy task because those who are placed in "a situation of multiple
identities and loyalties as a permanent, day-to-day, existential condition"
must "constantly negotiate, often without the benefit of clear guidelines
and helpful models."[27]

---

[20] Phan, "The Dragon and the Eagle," 235.
[21] Phan, "Betwixt and Between," 113.
[22] Ibid.
[23] Ibid.
[24] Peter Phan, "The Experience of Migration as Source of Intercultural Theology
in the United States," in *Christianity with an Asian Face: Asian American Theology in the
Making* (Maryknoll, NY: Orbis Books, 2003), 3–25, at 9.
[25] Phan, "The Dragon and the Eagle," 235.
[26] Phan, "Betwixt and Between," 113.
[27] Phan, "The Dragon and the Eagle," 235.

Phan proceeds to delineate this particular approach's rich promise for Christian theology in general. What is the shape of a theology that has, as locus, the betwixt and between state?[28] For Phan, it is "thinking religiously from both sides of the boundaries"; it is specifically an "intercultural theology" which has the "global village" as horizon. Significantly, Phan posits that doing theology betwixt and between worlds is "predicated on the conviction that no culture is totally devoid of divine presence" because God continues to self-communicate to all peoples in all cultures. It is imperative then for such a theology to develop a method that can seriously take into account "expressions of God's message that are different from those that have grown out of one's own philosophical, religious, political, and ethical traditions." Hence, such a theology and its methods will be able to contribute in a significant manner to the struggle against "prejudice, racism, colonialism, and ethnocentrism, on the one hand, and inferiority complex and loss of cultural identity on the other."[29]

Tools: Memory and Imagination

Phan suggests that a theology that is betwixt and between worlds utilizes the tools of "memory and imagination."[30] This refers to the process of "contemplating the past and creating the future at the same time."[31] Memory anchors the theologian in history and tradition (both Christianity's and one's own culture[s]). It serves as an important means to prevent a theology from becoming mere "phantasmagoria."[32] In that light, Phan is reluctant, for example, to agree with proposals, even when they are made by Asian/Asian American theologians, "to bypass the development of Western theology in constructing a theology appropriate to the Asian [and I would add, also the Asian North American] context."[33] In the face of its growing unpopularity in certain academic circles, he upholds the continuing importance of—what is the proud child of the Enlightenment—the historical–critical method, for the purpose of retrieving the world *behind* the text, not only in order to explain it better historically, but, more importantly, to serve as a catalyst for the world *in front of the text* (ourselves/the readers); a catalyst that allows

---

[28] The descriptions that follow come from Phan, "Betwixt and Between," 114–15.

[29] Ibid.

[30] Ibid., 127. I have inverted Phan's original order to put memory first because for me that often seems to be the first action, chronologically speaking.

[31] Ibid., 114.

[32] Ibid., 128.

[33] Ibid.

us to enter more accurately and profitably into the world *of* the text and be transformed through grace working throughout the whole process.[34] A betwixt and between theology then does not—according to Phan—totally dispense with the analytical tools that the West has devised and utilized. In fact, he concurs with the Korean American theologian Anselm Kyongsuk Min that the first task of an ethnic theology (such as Asian or Asian North American theology) is "to retrieve both *the Western*[35] and the Asian traditions for the needs of Asian communities in America."[36]

For Phan, Western methodologies and analytical tools do not have a monopoly in the search for the truth because there are other alternative ways of acquiring knowledge, such as those utilized in Asia, some of which are radically different from those in vogue in the West.[37] Many of these epistemological strategies are more intuitive and circular in their logic (as opposed to Western linear logic), such as storytelling in the style, for example, of the well-known Taiwanese theologian C. S. Song.[38] This delicate balancing act shows us clearly once more how Phan is poised betwixt and between the worlds of Asia and the West.

Phan is adamant that theology should be well aware that "the stability and security it [the static memory of history and tradition] affords is impermanent and illusory." Rather, he emphasizes that memory is re-creating history and tradition imaginatively; it is "re-*membering* disparate fragments of the past together and forming them into a new pattern under the pressure of present experiences, with a view to shaping a possible future."[39]

The faculty of imagination enables the theologian to enter into a new way of being-in-the-world. It empowers one "to break out of the limits of the past and bring human potentialities to full flourishing."[40] In summary, let us allow Phan to describe his vision:

> Like a pair of wings, memory and imagination carry the theologian aloft in the work of linking past and future, east and west, north and south, earth and heaven. Both memory and imagination in their

---

[34] Ibid., 129–30.

[35] Emphasis added.

[36] Phan, "The Dragon and the Eagle," 240.

[37] Phan, "Betwixt and Between," 131–32.

[38] Peter Phan, "Jesus with a Chinese Face: Choan-Seng Song's Jesus-Oriented Christology," in *Christianity with an Asian Face: Asian American Theology in the Making* (Maryknoll, NY: Orbis Books, 2003), 146–70.

[39] Phan, "Betwixt and Between," 114.

[40] Ibid.

mutual interaction are indispensable tools for theology. Without memory, theology would be empty; without imagination, it would be blind. They are the epistemological equivalent of *yin* and *yang*, ever in movement, ever transmuting into each other, ever complementing each other, to capture reality in its wholeness."[41]

Contexts:
The Underside of History and Inter/Multireligiosity

There are arguably two other defining characteristics in the theological style rooted both in Asia and Asian North America advocated by Phan. Phan uses the following Vietnamese proverb to explain: "Come back and bathe in your own pond; clear or muddy, the home pond is always better."[42] Interpreted theologically, that proverb suggests that the use of resources particular to and characteristic of one's own context(s) might be the most helpful way to do theology. In Phan's case, a major source (in addition to the North American one) from which he draws his theology is, of course, the Asian context in general and the Vietnamese in particular. Drawing from that particularly Asian source, Phan advocates that theology should also have the following ingredients: first, it should be undertaken in a spirit of solidarity with the underprivileged, the poor and the suffering; and, second, it should be in a dynamic conversation with and openness to multi/inter-religious realities.

The first reveals an inseparable link to liberation theology. Phan firmly stands in the line of what theologies of liberation hold as a *sine qua non* in the methodological principles that undergird theology, namely, that any theological method should pay attention to—in Gustavo Gutiérrez's words—"the underside of history"[43] in order to unmask forms of repression and oppression embedded in whatever theme theology takes as its object of study. The second element is more typically and peculiarly Asian in origin. Being a continent of diverse and ancient religions that often coexist with each other and even mix and fuse with each other,[44] one cannot avoid the

---

[41] Ibid., 114–15.

[42] Ibid., 131.

[43] James Nickoloff, *Gustavo Gutiérrez: Essential Writings* (Maryknoll, NY: Orbis Books, 1996), 40.

[44] Jan Van Bragt, "Multiple Religious Belonging of the Japanese People," in *Many Mansions? Multiple Religious Belonging and Christian Identity*, ed. Catherine Cornille (Maryknoll, NY: Orbis Books, 2002), 7–19.

inter/multireligious context in any discussion of Asia or even of Asian North America. Moreover, since many parts of Asia (as well as many Asian North American immigrant lives) are characterized both by various ways of participation in the underside of history as well as deep religiosity, any theology which touches Asia/Asian North America must in some way take these two factors into account in a serious way.[45] A case in point, in his work, Phan has tirelessly echoed the call of the Federation of Asian Bishops' Conferences (FABC) since the 1970s to carry out an intensive dialogue with the most important of Asian contexts.[46] They style this as a *triple dialogue*, first, with the cultures of Asia; second, with the many and manifold religions found in this vast continent; and, third, with the poor who make up a great majority of the peoples of Asia. Such a triple dialogue must be characterized by a real dialogue of presence and action, a dialogue of discourse and of spirituality,[47] and not merely by words alone.

Theology and Migration

In recent years, Phan has concretely expressed his theological approach from the underside of history through his extensive work on the relation of migration with theology. Phan's 2003 essay titled "The Experience of Migration as Source of Intercultural Theology in the United States"[48] is an important key to understanding his thinking on this theme.[49]

Phan maintains that an important contextual factor to keep in mind is that, with the US Immigration and Nationality Act of 1965, which did away with the official preference for immigrants of European origin, a new

---

[45] Phan, "Betwixt and Between," 131–32.

[46] For example, Peter Phan, "Human Development and Evangelization," in *Christianity with an Asian Face: Asian American Theology in the Making*, 184–201.

[47] Peter Phan, *In Our Own Tongues: Perspectives from Asia on Mission and Inculturation* (Maryknoll, NY: Orbis Books, 2003), 17–31.

[48] Peter Phan, "The Experience of Migration as Source of Intercultural Theology in the United States," in *Christianity with an Asian Face*, 3–25. Also recently revised in the following work within an explicit context of migration: Elaine Padilla and Peter C. Phan, eds., *Contemporary Issues of Migration and Theology* (New York: Palgrave Macmillan, 2013), 179–209.

[49] As shown by his recent research activity. In addition to his coedited 2013 work mentioned above, there are also the following: Elaine Padilla and Peter Phan, eds., *Theologies of Migration in the Abrahamic Religions* (New York: Palgrave Macmillan, 2014); and Elaine Padilla and Peter Phan, eds., *Migrations in World Christianity* (New York: Palgrave Macmillan, forthcoming).

era of unprecedented immigration from non-European countries began, resulting in what is sometimes called "the browning of America."[50] Whereas earlier immigrants were strongly subjected to the process of "assimilation," more recent immigrants are less inclined to blend fully with the mainstream society, preferring instead to maintain their own heritages and cultures to some extent, while also adapting to life in North America.[51] Phan observes that the dominant presence of non-European immigrants now has important consequences for how theology is to be done in the North American context. The most prominent one is that theology cannot anymore rely exclusively on sources traditionally used up to this point by Western theologians. Theology must likewise adopt new, unfamiliar sources and resources; it must anchor itself in the nature and sensibility of the immigrant and refugee, and it must develop a distinct epistemology and hermeneutics, that is, a way of perceiving and interpreting reality (oneself, others, the cosmos, and God) from the standpoint of migration.

The specific factors with which a theology speaking out of the context of migration will necessarily have to grapple are the salient experiences of the immigrants themselves, more precisely, two in particular: (1) displacement and suffering, and—as has been already described above—(2) being betwixt and between different cultures. The former experience frequently includes violent uprooting, economic poverty, anxiety about the future, and a loss of national identity, political freedom, and personal dignity.[52] Phan is convinced that a theology rooted in the experience of migration will begin "with personal solidarity with the victims of this abject condition of human, often innocent suffering."[53] The theologian will "see" for him or herself the nature of the immigrants' plight, will "listen" to the stories of victims, will "preserve" this "dangerous memory," and "accompany" these oppressed people in their struggle to attain liberation and human dignity.[54]

As for theology taking the immigrants' experience of living betwixt and between cultures more seriously, Phan utilizes—what he calls—inter-multi-culturality to unpack what such a theology is supposed to be and do. An

---

[50] Peter Phan, "The Experience of Migration," 6.

[51] See James H. Johnson Jr., Walter C. Farrell, and Chandra Guinn, "Immigration Reform and the Browning of America: Tensions, Conflicts, and Community Instability in Metropolitan Los Angeles," in *The Handbook of International Migration*, ed. Charles Hirchman, Philip Kasinitz, and Josh Dewind (New York: Russell Sage Foundation Publications, 1999), 390–411.

[52] Phan, "The Experience of Migration," 8.

[53] Ibid.

[54] Ibid.

inter-multicultural theology in the North American setting would be one that is "not only shaped by the encounter between *two* cultures, the dominant (Anglo/European/white) culture and a minority culture (for example, Vietnamese), but by the much more complex and challenging encounter of several cultures at the same time (white and Latino and black and Asian and Native American and so on)."[55] It is, therefore, a theology of encounter not only *between* but *among* cultures. Such an inter-multicultural character of the immigrant experience must be adopted as "the epistemological, hermeneutical, and methodological vantage point"[56] for this theological approach. To elaborate, Asian North Americans bear within their histories and within themselves a mixture of cultures. Sometimes, that stretches very far back in time such as in the case of the relationship of Chinese/Confucian culture with the local cultures that are found, for example, in Korea, Japan, and Vietnam. But the mixture becomes a significant experience as soon as immigrants come to North America and are faced with the dominant culture. Moreover, they also have to deal with a myriad of other subcultures found here. How is theology to speak to such an experience? In response, Phan asserts that theology must "take this preexisting multicultural experience of these new arrivals as the vantage point from which to perceive and know reality (epistemology), to interpret it (hermeneutics), and to guide the articulation of a Christian understanding appropriate for and relevant to the betwixt and between predicament of immigrants facing multiple cultures (methodology)."[57] Only then would theology truly be inter-multicultural, and will likewise truly be able to claim to speak out of and to the experience of immigrants.

The theologian has to retrieve the *underside of history* as embodied in immigrants' experiences. This often overlooked side of history is contained in immigrant stories, which are

> stories of hard struggle for physical survival and for human dignity, especially stories of women who are triply discriminated against (because they are poor, are a minority and female); stories of how their faith in the God who vindicated Jesus . . . inspired and sustained them to overcome bouts of self-doubt and despair; stories of hope; stories of effective solidarity of immigrants with one another in a community of love and mutual acceptance, of shared

---

[55] Ibid., 10.
[56] Ibid., 11.
[57] Ibid., 12.

spiritual and material resources, of common work to build a more just and equitable society across gender, racial, ethnic, economic, and political differences; and, yes, even stories of immigrants' mutual suspicion and jealousy, of self-reliant "model immigrants" over against public-welfare-dependent ones, of earlier immigrants scapegoating and discriminating against more recent ones, for fear that the American pie would be cut into too many slices.[58]

Inter/Multireligiosity

Going to the Asian and Asian North American inter/multireligious dimension, even a cursory survey of Phan's corpus to date will show clearly that this is an area that Phan has given much thought to and written quite voluminously about because he maintains—as what is arguably his most well-known book to date proclaims in its title—that "being religious" (and I add, particularly, in a context rooted in Asia or Asian North America) should be "interreligious."[59] Christians in Asia continue to comprise a small minority of the total population. That is correspondingly reflected in the significant number of non-Christians among Asian North Americans. The presence of a majority non-Christian population constitutes such an undeniable and dominating factor in Asia (as well as a significant non-Christian segment in Asian North America) that grappling with inter/multireligiosity is not a luxury but an urgent necessity. This boils down to the fact that an Asian and Asian North American theology will keep in mind that its—to use theologian David Tracy's term—"public"[60] is composed of a substantial number of adherents of other religions. Hence, it must seek to maintain

---

[58] Ibid., 17.

[59] Peter Phan, *Being Religious Interreligiously: Asian Perspectives on Interfaith Dialogue* (Maryknoll, NY: Orbis Books, 2004). Other recent representative works include Peter Phan and Jonathan Ray, eds., *Journal of Ecumenical Studies: Special Issue on Understanding Religious Pluralism: Perspectives from Religious Studies and Theology*—a conference held at Georgetown University in May, 2012—48/3 (2013); Peter Phan and Jonathan Y. Tan, "Interreligious Majority-Minority Dynamics," in *Understanding Interreligious Relations*, ed. David Cheetham, Douglas Pratt, and David Thomas (Oxford: Oxford University Press, 2013), 218–40; Peter Phan, "Can We Read Religious Texts Interreligiously? Possibilities, Challenges, and Experiments," in *Postcolonial Interruptions*, ed. Tat-siong Benny Liew (Sheffield, UK: Sheffield Phoenix Press, 2009), 313–31.

[60] David Tracy, *The Analogical Imagination: Christian Theology and the Culture of Pluralism* (New York: Crossroad Publishing, 1981), 5.

certain principles that would not necessarily carry as much weight in a *public* that has Christians (or at least cultural Christians) as the majority. A case in point would be the principle that the sacred texts of other religions are to be given due consideration. This implies that the Bible might not be a priori granted universal and normative value or that Jesus might not necessarily be accepted as universal and lone savior, etc. Since a significant number of Asians and Asian North Americans draw their inspiration from many religions among which Christianity is only one option, a theology based on Asian North American experience is not only inter-multicultural, but also, by necessity, interreligious.[61]

It is also significant to note that his 2004 book *Being Religious Interreligiously* became the subject of investigation by local and Roman authorities of the Roman Catholic hierarchy because it warned that Phan's cutting-edge theological reflection—which is arguably representative of general trends in Asian and Asian North American theological efforts—"could easily confuse or mislead the faithful."[62] The book deals with many issues concerning the relation of Christianity with other religions, but its core message is nothing more than what is stated in the title: in this globalized and postmodern era, the religiosity of Catholics should by necessity be interreligious in nature. The book proposes some factors that were apparently thought of by the Catholic hierarchy as pushing the envelope too far, particularly in the realms of Christology and ecclesiology. The details are beyond the point here, but this affair is another proof that Phan's thinking on inter-multireligiosity is cutting edge in terms of its extraordinary openness to, and valorization of, other religions on the bigger world stage. This is why it can seem threatening to Christian circles that tend to emphasize their own uniqueness and even superiority.

This inter/multireligious dimension, if pushed to its most radical form, takes the form of multiple religious belonging.[63] The fact is that

---

[61] See Phan, *Being Religious Interreligiously*. See also Phan, "Can We Read Religious Texts Interreligiously?" 313–31.

[62] US Conference of Catholic Bishops Committee on Doctrine, "Clarifications Required by the Book *Being Religious Interreligiously: Asian Perspectives on Interfaith Dialogue* by Reverend Peter C. Phan" (December 10, 2007), http://www.usccb.org/about/doctrine/publications/upload/statement-on-being-religious-interreligiouly.pdf.

[63] For more on this topic, consult Gideon Goosen, *Hyphenated Christians: Towards an Understanding of Dual Religious Belonging* (Bern, Switzerland: Peter Lang, 2011); Judith Berling, *Understanding Other Religious Worlds: A Guide for Interreligious Education* (Maryknoll, NY: Orbis Books, 2004); and Catherine Cornille, ed., *Many Mansions? Multiple Religious Belonging and Christian Identity* (Maryknoll, NY: Orbis Books, 2002).

this phenomenon of identifying with more than one religious tradition, common in certain parts of Asia for a long time now,[64] is being encountered in the West with increasing frequency. This compulsion toward multiple religious affiliations is felt keenly by a good number of Asians and Asian North Americans.[65] The reason is simple. Their roots are sunk deeply in the cultural grounds of some of the world's great religions, such as Buddhism and Hinduism, where Christianity is often deemed as a foreign entity by a majority of their particular country's populace. In this context, Kwok Pui-lan's remark is particularly telling: "an Asian reads the Bible from a situation of great alienation."[66] Peter Phan has also reflected on this contemporary phenomenon and its implications for today, particularly for theological education, and has made some very enlightening suggestions.[67] He concedes that this is still a substantial challenge for traditional Christianity.

> Multiple religious belonging is not for the fainthearted or the dilettante. . . . it is a demanding vocation, a special call to holiness, which up till now God has granted only to a few. It is not unlike martyrdom. Ultimately it is not something one looks for or demands at will. It is a gift to be received in fear and trembling and in gratitude and joy.[68]

---

[64] For example, in Japan, the *common person* practically identifies with *both* Shintoism and Buddhism. Van Bragt, "Multiple Religious Belonging of the Japanese People," 7–19.

[65] See, for example, Fumitaka Matsuoka's thought-provoking reflections in *Learning to Speak a New Tongue: Imagining a Way that Holds People Together—An Asian American Conversation* (Eugene, OR: Pickwick, 2011), chap. 4, "Amphibolous Faith: Reality Is Multiple."

[66] Kwok Pui-lan. *Postcolonial Imagination and Feminist Theology* (Louisville, KY: Westminster John Knox Press, 2005), 39.

[67] Peter Phan, "Multiple Religious Belonging: Opportunities and Challenges for Theology and Church," in *Being Religious Interreligiously*, 60–81.

[68] Ibid., 81.

20

PETER C. PHAN:
A PERSON OF THE WORLD CHURCH

Gerard Mannion

When I was a student, long before he became a much-treasured friend, inspiration, collaborator, and eventually a colleague, I believed that there were at least two and perhaps even an abundance of Peter C. Phans. Now, of course, the name is indeed very common in Vietnam, just as, say, Kelly or Murphy is in Ireland and Smith is in the United Kingdom (and all three names, thanks to waves of migration, in the United States). However, what I mean more specifically is my expectation that *within the world of theology* there might possibly be multiple learned scholars at work who shared the same name, a name that spoke of far-off and exotic origins. After all, in the world of theology, there are often two people or more who share the same or a similar name.

The first time I came across a Peter C. Phan was as the editor of a collection mined from the early church fathers and other sources from the patristic era on social thought.[1] This is an excellent collection that I still use with students to this very day, never ceasing to surprise a class when they read about the strength of the social message of the early Christian centuries and how uncompromising it was with regard to those with greater wealth and resources who failed to help their sisters and brothers in need. In many ways that collection helps show that the world of today and then are not so dissimilar. This collection was in fact Peter Phan's very first book.

Subsequently, I would come across Peter C. Phan writing on Orthodox theology, Peter C. Phan who works on grace and the human condition; the Peter C. Phan who authored the definitive study of Karl Rahner's eschatology, possibly the same man as the Phan who writes on death and eternal life in general. Likewise, Peter C. Phan on missiology, inculturation, liberation, and aspects of what some would call contextual theology. There were

---

[1] Peter C. Phan, *Social Thought* (Wilmington, DE: Michael Glazier, 1984).

Peter Phans writing and editing work on liturgy and on multiple aspects of ecclesiology. By this stage, I had twigged that, amazingly, these works were all from the same person and, just as many others did, I marveled at the breadth and above all scholarly and groundbreaking depth of his work.

A Martian theologian landing on earth who might not have had the good fortune to meet the scholar in question, as I was fortunate enough to do so in 2003, might be forgiven for thinking that the world of theology was awash with Peter C. Phans. There is Peter C. Phan who worked on Christianity and the new, *wider ecumenism*, the editor and author of that groundbreaking work on the Asian synod, the Peter Phan who wrote about Asian American theology, not to be confused with perhaps the Peter Phan writing about Asian Christianity in its own right. Then, there is the Peter Phan who writes about Vietnamese and American Catholicism, the pioneering Peter Phan who began to write about being religious in religiously pluralistic contexts, the Phan who edited the *Cambridge Companion to the Trinity*, the Phan who was among the pioneers raising awareness about the plight of migrants and helping to shape the theology of migration, and the Phan who was one of the leading figures in helping develop what has come to be termed *World Christianity* as an academic area of study in its own right, one that cuts across multiple different disciplines.

Who could fail to be amazed by the ubiquity of this scholar–teacher's influence? It is little wonder that eventually his attention would come to focus on World Christianity because his sharp-eyed attention had covered so many differing areas of the theological subdisciplines, the net had to be cast across the whole globe in order that he could find new stimulation to satisfy the great yearning for learning and discourse that had led to these dozens of great books and countless articles and chapters elsewhere to come into being. All of this is aside from the three book series he has edited and the countless students he has taught in multiple different institutions along the way.

If there is a common thread to all of this learning and ubiquitous influence, I might suggest that it is twofold. First, Peter C. Phan is a person of the church—shaped by it, immersed in it, and a lifelong servant of it. But it is not church as institution I mean here, nor do I make such a statement in the sense of how it might often be employed of, say, a scholar or pastoral worker, cleric, or religious in Europe or North America. Peter C. Phan is, first and foremost, a person of the church understood as the people of God; given his own upbringing and early career in Vietnam, his schooling, ministry, and work in many other nations—including China

(Hong Kong), Italy (Rome), Ireland (Limerick), England (London), and the United States (Dallas, Washington DC), not to mention his countless talks and presentations on almost every continent of the planet)—he is a person of the people of God in its most richly fluid, diverse, and globally reaching sense. If the church helped to shape this giant of world theology, then so, also, in turn, has he had an enormous influence on the church itself, and by church, here, I mean the world church that embraces the Christian family in its entirety.

Peter Phan was born into a pluralistic culture; he has lived and worked in multiple diverse international cultures. He has also, at times, lived and worked in places and in times where more rigid and narrower understandings of what it is to be church have prevailed. In all of his rich experience, however, he has learned that the church cannot be confined to the conceptual, liturgical, and cultural confines of any particular time and context. And so his work (increasingly so in recent times) bears testimony to the great breadth and depth of the church's richly pluralistic reality—a reality that Pope Francis, as we have seen in Chapter 11, has equally said is one we must not only recognize as true but also embrace as necessary.

Peter Phan's pioneering work in interreligious coexistence and Asian theology, as well as his contributions to the study of World Christianity, equally reflect and demonstrate his own background, his schooling as a *world citizen*, his journeys into the multiple disciplines of the theological sciences, and his long and illustrious career as a theologian who traveled so very far from home in troubled times only to end up, through his work, making that home and the enormous continent in which it sits so much better known and understood and all that much closer to those throughout the rest of the church and the world.

Peter Phan is passionately committed to dialogue—among Christians, among people of differing faiths and religions, and between those who follow religious pathways and those who do not do so. Peter's overall work can collectively be lauded as helping to enhance understanding and dialogue across many differing divides—cultural, ethnic, religious, even political. Peter Phan, then, is a person and servant of the *world* church. And the test of time will also hopefully demonstrate that, in fact, he has been among its most creative and inspiring theological prophets for our times.

Indeed, there is a prophetic timbre to so much of his writing, his teaching and speaking, to his work in general. He is a migrant theologian who has helped transform theology around the globe, including the theology of migration and theological interaction between differing migrant communities and the cultures in which multiple migrants have found themselves living.

Peter Phan's work helps to make the world, in a good sense, a more interconnected place, and this certainly without diluting its rich diversity or playing down the serious social and cultural challenges and differences that must be tackled throughout the human family. His life and work alike have equally reflected the great transformative developments that Christianity had undergone in recent decades, but he has been no mere observer in much of this. He has actively contributed to many of the most positive changes that the church and theology has seen in recent times.

If the notion of Peter Phan as person of the world church might therefore serve as a hermeneutical key for drawing together his many diverse and inspiring contributions to theology and the communities that theology serves in general, then I might go one step further and suggest that, in fact, the shadow of ecclesiology is never very far from the thinking and writing of Peter Phan. His work *in toto* helps people to better appreciate, understand, and enhance the church and its mission in these and future times, as well as to appreciate better its story and challenges in former times. Through his writing, teaching, and multiple leadership roles, as well as in the friendships and networks he has helped build across this planet, Peter Phan has served the church in so many different ways and helped countless people come to appreciate that there are important and more life-giving ways of not simply understanding and explaining the church, but also such ways of being, organizing, and ministering church. From his myriad contributions then, ecclesiology and those who practice it can gain much in these times and long into the future.

Peter Phan's deep influence upon ecclesiology in recent times is illustrated most vividly, of course, by his leading role in helping to bring about the turn toward a much greater and wide-reaching focus on World Christianity or, better still, as the man himself has said, a turn to the realization that in truth we must today speak about and study world Christiani*ties* in the plural. This great realization is not intended to be reductive; rather it is intended to be *instructive* and indeed inspiring. Once again, as we sought to illustrate in Chapter 11, we can judge this to be prophetic too.

Peter Phan's many works have helped demonstrate clearly the impact that the cultures and contexts that Christianity comes to anew have in turn upon the wider faith itself—the wonderfully transformative marvels of inculturation and its multiple directions and spheres of influence have been so eloquently explicated by this brilliant scholar. In the works of Peter

C. Phan, a man who has spent his life transcending boundaries, building bridges, and serving the world church, we find an abundance of treasures that contemporary and future ecclesiologists will forever be grateful for as they continue to seek to make sense of and in turn help further serve the church and Christianity—that world religion that is always local and universal.

INDEX